Theorising Undergraduate Entrepreneurship Education

Guillermo J. Larios-Hernandez ·
Andreas Walmsley · Itzel Lopez-Castro
Editors

Theorising Undergraduate Entrepreneurship Education

Reflections on the Development of the Entrepreneurial Mindset

Editors
Guillermo J. Larios-Hernandez (iD)
Universidad Anáhuac
Mexico, Mexico

Andreas Walmsley (iD)
Plymouth Marjon University
Plymouth, UK

Itzel Lopez-Castro
Universidad Anáhuac
Mexico, Mexico

ISBN 978-3-030-87864-1   ISBN 978-3-030-87865-8   (eBook)
https://doi.org/10.1007/978-3-030-87865-8

© The Editor(s) (if applicable) and The Author(s), under exclusive license to Springer
Nature Switzerland AG 2022
This work is subject to copyright. All rights are solely and exclusively licensed by the
Publisher, whether the whole or part of the material is concerned, specifically the rights
of translation, reprinting, reuse of illustrations, recitation, broadcasting, reproduction on
microfilms or in any other physical way, and transmission or information storage and
retrieval, electronic adaptation, computer software, or by similar or dissimilar methodology
now known or hereafter developed.
The use of general descriptive names, registered names, trademarks, service marks, etc.
in this publication does not imply, even in the absence of a specific statement, that such
names are exempt from the relevant protective laws and regulations and therefore free for
general use.
The publisher, the authors and the editors are safe to assume that the advice and information in this book are believed to be true and accurate at the date of publication. Neither
the publisher nor the authors or the editors give a warranty, expressed or implied, with
respect to the material contained herein or for any errors or omissions that may have been
made. The publisher remains neutral with regard to jurisdictional claims in published maps
and institutional affiliations.

This Palgrave Macmillan imprint is published by the registered company Springer Nature
Switzerland AG
The registered company address is: Gewerbestrasse 11, 6330 Cham, Switzerland

Contents

**Introduction: The 'Why', the 'What' and the 'How'
of Entrepreneurship Education**   1
Guillermo J. Larios-Hernandez, Andreas Walmsley,
and Itzel Lopez-Castro

**Distinctive Approaches to Undergraduate
Entrepreneurship Education**

**Setting the Scene: The Student-Process-Educator Nexus
in Entrepreneurship Education**   15
Birgitte Wraae

**Guiding the First-Year Student Entrepreneur:
A Conceptual Map to Nudge Towards the Reversal Effect
in Learning**   33
Gustav Hägg and Agnieszka Kurczewska

**Teaching Entrepreneurship to Undergraduates:
A Vygotskian Perspective**   49
Daniele Morselli and Alexandros Kakouris

The Elusive Role of Play in Entrepreneurship Education   69
Heidi Neck, Elissa Grossman, Doan Winkel, and Jeffrey Stamp

Conceptualising the Entrepreneurship Education and Employability Nexus 97
Andreas Walmsley, Carolin Decker-Lange, and Knut Lange

Dual Learning Space in Undergraduate Entrepreneurship Education: A Framework Proposal 115
Guillermo J. Larios-Hernandez and Itzel Lopez-Castro

Impacting the Mindset of the Undergraduate

What Do We Talk About When We Talk About Entrepreneurial Mindset Training? 137
Lucrezia Casulli

Supporting Students and Society: Underpinning Entrepreneurship Education with a Humanistic Philosophy 157
Robin Bell

Success Through Failure: Towards a Problem-Based Approach to Entrepreneurship Education 173
John Alver Dobson and Lisa Dobson

Exploring the Professional Identity and Career Trajectories of Undergraduates on a Team-Based, Experiential Degree Programme 191
Lauren Davies, Berrbizne Urzelai, and Karolina Ozadowicz

Delivering Entrepreneurship Education for Would-Be and Existing Small Business Entrepreneurs 211
Peter Wyer, Seynam Kwakuvi-Zagbedeh, and Jonathan Nii Okai Welbeck

Pedagogy and Andragogy, a Shared Approach to Education in Entrepreneurship for Students in Higher Education 233
Glorimar Santini-Hernández

Ecosystem experiences in UEE

Innovative Educators: The State of Undergraduate Entrepreneurship Education in the United States 255
Sara L. Cochran

CONTENTS   vii

**Ecosystem Engagement in Entrepreneurship Education:
A View from Sri Lanka**   271
Nilusha Gallage, Richard Laferriere,
and Christopher Selvarajah

**University-Based Entrepreneurship Ecosystems: The
Role of the Sustainable Family Business Theory
and Entrepreneurship Education**   291
Edgar Rogelio Ramírez-Solís, Lucía Rodríguez-Aceves,
and Verónica Ilián Baños-Monroy

**Digital Skills and Entrepreneurial Education in Malaysia:
Evidence from Experiential Learning**   311
Zatun Najahah Yusof, Najib Murad, and Borhannudin Yusof

**Experiential Learning in Online Entrepreneurship
Education: Lessons from an Undergraduate
Entrepreneurship Course**   333
Mavis S. B. Mensah, Keren N. A. Arthur,
and Enoch Mensah-Williams

**Conclusion: Entrepreneurship Education
for an Undergraduate Audience—A Review and Future
Directions**   353
Guillermo J. Larios-Hernandez, Andreas Walmsley,
and Itzel Lopez-Castro

Index   361

LIST OF CONTRIBUTORS

Keren N. A. Arthur Centre for Entrepreneurship and Small Enterprise Development, School of Business, University of Cape Coast, Cape Coast, Ghana

Verónica Ilián Baños-Monroy Tecnológico de Monterrey, Guadalajara, Mexico

Robin Bell Worcester Business School, University of Worcester, Worcester, UK

Lucrezia Casulli Hunter Centre for Entrepreneurship, University of Strathclyde Business School, Glasgow, Scotland, UK

Sara L. Cochran Indiana University, Bloomington, IN, USA

Lauren Davies Team Entrepreneurship Programme, Faculty of Business & Law, University of the West of England, Bristol, England

Carolin Decker-Lange The Open University, Milton Keynes, UK

John Alver Dobson Clark University, Worcester, MA, USA

Lisa Dobson DYME Institute, Worcester, MA, USA

Nilusha Gallage School of Business, Law and Entrepreneurship, Swinburne University of Technology, Melbourne, VIC, Australia

x LIST OF CONTRIBUTORS

Elissa Grossman University of Southern California, Los Angeles, CA, USA

Gustav Hägg Department of Urban Studies, Malmö University, Malmö, Sweden;
Sten K. Johnson Centre for Entrepreneurship, Lund University, Lund, Sweden

Alexandros Kakouris University of Peloponnese, Tripolis, Greece

Agnieszka Kurczewska Faculty of Economics and Sociology, University of Lodz, Lodz, Poland

Seynam Kwakuvi-Zagbedeh Bank of Ghana, Accra, Ghana

Richard Laferriere School of Business, Law and Entrepreneurship, Swinburne University of Technology, Melbourne, VIC, Australia

Knut Lange Royal Holloway University of London, London, UK

Guillermo J. Larios-Hernandez Universidad Anáhuac, Mexico, Mexico

Itzel Lopez-Castro Universidad Anáhuac, Mexico, Mexico

Mavis S. B. Mensah Centre for Entrepreneurship and Small Enterprise Development, School of Business, University of Cape Coast, Cape Coast, Ghana

Enoch Mensah-Williams Centre for Entrepreneurship and Small Enterprise Development, School of Business, University of Cape Coast, Cape Coast, Ghana

Daniele Morselli Free University of Bozen-Bolzano, Bolzano, Italy

Najib Murad University of Stirling, Scotland, UK

Heidi Neck Babson College, Wellesley, MA, USA

Karolina Ozadowicz University of the West of England, Bristol, England

Edgar Rogelio Ramírez-Solís Tecnológico de Monterrey, Guadalajara, Mexico

Lucía Rodríguez-Aceves Tecnológico de Monterrey, Guadalajara, Mexico

Glorimar Santini-Hernández EDP University of Puerto Rico, San Juan, Puerto Rico, USA

Christopher Selvarajah School of Business, Law and Entrepreneurship, Swinburne University of Technology, Melbourne, VIC, Australia

Jeffrey Stamp University of Minnesota, Minneapolis, MN, USA

Berrbizne Urzelai University of the West of England, Bristol, England

Andreas Walmsley Plymouth Marjon University, Plymouth, UK

Jonathan Nii Okai Welbeck Founder & Director Enterprise Risk Management Institute, University of Ghana, Accra, Ghana

Doan Winkel John Carroll University, University Heights, OH, USA

Birgitte Wraae Faculty of Business and Technology, Department of Finance and Administration, UCL University College, Odense, Denmark; Applied Research in Business and Technology, UCL University College, Odense, Denmark

Peter Wyer Institute of Continuing Education, University of Cambridge, Cambridge, UK

Borhannudin Yusof Universiti Malaysia Terengganu, Kuala Terengganu, Malaysia

Zatun Najahah Yusof University of Strathclyde, Scotland, UK

LIST OF FIGURES

Setting the Scene: The Student-Process-Educator Nexus in Entrepreneurship Education

Fig. 1	Three central components on the entrepreneurship education scene (*Source* Own depiction)	18
Fig. 2	The nexus between the entrepreneurship educator, learning space and the student (*Source* Own depiction)	24

Guiding the First-Year Student Entrepreneur: A Conceptual Map to Nudge Towards the Reversal Effect in Learning

Fig. 1	A conceptual map to nudge first-year students towards the reversal effect (*with an example of how to engage students in academic reading and enable them to understand key concepts related to the discovery or creation of opportunities*)	43

The Elusive Role of Play in Entrepreneurship Education

Fig. 1	Philosophy of play model	78
Fig. 2	Escalation of play	84

Dual Learning Space in Undergraduate Entrepreneurship Education: A Framework Proposal

Fig. 1	Dual Entrepreneurship Learning Space (DELS) Framework	125
Fig. 2	Design, execution and assessment learning process	127

What Do We Talk About When We Talk About Entrepreneurial Mindset Training?

Fig. 1	Mindsets and applications underpinning entrepreneurial behaviour	144

Delivering Entrepreneurship Education for Would-Be and Existing Small Business Entrepreneurs

Fig. 1	Small Business Strategic Planning and Development Frame	227
Fig. 2	Personal construct theory-based action learning and development path (Co-driven—Student and Owner Manager)	229

Pedagogy and Andragogy, a Shared Approach to Education in Entrepreneurship for Students in Higher Education

Fig. 1	The Pedagogy-Andragogy shared approach model for entrepreneurship education	242

Ecosystem Engagement in Entrepreneurship Education: A View from Sri Lanka

Fig. 1	External stakeholders contributing to U-BEE factors	282

University-Based Entrepreneurship Ecosystems: The Role of the Sustainable Family Business Theory and Entrepreneurship Education

Fig. 1	The relationship between family business and U-BEE systems	300

Digital Skills and Entrepreneurial Education in Malaysia: Evidence from Experiential Learning

Fig. 1	Structure of basic entrepreneurship course	319
Fig. 2	Perception of experiential learning by learning activities	324

| Fig. 3 | Perception of e-commerce and digital business experience by category of student | 324 |

Experiential Learning in Online Entrepreneurship Education: Lessons from an Undergraduate Entrepreneurship Course

| Fig. 1 | Online Experiential Learning (OEL) | 348 |

LIST OF TABLES

The Elusive Role of Play in Entrepreneurship Education

Table 1	Six types of play	72
Table 2	Qualities of play and In-class observation guidelines	74

Success Through Failure: Towards a Problem-Based Approach to Entrepreneurship Education

Table 1	Comparison between process-based and problem-based EE	182

Exploring the Professional Identity and Career Trajectories of Undergraduates on a Team-Based, Experiential Degree Programme

Table 1	Research participants	206

Ecosystem Engagement in Entrepreneurship Education: A View from Sri Lanka

Table 1	Actors engagement in U-BEE factors	283

Digital Skills and Entrepreneurial Education in Malaysia: Evidence from Experiential Learning

Table 1	Entrepreneurial and digital business knowledge	322

Experiential Learning in Online Entrepreneurship Education: Lessons from an Undergraduate Entrepreneurship Course

Table 1   Operationalising experiential learning   340

Introduction: The 'Why', the 'What' and the 'How' of Entrepreneurship Education

Guillermo J. Larios-Hernandez, Andreas Walmsley, and Itzel Lopez-Castro

It is no longer possible to convincingly argue that entrepreneurship education (EE), its practice or underpinning theory are nascent. As interest in entrepreneurship on the part of policymakers and scholars has grown rapidly in the last two decades, so has the literature on entrepreneurship education (EE). A growing body of literature in the form of academic articles, books and even journals are now dedicated specifically to EE. Following in the footsteps of a surge in interest in entrepreneurship, scholarship in the area of EE has proliferated since

---

G. J. Larios-Hernandez (✉) · I. Lopez-Castro
Universidad Anáhuac, Mexico, Mexico
e-mail: guillermo.lariosh@anahuac.mx

I. Lopez-Castro
e-mail: itzel.lopez@anahuac.mx

A. Walmsley
Plymouth Marjon University, Plymouth, UK
e-mail: awalmsley@marjon.ac.uk

© The Author(s), under exclusive license to Springer Nature Switzerland AG 2022
G. J. Larios-Hernandez et al. (eds.), *Theorising Undergraduate Entrepreneurship Education*,
https://doi.org/10.1007/978-3-030-87865-8_1

calls were made to seek to further its legitimacy (Kuratko, 2005), more recently seeing the creation of dedicated journals such as the Journal of Entrepreneurship Education and Pedagogy (its first issue being published in January 2018). Special issues on entrepreneurship education in other journals similarly point to a lively interest in EE (for example Vol. 6, No. 5 of the International Journal of Entrepreneurial Behaviour and Research, or several special issues in the journal Education and Training). This mirrors interest in the teaching of entrepreneurship where globally growth in entrepreneurship programmes has taken off. However, despite recent advances, the scholarship of EE has not kept pace with practice (Morris & Liguori, 2016), whereby entrepreneurship educators are still grappling with the 'how', 'what', 'why' and 'for whom' of EE (see, for example, Lackéus, 2015; Fayolle & Gailly, 2008).

Nonetheless, though it seems that we are reaching a tipping point in EE (Neck & Corbett, 2018), many scholars appear to have neglected, at least explicitly, the type of EE that focuses on the largest group of university students: undergraduates, their needs and ambitions (e.g. psychological needs, career developmental needs, generational needs [role of generation theory], experiential needs, etc.). As such, these needs are likely to be quite different from the requirements of other cohorts, e.g. postgraduate students, mid-life and mature entrepreneurs, pre-university students. It is upon this backdrop that we are delighted to have been able to pull together 19 chapters covering a range of topics relating to EE set within the context of the undergraduate student specifically.

A focus in particular on the undergraduate student of higher education is offered for a number of reasons. Firstly, alongside entrepreneurship's potential in driving economic renewal, it offers a means for many people to join the economic mainstream. Although this is usually understood as entrepreneurial firms creating jobs, it also relates to graduate entrepreneurship. Setting up a business upon graduating, or even during one's studies, should be seen as an alternative to traditional labour market entry. It is too early to say what the impact of the COVID-19 pandemic will have on self-employment rates: on the one hand it has raised awareness among the self-employed of the risks of 'going it alone' (Strauss, 2020) but at the same time it may serve as a wakeup call to those unsatisfied in their current positions, or worse, who have been made redundant as a result of digitalisation and organisational change, situations that may have encouraged a type of necessity entrepreneurship. Nonetheless, UEE is instrumental not as a result of lack of opportunities in local labour markets, but because the business start-up is now increasingly recognised as a legitimate goal of higher education alongside the traditional route into employment.

More generally, even before the pandemic or the 2007/2008 financial crisis had arisen, attention was being drawn to the changing nature of the world of work. In fact, notions of Boundaryless (Arthur & Rousseau, 1996) and Protean careers (Hall, 1996) that characterise the fluidity of modern careers, and indeed lives, were coined some time ago. Yet continued rapid advances in technology, shifting societal norms and expectations, economic structures and sustainability considerations shape the nature of work and young people's career aspirations. Hence, beyond a simple response to unemployment, the need to be enterprising in one's career is likely to grow in the foreseeable future.

Rather than a sole focus on business start-up, EE can develop enterprising graduates who can contribute to the dynamism of firms (via intra- or corporate entrepreneurship). This relates to a distinction sometimes clarified by the use of explicit terminology: entrepreneurship education pointing to business start-up and enterprise education a more general development of enterprise skills and attributes; in this book we are interested in both, especially considering the rise of enterprise education in disciplines other than business.

Benefits to the individual aside, policymakers may be keen to promote EE as a form of human capital development. Thus, despite underlying complexities, a positive relationship between human capital development via education and economic growth is widely accepted (Barro, 2001; Mincer, 1984). Theoretically, if EE adds to a nation's human capital stock individuals with an enterprising mindset, then there is a strong case to be made for EE as a driver of economic growth and renewal, even more so at a time of rapidly changing, uncertain, environments that call for those able to adapt, identify and evaluate new opportunities. In a fast-paced business environment, the benefits to the individual and also to society of having an entrepreneurial mindset are clearly augmented. The potential of EE to support the development of these mindsets in undergraduates is something worthy of study (Gibb, 2011).

A further reason we wanted to focus on undergraduates is because they constitute the most widely reported group of individuals who have received EE. Because of this, their specific needs and circumstances are not always directly acknowledged, however; they are simply assumed. In pulling together the contributions for this text we wanted to draw attention to the fact that they are a distinct analytical category, deserving of a deliberate rather than accidental focus. Here, although higher education is not exclusive to young people, especially if we consider the promotion of the idea of lifelong learning, the majority of undergraduates are still youth (taking the UN definition of youth as those aged between 15 and 24). This period in an individual's life presents a number of challenges as they transition from childhood to adulthood, so-called rights of passage (Irwin, 1995): finding one's place in the world, developing one's identity and career interests are all associated with this phase. Donald Super's work on the theory of career development (1957, 1990) calls this period an exploration phase, where the individual experiments with different career options, something reflected also in Gottfredson's theory of career development (2002) where the individual seeks to identify suitable career options and then makes compromises based on personal ability and congruence with self-concept. Generation Theory (Mannheim, 1952), which has attracted much scholarly interest, draws on the notion that youth are more open and impressionable, and that experiences gained in youth may shape our values and outlook even later in life.

Moreover, transitions to adulthood are becoming longer and more complex (Keep, 2012), a situation brought about by rapid change in many spheres of life, in an era termed 'liquid modernity' by Baumann (2000). In many respects youth today are offered more opportunities than ever before and yet there are fewer certainties. Frequently we hear about technological obsolescence, about preparing youth for jobs that do not even exist yet, about being in a state of constant disruption. Statistics vary, of course, but according to one Canadian source Generation X spends over 20% longer in each job they hold than Gen Y does. The US Labour Bureau said Late Baby Boomers (those born between 1957 and 1964) held on average 12 jobs in their lifetime; nearly half of these jobs were between 18 and 24. The general view now is that young people will have even more jobs, and indeed careers, than this.

Youth (un)employment continues to pose a serious challenge to society. Young people are three times more likely to be unemployed than adults, a statistic that has worsened since the COVID-19 crisis struck (ILO, 2021); unsurprisingly it is something policymakers are keen to address. The extent to which EE can provide youth with the skills and attributes needed to navigate the shifting sands of the world of work is an important question. It seems youth today are going to have to be more self-reliant, adaptable, willing to take calculated risks and generally adopt an 'opportunity identification logic' (Lackéus, 2018). Nowadays, these skills are essential considering the grand challenges that this generation would have to face in the foreseeable future, whose entrepreneurial action turns out necessary for sustainable change. Only such an entrepreneurial mindset might be in position to develop bottom-up value-creation initiatives that tap into opportunities to act. In that regard, alternative proposals to solve problems (value creation) are required to incorporate a higher market value proposition, which becomes a compulsory requirement if the entrepreneurial initiative is to survive. This is another message that EE intends to convey to HE students, who must be trained to understand that created value can also be captured.

Theorising Undergraduate Entrepreneurship Education aims to tap into and extend ongoing debates about the nature, manifestation and purpose of EE. This is a book intended for a global audience, which presents state-of-the art contributions on the challenges and opportunities that entrepreneurship educators face around the world to equip undergraduate students with entrepreneurial skills, develop their entrepreneurial mindsets and capabilities, and more generally, take advantage of programmes and curricula available in their ecosystem. This is why this book has been organised in three parts. The first part has compiled a variety of theoretical perspectives that emphasise distinctive theories, reflections, ideas and models that build an Undergraduate Entrepreneurship Education (UEE) scaffolding.

In the second chapter, entitled "Setting the Scene: The Student-Process-Educator Nexus in Entrepreneurship Education", Wraae has emphasised the social process that supports EE, in which educators and students relate to each other through a dialogic experience that takes place in a safe learning space. According to the author, it is the educator's responsibility to encourage the creation of such a space (together with each student), which is determinant to assist UEE in developing their entrepreneurial identity, inviting scholars to reinterpret the role of the educator in EE. Following a cognitive approach to instruction, Hägg and Kurczewska propose the concept of Odigogy in chapter "Guiding the First-Year Student Entrepreneur: A Conceptual Map to Nudge Towards the Reversal Effect in Learning", which is an approach to UEE that takes into consideration students' developmental stage, identifying guidance and precise instructions as the educator's expected effort, who orchestrate activities according to the learner's absorptive capacity. In their proposal, Odigogy considers youngsters' limited experience and knowledge, offering a practical framework, which progressively guides the HE student, particularly in the first year, to execute activities that help them accomplish responsibility for learning according to a particular context.

In other words, entrepreneurial knowledge is constructed through the educator's intervention, who uses mediating artefacts (a problem or an intended solution) as auxiliary stimulus to guide students towards the development of their own agency. This is the social constructivist viewpoint covered by Morselli and Kakouris in chapter "Teaching Entrepreneurship to Undergraduates: A Vygotskian Perspective", who base their analysis on the Vygotskian principles of mediation and double stimulation, presenting a socio-cultural approach to UEE exemplified in two instructional case studies. An instance of such a mediating artefact is the function of play, which is exposed by Neck, Grossman, Winkel and Stamp in chapter "The Elusive Role of Play in Entrepreneurship Education". In this chapter, the role of play is emphasised as an educational tool to foster flexibility and action in the face of uncertainty, leading to self-discovery and learning. Neck et al. have proposed four guiding principles to design scalable play experiences, leading to the development of a shared and co-created curiosity and courage, new perspectives, sense-making, and fun, whose educational outcomes involve the creation of an entrepreneurial mindset (EM) that is developed when students are able to challenge the status quo.

Hence, EE goes beyond enterprising in a pure business start-up sense, and includes other career-related dimensions of particular importance for youth. This is an approach covered by Walmsley, Decker-Lange and Lange in chapter "Conceptualising the Entrepreneurship Education and Employability Nexus". In this part of the book, the authors review the association between EE and employability, proposing three dimensions of action that include the start-up, the concept of entrepreneurship and career development. From this perspective, EE becomes relevant for a generation that embraces autonomy and career fluidity, challenging the typical employee-employer-society/economy logic to employability for an entrepreneur-society/economy. Also, skills for new venture creation are also useful in established businesses, indicating the upsurge of another type of employability skills that require HE students to be ready for alternative labour market contexts or develop their own employability rather than seek employment.

This part closes with design considerations about the learning space where the EE process takes place, including the educator's orchestrated activities as mediating artefacts, according to the learning objectives and needs of young HE students. Based on the maturity level of young learners, chapter "Dual Learning Space in Undergraduate Entrepreneurship Education: A Framework Proposal" focuses on the development of a framework to describe the advancement of UEE in a dual learning space: one led by the educator and another one taking place in a business-like real situation, with implications in didactic methods and instructional design. The model emphasises the role of subjective mentorship to guide divergent and convergent thinking in UEE.

On the other hand, EE has particularly emphasised a variety of techniques, methods and processes with little consideration to the context and psycho-educational qualities of the young university recipients. In particular, today's young undergraduate students have adopted and are keen to explore perspectives of EE that go beyond the purely economic, i.e. EE for responsible, sustainable, social and transformational entrepreneurship as well as a focus on eco-preneurship. The deliberate focus on broader perspectives of the purpose of EE is fairly novel. For this reason, Part II in this book, 'Impacting the Mindset of the Undergraduate', aims to contribute to the discussion of entrepreneurial mindset (EM) from a different approach: that of the typical, young undergraduate student, its characteristic archetypes and needs for entrepreneurial skills development. Chapter "What Do We Talk About When We Talk About Entrepreneurial Mindset Training?", by Casulli, introduces the concept of entrepreneurial mindset beyond the typical approach to creativity and ideation, emphasising uncertainty and ambiguity as key components of the construction of an EM. This viewpoint implies that education of the EM involves a psychological intervention to encourage an entrepreneurial behaviour among youngsters, considering the development of skills such as failure tolerance, empathy, team building and openness to feedback. Regarding those EE angles that extend beyond the pure economic logic, Bell in chapter "Supporting Students and Society Underpinning Entrepreneurship Education with a Humanistic Philosophy" emphasises the relevance of humanistic philosophy to UEE, demonstrating that compassion within entrepreneurship should be a core objective to develop students' integrative judgement and value-oriented skills. This approach involves learning through human interactions to develop attitudes, morals, values and skills, personal growth, leading to a type of mission-entrepreneurship.

Additionally, Dobson and Dobson in chapter "Success Through Failure: Towards a Problem-Based Approach to Entrepreneurship Education" find in pedagogical approaches an explanation for why new venture creation hasn't increased as a result of EE, particularly in the United States. This chapter highlights autonomy and passion over traditional process-based learning for a generation of young students that want to change the world but are risk-averse and overlook their true efficacy. The authors advocate for a type of EE practice that encourages self-reflection and autonomy through a problem-based approach in a learning environment that provides experiences outside the classroom, involving failure as a key element of EE. In this sense, Davies, Urzelai and Ozadowicz in chapter "Exploring the Professional Identity and Career Trajectories of Undergraduates on a Team-Based, Experiential Degree Programme" warn against programmes that place students into too protective 'bubbles', education-safe environments that ignore the reality of failure. They stress the importance of reflective skills, which help students determine their preferred career trajectory, based on their own values and personal drivers that encourage them to create opportunities, not just identify them, away from the venture creation metric and closer to the EM required to navigate uncertainty. Based on an assessment of the impact of an entrepreneurship programme in the UK (Team Academy), the authors conceptualise learning as team-based, self-managed and experiential, leading to the self-determination of career identity.

Pedagogical underpinnings of EM development are provided by Wyer, Kwakuvi-Zagbedeh and Welbeck. Informed by the experience of a SME owner, Wyer et al. propose Personal Construct Theory [PCT] to explain the EE learning process, considering it a theoretical framework that implicitly conceptualises learning as embedded in personal constructs, where the role of EE is to reflect on adequacy of existing constructs. Based on knowledge offered by the educator, students identify potential for construction of new meanings, where construct definition and redefinition represent a process of learning to learn. Serendipity and experimentation with real people are resources for what they call a 'learning conversation', which lead to personal construing/re-construing processes. In line with this approach, Santini (chapter "Pedagogy and Andragogy, a Shared Approach to Education in Entrepreneurship for Students in Higher Education") closes this part, acknowledging that HE students constitute a heterogeneous population, where EE is conceived as a dynamic and iterative contextualised progression of learning stages that make use of pedagogical and andragogical education techniques, particularly related to experiential learning, mindset develop and mentoring.

Considering that the educator's perspective has remained somewhat silent in the discussions around EE (Neck & Corbett, 2018; Wraae & Walmsley, 2020), the final chapters included in this title provide educators with a voice to explain how they participate in the topic of entrepreneurship education, how undergraduate students engage and respond to EE, and how institutional frameworks for EE may support it. This is the focus of Part III: 'Ecosystem Experiences in UEE', which presents applied research on EE in HE at a global level. To initiate this part (chapter "Innovative Educators: The State of Undergraduate Entrepreneurship Education in the United States"), Cochran revisits some of the EE programmes in the United States to derive core research topics discussed in this ecosystem, exemplifying relevant programmes and courses, usable techniques types of extra(co)-curricular programmes, and outcomes to realise that educators continue to act entrepreneurially. To exemplify such a scholarly innovation, Gallage, Laferriere and Selvarajah (chapter "Ecosystem Engagement in Entrepreneurship Education: A View from Sri Lanka") derive, from case interviews in Sri Lanka, a proposed expansion of the university-based entrepreneurship ecosystem (U-BEE) to include the role of parents, alumni entrepreneurs' tutorials and student involvement in start-ups/SMEs projects, confronting traditional viewpoints that consider internal stakeholders such as students, faculty or university incubator staff. In the same line of thought, chapter "University-Based Entrepreneurship Ecosystems: The Role of the Sustainable Family Business Theory and Entrepreneurship Education" makes a conceptual proposal to connect family business principles (based on the sustainable family business theory or SFBT) and the elements of a U-BEE that may provide HE students (the heirs) with integrated formal and informal EE. Business continuity and success is a topic that could arguably be included in more UEE courses, especially in communities where it is quite typical for a son or daughter to take over the family business (in rural communities, for example).

Another instance of innovative EE is provided by Yusof, Murad and Yusof in chapter "Digital Skills and Entrepreneurial Education in Malaysia: Evidence from Experiential Learning", who analyse the outcome of the application of a digital business project to a UEE class, documenting the students' experience in terms of entrepreneurial mindset and digital literacy. These results are derived from an EE programme study in Malaysia, in which students are required to launch and manage a business developed on a government-supported online entrepreneurial platform. The authors consider that the goal of EE is the creation of the entrepreneur, whose skills should be developed in a controlled environment that allows for experimentation.

To end this book, Mensah, Arthur and Mensah-Williams (chapter "Experiential Learning in Online Entrepreneurship Education: Lessons from an Undergraduate Entrepreneurship Course") highlight a case of experiential learning in an online EE programme in Ghana, proposing a framework that combines senses, cognition and experiences to drive reflection. Based on the analysis of audio-visuals and discussion forums, the authors provide a narrative of students' behaviour, providing examples of experience participation and reflection.

In summary, *Theorising Undergraduate Entrepreneurship Education* offers a variety of reflections and perspectives of EE, e.g. pedagogy, humanism, COVID-19, employability-entrepreneurship liaison, digital skills, etc., that go beyond traditional approaches, considering a global audience with examples from around the world. The deliberate focus on undergraduate students, their needs and ambitions has added novelty, combining theory of EE with its practice, which grants support to undergraduate educators in their efforts to understand why and how entrepreneurship is to be taught to this generational cohort. For the reasons expressed in this Introduction, we maintain it is crucial for educators to continue to explore how to teach entrepreneurship, to consider which outcomes should be achieved, and how these may be measured. How and what we teach must take into account who we are teaching to; this being a consideration that becomes particularly challenging in a field that has been traditionally non-routine activity for universities. Yet, HE and young students have evolved together and UEE continues to extend its influence to more university curricula. Our text seeks to offer insights that may help institutions and educators adapt to this new reality, hoping to contribute to the creation of higher-order skills and competences that interrelate the business, academic and personal worlds that converge nowadays in our university milieus.

References

Arthur, M., & Rousseau, D. M. (1996). *The Boundaryless career: A new employment principle for a new organizational era*. Oxford University Press.

Barro, R. (2001). Human capital and growth (Conference proceeding). *American Economic Review, 91*(2), 12–17.

Bauman, Z. (2000). *Liquid modernity*. Polity Press.

Fayolle, A., & Gailly, B. (2008). From craft to science - Teaching models and learning processes in entrepreneurship education. *Journal of European Industrial Training, 32*, 569–593. https://doi.org/10.1108/03090590810899838

Gottfredson, L. S. (2002). Gottfredson's theory of circumscription, compromise, and self-creation. In D. Brown (Ed.), *Career choice and development* (4th ed., pp. 85–148). Jossey-Bass.

Gibb, A. (2011). Concepts into practice: Meeting the challenge of development of entrepreneurship educators around an innovative paradigm: The case of the International Entrepreneurship Educators' Programme (IEEP). *International Journal of Entrepreneurial Behavior & Research, 17*(2), 146–165. https://doi.org/10.1108/13552551111114914

Hall, D. T. (1996). Protean careers of the 21st century. *Academy of Management Executive, 10*(4), 8–16. https://doi.org/10.5465/ame.1996.3145315

International Labour Office. (2021). *Statistical brief: An update on the youth labour market impact of the COVID-19 crisis*. ILO. https://www.ilo.org/wcmsp5/groups/public/---ed_emp/documents/briefingnote/wcms_795479.pdf

Irwin, S. (1995). *Rights of passage. Social change and the transition from youth to adulthood*. UCL Press.

Keep, E. (2012). *Youth transitions, the labour market and entry into employment: some reflections and questions*. Skope Publications.

Kuratko, D. F. (2005). The emergence of entrepreneurship education: development, trends, and challenges. *Entrepreneurship Theory and Practice, 29*(5), 577–597. https://doi.org/10.1111/j.1540-6520.2005.00099.x

Lackéus, M. (2015). *Entrepreneurship in education: What, when, why, how*. Europe: OECD. Recovered from https://www.oecd.org/cfe/leed/BGP_Entrepreneurship-in-Education.pdf

Lackéus, M. (2018). Making enterprise education more relevant through mission creep. In G. Mulholland & J. Turner (Eds.). *Enterprising education in UK higher education: Challenges for theory and practice*. Routledge.

Mannheim, K. (1952). *The problem of generations. Essays on the sociology of knowledge*. Routledge.

Mincer, J. (1984). Human capital and economic growth. *Economics of Education Review, 3*(3), 195–205. https://doi.org/10.1016/0272-7757(84)90032-3

Morris, M. H., & Liguori, E. (2016). Preface: Teaching reason and the unreasonable. In M. H. Morris & E. Ligouri (Eds.). *Annals of entrepreneurship education and pedagogy* (pp. xiv–xxii). Edward Elgar.

Neck, H. M., & Corbett, A. C. (2018). The scholarship of teaching and learning entrepreneurship. *Entrepreneurship Education and Pedagogy, 1*(1), 8–41. https://doi.org/10.1177%2F2515127417737286

Strauss, D. (2020, November 23). Covid crisis threatens UK boom in self-employed work. *Financial Times*. https://www.ft.com/content/3d94b170-c6be-44dd-95ac-436284693090

Super, D. (1957). *The psychology of careers*. Harper.

Super, D. (1990). A life-span, life space approach to career development. In D. Brown, L. Brooks & Associates (Eds.), *Career choice and development* (2nd ed., pp. 197–261). Jossey Bass.

Wraae, B., & Walmsley, A. (2020). Behind the scenes: Spotlight on the entrepreneurship educator. *Education + Training, 62*(3), 255–270. https://doi.org/10.1108/ET-01-2019-0009

Distinctive Approaches to Undergraduate Entrepreneurship Education

Setting the Scene: The Student-Process-Educator Nexus in Entrepreneurship Education

Birgitte Wraae

1 INTRODUCTION

Teaching entrepreneurship to undergraduates and what takes places in the classroom can in many ways be compared to setting a scene in the theatre. Students are the leading actors surrounded by elements in supporting roles. While not a cultural art scene entrepreneurship education (EE) is yet a similar scene with actors assigned to different roles. The scene of EE can best be described as dialogic system with elements such as the institution, the community, the educational process and the entrepreneurship educator that evolves around each student (Jones & Matlay, 2011). While each student is the star of their own show the star cannot shine

---

B. Wraae (✉)
Faculty of Business and Technology, Department of Finance and Administration, UCL University College, Odense, Denmark
e-mail: biwr@ucl.dk

Applied Research in Business and Technology, UCL University College, Odense, Denmark

© The Author(s), under exclusive license to Springer Nature Switzerland AG 2022
G. J. Larios-Hernandez et al. (eds.), *Theorising Undergraduate Entrepreneurship Education*,
https://doi.org/10.1007/978-3-030-87865-8_2

without the necessary support. Unclear directions from the entrepreneurship educator add to the probability that only very skilled stars will manage to obtain a personal success. However, EE is for all and as such the entrepreneurial classroom should offer possibilities for all. This is the setup for this chapter.

From a research perspective, EE research is rather diverse, however, the dominant focus concerning entrepreneurial pedagogy and teaching approaches has been on the outcome and less on 'how' to teach entrepreneurship and even lesser on how both students and educators should act in this perspective. This chapter zooms into the roles, relationship and interaction between the educator and student using the entrepreneurial classroom or learning space as a scene for student identity development. It proposes a framework that assists the entrepreneurship educator to direct the play on the entrepreneurial learning scene, that could act as an inspirational manual for the entrepreneurship educator who wishes to develop students' entrepreneurial identity by focusing on how the entrepreneurial learning space is created. The chapter ends with some practical propositions of what the entrepreneurship educator could do to put the framework into play in an undergraduate setting.

2 Understanding the Context in Entrepreneurship Education

Often EE is linked to the purpose of creating a business plan and starting up a business which affects the teaching focus and learning approach. However, as the purpose of the chapter is to discuss and propose how the entrepreneurship educator can assist in students' entrepreneurial identity development a wider focus on EE is needed. In this context, EE acts as the scene for becoming entrepreneurial hence a movement from the 'starting up' perspective towards the 'stepping up' perspective that embraces both the purpose of either being an entrepreneur or becoming entrepreneurial (Jones & Matlay, 2011). In the wider context of EE becoming entrepreneurial relates to each students' personal development, being creative, taking initiative and building self-reliance among other things (Lackéus, 2015). As an entrepreneurship educator, it is important to consider one's own understanding of the EE context, the definitions, and purposes. The approach to entrepreneurship stems from these clarifications and act as the thread that binds plan, content and execution including the perception of learning objectives and assessment of the students together (Samwel Mwasalwiba, 2010).

In this chapter, EE is defined broadly as developing the mindset, skill set and practice necessary for starting new ventures, yet the outcomes of such education are far-reaching supporting the life skills necessary to live productive lives even if one does not start a business thus empowering each student through EE (Lackéus, 2015; Neck & Corbett, 2018). This definition of EE implies an entrepreneurial learning approach that reaches further than using conventional teaching methods only, while at the same time emphasises the potential of EE as a driver for students to undergo a personal transition as well.

To set the scene further, this chapter moves beyond the traditional view on the classroom denominating the entrepreneurial learning space. The reasoning is that the classroom is more than 'only' a physical room where the students and the educator meet. Alongside the traditional understanding of a room a mental room appears in which the educator has a large degree of influence. This mental room includes content, methods and approaches used in class when setting the scene of EE. The mental room represents the entrepreneurship educator's interpretation of how to teach entrepreneurship, how the educator will allow and encourage student development (Sagar, 2015). The understanding of the entrepreneurial learning space challenges the conventional assumption that students only learn during their presence and meeting with their educator in the classroom. Learning can take place everywhere, for instance when the entrepreneurial learning approach includes applying a practical element to the course content that sends the students out of the classroom to test their ideas in practice. Moreover, students interact with fellow students outside the classroom which reinforces the assumption that entrepreneurial learning takes places both inside and outside of the classroom.

Presenting the Components of the Play

Something 'magical' can and should happen in the entrepreneurial learning space. As illustrated in Fig. 1, there is a deeply connected dialogical relationship between the entrepreneurship educator and each student through the educational process. This dialogic relationship influences how the educator teaches entrepreneurship and impact the development of what happens in the classroom. The entrepreneurship educators influence

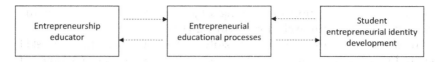

Fig. 1 Three central components on the entrepreneurship education scene (*Source* Own depiction)

students in their 'becoming' towards their entrepreneurial identity development where they acknowledge themselves being able to act in that role. Likewise, the students' interaction and feedback influence the role of the entrepreneurship educator as well.

The three components in Fig. 1 represent the backbone of this chapter. At a first glance, the illustrated relationships seem simple; however, each element represents a complexity bound by dialogic relationships that together 'form a system that cannot be divided if it is to be understood' (Bruyat & Julien, 2001, p. 169). The entrepreneurial educational processes are the stage where the story unfolds with each student as the lead actor and the entrepreneurship educator as the primary director of the play bound together through interactions in the entrepreneurial learning space.

Behind the scenes, the entrepreneurship educator is embedded in a system of own dialogic relationships with a range of stakeholders (Wraae & Walmsley, 2020). Hannon (2018) even views entrepreneurship educators in the role of entrepreneurial leaders within the organisation. The educator is (re)acting to how the educational frames of reference are decided by the institution in order to plan and execute teaching entrepreneurship. Further, they act as the link between the students and the outside world, for instance by creating contact to incubator environments and the private sector. In many ways, the entrepreneurship educator is the 'buffer' between the students and the elements that surrounds the students in their daily lives as students. How the educators take on the role of being and acting as an entrepreneurship educator is based on the view of their own role in relation to the dialogic relationships (Wraae & Walmsley, 2020) and their previous entrepreneurial experience as well as their experience as educators (Wraae et al., 2021).

The scene, the entrepreneurial educational processes, is the entrepreneurial learning space and the delivery of teaching. Its focus is not exclusively on the immediate creation of new businesses, rather it evolves around developing certain personal qualities, entrepreneurial attitudes, and skills. It is the scene where students have their rehearsals through a wide variety of situations, aims, methods, and teaching approaches (Fayolle et al., 2006; Harmeling, 2011; Pittaway & Thorpe, 2012; Svensson et al., 2017).

On the centre stage, the entrepreneurial play unfolds with each student, that is expected to take on a leading role on their entrepreneurial identity development journey. Having the leading role really means to take an active role. The student cannot act as an extra on their own show. They must act in the role of (future) entrepreneurs. At the same time, students enter the entrepreneurial learning space with different backgrounds, life experiences (thus far), skills and competences. In other words, they represent a wide span of differences, that the entrepreneurship educator needs to be aware of in the student's journey towards a future career (Jones & Matlay, 2011).

Setting a Transformative Scene—The Educational Entrepreneurial Processes

Zooming in on the scene, the educational entrepreneurial processes, is where the entrepreneurship educator and the students meet and play out their role in students' entrepreneurial learning journey and identity formation. This is the stage for both the rehearsals and where the opening show takes place.

While it can be discussed whether the entrepreneurial learning approaches can be considered a process (Sagar, 2015) or a method (Neck & Greene, 2011)—this relates to the unpredictability of acting entrepreneurially—there is an agreement that teaching entrepreneurship should include students learning through a practical and experiential context where the gained knowledge, learned tools and theories are put into practice while giving the students the possibility to reflect on that practice and their own role (Sagar, 2015; Wraae et al., 2020).

Transformative learning relates to EE as it: 'refers to the process by which we transform our taken-for-granted frames of reference (meaning perspectives, habits of mind, mind-sets) to make them more inclusive, discriminating, open, emotionally capable of change, and reflective so that they may generate beliefs and opinions that will prove more true or justified to guide action' (Mezirow, 2000, pp. 7–8).

To implement transformative learning a series of teaching approaches are possible. Each represents different purposes in terms of content and role distribution. The 'for' and 'through' approaches are each linked to activity-based learning as a means to develop entrepreneurial students (Neck & Greene, 2011; Robinson & Blenker, 2014). The 'demand' and 'competence' models are related to the entrepreneurship educator's view on education and the role of respectively student and educator (Béchard & Grégoire, 2005; Nabi et al., 2016). As such, the entrepreneurship educator faces possibilities and choices when deciding what should take place in the entrepreneurial learning space. However, keeping the transformative learning approach in mind, the overall role of the educator is to assist students to become both aware and critical of their own assumptions and others' assumptions as well in order to use their imagination to look at and redefine problems from a different perspective to facilitate transformative learning (Mezirow, 1997).

Mezirow's (1997, 2000) transformative learning approach aligns with the principles of andragogy and heutagogy (Jones, 2015, 2019; Neck & Corbett, 2018). Each principle resonates around the interaction between the student and the educator either in the form of a mutual agreement between each student and the educator on the outcome (andragogy) or the activities the students initiate (heutagogy), thus self-determined learning and facilitating their own learning process (Jones, 2015). Each student is encouraged to take a personal responsibility to make meaning of the learned, however not in isolation but in cooperation with the educator, that facilitates a learning environment where this is possible (Garrison, 1997). Each student must claim ownership over their own learning and make sense of acting entrepreneurially and achieve a sense of belonging in the entrepreneurial learning space and to the actors in that space (Donnellon et al., 2014; Nielsen & Gartner, 2017).

Students having a real-world experience rather than simply re-producing theoretical concepts experience 'learning by doing' or 'doing by learning' producing problem-solving and solutions and having to use their knowledge to make a case for the important aspects of the given task. By doing so, the entrepreneurship educator is engaging the student's senses, feelings and thinking (Jones & Matlay, 2011), hence: 'Learning is best facilitated by a process that draws out the students' beliefs and ideas about a topic so that they can be examined, tested, and integrated with new, more refined ideas' (Kolb & Kolb, 2005, p. 194). Further, learning takes place when students interact with the surrounding environment (Kolb & Kolb, 2005). Therefore, real-world experience should be a part of the transformative learning approach as an important contributor to students' learning and their making sense, meaning and purpose of their experiences.

Entrepreneurship as the Scene for Student Identity Development

A part of being an undergraduate student includes undergoing an identity development journey that makes sense of 'who am I' and making sense of what each student is going to become (Nielsen & Gartner, 2017). Being a student includes building 'identity capital' that defines themselves internally and how others define them externally in different contexts (Varelas, 2012). The role transformation is an ongoing part of every student's life. In the educational context, the general student role conception is that a student is someone that prepare for class, show up and participate, have an attitude (being active or passive), hand in assignments and finally, pass their exam to get their grade.

However, upon entering the entrepreneurial learning space that role conception is challenged more than in the traditional sense when each student is expected to take on the role as an active student that is responsible for own learning while experiencing an entrepreneurial transformation through the offered learning processes. As such, students' entrepreneurial learning experience is strongly linked to their identity construction (Brush & Gale, 2015) however sensing multiple identities in the process, for instance as both students, entrepreneurs and predefined future worker identity (Nielsen & Gartner, 2017).

While identity transformation can be explained by a shift in roles, it can also be explained as a result of an individual socialisation process when the student creates meaning through the interaction with the educator and the other students (Donnellon et al., 2014). Further, the narrative or the dialogue assist in the identity formation. When the student experiences dialogues with him or herself and with others as a part of the entrepreneurial process, it creates experiences that contribute to the entrepreneurial identity construction (Donnellon et al., 2014).

The student can also adopt an entrepreneurial identity by claiming to be an entrepreneur while in the process of creating a new venture (Rigg &

O'Dwyer, 2012). Finally, symbols contribute to entrepreneurial development, for instance when the student presents a prototype or pitch an idea or dresses up to make an impact to an audience (Donnellon et al., 2014).

The student entrepreneurial identity construction, therefore, links to different theoretical identity perspectives. The students themselves must perceive their own entrepreneurial role (identity theory) as well as a shared construction of entrepreneurship in groups (social identity theory). Furthermore, students are formed in a social process by their educator, their student peers and what happens both inside and beyond the classroom and the educational facilities (Kolb & Kolb, 2005; Nielsen & Gartner, 2017). Finally, the students must consider themselves in a future job-related perspective and how they will act either as entrepreneurs or intrapreneurs for that matter (professional identity theory).

As the focus of the chapter is the entrepreneurship educator assists the students in their becoming—their entrepreneurial identity development—the role of the entrepreneurship educator is to give each student a sense of belonging through enabling students with meaning, motivation and decision-making competences (Donnellon et al., 2014; Hytti & Heinonen, 2013).

Reflection as a Supporting Role to Student Identity Development

For each student to make sense of the 'who am I' question, they must engage in a complex reflective process and find meaning through the entrepreneurial learning processes (Donnellon et al., 2014). As such, reflection serves to understand, recognise, and even acknowledge own identity development in EE. Reflection triggers insights about learning and about the entrepreneurial process including which skills that are needed to act through entrepreneurship. Students become empowered to understand their own identity and their identity formation. Further, they obtain an awareness of the transformation they are going through and the shift between different identities; that they leave something and move towards a new understanding of themselves. In short, they obtain self-insights into their own personal transformation (Wraae et al., 2020).

Self-reflective and self-assessment tools have proven useful to connect the learned to own learning and identity development. Moreover, such tools enhance critical thinking when the students assess themselves in the light of own skills and competences. Reflections in EE can have various goals and foci from doing self-observations of self, of experiences, of relations to others to assessment of dreams and future career aspirations (Lindh, 2017; Pittaway & Thorpe, 2012). The latter is especially important for undergraduate students as they are in their early stage of career development.

For students to obtain self-insights and understanding of own self and future role towards an identity development, Wraae et al. (2020) suggest individual video clip as a concrete and effective tool that allows students the possibility to reflect on their themselves in an entrepreneurial perspective without any interruptions from anyone. Individual assignments 'force' each student to reflect on themselves. Alongside the tool, however, the educator must give room for reflection to happen and there must be something to reflect upon. Only then, are the students capable of reflecting on themselves in an entrepreneurial perspective and obtaining crucial personal insights and transformations about themselves in an entrepreneurial perspective (Wraae et al., 2020). The role of the entrepreneurship educator is therefore to encourage students to learn how to learn and assist the students to develop the right capabilities to be able to do so.

The Framework and the Nexus Between the Actors in EE

The dialogic relationship between educator and student relates to andragogy and heutagogy as the entrepreneurship educator must view each student as an individual and give each student an active role in their own learning process. On the other hand, student identity development can only happen in cooperation with each student. Based on the discussions so far this section proposes how the educator can contribute to students' entrepreneurial identity development.

Figure 2 illustrates a suggested framework—a proposal for how to develop students' entrepreneurial identities. It acts as an illustration of the dialogical relationship and the interdependence between the actors and shows that the role of the entrepreneurship educator is to create an entrepreneurial learning space along with each student. In turn, each student delivers active engagement and through that experience and entrepreneurial identity formation. Thus, the entrepreneurship educators are highly dependent on the students as they must be able to self-direct their own learning in the entrepreneurial learning space (Jones, 2015; Neck & Corbett, 2018).

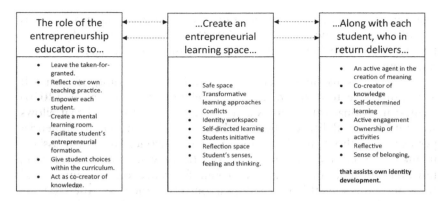

Fig. 2 The nexus between the entrepreneurship educator, learning space and the student (*Source* Own depiction)

Even while the expectations of the entrepreneurship educators can seem overpowering in terms of content relative to the goal of EE (Henry, 2020), they still need to be experts and understand the key concepts of both entrepreneurship and education and be able to incorporate 'softer' entrepreneurial topics, for instance teaching about the entrepreneurial mindset, work-life balance and talk to the students how to cope and learn from the failures that are unavoidable (Fayolle, 2013).

Entrepreneurship educators must be aware of their own role in the entrepreneurial learning space and how that role aligns with their teaching focus (Wraae et al., 2021). They need to recognise that role shifts are necessary if they want to empower the students and contribute to students' identity formation (Wraae & Walmsley, 2020). As such, the educators must let go of the known world and the 'taken-for-granted' educator position, a term adopted from Fayolle (2013) to develop new practices. Along with each student, the entrepreneurship educator must move into unknown territory and even give the student a leading role on their entrepreneurial learning journey and accordingly fulfilling the learning goals and the frame for teaching set by the educational institution. In fact, the entrepreneurship educators act as supporters in the interaction with the students as they use students' feedback and their experiences to support and improve students' learning and through that take part in students' identity development (Wraae & Walmsley, 2020).

The educators are even learners themselves when they use students' feedback and responses to reflect on their own teaching practices.

Summarising the chapter so far, to implement the framework the entrepreneurship educator must first acknowledge the existence of the entrepreneurial learning space that goes beyond the traditional understanding of a classroom.

Second, the students must be given the space and the opportunity to act entrepreneurially in practice which in turn means that the students must claim ownership and responsibility for their own learning. In that process each student must be viewed individually with their own individual direction to follow. Thus, empowering students and assisting them in their identity development. When that happens more than just learning takes place in this shared learning space, identity development starts to happen.

Third, the entrepreneurship educator must plan and execute teaching entrepreneurship accordingly and include practical elements, 'conflict' and room for reflection as a platform for identity development. As such, each student must be given the entrepreneurial knowledge and entrepreneurial tools to deal with the issues related to entrepreneurship (Gibb, 2002; Wraae & Walmsley, 2020). Through transformative learning, it is possible to appeal to student's senses, feeling and thinking (Jones & Matlay, 2011) and thereby creating a learning space with an included possibility to experience and develop their identity. While a part of learning approach involves conflict and tension, the learning space must be considered a safe space to build on mutual trust and where each student can take the initiative and action in relation to their own learning. If the students do not feel safe, they might act on the incorporated learning elements, but it might have a different outcome than the expected.

Fourth, both the entrepreneurship educator and the students must understand, acknowledge and accept new role distributions (re. andragogy and heutagogy) and leave their respective own traditional role perception and accept the idea about them being in a 'community of practice'. Sharing the responsibility as co-creators of knowledge in the entrepreneurial learning space establish all parts as both directors and learners as they all learn from each other and are acting and executing on a common learning and personal development journey (Jones, 2015, 2019; Kolb & Kolb, 2005).

While the educator must give room and surrender a piece of the responsibility, the students must take that responsibility and bring that newfound responsibility into use as well. It can be done. The following quote describes how a student views the co-creational role and shared responsibility: 'Normally we get told what to do – now we have to make our own decisions' (Wraae, 2017, p. 147) which illustrates how the educational process aids forming the student (Kolb & Kolb, 2005; Nielsen & Gartner, 2017). When a student takes ownership of own and others' learning, the students experience new insights into that role which leads to their own identity development (Nielsen & Gartner, 2017). However, the entrepreneurship educator plays a critical role in creating the entrepreneurial learning space which, depending on how this learning space is created, leads to varying levels of student engagement.

The framework presents the paradox in EE with on one hand arguing for how educators need to direct and by that set all actors free and create a more democratic entrepreneurial leaning space by relinquishing power and hand it over to the students while on the other hand doing it through a restrictive framework. The necessity lays in the EE context that is both complex (Neck & Greene, 2011) and heterogeneous (Jones & Matlay, 2011) and if the purpose of EE is to act as an arena for identity formation (Hytti & Heinonen, 2013) the entrepreneurship educator cannot do it alone. The entrepreneurship educator should accept that when you ask the students to go through an entrepreneurial process and ask them to act and think on their own as well as asking them to reflect on what happens it will be messy and chaotic. The vital role of the entrepreneurship educator is to create 'a safe space, a quasi safe zone in the mind' before the comma to replace 'such a mental room', that allows and encourages students' development. Therefore, a framework—a script is necessary and even while the script encourages students to 'improvise' this must be orchestrated by the educator who is—after all—responsible for the process and the frames set by the institution and who navigates these relationships in a complex world of delivering EE. Even more so, because in the end the entrepreneurship educator must assess the outcome of the process and as such, a framework and some guidelines are in order.

3   Putting the Framework into Play

Based on the theoretical discussion and the analysis that led to the presented framework and own experiences as an entrepreneurship educator, this section will offer some practical suggestions on how to put the framework into play and turn the classroom into an entrepreneurial learning space.

First of all, be aware of who is present is the learning space. As an educator you should know your students. In contrast to what is commonly believed, students sign up for an entrepreneurial course for a lot of different reasons. True, some are there to become entrepreneurs, but many enter the entrepreneurial learnings space with another motivation entirely, ranging from that entrepreneurship is an important skill to learn, to choosing the course for convenient reasons only. No matter the reasons and motivations each student brings skills, capabilities and competencies into the classroom that can be put into use. They all bring active assets to the learning space. Therefore, know your students. Moreover, know yourself. Be aware of own role as an entrepreneurship educator and the change in roles throughout the course: "Teachers are conceived as 'coaches' and 'developers' – while students are seen as individuals who actively construct their knowledge through their interaction with their educator(s) and peers" (Béchard & Grégoire, 2007, pp. 264–265).

Second, be in control to be able to give up control. The entrepreneurship educator must have an overview of the purpose, the goals and the outcome of asking the students to act accordingly in this learning space. Be transparent. Always convey all information possible so there will be no surprises during the course and also, to align expectations with the students. This includes an explanation of the learning approach and the (new) role distribution between the educator and the students, including highlighting the difference to what they are used to. The students must be encouraged to take responsibility for their own learning through an action-based approach with a goal of creating something of value for others, in reality work with an idea that has turned into an opportunity.

Third, let the students be co-creators of their own learning: 'To some extent, the teacher engages the students in defining the learning objectives (what) and how, when, where and with whom this is to be learned. The discussion is focused on the creation of value for the student in the learning process' (Sagar, 2015). The choices could for instance be to have students add one or two personal learning goals and/or add a personal curriculum to the official one that is of relevance the idea, they are working with and to whom they are as students. Both can be incorporated in the final assessment of the course. The goal is to provide the students with an opportunity to focus on something that has their personal interests at heart. Further, let the students have a voice and let them decide the narrative. Some students find the business plan an easy tool while others prefer to call it an innovation plan (intrapreneurship) and others prefer to expand on the business model canvas. Let the students argue for their choice relative to the idea they are acting on (Wraae, 2017). This is about empowering students and facilitate their identity formation.

Then, create a safe space. In the shared learning space, the students need to know, that even while they act independently, they are not alone. Self-directed learning does not mean that students are given responsibility for their own learning alone (Garrison, 1997). Therefore, the entrepreneurial learning space should include room for supervision of the teams and room for students making decisions on their learning direction. This is a safe room for students to talk about their progress and their setbacks and how to proceed. Here the role of the educator is to coach and ask questions that leads students to deduct their next step. For the educator this is a balance as too much support from the educator is at risk of being counterproductive to the achievement of learning goals.

Finally, make room for reflection to contribute to personal identity formation for instance by using video-clips as previously described (Wraae, 2017; Wraae et al., 2020). Give each student the task to describe him or herself in an either entrepreneurial or intrapreneurial perspective in a 2–3-min video clip to for instance be handed in as a part of the final assessment. Alternatively, in the beginning and the end of the entrepreneurial course to discuss the transformation. It is important not to provide too many guidelines on how to solve the reflective practice itself and emphasise that the creation of the clip, including layout and editing is less important. The focus must be on how each student interpret the assignment and reflect on themselves in a free room where they are in decision on how to solve the given task.

Finally, remember that being an entrepreneurship educator is messy and chaotic at times. Still, the students will be more than ready for the opening show—they will have found a direction towards who they are and where that could take them.

4   Conclusion

The purpose of this chapter was to present a framework for how the entrepreneurship educator can plan and execute EE in a transformative learning environment with the goal of assisting undergraduate students' entrepreneurial identity development. The actors in the entrepreneurial learning space and the assumptions linked to them were introduced as being bound by dialogic relationship to be understood in its whole. The presented framework in Fig. 2 illustrates this relationship underlining that the educator cannot do it alone but must work together with the students and understand the possibilities of the entrepreneurial learning processes.

Applying the framework in practice contributes to assisting students to both gain entrepreneurial skills and a transformation towards an entrepreneurial 'becoming'. Entrepreneurship educators can view each of the presented bullet points in Fig. 2 along with the practical suggestions at the planning and executing stages of an entrepreneurial course. If the entrepreneurship educator acts as proposed, then the likely outcome is that each student develops their entrepreneurial identity.

As the entrepreneurship educators act on behalf of the institution, this chapter can serve as an inspiration for the management level with the importance of offering entrepreneurial courses as well as understanding the importance of what is offered as a part of an entrepreneurial course in the undergraduate setting.

On a final note, while each student in EE is the star of the show, the role of the educator and the cooperation between the two in the entrepreneurial learning space is important for delivering educational outcomes.

References

Béchard, J.-P., & Grégoire, D. (2005). Understanding teaching models in entrepreneurship for higher education. *The Dynamics of Learning Entrepreneursh Ip in a Cross-Cultural University Context, Edited by Paula Kÿro and Camille Carrier, 2*, 104–134.

Béchard, J.-P., & Grégoire, D. (2007). Archetypes of pedagogical innovation for entrepreneurship in higher education: Model and illustrations. In A. Fayolle (Ed.), *Handbook of research in entrepreneurship education, Volume 1 A General Perspective* (p. 311). Edward Elgar.

Brush, C. G., & Gale, M. (2015). Becoming entrepreneurial: constructing an entrepreneurial identity in elective entrepreneurship courses. In V. L. Crittenden, K. Esper, R. Slegers, & N. Karst (Eds.), *Evolving entrepreneurial education: Innovation in the Babson classroom* (pp. 305–322). Emerald Group Publishing Limited.

Bruyat, C., & Julien, P.-A. (2001). Defining the field of research in entrepreneurship. *Journal of Business Venturing, 16*(2), 165–180.

Donnellon, A., Ollila, S., & Middleton, K. W. (2014). Constructing entrepreneurial identity in entrepreneurship education. *The International Journal of Management Education, 12*, 490–499.

Fayolle, A., Gailly, B., & Lassas-Clerc, N. (2006). Assessing the impact of entrepreneurship education programmes: A new methodology. *Journal of European Industrial Training, 30*(9), 701–720. https://doi.org/10.1108/03090590610715022

Fayolle, A. (2013). Personal views on the future of entrepreneurship education. *Entrepreneurship & Regional Development, 25*(7–8), 692–701. https://doi.org/10.1080/08985626.2013.821318

Garrison, D. R. (1997). Self-directed learning: Toward a comprehensive model. *Adult Education Quarterly, 48*(1), 18–33. https://doi.org/10.1177/074171369704800103

Gibb, A. (2002). In pursuit of a new 'enterprise' and 'entrepreneurship' paradigm for learning: Creative destruction, new values, new ways of doing things and new combinations of knowledge. *International Journal of Management Reviews, 4*(3), 233–269. https://doi.org/10.1111/1468-2370.00086

Hannon, P. D. (2018). On becoming and being an entrepreneurship educator: A personal reflection. *Entrepreneurship & Regional Development, 30*(7–8), 698–721. https://doi.org/10.1080/08985626.2018.1464259

Harmeling, S. S. (2011). Re-storying an entrepreneurial identity: Education, experience and self-narrative. *Education + Training, 53*(8/9), 741–749. https://doi.org/10.1108/00400911111185053

Henry, C. (2020). Reconceptualizing the role of the future entrepreneurship educator: An exploration of the content challenge. *Entrepreneurship & Regional Development*, 1– 20. https://doi.org/10.1080/08985626.2020.1737416

Hytti, U., & Heinonen, J. (2013). Heroic and humane entrepreneurs: Identity work in entrepreneurship education. *Education + Training, 55*(8/9), 886–898. https://doi.org/10.1108/ET-06-2013-0086

Jones, C. (2015). *31 Emerging laws of entrepreneurship education: Vol. 1* (Kindle ed.). Amazon Digital Services LLC.

Jones, C. (2019). *How to teach entrepreneurship*. Edward Elgar Publishing.

Jones, C., & Matlay, H. (2011). Understanding the heterogeneity of entrepreneurship education: Going beyond Gartner. *Education + Training, 53*(8/9), 692–703. https://doi.org/10.1108/00400911111185026

Kolb, A. Y., & Kolb, D. A. (2005). Learning styles and learning spaces: Enhancing experiential learning in higher education. *Academy of Management Learning & Education, 4*(2), 193–212. https://doi.org/10.5465/AMLE.2005.17268566

Lackéus, M. (2015). *Entrepreneurship in education: What, why, when, how. Entrepreneurship 360* (p. 45) (Background paper). OECD.

Lindh, I. (2017). Entrepreneurial development and the different aspects of reflection. *The International Journal of Management Education, 15*(1), 26–38. https://doi.org/10.1016/j.ijme.2016.12.001

Mezirow, J. (1997). Transformative learning: Theory to practice. *New Directions for Adult and Continuing Education, 1997*(74), 5–12.

Mezirow, J. (2000). Learning to think like an adult. In J. Mezirow & Associates (Eds.), *Learning as transformation. Critical perspectives on a theory in progress.* (pp. 3–33). Jossey-Bass.

Nabi, G., Liñán, F., Krueger, N., Fayolle, A., & Walmsley, A. (2016). The impact of entrepreneurship education in higher education: A systematic review and research agenda. *Academy of Management Learning & Education, 16*(2), 277–299. https://doi.org/10.5465/amle.2015.0026

Neck, H. M., & Corbett, A. C. (2018). The scholarship of teaching and learning entrepreneurship. *Entrepreneurship Education and Pedagogy, 1*(1), 8–41. https://doi.org/10.1177/2515127417737286

Neck, H. M., & Greene, P. G. (2011). Entrepreneurship education: Known worlds and new frontiers. *Journal of Small Business Management, 49*(1), 55–70.

Nielsen, S. L., & Gartner, W. B. (2017). Am I a student and/or entrepreneur? Multiple identities in student entrepreneurship. *Education + Training, 59*(2), 135–154. https://doi.org/10.1108/ET-09-2014-0122

Pittaway, L., & Thorpe, R. (2012). A framework for entrepreneurial learning: A tribute to Jason Cope. *Entrepreneurship & Regional Development, 24*(9–10), 837–859. https://doi.org/10.1080/08985626.2012.694268

Rigg, C., & O'Dwyer, B. (2012). Becoming an entrepreneur: Researching the role of mentors in identity construction. *Education + Training, 54*(4), 319–329. https://doi.org/10.1108/00400911211236181

Robinson, S., & Blenker, P. (2014). Tensions between rhetoric and practice in entrepreneurship education; an ethnography from Danish higher education. *European Journal of Higher Education, 4*(1), 80–93. https://doi.org/10.1080/21568235.2013.853621

Sagar, H. (2015). *Entrepreneurial schools. Part 2—Entrepreneurial learning environments and a changed role for teachers. Entrepreneurship 360* (pp. 1–38) (Thematic paper). OECD. http://www.oecd.org/cfe/leed/Entrepreneurial-School-pt2.pdf

Samwel Mwasalwiba, E. (2010). Entrepreneurship education: A review of its objectives, teaching methods, and impact indicators. *Education + Training, 52*(1), 20–47. https://doi.org/10.1108/00400911011017663

Svensson, O. H., Lundqvist, M., & Middleton, K. W. (2017). *Transformative, transactional and transmissive modes of teaching in action-based entrepreneurial education,* 15. http://publications.lib.chalmers.se/records/fulltext/248686/local_248686.pdf

Varelas, M. (Ed.). (2012). *Identity construction and science education research: Learning, teaching and being in multiple contexts*. Sense Publishers.

Wraae, B. (2017). How to create entrepreneurial thinking among non-business students in ten weeks. In D. Remenyi (Ed.), *Innovation and entrepreneurship teaching excellence awards 2017. An anthology of case histories* (p. 150). Academic Conferences and Publishing International.

Wraae, B., Brush, C., & Nikou, S. (2021). The entrepreneurial educator: Understanding role identity. *Entrepreneurship Education and Pedagogy*, Online. https://doi.org/10.1177/2515127420979662

Wraae, B., Tigerstedt, C., & Walmsley, A. (2020). Using Reflective Videos to Enhance Entrepreneurial Learning. *Entrepreneurship Education and Pedagogy*, 251512742093695. https://doi.org/10.1177/2515127420936955

Wraae, B., & Walmsley, A. (2020). Behind the scenes: Spotlight on the entrepreneurship educator. *Education + Training*, *62*(3), 255–270. https://doi.org/10.1108/ET-01-2019-0009

Guiding the First-Year Student Entrepreneur: A Conceptual Map to Nudge Towards the Reversal Effect in Learning

Gustav Hägg and Agnieszka Kurczewska

1 INTRODUCTION

In the process of legitimising itself as an academic subject, entrepreneurship education has come a long way over the last forty years (Fayolle et al., 2016; Gabrielsson et al., 2020). Nevertheless, the challenge of how to structure and develop sound theoretical foundations for learning entrepreneurship in higher education through a cross-fertilisation of educational science and educational psychology is still at an infant stage (Hägg & Gabrielsson, 2020; Pittaway & Cope, 2007; Rideout & Gray, 2013). The call to strengthen these ties has been made by several scholars over the decades, but so far little agreement and unity has been achieved.

G. Hägg (✉)
Department of Urban Studies, Malmö University, Malmö, Sweden
e-mail: gustav.hagg@mau.se

Sten K. Johnson Centre for Entrepreneurship, Lund University, Lund, Sweden

A. Kurczewska
Faculty of Economics and Sociology, University of Lodz, Lodz, Poland
e-mail: agnieszka.kurczewska@uni.lodz.pl

© The Author(s), under exclusive license to Springer Nature
Switzerland AG 2022
G. J. Larios-Hernandez et al. (eds.), *Theorising Undergraduate Entrepreneurship Education*,
https://doi.org/10.1007/978-3-030-87865-8_3

We know that entrepreneurs learn through and from experience (Politis, 2005), but when we take these insights into the educational process and meet a different group of individuals, the playing field is no longer the same. Hence the experiential learning process of practicing entrepreneurs requires modification (Hägg & Kurczewska, 2020b) to fit the educational context and the characteristics of student entrepreneurs, often positioned in the phase termed emergent adulthood (see Cohen et al., 2020 for an interesting method that discusses the difference between novice and expert).

Taking it one step further, we know from Cognitive Load Theory (Sweller, 1988, 2016) and evolutionary educational psychology (Geary, 2002, 2007) that learning subject matter is based on biologically secondary knowledge (i.e. developed through cultural artefacts over time) that differs greatly from biologically primary knowledge that is learnt epigenetically (such as learning to talk). Learning subject matter such as entrepreneurship requires more structured processes and instructional clarity in the initial stage until the tipping point has been reached, known as the reversal effect in learning, which is when instructions no longer advance learning but rather impede a learner in their development.

Based on the above arguments, there has been a recent call for a term such as odigogy, meaning to guide, in entrepreneurship education (see Hägg & Kurczewska, 2019, 2020a). The idea of guidance is not a completely new phenomenon nor is it something exclusively associated with entrepreneurship education, but rather a universal thought practiced both in ancient forms of adult learning (e.g. Aristotle and Socrates) and in progressive views on schooling (Dewey & Dewey, 1915). The role of guidance has also been addressed in other ways related to the balance between pedagogy and andragogy as well as between teacher- and student-led learning (Jones et al., 2014, 2019; Lackéus et al., 2016; Robinson et al., 2016). Without casting a shadow on previous thoughts that have greatly advanced our thinking about balance and guidance in entrepreneurship as well as enterprise education, odigogy is an attempt to raise the importance of guidance and potentially position its conceptualisation on a par with terms such as pedagogy and andragogy as well as the more contemporary development of heutagogy. Given the development in research on how learners accumulate knowledge and the distinctions between adolescents, emergent adults and adults in developmental psychology, there is a need to acknowledge that the traditional division into andragogy and pedagogy no longer fully fills the blanks left by recent research knowledge on student characteristics. As a key part of the discussion on odigogy is based on understanding the student entrepreneur, a potential next step in its evolution is to address novice learners, in particular the first-year student exposed to entrepreneurship education. It is at this stage that the first seeds of knowledge and understanding of higher education and the academic learning process become apparent.

Consequently, the purpose of this chapter is to respond to the call to develop odigogy and conceptualise a potential map for how to reason and teach when facing first-year student entrepreneurs and the challenges they encounter when entering higher education. The goal is not to provide a toolbox that can be placed in the classroom, as that is contextually impossible and would be imprudent due to lecturers' academic freedom in managing classroom activities. Instead, we offer a conceptual map that might serve as an inspiration for refining learning processes for novice learners. Hence, we hope to further contribute to the discussion on how to synthesise knowledge from different educational theories when developing our understanding of how to create conducive and progressive learning environments in entrepreneurship education tailored to novice learners, i.e. first-year students. To achieve this we start by providing a theoretical backup to highlight unique features of novice students, which leads us to the conceptual map addressing the reversal effect in learning and ends with conclusions and implications for entrepreneurship education theory and practice.

2   STREAMS OF LITERATURE

To highlight the specificity of novice learners and its implications for learning and teaching practice, in the following sections we will address some insights from developmental psychology. In particular, we will explain the emerging adulthood concept and its relevance to first-year students of entrepreneurship, as well as the foundation of Cognitive Load Theory that will help us to grasp the process of moving from novice to expert learner, where odigogy could facilitate the transition from an instructional perspective. We will also discuss the recent developments in entrepreneurship education for undergraduate students to better understand the main challenges it entails and end with a short discussion on odigogy, which is followed in the next section by the conceptual map illustrating a typical classroom situation, where entrepreneurship constitutes a new domain-specific knowledge.

Emergent Adult and the First-Year Student

Entrepreneurship education research has tended to focus more on student learning and pedagogical methods than on the developmental stages of students taking courses in entrepreneurship (Hägg & Kurczewska, 2019). The limited attention to student characteristics and their relation to developmental psychology is, however, natural as the field is young and still seeking boundary conditions for the subject domain as well as legitimacy (Fayolle et al., 2016). Nevertheless, understanding cognitive development and its dynamics and characteristics in relation to how young individuals learn skills and develop attitudes seems promising for the creation of a progressive and supportive learning environment in entrepreneurship education (2020a; Hägg & Kurczewska, 2019). In particular, knowing more about who we really have in the classroom from the perspective of cognitive studies could be beneficial. Therefore, we start our theoretical discussion with the culturally constructed concept of emerging adulthood established by the developmental psychologist Jeffrey Arnett and presented in the "American Psychologist" in 2000 (Arnett, 2000). The phase of emerging adulthood concerns a specific period of human development between adolescence and adulthood and includes alterations related to demography, subjectivity as well as identity exploration (Swanson, 2016). The period of emerging adulthood occurs between the ages of 18 and 29 years (Arnett et al., 2014) and refers to a transition full of turbulence, where complex forms of thinking, including self-reflection, are developed (Arnett, 2006). It is the distinct time when young people usually enter higher education, leave their family homes to live alone, take up their first job and begin a more independent life. During this phase the emerging adult faces many new problems and needs to learn how to make more enduring choices (Arnett et al., 2014). Young individuals, still being relatively independent from social roles and normative expectations (Arnett, 2000, 2015), tend to use this phase of transition to explore and experiment to determine their roles and identities when entering the phase of adulthood. Therefore, emerging adulthood is characterised by instability, a feeling of being in-between and ambiguity but also self-focus and checking out various life options to seek "true selves".

The development of emerging adulthood is explained by the fact that "longer and more widespread education, later entry to marriage and parenthood, and a prolonged and erratic transition to stable work have opened up a space for a new life stage in between adolescence and young adulthood" (Arnett, 2015, p. 8). On the educational level, the suspension between being an adolescent and an adult often means that students need to take more responsibility for their learning and become accustomed to a less structured form of education. In the context of this chapter's research question, we may consider the characteristics of today's first-year students as emerging adults. With high probability, many of our students on entrepreneurship courses, particularly in their first years of study, are emerging adults and therefore face a quite dynamic and transformative period in their lives. This stage of development requires understanding from the instructor/teacher as well as careful and well though-out guidance to facilitate learning and allow more complex forms of thinking to grow and materialise. Students need more "anchors" that they can refer to and more support that they can reach for. The instructor/teacher should be available with guidance related to the merits of the entrepreneurship domain but also in terms how to learn in a more mature and independent way.

3   Cognitive Load Theory

Drawing from developmental psychology also leads us to Cognitive Load Theory (CLT) that addresses a cognitive approach to instruction for creating a prosperous learning process. The rationale behind CLT, developed by the psychologist John Sweller, is a need to create learning content suited to the learner's pace, level and absorptive capacity (Sweller, 1988, 1994). Creating such learning content requires interplay between long-term and short-term/working memories. Information gained through learning is constructed in the short-term memory but kept in the long-term memory due to the mental structures (schemas), enabling better organisation of knowledge. However, novice learners who possess limited prior knowledge and less developed schemas in the long-term memory rely heavily on processing new information in the working memory, which is not only short-term but also quite limited (Cowan, 2001). Therefore, learning might become inefficient if its contents block learners' working memory, leading to cognitive overload and a reduction of transfer to the unlimited long-term memory (Sweller, 1994, 2016).

In contrast, reducing the load on the working memory and using the long-term memory make learning more powerful and productive. The mental processing power (cognitive load) depends on the complexity of concepts, instructional design and effort to process and construct schema (Sweller). Thus, CLT provides more understanding of how various stages of development impact learners and how different levels of instruction are important when tailoring and developing a conducive educational learning environment for student entrepreneurs, especially in the initial formative part of higher education studies.

When translating CLT into the entrepreneurship education context, the risk of cognitive overload is a particular concern for novice learners, such as first-year students, due to new content as well as new forms of instruction (Kirschner et al., 2006). Learners exposed to entrepreneurship education for the first time are often confronted with a progressive and student-centred type of teaching (Robinson et al., 2016) that requires more action and higher degrees of independence when making decisions in problem-solving situations. They do not have many, if any, (entrepreneurial) experiences (Cohen et al., 2020; Hägg & Kurczewska, 2019) to lean on in learning activities in order to grasp the process (Kalyuga et al., 2003). Hence, in relation to CLT one could argue that first-year students in entrepreneurship education lack appropriate cognitive schemas for processing information. Therefore, to make learning entrepreneurship effective, novices in the field require more precise instruction and guidance. However, the instructor/teacher needs to be aware that when students increase their domain-specific knowledge and expertise (i.e. develop schemas in their long-term memory), instruction-based learning becomes less efficient and may lead to a slowdown of the learning process, known as the expertise reversal effect (Kalyuga et al., 2003).

4   Entrepreneurship Education—What Do We Know About Undergraduate Studies?

In general, entrepreneurship education research concerning university level does not differentiate to any great degree between undergraduate and postgraduate studies in terms of what and how to teach (although the various chapters in the present book are seeking to change this), which means that the maturity of learners as well as the diversity and depth of their experiences has received less consideration (see, e.g., Cohen et al., 2020; Hägg & Kurczewska, 2020b). Undergraduate studies alone, if discussed at all, appear more as a context of research (for example, a review of top programmes in experiential entrepreneurship education by Mandel and Noyes (2016), or the review of entrepreneurship education programmes by Myrah and Currie [2006]), not as a subject of investigation of some specific characteristic, nor as an entry point to discuss the profile of learners. More attention has been focused on outcomes such as entrepreneurial intentions, where large cohorts of students are often found at undergraduate level (Kassean et al., 2015), but less of an attempt is made to differentiate the progressive nature of learning that most likely impacts on how to organise curricula and the educational process from freshman towards postgraduate studies. This is surprising, as at the same time entrepreneurship education is seen as drifting towards a student-driven approach and a constructivist perspective on learning (Krueger, 2007; Löbler, 2006). The studies acknowledging the division between undergraduate and postgraduate studies do not describe a particular difference between the levels (Pittaway & Edwards, 2012). In the rare studies concerning only the undergraduate level of entrepreneurship education, such as Katz et al. (2016), the authors try to suggest a direction for the development of undergraduate curricula in entrepreneurship and make some recommendations for its modelling. However, even in these studies, the focus is placed on the content and method, not on the learners and their abilities or entry level characteristics for learning.

5   Odigogy—An Intermediary Phase for Meeting the Emerging Adult

Drawing from developmental psychology, namely the concept of emerging adulthood and Cognitive Load Theory but also by synthetising previous research output on entrepreneurship education during undergraduate studies, we infer that, firstly, novice students possess some unique cognitive characteristics and require adequate attention from their teachers/instructors. Secondly, the role of guidance is greater than commonly acknowledged both in entrepreneurship education literature and as a classroom practice. Thirdly, the undergraduate level of entrepreneurship education has been marginalised in research and mainly treated without appropriate attention to the progressive nature that is ingrained in the higher education process, where a focus on seeing entrepreneurship from a method perspective has perhaps reduced the process perspective that underpins learning. Thus, the idea of odigogy has a particular meaning for learning and teaching entrepreneurship among novice learners. Its further conceptual development is captured in the following section in relation to first-year students.

Building further on the conceptualisation by Hägg and Kurczewska (2019, 2020a), odigogy implies a constant guiding process in-between the continuum of pedagogy and andragogy. As Hägg and Kurczewska (2020a, p. 771) argue: "Odigogy explains this continuum for students who are in a transitional stage between adolescence and adulthood". Like pedagogy and andragogy, odigogy departs from a specific group of individuals. In the same way as pedagogy departs from and builds its assumptions on how to teach children and adolescents, and the learning process in andragogy is based on adults, odigogy departs from the assumption of emergent adults and their specific characteristics. Being placed in the higher education context, odigogy neatly targets the needs of emerging adults. To highlight its characteristics, Hägg and Kurczewska (2020a) contrast it with pedagogy and andragogy in terms of educational context (higher education), features of learning (guided) and how knowledge is developed (as explored), role of teacher (as a guide), motivation to learn (as being both external and internally driven), as well as responsibility for learning (reversal effect). If odigogy is applied to education, the learning process is developed through tailored guidance by teachers throughout the learning process by employing instructional design and content expertise. Students are encouraged to immerse in educative experience through which they accumulate knowledge and motivation for learning moves from external to internally driven. In this sense, knowledge is discovered and co-created by students and teachers. Also, responsibility for learning is shared between student and teacher but shifts with proficiency level as part of the learning process.

The initial paper by Hägg and Kurczewska (2019) addressed the void in the continuum of pedagogy and andragogy and the importance of tailoring learning activities, as well as adopting learning theories that take account of student characteristics and proficiency level. This was then followed up in the next study by Hägg and Kurczewska (2020a), where four main assumptions were proposed to demarcate the scope of the term. In the present chapter, the initial stage of how to approach first-year students (emergent adults) is further discussed, where the following section seeks to describe the attempts to model a map to aid in developing the initial phase of entrepreneurship studies in higher education.

6 A Conceptual Map to Nudge First-Year Students Towards the Reversal Effect

We are surrounded by a highly constructivist paradigm of teaching and learning, where the mixture and functions of pedagogical, andragogical and to some extent also heutagogical views on learning are superimposed in the discussion of best practices for educating entrepreneurial individuals. In the previous sections we have sought to address a number of theoretical streams that together could cast light on this conundrum that has materialised in the search for, in the absence of a better term, "the holy grail" for how to teach. We are not going to argue that the conceptual map is a contender for "the holy grail" as that would be thoughtless. But we are arguing that, given what current research has achieved in developmental psychology and also in CLT, the role of guidance has an important place when considering first-year students lack of knowledge in the subject and have little insight into the educational process in higher education.

We propose a conceptual map that might serve as an inspiration for developing learning processes for novice learners. Although it helps us to find a direction and guides us when we feel lost, it does not do the job for us and should not be treated as the only tool to use. Here, the academic freedom of deciding what to teach becomes the lifeblood of the individual lecturer and something beyond the map. The map focuses on achieving the reversal effect in learning (which in some sub-processes might be fast and in others could take months or even years). The reversal effect is attentive to the development of the learner and focuses on the shift in responsibility for the learning process. In accordance with the ideas of CLT, we posit that working closely with explicit instructions, worked examples and from the start transferring the authority for the learning process create a fruitful foundation that accelerates the learning process and the ability to take responsibility for one's own learning.

Model one illustrates our previously presented thoughts on how to nudge a novice learner towards the very basic ability to digest academic reading, which is not a self-explanatory process but most likely requires explicit instructions and clear guidance. The model outlines what to pay attention to, how to focus one's reading and why different academic texts require diverse forms of understanding from the reader. This basic activity of nudging a novice learner in higher education creates a first step for how to orchestrate other learning activities, as student characteristics differ due to the difference in their previous knowledge. Creating an equal starting point for continued guidance in the learning process provides opportunities for blended and experiential learning processes, where less attention may need to be given to covering the content, instead focusing on developing the how and the why in order to find the balance between theory and practice. This thought accords with the idea from experiential education on teaching people, not content (Roberts, 2015). Although content is necessary to develop domain-knowledge, it can be covered in many different ways. By developing understanding in the early stage of, for example, how to read in order to digest the content of academic articles, the focus can be altered towards working with the content and developing skills and understanding how to apply it and also why and when to use content in different situations. Although the example is prosaic in scope, we believe it is essential to free up time for more experiential and deeper learning activities where the responsibility of the learner is higher (Fig. 1).

To help read the map, we provided a very simple example of how to engage with academic reading and understanding key concepts related to the discovery or creation of opportunities. Although it might sound like a very ordinary example, it is also essential when starting entrepreneurship education. In the first place, the idea of guiding the novice learner with clear instructions on how to read an academic article enables her/him to understand the process, thus reducing the uncertainty about what to do, how to do it and why. But it is also a key to nudging the novice learner towards the next step to becoming proficient and achieving the reversal effect, perhaps in the long run becoming a self-directed expert learner (Dreyfus, 2004; Ertmer & Newby, 1996). The map and the example also address the importance of meeting the learner at her/his level and being aware of the fact that what is clear and simple for one learner might be fuzzy and unclear for another, given that most learners come with different backpacks of prior experience, thus creating a common ground from which to move forward. This is also an important difference between odigogy and andragogy when it comes to creating a starting point for the experiential learning process. The map could be used when thinking about how to create understanding for the novice learner and also to nudge them towards taking more responsibility. This is especially important in the context of experiential learning, as it is a learning context that emphasises individual responsibility through the interplay between

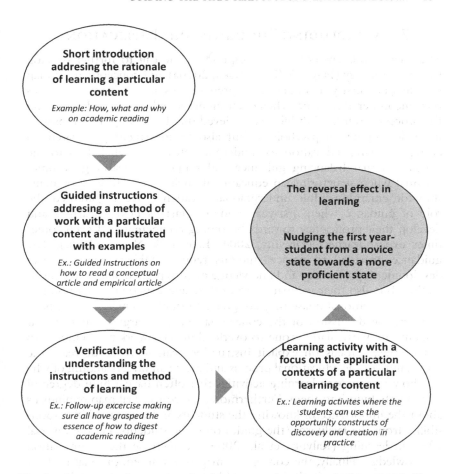

Fig. 1 A conceptual map to nudge first-year students towards the reversal effect (*with an example of how to engage students in academic reading and enable them to understand key concepts related to the discovery or creation of opportunities*)

knowing and doing. Odigogy and the guiding assumption that underlies it are sprung from the interplay between instructional design and experiential education literature (see Hägg & Kurczewska, 2020a).

7 Concluding Thoughts and Implications

The idea of this chapter was to respond to the call to further develop the term odigogy (Hägg & Kurczewska, 2020a) and conceptualise a map to help guide first-year student entrepreneurs despite the many challenges they encounter as students when entering higher education and beginning the process towards adult life. We achieved that by making use of insights from developmental psychology, but also by investigating research on entrepreneurship education for undergraduates. They all led us to the conclusion that balancing guidance and support for learning becomes essential when structuring an educational environment in entrepreneurship for emerging adult undergraduate students. We highlighted the role of guidance when first-year students start as novice learners and develop their proficiency towards becoming competent and even sometimes expert learners (Dreyfus, 2004; Ertmer & Newby, 1996). The guidance provided to novice students requires taking their cognitive development, proficiency and knowledge of entrepreneurship into consideration, but also their inclination to explore and experience as a result of the transformational phase they are going through as emergent adults.

From the discussion of the conceptual map, we argue that first-year students are particularly prone to overload in their working memory. To reduce this, a focus on explicit instructions can serve to decrease the uncertainty of the educational process and create an understanding of why and how to approach learning activities that often have a high degree of uncertainty built into them. Furthermore, the conceptual map reminds us about the importance of knowing the students and when to shift responsibility from the facilitator (the guide) onto the students, i.e. the reversal effect in learning (Kalyuga et al., 2003), to increase the accumulation of knowledge. Finally, the conceptual map is not an educational tool for classroom practice in itself, but should be viewed as a mental model when thinking about how to develop a learning process by keeping the student characteristics in mind on a par with learning theories and various experiential learning activities that have been acknowledged as foundational for teaching entrepreneurship.

By writing this chapter we hope to start a more thorough discussion on how to design teaching when engaging students in entrepreneurship education at undergraduate level. Highlighting well-grounded theoretical backup, we further theorise around the concept of odigogy, but also make it more applicable. Therefore, as far as practical implications are concerned, the discussion in this chapter might be helpful for entrepreneurship teachers/instructors, where the proposed conceptual map may stimulate the development of teaching. Furthermore, signalling the need to consider odigogy in teaching and the significance of guidance for novice learners with characteristics typical of emerging adults could help to define the role of the teacher/instructor as the process evolves. It also contributes to the ongoing discussion on the balance between pedagogy, andragogy and heutagogy that is currently being voiced in research discussions in entrepreneurship and enterprise education (e.g. Hägg & Kurczewska, 2020a; Jones et al., 2019; Neck & Corbett, 2018).

Despite all efforts, our line of thought has some limitations. The key limitation concerns the fact that our reasoning is not universal in the sense that it is only useful for a limited group of students who are emerging adults. The emergent adult is fairly typical of the Western part of the world and not all students in the classroom might be this specific type of student (Hendry & Kloep, 2010). However, the phenomenon of emerging adulthood is spreading and together with the growing trend towards experience-based, constructivist, inquiry-based education as well as the progressive trajectory in entrepreneurship education offerings around the world, legitimises the introduction of odigogy into entrepreneurship education. We are also aware that the reasoning presented in this chapter relates to the quite narrow context of undergraduate studies and novice learners. However, odigogy is not supposed to be a generic term fitting all aspects of entrepreneurship education, but more a helpful way of thinking when designing learning environments for students and considering the progressive nature of the educational process (Hägg & Kurczewska, 2019). In this study, we justified its rationale for a specific context and hopefully opened the door for future empirical verification.

References

Arnett, J. J. (2000). Emerging adulthood: A theory of development from the late teens through the twenties. *American Psychologist, 55*(5), 469–480.

Arnett, J. J. (2006). Emerging adulthood in Europe: A response to Bynner. *Journal of Youth Studies, 9*(1), 111–123.

Arnett, J. J. (2015). *Emerging adulthood: The winding road from the late teens through the twenties* (2nd ed.). Oxford University Press.

Arnett, J. J., Žukauskienė, R., & Sugimura, K. (2014). The new life stage of emerging adulthood at ages 18–29 years: Implications for mental health. *The Lancet Psychiatry, 1*(7), 569–576.

Cohen, D., Hsu, D. K., & Shinnar, R. S. (2020). Identifying innovative opportunities in the entrepreneurship classroom: A new approach and empirical test. *Small Business Economics,* 1–25.

Cowan, N. (2001). Metatheory of storage capacity limits. *Behavioral and Brain Sciences, 24*(1), 154–176.

Dewey, J., & Dewey, E. (1915). *Schools of tomorrow.* E. P. Dutton & company.

Dreyfus, S. E. (2004). The five-stage model of adult skill acquisition. *Bulletin of Science, Technology & Society, 24*(3), 177–181.

Ertmer, P. A., & Newby, T. J. (1996). The expert learner: Strategic, self-regulated, and reflective. *Instructional Science, 24*(1), 1–24.

Fayolle, A., Verzat, C., & Wapshott, R. (2016). In quest of legitimacy: The theoretical and methodological foundations of entrepreneurship education research. *International Small Business Journal, 34*(7), 895–904.

Gabrielsson, J., Hägg, G., Landström, H., & Politis, D. (2020). Connecting the past with the present: The development of research on pedagogy in entrepreneurial education. *Education+ Training, 62,* 1061–1086.

Geary, D. C. (2002). Principles of evolutionary educational psychology. *Learning and Individual Differences, 12*(4), 317–345.

Geary, D. C. (2007). Educating the evolved mind: Conceptual foundations for an evolutionary educational psychology. In J. S. Carlson & J. R. Levin (Eds.), *Educating the evolved mind: Conceptual foundations for an evolutionary educational psychology* (pp. 1–100). Information Age Publishing.

Hendry, L. B., & Kloep, M. (2010). How universal is emerging adulthood? An empirical example. *Journal of Youth Studies, 13*(2), 169–179.

Hägg, G., & Gabrielsson, J. (2020). A systematic literature review of the evolution of pedagogy in entrepreneurial education research. *International Journal of Entrepreneurial Behavior & Research, 26*(5), 829–861.

Hägg, G., & Kurczewska, A. (2019). Who is the student entrepreneur? Understanding the emergent adult through the pedagogy and andragogy interplay. *Journal of Small Business Management, 57*(S1), 130–147.

Hägg, G., & Kurczewska, A. (2020a). Guiding the student entrepreneur–Considering the emergent adult within the pedagogy–andragogy continuum in entrepreneurship education. *Education+ Training, 62*(7/8), 759–777.

Hägg, G., & Kurczewska, A. (2020). Towards a learning philosophy based on experience in entrepreneurship education. *Entrepreneurship Education & Pedagogy, 3*(2), 129–153.

Jones, C., Matlay, H., Penaluna, K., & Penaluna, A. (2014). Claiming the future of enterprise education. *Education+ Training, 56*(8/9), 764–775.

Jones, C., Penaluna, K., & Penaluna, A. (2019). The promise of andragogy, heutagogy and academagogy to enterprise and entrepreneurship education pedagogy. *Education+ Training, 61*(9), 1170–1186.

Kalyuga, S., Ayres, P., Chandler, P., & Sweller, J. (2003). The Expertise reversal effect. *Educational Psychologist, 38*(1), 23–31.

Kassean, H., Vanevenhoven, J., Liguori, E., & Winkel, D. E. (2015). Entrepreneurship education: A need for reflection, real-world experience and action. *International Journal of Entrepreneurial Behavior & Research, 21*(5), 690–708.

Katz, J. A., Hanke, R., Maidment, F., Weaver, K. M., & Alpi, S. (2016). Proposal for two model undergraduate curricula in entrepreneurship. *International Entrepreneurship and Management Journal, 12*(2), 487–506.

Kirschner, P. A., Sweller, J., & Clark, R. E. (2006). Why minimal guidance during instruction does not work: An analysis of the failure of constructivist, discovery, problem-based, experiential, and inquiry-based teaching. *Educational Psychologist, 41*(2), 75–86.

Krueger, N. F. (2007). What lies beneath? The experiential essence of entrepreneurial thinking. *Entrepreneurship Theory and Practice, 31*(1), 123–138.

Lackéus, M., Lundqvist, M., & Middleton, K. W. (2016). Bridging the traditional-progressive education rift through entrepreneurship. *International Journal of Entrepreneurial Behavior & Research, 22*(6), 777–803.

Löbler, H. (2006). Learning entrepreneurship from a constructivist perspective. *Technology Analysis & Strategic Management, 18*(1), 19–38.

Mandel, R., & Noyes, E. (2016). Survey of experiential entrepreneurship education offerings among top undergraduate entrepreneurship programs. *Education+ Training, 58*(2), 164–178.

Myrah, K. K., & Currie, R. R. (2006). Examining undergraduate entrepreneurship education. *Journal of Small Business & Entrepreneurship, 19*(3), 233–253.

Neck, H. M., & Corbett, A. C. (2018). The scholarship of teaching and learning entrepreneurship. *Entrepreneurship Education and Pedagogy, 1*(1), 8–41.

Pittaway, L., & Cope, J. (2007). Entrepreneurship education a systematic review of the evidence. *International Small Business Journal, 25*(5), 479–510.

Pittaway, L., & Edwards, C. (2012). Assessment: Examining practice in entrepreneurship education. *Education+ Training, 54*(8/9), 778–800.

Politis, D. (2005). The process of entrepreneurial learning: A conceptual framework. *Entrepreneurship Theory and Practice, 29*(4), 399–424.

Rideout, E. C., & Gray, D. O. (2013). Does Entrepreneurship education really work? A review and methodological critique of the empirical literature on the effects of university-based entrepreneurship education. *Journal of Small Business Management, 51*(3), 329–351.

Roberts, J. W. (2015). *Experiential education in the college context: What it is, how it works, and why it matters*. Routledge.

Robinson, S., Neergaard, H., Tanggaard, L., & Krueger, N. (2016). New horizons in entrepreneurship: from teacher-led to student-centered learning. *Education+ Training, 58*(7/8), 661–683.

Swanson, J. A. (2016). Trends in literature about emerging adulthood: Review of empirical studies. *Emerging Adulthood, 4*(6), 391–402.

Sweller, J. (1988). Cognitive load during problem solving: Effects on learning. *Cognitive Science, 12*(2), 257–285.

Sweller, J. (1994). Cognitive load theory, learning difficulty, and instructional design. *Learning and Instruction, 4*(4), 295–312.

Sweller, J. (2015). In academe, what is learned, and how is it learned? *Current Directions in Psychological Science, 24*(3), 190–194.

Sweller, J. (2016). Working memory, long-term memory, and instructional design. *Journal of Applied Research in Memory and Cognition, 5*(4), 360–367.

Teaching Entrepreneurship to Undergraduates: A Vygotskian Perspective

Daniele Morselli and Alexandros Kakouris

1 INTRODUCTION

Unequivocally, entrepreneurship is rapidly evolving as a standalone or supplementary subject embedded in curricula of all educational levels. As a distinct teachable subject, it currently encounters Katz's (2007) remarks for a "third wave" of expansion. Gabrielsson et al. (2020, p. 1063), who recently reviewed the field, contend that "entrepreneurial education has evolved into a distinct research field in its own right". Through the correspondent educational research along with bibliometrics (e.g. Durán-Sánchez et al., 2019; Fellnhofer, 2019; Hägg & Gabrielsson, 2019; Kakouris & Georgiadis, 2016; Nabi et al., 2017), a consensus has emerged whereby after teaching entrepreneurship initially focused on the relevant notions, it was realigned more closely with the content

---

D. Morselli (✉)
Free University of Bozen-Bolzano, Bolzano, Italy
e-mail: Daniele.Morselli@unibz.it

A. Kakouris
University of Peloponnese, Tripolis, Greece
e-mail: a.kakouris@uop.gr

© The Author(s), under exclusive license to Springer Nature
Switzerland AG 2022
G. J. Larios-Hernandez et al. (eds.), *Theorising Undergraduate Entrepreneurship Education*,
https://doi.org/10.1007/978-3-030-87865-8_4

so it now systematically confronts the teaching methods (i.e. the pedagogy). As well-documented in Hägg and Gabrielsson (2019), a move from "teachability" to "learnability" has taken place within the field. Ergo, a theoretical reflection on how entrepreneurship is taught within universities is timely since disparate implementations have taken place over two decades. Hindle (2007, p. 111) has noted early that "For an entrepreneurship education program to be truly worthy of a university setting, it needs some intellectual challenges that take it beyond mere training and give it claim to being education".

From the educational perspective, it has been maintained by the authors (Kakouris & Morselli, 2020) that entrepreneurial pedagogies have to be grounded on well-established learning theories in order to articulate concrete objectives that can be materialised by the educators. Such a connection of practice to theory enables the systematic evaluation of entrepreneurship education and its impact that has been an underdeveloped subject in the literature so far (e.g. Duval-Couetil, 2013). Therefore, different learning theories have been recommended as more suitable to inform the pedagogy in different levels of education. For tertiary settings, Kolb's experiential learning along with Dewey's learning-by-doing have dominated the entrepreneurial pedagogy (Fellnhofer, 2019). These theories emanate from the general standpoint of constructivism, thus pointing out the active role of the learner in constructing his or her own knowledge.

Unlike entrepreneurship in secondary education and in lifelong learning settings, addressed elsewhere, the present chapter focuses on undergraduates as a separate audience that needs specific attention for the implementation of entrepreneurial teaching and courses. University studies are highly structured through curricula which aim to provide scientific knowledge on specific disciplines attested by certificates. Thus, learning in universities is institutionalised and consequently, in such environments entrepreneuring may be considered academically illegitimate (e.g. Fayolle & Gailly, 2008; Johannisson, 2016; Kuratko, 2005). A driver on how entrepreneurship is taught, or ought to be taught, in universities can be based on the early remarks of Hindle (2007) who clearly dissociates entrepreneurship from the Business School paradigm requiring the presence of the "vocational component" in entrepreneurial teaching. Entrepreneurship in economics and business studies, for instance, has always been met in its informative manifestation, such as how it relates to macroeconomic indices, how it conforms with the theory of the firm, how businesses are financially managed, how corporations organise resources to create value, etc.; called as the "about" mode of entrepreneurship education. This type of instruction is significantly cognitive, which is a characteristic consistent with how it is addressed in many other disciplines.

Nonetheless, entrepreneurship education in the 2000s departed from the previous traditional teaching by embracing broader perspectives; that is to cultivate skills and affect attitudes capable of resulting in more entrepreneurial alumni (Kakouris & Liargovas, 2020). It has also embraced social entrepreneurship, sustainability and social responsibility. To this end, the adopted pedagogies pursue, to an extent, the learning paradigm of constructivism (Hägg & Gabrielsson, 2019) whilst the relevant courses penetrate different disciplines and appear in the last two years of study. In this way, basic entrepreneurial knowledge has to be constructed from the extant scientific knowledge of students, following a cognitive constructivist logic. Further, entrepreneurship needs to be considered through a social constructivist lens, that it can be socio-culturally mediated through scheduled interventions from educators. Whilst cognitive constructivism embraces different types of learning, introduced by Piaget in the process of equilibration, social constructivism introduces the Vygotskian concepts of zone of proximal development and mediated act. Both these learning paradigms are useful in undergraduate entrepreneurial teaching depending on the level and scope of the implemented entrepreneurial teaching. The present chapter focuses on the Vygotskian theory of learning for teaching entrepreneurship to undergraduates. The impetus to focus on social constructivism pursues cross-national studies which indicate that students' entrepreneurial intentions and motivations conform with national cultures and local social norms (Fleck et al., 2020).

During the 1960s and the 1980s there has been a growing interest in the Western World on the ideas of Lev Vygotsky, a psychologist and educator lived in Russia between 1896 and 1934, since his theories changed dramatically the prevailing theory of child development. According to Mecacci (2017), the first impulse came in 1962 when Vygotsky's masterpiece "Thinking and Language" was partially translated into English. However, in the 1980s Vygotsky's representation started to change to acknowledge that his work had been more far reaching than child psychology, whilst a larger number of his writings were translated into Western languages. A new phase of historical research started with the fall of the Soviet Union, thus showing the complex figure of a politically engaged intellectual and the absence of a compact Vygotskian school. Such "revisionist phase" also identified a "neo-Vygotskian school" represented for example by Cole, Wertsch and Bruner. Nowadays, a new review of Vygotsky is called for in the light of the revisionist phase and the unpublished materials that are being discovered.

Accordingly, this chapter will review the main tenets of Vygotsky, which are: mediation in human interaction, the selection of the unit of analysis, the zone of proximal development (ZPD) and the principle of double stimulation. These concepts can be used differently according to the level of education, with undergraduate education seen as appropriation of existing tools and adult education seen as development of new tools. A literature review is included on Vygotsky's principles within the realm of entrepreneurship education. In line with the scope of this volume, most of the articles reviewed concern tertiary educational settings. Two practical examples with a potential for undergraduate teaching are subsequently described: a discourse on Pareto's 80/20 principle in entrepreneurship performed online and course on social entrepreneurship based on problem-based learning. The first example focuses on the appropriation of entrepreneurial tools, whilst the second on transformation (agency and creativity). The chapter closes with a discussion of implications for educators and researchers towards developing effective entrepreneurial teaching based on Vygotsky's theory at the undergraduate level.

2   THE BASICS OF THE VYGOTSKIAN THEORY

The first reason to introduce a Vygotskian perspective is methodological (Kakouris & Morselli, 2020), to offer a strong alternative to the cognitive studies characterised by a Cartesian split between cognition and learning, thus depicting humans as a computer isolated from their cultural context (Engeström, 2015). The second methodological reason is that, whilst the cognitive studies were predominantly analytical and observational, the Vygotskian studies are characterised by an activist and interventionist legacy. Such transformational aim "to make the world better" is close to the meaning of entrepreneurship, on the one hand with its aim as value creation, and on the other hand to cultural entrepreneurship (Kyrö, 2005), with entrepreneurship allowing both new practices and breaking down old institutions and systems.

The ideas of Vygotsky can be summarised into three main tenets, these pertain to the mediated act as unit of analysis, the ZPD and double stimulation. For Vygotsky (1987) the selection of an appropriate unit of analysis was particularly important. If the analysis was based on single elements, the relationships between elements would be lost. Instead, an appropriate unit is based on a set of elements that maintains the property of the whole phenomenon. In the study of the relationship between thinking and thought for example, the content of thought is expressed through words, the unit of analysis is the meaning. The first idea of "mediated act" as unit of analysis (Vygotsky, 1978) embeds the fundamental idea that a human act cannot be considered a mere response (R) to an external stimulus (S). Instead, human behaviour is mediated by an auxiliary stimulus (X) that is drawn into the situation, and creates a new link between S and R. To be "drawn" here means the human is actively engaged in the establishment of the relationship which inhibits the impulse to react immediately. Following Marx, such unit of analysis represents an attempt to embed dialectic materialism into human action (Sannino, 2011), and in doing so, it overcomes the division between the individual and the societal structures: whilst the individual had to be understood in the light of cultural means, the society had to be understood with the individuals' agency which produces and uses artefacts (Engeström, 2015). This organisation is thus fundamental for all the higher psychological functions and allows humans to control their behaviour from outside with the help of auxiliary stimuli, allowing them to break away from biological determinism and creating new forms of psychological process based on culture. Vygotsky (1978) distinguished between two types of auxiliary stimuli in human behaviour: tools and signs. Whilst tools are oriented externally and aim to change the object of activity and ultimately to master nature, signs are part of psychological tools and aim to control the behavioural processes—own or someone else's. Examples of psychological tools are language, mathematics, writing, schemas, diagrams, maps, etc. Drawing from Vygotsky's mediated act S-X-R, Engeström (2015, p. 63) reconceptualised this relationship into a triangle connecting the subject, the mediating artefact (sign or tool) and the object to which a human activity is oriented.

Through the mediated act as unit of analysis, Vygotsky (1978) argues that learning is social in nature, and that social learning anticipates the development of the individual mental functioning. This thinking leads to the second tenet, the ZPD, which is defined as "the distance between the actual developmental level as determined by independent problem-solving and the level of potential development as determined through problem-solving under adult guidance or in collaboration with more capable peers" (p. 86). Whilst Vygotsky stresses the power of relationships with adults or peers to structure significative learning in pupils, Engeström (2015) has extended this concept to collectives when groups or even organisations engage in formative interventions to analyse and find solutions to the problems affecting their organisations seen as activity systems, and subsequently envision the ZPD of their organisation through novel concepts or models.

The third tenet of Vygotsky, important for entrepreneurship and probably the least researched (Morselli & Sannino, 2021), is double stimulation. Caused by an initial problem (the first stimulus), the second stimulus is an artefact that is turned into a sign, that is a connection between the external world and the human's psychological functioning (Sannino, 2015). Besides being a method, double stimulation is a principle of volitional action distinguishing higher psychological functions, with which humans wilfully change their behaviour and environment. This principle of volition should be considered as distinct from the mediated action described above, since it also entails a conflict of motives. Consequently, it is also a collision between antithetic tendencies or aspirations that happens in conditions of uncertainty and demands the audacity to take a deliberate decision. Hence, an action is considered volitional only when there are obstacles hindering its realisation.

In an experimental situation on double stimulation, Vygotsky (1978) gave a child a problem beyond her abilities, which is the first stimulus. What he frequently observed was that, when a neutral object was placed next to the child, she would draw it into the situation to solve the problem, and in doing so, the second stimulus became a meaningful sign that mediated the solution (van der Veer & Valsiner, 1991). However, the experimenter does not have necessarily to provide the subject with any ready-made second stimulus, since it is the subject who can build the second stimulus on their own (Engeström, 2007). Furthermore, double stimulation can be used in structured, collaborative problem-solving such as in formative interventions, and in this case the researcher or instructor could provide the participants with specific concepts, models or schemas. However, since this process can be hardly controlled externally, and in fact it is the basic mechanism for the genesis of the will, the participants end up by developing their own concept or model as an indicator of their agency.

3 VYGOTSKYAN CONCEPTS IN ENTREPRENEURSHIP EDUCATION

Whilst the ideas of Vygotsky have certainly represented a turnaround in education to overcome the cognitive view of the individual as separated from their cultural context, this chapter focuses on how his principles have been used in entrepreneurship education. A search in the literature with the keywords "Vygotsky" and "entrepreneurship" gave at least 50 articles citing his works. Although the following literature review is by no means exhaustive, it shows in our view the most interesting research that embedded Vygotsky's principles to entrepreneurship education.

Concerning Vygotsky's notion of mediation, it has only been applied by few authors. Drawing from Engeström (2015) reformulation subject-artefact-object, Thorpe et al. (2006) conceptualise the entrepreneurial activity as an artefact mediated activity: "a similar relationship holds between the identity of the entrepreneurs, the recognition of an opportunity and the pursuit within the activity of venture creation" (p. 236). Almeida and Duque (2017) highlight the importance of mediation of tools and artefacts for the development of entrepreneurial minds, whilst Lackéus et al. (2016) suggest the use of tools to bridge the rift between traditional-progressive pedagogies in entrepreneurship. Similarly, Lahn, Leif and Erikson (2016) conceptualise the development of entrepreneurial competence as an activity mediated by artefacts which allows the transformation of the object for certain purposes. Additionally, Holt (2008) makes use of the mediated act to understand the search of entrepreneurial opportunities. By using Engeström's (2015) reformulation of the mediated act, that is the relation between the subject, the object and the artefact, Holt (2008) suggests that "The opportunity recognition and pursuit can be understood as the skilful integration of prevailing and emerging objects and relations of business activity typically articulated through collaborative enterprise" (p. 52).

Other authors focus on the social nature of cognition in tertiary settings, for example to understand the entrepreneurial learning process (Kakouris, 2017; Mueller & Anderson, 2014), to develop a framework for the delivery of experiential entrepreneurship (Bell & Bell, 2020), to nurture entrepreneurial women's insights (Rao, 2014) or to develop an innovative paradigm for entrepreneurship education (Gibb, 2011). Ementa et al. (2018) suggest that integrated web-based instructional technology can promote learning through social interactions and collaboration in students, whilst Almeida and Duque (2017) contend that teachers, learners and entrepreneurs are active participants in understanding the concepts related to business. Philipson (2015) recommends that the teachers develop the caring aspects of the relationship with the students suggesting collaborative learning amongst students.

Drawing on the social origin of cognition, other scholars focus on the situational conditions to awaken students' motivation, problem-solving and creativity. Musa et al. (2019) suggest that teaching should build on students' interests, since learning happens only when there is novelty that awakens higher cognitive functions. To do so, entrepreneurial learning should happen in authentic contexts (Thorpe et al., 2006; Toutain et al., 2017). Similarly, for Hjorth and Johannisson (2007) the ideas of Vygotsky and Bakhtin (an influential Russian philosopher contemporaneous of Vygotsky) are fruitfully combined in problem-based learning (PBL). Most importantly, in line with the careful selection of an appropriate unit of analysis, it is noteworthy that the problems are selected in relation to a whole situation rather than fragmented and therefore without an appropriate context. In line with Vygotsky's idea that imagination is related to creativity, Kier and McMullen (2018) study venture creation through imagination and suggest that by learning to connect unrelated information, students imagine potential solutions.

Moreover, the ZPD had some fortune amongst the scholars writing about entrepreneurship education. Ehrlin et al. (2015) use the ZPD to highlight that children can collaborate with their peers and their community outside the school, whilst in higher education they suggest that programmes are broken down to fall within the students' ZPD, and that instructors should seek to identify the students' individual ZPD. In secondary education (Hietanen, 2015) and in tertiary education settings (Ibraheem & Aijaz, 2011; Menzies, 2011) the ZPD means that students need well timed support from both peers and the teacher to learn entrepreneurship. Additionally, from an historical perspective, the ZPD suggests that the hierarchical relation between teacher and students is reduced, and that entrepreneurship education promotes learning from peers (Hjorth & Johannisson, 2007). An interesting proposal to apply a social constructivist perspective (including ZPD) to entrepreneurship education comes from Man (2019), who suggests five leading principles to structure activities in university-based entrepreneurship centres. Hence, these centres: (1) have the participants experiment actively; (2) offer authentic contexts; (3) provide many opportunities for social interaction; (4) develop in students a strong sense of ownership through participation; and (5) offer scaffolding support.

The following section discusses two case studies that show two different principles of Vygotsky applied to entrepreneurship education at the undergraduate level. The first example entails mediation, that is appropriation of entrepreneurial tools and concepts, whilst the second example focuses on nurturing innovation through the principle of double stimulation.

A case study is a contemporary, real-life event bound in space and time (Yin, 2009). For Blenker et al. (2014) case studies represent the favoured form of entrepreneurship research strategy since entrepreneurship education comprises entities and activities that can be easily identified despite their embeddedness in the context.

4   Case Studies

An Activity Based on Pareto's 80/20 Principle: The Appropriation of Entrepreneurial Tools and Concepts

Learning through the online environment of TeleCC (http://telecc.org/) can be considered an example of social learning in entrepreneurship. In Kakouris (2017) a specific TeleCC learning programme in Greece has been discussed seeking for incidents of reflection and critical thinking of individuals. In the present Vygotskian approach, the same example can be examined as the internalisation of new instruments, once internalised they can be externalised, thus mediating entrepreneurial action. The TeleCC project gathered more than 250 participants of different backgrounds all over Greece in five-month online courses. Two learning groups in entrepreneurship were formed of 70 attendees each, taught by one of the co-authors. The main goal of the programme was to introduce the attendees into entrepreneurship whilst the whole instruction had been organised through activities and asynchronous online discussions. The relevant learning tools (documents, videos, games, websites, etc.) were developed and introduced by the educator who was initiating the discussion after each scheduled experience. Later on, the educator simply facilitated the discussion, enabling peer-learning, and finally he summarised the conclusions. One of the performed activities (out of 15) is described in the sequel.

The specific activity aimed at introducing the Pareto 80/20 principle into entrepreneurship. This simple empirical law is met in management and economic studies but has scarce direct implementations to entrepreneurship. It implies that 20% of the factors result for the 80% of the results and could feature the mindset of some entrepreneurs. Hence, the authentic problem posed to trainees (subjects) is to optimise the resources of a company to achieve maximum performance (object). This purpose is considered as the working unit of analysis. It is holistic and meaningful to the trainees without pre-given answers. Trainees experimented with an online game (tool) where 100 units of resources can be delivered to 38 corporate processes (cells) organised through the Business Model Canvas template (Osterwalder & Pigneur, 2010) which is an important tool to mediate entrepreneurship. Some constraints are posed (e.g. a maximum number of resource units per cell, fill of all cells, etc.) whilst the system records the time everyone spends on the game along with the maximum performance she achieves. Each cell contributes with a hidden coefficient to the performance and the cell coefficients obey the Pareto 80/20 rule. According to Wartofsky (1979), tools can be primary, secondary or tertiary. The first category includes physical and tangible objects whilst the other two psychological and cultural. The TeleCC online platform and the specific business game are primary tools whereas the Canvas model is a secondary one. Tertiary tools involve the culture and the context and will be discussed below. The business game facilitates, as a mediated act, the internalisation process of the subjects (trainees) who are left free to practice solutions.

After the game was over, a discussion followed amongst the learners in the virtual classroom. The trainees were asked to externalise what they learned from their experience and to share this knowledge with their peers. The educator undertook the interventionist role to extract the shared knowledge. The trainees described different creative strategies to solve the problem. Some tried to solve it mechanistically, such as by way of a mathematical quiz, whilst others considered which specific Canvas domain each cell belongs to and accordingly, its significance to the company's performance. In this way the trainees learn from peers and from a more knowledgeable other (educator). A common result was that it was quick to achieve a 50% performance outcome but much more time consuming to attain higher levels. It came out, as scheduled, that those who achieved more than 90% had spent almost quadruple time online. At this point the Pareto 80/20 principle was presented triggering individual reflections. The 80/20 principle had served as a mediating concept to be internalised by the students using it towards developing better solutions within their ZPD. Nonetheless, some contradictions arose which is a key-element for the learning process. Was the goal to achieve a 100% performance or to save time? Was the coefficient of each cell irrelevant to the Canvas domain and why? To resolve the different views, the context of entrepreneurship was used as a tertiary tool (i.e. another mediating concept). What does "maximum performance" mean for an entrepreneur and for an employee? How do people from different backgrounds and experiences understand a task to optimise the performance of something? Under the prism of entrepreneurship, an 80% outcome might be desirable if it preserves time. That said, such a realisation or interpretation has to do with the context of entrepreneurship and the cultural influences that students possibly carry. As a final stage of the discussion, the group expressed the view that Pareto 80/20 could be used creatively in the organisation of a new firm but which 20% of factors is important depends on the specific venture. Thus, the entrepreneur has to learn her own business during the first stages of its life. This conclusion indicates the externalisation process of the activity. Due to mediating concepts, the trainees invented own ways of how to integrate the Pareto 80/20 law into the optimisation process of a new firm. To this end, peer-learning in a social context under the interventions of the educator was crucial whilst the current example illustrates acquisition of extant mediating tools for entrepreneurship.

Course on Social Entrepreneurship for Social Educators: Towards Innovation Through Double Stimulation

The Bachelor for Social Educators at the University of Bolzano offers a course on "Methods of Groupwork" which is based on a challenge in context delivered by a local entrepreneur (see Korda, 2019; Morselli, 2019). The students work in small groups, and in few intensive weeks of work they develop their solution and eventually pitch it to the entrepreneur. The first step to design this part in the course entails finding an entrepreneur who has a real challenge that challenges their business, such as a strategic decision to take or how to increase sales. In one edition of the course, the challenge dealt with the formulation of a proposal for the families having kids suffering from hyperactive disorders in times of COVID-19 pandemic. In the previous edition, the challenge was to formulate a proposal for an inclusive programme for both kids with and without learning disabilities to increase their learning to learn skills.

In line with a Vygotskyan approach: (a) the unit of analysis is preserved as holistic, that is the challenge that the students work out tackles a complex unit rather than scattered elements; (b) the challenge is real-life, as it comes from the entrepreneur's social environment and deals with the students' professionalism, and as such it is meaningful for the students, thus pointing out the social nature of learning. Students are then divided into small groups to start working on the challenge and find an innovative solution. However, learn does not proceed on its own without a guide, and this pedagogy implements the ZPD concept of progressive and structured learning in two ways.

Firstly, similar to the example of 4.1, the teacher provides tools and concepts for groupwork and innovation that the students appropriate. An example is the jigsaw for group work (Aronson & Patnoe, 2011), where through having several articles to read and summarise, the students realise the importance of cooperation and at the same time gain basic knowledge on the topic. Another example of tool conductive for entrepreneurship is Design Thinking (Kelley & Kelley, 2013), to develop a solution through cycles of ideation, prototyping and testing. The instructor can also provide mediating concepts through having students watching video and making consequent reflection and discussion, for example on how ideation works. Concerning the tools that mediate online cooperation and ideation, Google Jam-Boards helps the students brainstorm and keep track of their ideas. Moreover, whilst providing tools and concepts, the instructor also provides a structured setting and rules on how to work in groups, regarding how different roles and labour is divided between the group (timekeeper, coordinator, minute taker, etc.), so that the students progressively internalise the rules and tools on how to structure groupwork productivity.

Secondly, the teacher provides individualised support, and once a week meets the groups for share-out meetings. The format is the following: the students deliver a presentation on what they have done so far, what they have learnt, what they are doing next and what they are keeping in mind. After having listened to the presentation, the instructor answers the students' questions and gives them advice on what they could do. The social nature of learning is evidenced not only by the real-life challenge, but also by the groupwork, where students learn from each other. During the share-out meetings or the quick workshops, the students learn also from a more knowledgeable other, the instructor. Progressively, thanks to the graduality given by the instructor guidance, increasingly structured groupwork, new tools and concepts, the challenge falls within the students' ZPD.

The fact that students have only few weeks to deal with the challenge makes it cogent, that is something must be done for the finals. All in all, the double stimulation works as a principle for problem-solving and agency development. The first stimulus is the challenge combined with the tight deadline that makes it a cogent motive. Concerning possible second stimuli, these are the entrepreneurial concepts and tools provided by the teacher, or even found by the students during their web searches or heard in other lectures. Students select one stimulus, or combine two stimuli to make a new one, or even create a new stimulus from scratch. This stimulus becomes their second stimulus: in Vygotskian terms, such stimulus from "neutral" becomes meaningful to tackle the first stimulus, that is the problematic situation (Engeström, 2011). During this process, the students design, enrich, prototype, and test their second stimulus, and finally pitch it to the social entrepreneur the day of the finals. Such learning process can be seen as a mini cycle of expansive learning (Rantavuori et al., 2016), where the participants learn something that is not yet there. The final presentation is another important learning experience, not only because it gives meaning to the students work, but also because the students get feedback on their proposal, its feasibility, potential and limitations.

This pedagogy calls the students to demonstrate more effort compared to other teaching methods such as lectures, as the students feel they are immediately "thrown" into the practice; they value, however, such hands-on approach where they work always in their small group, and consider the course almost "work experience", since it tackles real-life challenges related to their vocation. Furthermore, the social entrepreneur is often impressed by the students' solutions and finds that the pitches are delivered more professionally than the presentations delivered by the "alleged" experts. Sometimes the students are so confident about their idea that they decide to take further steps to its implementation to the market, which is an unusual outcome for second year's students in social education.

5 Conclusions

This chapter started by introducing the basic tenets of Vygotsky (1978, 1987), these are: the unit of analysis of the mediated act, the ZPD, and double stimulation. This chapter reviewed the most important articles that make use of Vygotsky's concepts in entrepreneurship education and found that six articles referred to the mediated act, whilst most articles (8) concentrated on the social nature of learning and the environmental conditions (5) promoting learning. Another six articles made use of the ZPD, whilst we could find no articles using double stimulation in entrepreneurship education.

A summary of the review on Vygotsky and entrepreneurship suggests that teachers should pay attention to the social nature of learning (Kakouris, 2017; Mueller & Anderson, 2014), having students working with their peers and cultivating social relationships (Man, 2019) to understand the entrepreneurship related concepts. Furthermore, the teacher should structure the working environment so that students can work within their ZPD (Ibraheem & Aijaz, 2011; Menzies, 2011). Concerning the selection of the unit of analysis, the students should tackle problems and challenges (Hjorth & Johannisson, 2007) that are meaningful for them, for example coming from their community (Musa et al., 2019); to do so, the course could tackle a problem holistically (Man, 2008, Thorpe et al., 2006; Toutain et al., 2017).

The results of this review are twofold. From one perspective, we found that most of the articles use only one concept rather than an integrated combination, which suggests that Vygotsky's thinking and principles could be better integrated to back entrepreneurship education. From another perspective, we were surprised by such flourishing of articles, most of them recent, which indicate a renewed discovery of Vygotsky. We hypothesise this trend has developed because scholars are becoming aware of the necessity of having a strong educational theory backing entrepreneurial learning, as we affirm in Kakouris and Morselli (2020).

Additionally, we described two cases that put into practice Vygotsky's principles in undergraduate education. The first case focuses on how specific tools and concepts (for example the Business Model Canvas and the Pareto 80/20 principle) can be internalised to mediate entrepreneurial action. The second case shows the power of double stimulation as a principle to develop agency and creativity. Through the examples we highlighted the importance of mediation as appropriation of tools and concepts, which in entrepreneurship at the undergraduate level could be the Business Model Canvas (Osterwalder & Pigneur, 2010), Design Thinking (Kelley & Kelley, 2013) and the Lean LaunchPad (Blank et al., 2014) or other tools and concepts (e.g. Mansoori & Lackéus, 2020). Beyond appropriation of entrepreneurial tools and concepts, however, students could learn how to signify them to devise something new through double stimulation. The first stimulus is the cogent problem that the students have to tackle, and for which there are no ready-made solutions (Engeström, 2011). The tools and concepts provided by the instructors are second stimuli that help the students build their own and unique second stimulus, that is a model of solution, which is progressively enriched, prototyped and finally pitched to the social entrepreneur.

Consequently, we see Vygotsky's theory in undergraduate education at a first level as appropriation of entrepreneurial artefacts (tools and concepts) that once well-internalised can be externalised, thus mediating entrepreneurial action. However, beyond appropriation of tools, a second level of entrepreneurship education can be re-mediation through double stimulation, which brings innovation by creating new tools and concepts. The result of double stimulation is also the students' development of agency, which means that sooner or later learners end up developing their own solution which could take unexpected directions, and the teacher supports this process of agency development by acting as a coach, for example during the share out meetings. Whilst the second case study suggests that double stimulation is key for entrepreneurship education, in that it triggers creativity, problem-solving and commitment, the literature review shows that this concept has been rather unexploited. Despite much more research and practice are needed to show its potential, in our view it could become the key principle for scholars researching on entrepreneurship education. This is in line with Hindle's (2007) call to confront the "plus-zone challenge" in teaching entrepreneurship to undergraduates.

In sum, most of Hindle's remarks can be met once entrepreneurship education develops its own methods grounded on the pillars of educational theory. This is especially essential in university settings where entrepreneurship still seeks academic legitimacy. The experiential nature of teaching so far has infused the learning-by-doing approach of Dewey as an underpinning of pedagogy in various educational levels. Further adoption of theories like the social constructivism of Vygotsky, discussed here, will make the art and practice of teaching entrepreneurship more comprehensive to academics who may feel a step behind the rapid evolution of the field and the increased demand for tertiary entrepreneurial courses.

Acknowledgements AK is grateful the U.S. Embassy in Athens for financial support for the TeleCC implementation in Greece. The authors are also thankful to David Nally for the proofreading services.

REFERENCES

Almeida, E. V., & Duque, G. V. (2017). The importance of mediation in the development of entrepreneurial minds. *INNOVA Research Journal, 2*(8.1), 86–91.

Aronson, E., & Patnoe, S. (2011). *Cooperation in the classroom: The Jigsaw method.* Pinter & Martin Ltd.

Bell, R., & Bell, H. (2020). Applying educational theory to develop a framework to support the delivery of experiential entrepreneurship education. *Journal of Small Business and Enterprise Development, 27*(6), 987–1004.

Blank, S., Engel, J., & Hornthal, J. (2014). *Lean launchpad. Evidence-based entrepreneurship educators guide.* Retrieved from https://venturewell.org/wp-content/uploads/Educators-Guide-Final-w-cover-PDF.pdf. Accessed 28 January 2021.

Blenker, P., Trolle Elmholdt, S., Hedeboe Frederiksen, S., Korsgaard, S., & Wagner, K. (2014). Methods in entrepreneurship education research: A review and integrative framework. *Education+ Training, 56* (8/9), 697–715.

Durán-Sánchez, A., Del Río-Rama, M. d. l. C., Álvarez-García, J., & García-Vélez, D. F. (2019). Mapping of scientific coverage on education for entrepreneurship in higher education. *Journal of Enterprising Communities: People and Places in the Global Economy, 13*(1/2), 84–104.

Duval-Couetil, N. (2013). Assessing the impact of entrepreneurship education programs: Challenges and approaches. *Journal of Small Business Management, 51*(3), 394–409.

Ehrlin, A., Insulander, E., & Sandberg, A. (2015). Perspectives on entrepreneurial learning in the early years of education. *Journal of Education and Human Development, 4*(3), 151–159.

Ementa, C., Onokpaunu, M., & Okonkwo, M. (2018). Integration of web-based instructional technologies in teaching entrepreneurial courses in tertiary instituions in Delta State. *Nigerian Journal of Business Education, 4*(2), 248–259.

Engeström, Y. (2007). Putting Vygotsky to work: The change laboratory as an application of double stimulation. In H. Daniels, M. Cole, & J. V. Wertsch

(Eds.), *The Cambridge companion to Vygotsky* (pp. 363–382). Cambridge University Press.

Engeström, Y. (2011). From design experiments to formative interventions. *Theory & Psychology, 21*(5), 598-628.

Engeström, Y. (2015). Learning by expanding: Origins, applications, and challenges. In *Learning by expanding* (pp. Xiii–Xxxviii). Cambridge University Press.

Fayolle, A., & Gailly, B. (2008). From craft to science: Teaching models and learning processes in entrepreneurship education. *Journal of European Industrial Training, 32*(7), 569–593.

Fellnhofer, K. (2019). Toward a taxonomy of entrepreneurship education research literature: A bibliometric mapping and visualization. *Educational Research Review, 27*, 28–55.

Fleck, E., Kakouris, A., & Winkel, D. (2021). Cultural traits of entrepreneurship education: A cross-national study. *Journal of Entrepreneurship in Emerging Economies, 13*(5), 838-863. https://doi.org/10.1108/JEEE-02-2020-0030.

Gabrielsson, J., Hägg, G., Landström, H., & Politis, D. (2020). Connecting the past with the present: The development of research on pedagogy in entrepreneurial education. *Education+ Training, 62*(9), 1061–1086

Gibb, A. (2011). Concepts into practice: Meeting the challenge of development of entrepreneurship educators around an innovative paradigm. *International Journal of Entrepreneurial Behavior & Research, 17*(2), 146–165.

Hägg, G., & Gabrielsson, J. (2019). A systematic literature review of the evolution of pedagogy in entrepreneurial education research. *International Journal of Entrepreneurial Behavior & Research, 26*(5), 829–861.

Hietanen, L. (2015). Entrepreneurial learning environments: Supporting or hindering diverse learners? *Education+ Training, 57*(5), 512–531.

Hindle, K. (2007). Teaching entrepreneurship at university: From the wrong building to the right philosophy. In A. Fayolle (Ed.), *Handbook of research in entrepreneurship education: A general perspective* (Vol. 1, pp. 104–126). Edward Elgar.

Hjorth, D., & Johannisson, B. (2007). Learning as an entrepreneurial process. In A. Fayolle (Ed.), *Handbook of research in entrepreneurship education: A general perspective* (Vol. 1, pp. 46–66). Edward Elgar.

Holt, R. (2008). Using activity theory to understand entrepreneurial opportunity. *Mind, Culture, and Activity, 15*(1), 52–70.

Ibraheem, M., & Aijaz, N. (2011). Dynamics of peer assisted learning and teaching at an entrepreneurial university: An experience to share. *International Journal of Humanities and Social Science, 1*(12), 93–99.

Johannisson, B. (2016). Limits to and prospects of entrepreneurship education in the academic context. *Entrepreneurship & Regional Development, 28*(5–6), 403–423.

Kakouris, A. (2017). Constructivist entrepreneurial teaching: The TeleCC online approach in Greece. In P. Jones, G. Maas, & L. Pittaway (Eds.), *Entrepreneurship education* (Contemporary issues in entrepreneurship research, Vol. 7, pp. 235–258). Emerald.

Kakouris, A., & Georgiadis, P. (2016). Analysing entrepreneurship education: A bibliometric survey pattern. *Journal of Global Entrepreneurship Research*, 6(6), 1–18.

Kakouris, A., & Liargovas, P. (2020). On the about/for/through framework of entrepreneurship education: A critical analysis. *Entrepreneurship Education and Pedagogy*. 4(3),396-421. https://doi.org/10.1177/2515127420916740

Kakouris, A., & Morselli, D. (2020). Addressing the pre/post-university pedagogy of entrepreneurship coherent with learning theories. In S. Sawang (Ed.), *Entrepreneurship education: A lifelong learning approach* (pp. 35–58). Springer.

Katz, J. A. (2007). Foreword: The third wave of entrepreneurship education and the importance of fun in learning. In A. Fayolle (Ed.), *Handbook of research in entrepreneurship education: A general perspective* (Vol. 1, pp. xi–xv). Edward Elgar.

Kier, A. S., & McMullen, J. S. (2018). Entrepreneurial imaginativeness in new venture ideation. *Academy of Management Journal*, 61(6), 2265–2295.

Kelley, D., & Kelley, T. (2013). *Creative confidence: Unleashing the creative potential within us all*. Crown.

Korda, D. (2019). *What happens when we do school better?* Retrieved from: https://www.gettingsmart.com/2019/02/what-happens-when-we-do-school-better/. Accessed 28 January 2021.

Kuratko, D. F. (2005). The emergence of entrepreneurship education: Development, trends, and challenges. *Entrepreneurship Theory and Practice*, 29(5), 577–597.

Kyrö, P. (2005). Entrepreneurial learning in a cross-cultural context challenges previous learning paradigms. In P. Kyrö & C. Carrier (Eds.), *The dynamics of learning entrepreneurship in a cross-cultural university context: Entrepreneurship education series* (Vol. 2, pp. 68–102): University of Tampere, Faculty of Education, Research Center for Vocational and Professional Education.

Lackéus, M., Lundqvist, M., & Williams Middleton, K. (2016). Bridging the traditional-progressive education rift through entrepreneurship. *International Journal of Entrepreneurial Behavior & Research*, 22(6), 777–803.

Lahn Leif, C., & Erikson, T. (2016). Entrepreneurship education by design. *Education+ Training*, 58(7/8), 684–699.

Man, T. W. Y. (2019). Nurturing entrepreneurial competencies through university-based entrepreneurship centers: A social constructivist perspective. In J. A. Katz, & A. C. Corbet (Ed.) Seminal ideas for the next twenty-five years of advances (Advances in entrepreneurship, firm emergence and growth, Vol. 21, pp. 141–161). Emerald.

Mansoori, Y., & Lackéus, M. (2020). Comparing effectuation to discovery-driven planning, prescriptive entrepreneurship, business planning, lean startup, and design thinking. *Small Business Economics, 54,* 791–818.

Mecacci, L. (2017). *Lev Vygotskij: sviluppo, educazione e patologia della mente.* Giunti.

Menzies, T. V. (2011). Advancing teaching and learning in relation to university-based entrepreneurship education: A theoretical, model building approach. *International Journal of Arts & Sciences, 4*(11), 47–56.

Morselli, D. (2019). Teaching a sense of initiative and entrepreneurship through problem-based learning. *Form@re-Open Journal per la Formazione in Rete, 19*(2), 149–160.

Morselli, D., & Sannino, A. (2021). Testing the model of double stimulation in a change laboratory. *Teaching and Teacher Education, 97,* 1–8.

Mueller, S., & Anderson, A. R. (2014). Understanding the entrepreneurial learning process and its impact on students' personal development: A European perspective. *International Journal of Management Education, 12*(3), 500–511.

Musa, K. J., Ndu, A., & Musa, K. A. (2019). Collaborative learning by doing in tertiary institutions: A strategy for quality entrepreneurship in agricultural education. *African Scholar Publications & Research International, 15*(8), 166–175.

Nabi, G., Liñán, F., Fayolle, A., Krueger, N., & Walmsley, A. (2017). The impact of entrepreneurship education in higher education: A systematic review and research agenda. *Academy of Management Learning & Education, 16*(2), 277–299.

Osterwalder, A., & Pigneur, Y. (2010). *Business model generation: A handbook for visionaries, game changers, and challengers.* John Wiley & Sons.

Philipson, S. (2015). *A framework for entrepreneurial learning in higher education* (pp. 124–162). https://doi.org/10.15626/lld.201507

Rantavuori, J., Engeström, Y., & Lipponen, L. (2016). Learning actions, objects and types of interaction: A methodological analysis of expansive learning among pre-service teachers. *Frontline Learning Research, 4*(3), 1–27.

Rao, S. (2014). Nurturing entrepreneurial women. *Journal of Entrepreneurship in Emerging Economies, 6*(3), 268–297.

Sannino, A. (2011). Activity theory as an activist and interventionist theory. *Theory and Psychology, 21*(5), 571–597.

Sannino, A. (2015). The principle of double stimulation: A path to volitional action. *Learning, Culture and Social Interaction, 6,* 1–15.

Thorpe, R., Gold, J., Holt, R., & Clarke, J. (2006). Immaturity: The constraining of entrepreneurship. *International Small Business Journal, 24*(3), 232–250.

Toutain, O., Fayolle, A., Pittaway, L., & Politis, D. (2017). Role and impact of the environment on entrepreneurial learning. *Entrepreneurship & Regional Development, 29*(9–10), 869–888.

van der Veer, R., & Valsiner, J. (1991). *Understanding Vygotsky: A quest for synthesis*. Blackwell.

Vygotsky, L. S. (1978). *Mind in society: The development of higher psychological processes*. Harvard University Press.

Vygotsky, L. S. (1987). *Thinking and speech*. Plenum.

Wartofsky, M. W. (1979). Perception, representation, and the forms of action: Towards an historical epistemology. In R. S. Cohen & M. W. Wartofsky (Eds.), *A portrait of twenty-five years: Boston studies in the philosophy of science* (pp. 215–237). Springer.

Yin, R. H. (2009). *Case studies research: Design and methods* (4th ed.). Sage.

The Elusive Role of Play in Entrepreneurship Education

Heidi Neck, Elissa Grossman, Doan Winkel, and Jeffrey Stamp

1 Introduction

> You can learn more about a person in an hour of play than you can from a lifetime of conversation.—Plato

Play has long been linked to early childhood development—recognised by the United Nations High Commission for Human Rights as a fundamental right of all children (1989) and acknowledged by numerous reports from the American Academy of Pediatrics as foundational to cognitive, physical, social, and emotional well-being (Yogman et al.,

---

H. Neck (✉)
Babson College, Wellesley, MA, USA
e-mail: hneck@babson.edu

E. Grossman
University of Southern California, Los Angeles, CA, USA
e-mail: elissa.grossman@usc.edu

D. Winkel
John Carroll University, University Heights, OH, USA
e-mail: dwinkel@jcu.edu

© The Author(s), under exclusive license to Springer Nature Switzerland AG 2022
G. J. Larios-Hernandez et al. (eds.), *Theorising Undergraduate Entrepreneurship Education*,
https://doi.org/10.1007/978-3-030-87865-8_5

2018). Yet there is a point in time for most, in the journey from childhood to adulthood, when play takes on less positive, less inclusive connotations—no longer viewed as involving developmentally appropriate activities for all, but as describing activities too childish or frivolous to merit adult involvement or attention. This *perceived* lack of professionalism and productivity leads adults to shun play and feel guilty if caught playing in professional settings, including in higher education (Brown & Vaughn, 2009; Forbes, 2021). As Neck (2010) noted, adults often associate play with "a time of freedom and imagination where minutes turned into hours, backyards transformed into magical faraway kingdoms, living rooms were reconfigured into tent cities, swimming pools became uncharted waters littered with sunken treasure, and stuffed animals sat at attention waiting for assignment from the young seven-year-old teacher" (p. 41). Adults appreciate play as tourists, enjoying it as fond memories and as real-time experiences lived vicariously through the children in their lives. Few appreciate play as offering adults more direct developmental benefits.

The life-stage separation of play as something appropriate for children and questionable for adults, while common to those of the current generation, is in fact comparatively recent. Until the eighteenth century, the games of children and adults were the same (Bettelheim, 1972)—and the source of the subsequent divide is unknown. Today, though a robust literature on play in early childhood education exists, research efforts to understand play in higher education are minimal. Sir Ken Robinson, a prolific supporter of creativity in education with one of the most viewed TED Talks ("Do Schools Kill Creativity?"), has described the exclusion of play in higher education as a tragedy in learning. In a twist on the childhood chicken-egg riddle, the provenance of that "tragedy" remains unclear: did higher education stop play because the role of play was misunderstood, or did the role of play simply get set aside as higher education excluded it for its lack of *gravitas*? Forbes (2021) suggests insufficient understanding has stymied the use of adult play in college environments, noting that play helps foster more interactive, more

---

J. Stamp
University of Minnesota, Minneapolis, MN, USA
e-mail: stamp013@umn.edu

supportive classrooms in which student community and student growth are enhanced.

In recent years, as demand for and use of interactive, experiential, hands-on higher education has grown across myriad fields, the opportunity for more thoughtful consideration of play has emerged. Within entrepreneurship education, the role of play and its uses are of particular relevance—driven in substantial part by the field's history of applied, hands-on learning. Even in entrepreneurship, however, where we find students readily embracing the utility of play within the classroom, we find instructors who express some reluctance to teach adults so ... entrepreneurially. Neck et al. (2014, 2021) introduced five core practices of entrepreneurship education: creation, empathy, experimentation, reflection, and play. Though the first four are easily understood in the context of entrepreneurship education, the practice of play remains a source of mystery and scepticism. Help students *create* new products, services and processes? Check! Help students develop *empathy* for customers, to better understand their needs? Check! Help students *experiment*, test hypotheses, and understand the iterative nature of building a viable and sustainable business? Check! Guide students in a *reflective* practice, so learning from doing is codified into knowledge for longer-term use? Check! Encourage students to *play* with their free and imaginative mind and to immerse themselves in playful experiences. What?! As noted by Neck et al. (2021), "The connection between play and education is so taboo that an entire gaming category had to be labeled 'serious games' (Abt, 1987) to denote those games playable for education purposes only" (p. 6).

This chapter reflects our strongly held belief that well-constructed play can deliver profound "aha" moments, resonant lessons, and truly rigorous learning experiences, as driven by its ability to immerse, engage, and focus students—all while enhancing or reinvigorating the joy of learning and practicing entrepreneurship. In an effort to shed light on a concept that has so long been seen as elusive, we provide a brief overview of what we know about play from a childhood development perspective and then explore what is known about play in higher education. We introduce a philosophical model of using play in entrepreneurship education and conclude with some sample exercises.

2 Play in Early Learning and Development

Play has a rich and well-researched history with respect to early childhood development, dating back to Gross (1916) who theorised play as a governing force of instinct underlying many natural biological processes. Later theorists defined play as free activity standing outside the ordinary (Huizinga, 1944); unorganised and spontaneous, yet fun (Piaget, 1962); carried out in leisure for purposes of pleasure and self-expression (Kraus, 1971); make-believe (Vygotsky, 1978), and a by-product of superfluous energy left over when childrens' primary needs are met by parents (Rubin, 1982). The cumulative breadth of these definitions has facilitated rich empirical research affirming play's many benefits; these include enhanced cognitive development (Burriss & Tsao, 2002), increased executive function (Diamond et al., 2007), creative thinking (Russ & Wallace, 2013), better language skills (Pelligrini, 2013), self-regulation (Karpov, 2005), and improved short- and long-term academic achievement, motivation, and well-being (Hyson et al., 2006; Marcon, 2002). Additionally, play supports the development and maintenance of physical, behaviour, and perceptual skills (e.g. dancing encompasses all three) (Burghardt, 2010). That said, definitional breadth belies limitations with existing approaches as well—play now long lacking a unifying, specific, and accepted definition.

In an effort to frame play with more specificity, Lillard (2015) conducted an extensive literature review to support an initial taxonomy of play, encompassing the six categories most commonly discussed (Table 1). She notes that there is (1) overlap across categories, and (2) an inverted

Table 1 Six types of play

Play Type	Definition	Example
Sensorimotor or Object	Repetitive action with objects	Bouncing a ball
Physical or Locomotor	Using the full body	Climbing a tree
Rough and Tumble	Full body play with another	Play fighting
Exploratory	Multisensory play to satisfy curiosity	Blowing bubbles with different wands
Construction	Using materials to makes things	Using sand to build a castle
Symbolic	Using one object to stand in for another	Using a broomstick as horse

U relationship peaking at some point in childhood but continuing throughout life. The latter suggests a nod to play in adult development. For example, she found that pretend play appears at 12–18 months, peaks around 3–5 years and ceases (on average) at 11 years but that pretend behaviour does continue into adulthood in such contexts as theatre acting, role playing, and games like Charades (Lillard, 2017).

While Lillard's typology provides a valuable starting point for discussion, we propose an expansion that situates each type within an overarching continuum—ranging from open, free-form activities (at one end) to structured interactions with clear win-loss conditions (at the other end). The addition of this continuum helps clarify that each of the six types of play presented in Table 1 can be implemented in robustly diverse ways—ranging from simple to complex and limited to expansive. Consider Lillard's example of sensorimotor play, in which a ball is bounced. At one end of the continuum, ball bouncing might be an individual activity where the bounce is by itself the end goal of the action; at the other end of the continuum, ball bouncing might manifest in a competitive sport like basketball. Similarly, consider the difference between building a sand castle and competing in a sand sculpture competition (construction play) or the difference between climbing a tree and Yosemite rock-climbing (physical play).

3   Play in Adult Learning and Higher Education

Despite the perceived stigma of adult play, a growing (though still very limited) research stream has emerged in recent years that focuses on the role of play in higher education and with adult learners (cf. Brown & Vaughn, 2009; Forbes, 2021; Harris & Daley, 2008; James & Nerantzi, 2019; Melamed, 1987; Robinson, 2011). Of particular note within this work is the research of Harris and Daley—who, using a typology of play qualities developed by Melamed (1987), concluded that classroom play fosters greater levels of individual and group social capital (enriching learner engagement, building cooperation among learners, creating a sense of learner connectedness). Harris and Daley mapped each of Melamed's "qualities of play" (relational, experiential, metaphoric, integrative, empowering), to a set of in-class play categories (pretend play, role play, improvisation, other playful activities), shedding a new and bright light on the benefits of adult learning and providing a set of observational guidelines (Table 2) that could be used by others with an interest in adult higher education play.

In a more recent study, Forbes (2021) looked at the experience of college students where play was part of every class session. She offers educators a better understanding of what play is and how it can bring increased value to higher education by helping students cultivate relational safety and social inclusion in a classroom environment; remove cognitive barriers to learning; and awaken positive affect, motivation, and learning engagement.

However comparatively or absolutely sparse the literature on play in higher education appears to be, a consistent through-line is that its implementation tends to be positive for learners—in terms of both felt experience and learning outcomes. Against this backdrop, we ask: why have we, as entrepreneurship educators so long committed to experiential

Table 2 Qualities of play and In-class observation guidelines

Qualities of Play from Melamed (1987)	*In-Class Observation Guidelines from Harris and Daley (2008, p. 56)*
Relational	"Evidence of learners' connectedness and synergy among one another, and conversations that were enthusiastic and responsive in both real and pretend interactions"
Experiential	"Evidence of learners engaging in shared activities, sharing their experiences with one another, being absorbed in their play activity, finding common ground, and pooling and comparing one another's perspectives"
Metaphoric	"Evidence of learners' creative thinking, imagination, readiness to suspend reality, flexibility, engaging with both real and pretend layers of meaning, and creating make-believe situations, roles, and dialogue"
Integrative	"Evidence of learners making connections among people, events, ideas and resources, and connecting past, present and future times"
Empowering	"Evidence of learners talking about rising above physical realities and perceived limitations, breaking away from conformity, and innovating, experimenting and exploring"

and applied learning, not been more open to incorporating play (or more play) into our classrooms? Adulthood is known to have three distinct stages beginning at age 20—early, middle, and late—each of which is known to influence our continued cognitive development throughout life. Most entrepreneurship students at the university level are classified as early adults. If we do not catch them at this critical inflection point out of childhood, are we missing an important opportunity to help them further develop their creative, interactive, and social skill sets? Even worse, might the designed or intentional absence of play in higher education in fact limit student development to the extent that it reduces the likelihood that play (and its attendant benefits) will re-enter their lives at a later stage?

4 The State of Play in Entrepreneurship Education

Perhaps the most popular example at the intersection of play and entrepreneurship is LEGO® Serious Play® (LSP), created by Roos and Victor in the 1990s with a goal of "designing more imaginative, effective, and responsible ways to guide leaders and organizations in their strategy-making" (2018, p. 327). At the core of LSP is an exercise in which attendees use LEGO bricks to build a model that addresses a problem or challenge posed by a facilitator. The models incorporate metaphors, symbols, imagination, and object play to draw out innovative insights that could not have been developed in a more "professional" meeting. In sum, Roos and Victor used all that we know from childhood play research to create an adult play experience that has been called transformational (Hadida, 2013). LSP as an experience is a representation of the uncertainty, information asymmetry, and dynamism that business leaders face (Roos & Victor, 2018). As a result, it is no surprise that LSP has been used in entrepreneurship education with success (Kristiansen & Rasmussen, 2014; Tawalbeh et al., 2018; Zenk et al., 2018).

Beyond LSP, however, we find that the notion of play in entrepreneurship education has been somewhat limited—recognised primarily as important to creativity, but not as an impetus to robustly new pedagogic approaches. In a special issue of *Organization Studies*, Hjorth et al. (2018) explored the intersection of creativity, play and entrepreneurship, from an organisational perspective. They noted that play facilitates exploration not of what something is in concrete terms (i.e. space, object, time), but of what that something can become. Addressing the importance of the word part "entre" in entrepreneurship—translated from the French for "between," they contend that "entre" describes the condition that inspires entrepreneurship to emerge. Using the analogy of a stop light, they distinguish between the clarity of red and green (stop and go) and the interpretability of yellow (slow down vs. speed up). Play is created by a yellow light moment—an "open, dynamic event with transformative powers" (p. 39), enacted in the in-between space where ambiguity drives flexible interpretations and actions.

In the same special issue, Courpasson and Younes (2018) studied the allure of "playing" and innovating underground in organisations. The allure stemmed from working against the status quo, which felt a bit sneaky, but yielded higher levels of creativity. In a business school environment that emphasises traditional methods of education, entrepreneurship stands apart as a field known for disrupting norms; perhaps play fits in, thus, as "unconventional" or rule-breaking, in ways that galvanise student engagement and outcomes in part simply by being different. Through play students could be more motivated because of their "I'm not supposed to be doing this in college so I'm super engaged" feeling.

Other connections to play in entrepreneurship education have emphasised simulations, deprioritising more complex methods of play and practical embrace of "playfulness" as a teaching philosophy (cf, Cadotte, 2014; Fox et al., 2018; Pittaway & Cope, 2007; Wolfe & Bruton, 1994). Still other work, by Neck and Greene (2011) focuses on games—an activity category clearly within the scope of play. As noted by Greene (2011), educational games align with Piaget's (1962) early typology of play as based on shared assumptions of rules and fun. Emerging affirmation of these authors' work can be seen in today's more prevalent (but still not common) use of escape rooms, enacted founder scenarios (e.g. Wharton's "The Startup Game"), and board games (e.g. GoVenture Entrepreneur). All involve complex game-like interactions that deploy complex rule sets, clear win-loss conditions, and information asymmetries to engage and reawaken.

As we move forward, however, we also move slowly. As entrepreneurship educators, we tend to acknowledge, pervasively, that we craft and deliver learning experiences that are experience-based, experiential, practice-based, active, immersive, hands-on, self-directed, and student-centred (Damani & Ghura, 2021; Harrison & Leitch, 2005; Hart, 2018; Kassean et al., 2015; Mukesh et al., 2020; Neck & Corbett, 2018;

Neck et al., 2014; Pittaway & Cope, 2007; Rasmussen & Sørheim, 2006). We do not tend to acknowledge that these experiences should be *playful*. Why not? Why must we be serious? Alternatively, why must even playfulness be couched in serious terms?

Neck et al. (2021) ask four questions as part of an "Are you Teaching Entrepreneurially" self-assessment: (1) Do your students report a playful or fun environment regarding your classroom/course? (2) Do they play any games as part of coursework? (3) Do they experience any game mechanics, such as earning points and badges for completing challenges and assignments? (4) Do you use simulations or other means for students to engage in immersive entrepreneurial activities? These questions aren't asked solely or primarily to confirm a lack or presence of playfulness, but as a mechanism by which educators can begin to understand their own propensity to bring "play" to the forefront—play as an opportunity to experiment; to not only succeed, but fail and demonstrate adaptive resilience; to reflect; and to develop (not just ideas, but people). As noted by Stamp (2016), play allows individuals to practice experimentation, developing the muscle memory and skill set by which we as humans learn to incubate new and novel ideas.

5 TOWARD A MORE PLAYFUL TEACHING PHILOSOPHY IN ENTREPRENEURSHIP EDUCATION

Given the outcomes of play highlighted in the childhood development, adult learning, and higher education literatures—and those emerging in the entrepreneurship education literature—the rationale for introducing more play is beginning to take shape. Within entrepreneurship education in particular, which defines the practice of entrepreneurship (Neck et al., 2014) as involving far-reaching outcomes of mindset, skills, competencies, and attitudes (Neck & Corbett, 2018; White et al., 2016), most agree that creativity is critical (Stamp, 2016). Creativity supports the emergent novelty that drives value generation through new venture creation (Shane, 2003), and requires aptitude in a wide range of cognitive abilities such as convergent and divergent thinking, cognitive flexibility, conceptual combination, and analogical reasoning (Stamp, 2016; Ward, 2004). Thus, play represents a powerful catalyst for creative thinking that can be a part of the entrepreneur's toolbox. As noted by Neck et al. (2014), "play is about developing a free and imaginative mind, allowing one to see a wealth of possibilities, a world of opportunities, and a pathway to more innovative ways of being entrepreneurial" (p. 25). In so many respects, by being playful as educators and by encouraging our students to participate in intentional play, we help provide the foundational classroom space in which students can rediscover or first discover not solely their entrepreneurial selves, but also their entrepreneurial concepts.

Inspired by Jones' (2019) work that introduced a general philosophy to entrepreneurship education, complete with guiding principles that govern conduct, we here propose a simple philosophy related to incorporating play into entrepreneurship education. We further provide a simple framework to act as a guide as for those who choose to add playful elements into their courses moving forward—noting that starting small and building from there is helpful to managing the inherent risk and time requirements of curricular revision (Grossman & Means, 2014). After introducing our philosophy and framework—our "Philosophy of Play" model—we share a few examples from our own play portfolios! (Fig. 1).

Before we dive into a deeper discussion of our proposed principles, we address a specific point often raised in discussions with peer educators—namely, the distinction between "play" and "games." McGonigal (2011) discusses four commonly accepted traits of games: (1) a **goal**, providing a sense of purpose; (2) **rules**, defining boundaries and eliminating solutions that inhibit player creativity; (3) a **feedback system**, assigning points, badges, etc., to keep players motivated in real time; and (4) **voluntary** participation, in which all players "knowingly and willingly [accept] the goal, the rules, and the feedback" (p. 21). McGonigal submits that a win/loss scenario need not be a defining or requisite feature of games. We depart from this perspective, at the specific level of so-called serious games in higher education—in that we believe it creates too expansive a category to be operationally meaningful in a classroom. We contend that

Fig. 1 Philosophy of play model

destigmatising adult learner play requires clear categorical descriptions, including clear differentiation of game-like experiences vs. "true" games. While all games involve play, not all play is a game (defined by us as a finite experience with clear rules and win-loss conditions), nor is all play gamified (seen by us as a competitive or comparative activity set involving recognised or publicised bonuses for those who perform better and/or demerits for those who perform worse).

Guiding Principles

Our teaching philosophy of play includes four guiding principles based on our own experience and use of play in entrepreneurship education: (1) construct, don't control; (2) keep it kinesthetic; (3) create fun with meaning and purpose; and (4) engage students' authentic selves. One might consider these as design inputs into the play experience.

We begin with the educator's desire to maintain control in the classroom—a great thing insofar as it signals planning, organisation, and preparation. However, given the unpredictable nature of play, and that integral dependence of play on its players, educators need to get a little more comfortable with loosening the reins. We suggest that educators *construct* the play experience in a manner that does not *control* the play experience. That does not mean an avoidance of rules. Rather, it means the development of rules that are essential to guiding students in an educational direction. Rules define the play space, characterise what's entirely in bounds versus out of bounds, and help guide the outcome; rules should not pre-determine the outcome at too detailed a level. Consider the adult analogue to finger painting—where the paper and paint is provided, but freedom with respect to what is painted and what colours are created or used. Rules can set the stage for tremendously playful experiences, while supporting immense creativity and invention.

In addition to freedom, play requires movement, engaging all of our senses, and applied immersion. The kinesthetic nature of play is what makes play play! You can't play basketball without bouncing the ball. You cannot play chess without moving the pieces. You cannot role-play a negotiation unless you sit in front of your colleague and talk through the possibilities; cannot win a video game without a controller; and cannot pass Go if you're lacking in dice and a top hat (or train or dog). In other words, there is an inherent tactility to play that leads to multi-sensory learning and greater retention (Breckler & Azzam, 2011; Wagner, 2014;

Woolwine et al., 2019), even when we are just thinking we are touching something as in virtual reality. Play should be designed to get learners out of their chairs and into active and often interactive, collaborative roles—traversing the classroom or learning space, perhaps handing objects to each other, manipulating marshmallows, cards, raw spaghetti, LEGO, blocks on a screen, and more.

Well-constructed educational play is also purposive and intentional, designed to create a robust, rigorous, and resonant learning experience for participants. In the same way that many of us design courses or programs beginning first with learning objectives, play in the classroom should be designed with a set of learning goals (encompassing connections to core content). Play is meant to shake things up in a very fun way, but the *raison d'être* must be clear—to the instructors at the outset and to the students by the end. Adult learners can tend to chafe, for reasons of personal need and expected return on educational investment, when play is not linked to "aha" moments or rich lessons that render the rationale for "untraditional" education clear.

Finally, powerful, effective play experiences allow students to engage as their authentic selves rather than as "actors" in a business play of others' creation. Don't get us wrong: role plays can be marvellous ways to get students to ostensibly imagine and enact specific tasks or roles (e.g. pretend you are a VC negotiating a term sheet or a founder negotiating her founding team's equity split). But we so often see students take on the roles as they believe others fill them—reenacting, for example, their version of Mr. Wonderful on the popular TV show "Shark Tank." We believe that well-designed play can get students to shed the costumes and engage as their truest selves—not as they imagine themselves as characters showcased through mass media, guest speakers, and podcasts. It is through their reflection or post-play debrief that students can understand the implications for their future (in those or other roles).

Desired Student Outcomes

Inasmuch as the prior section's guiding principles provide an overarching ethos to designing play in entrepreneurship education, they also speak to some inputs that help generate positive learning outcomes. Though our own experiences as entrepreneurship educators, as affirmed by theory, we suggest that play be designed to generate four critical learner outcomes

(Fig. 1): (1) curiosity and courage; (2) perspective and sensemaking; (3) culture and community; and (4) FUN.

We believe that in asking people to engage authentically, in purposive ways not traditionally associated with higher education, that learners can be acculturated and accelerated toward new ways of thinking, to the value of tackling challenges in new ways, and to the utility of challenging the status quo—asking challenging questions, taking some risks, and revealing one's creativity. They thus can become more courageous in expressing their curiosity. Bruner (1983) described creativity as "figuring out how to use what you already know in order to go beyond what you currently think" (p. 183). Play gives entrepreneurship students license to see the world in a different way. Play also amplifies what is possible through its inherent promise of freedom to experiment, absent robust negative consequences for what might elsewhere be considered errors. As Gordon and Esbjörn-Hargens' (2007) note,

"New realities dislodge the players from familiar identities, enabling them to encounter difficult material with support and ease, to venture into their growing edge, and to integrate a wider spectrum of emotional responses. Play engenders the optimism needed to take risks and shows that taking risks can bring rewards" (p. 217).

The authors' "paradox of play" is evident here—curiosity and exploration leading students to consciously enact within the "unreal" classroom space the new ways of thinking, new possibilities, and new interpretations that can then generalise to new habits of in the "real" world. Play allows students to challenge the status quo in a manner consistent with developing lifelong, entrepreneurial mindsets.

Curiosity and courage, as key to mindset, flow directly into the notion that entrepreneurship students benefit from perspective building and sensemaking. Consider the student who pitches an idea and believes it will work without conducting true customer discovery. Often, we find that students seek confirmation of their extant beliefs through customer discovery—this despite the fact that some of customer discovery's power lies in discovering disconfirmatory data or insights one did not know they did not know (i.e. John Mullins' [2007] unknown-unknowns or unk-unks). Playful experiences allow students to engage in data in a very different way, creating a mechanism by which learners are motivated to see things from others' perspectives. Through play, students begin to make sense of new data in ways they may not have experienced. This process of sensemaking (Weick, 1993), giving meaning to experience, helps learners manage or make sense of uncertain, unknowable, or ambiguous situations—scenarios definitely produced by play and entrepreneurship too. Because playful learning is active and entrenched in ongoing sensemaking, dialogue with other students and through self-reflection further brings meaning to the experience (Melamed, 1987; Mezirow, 1997). As Weick (1993) so eloquently stated, "the basic idea of sensemaking is that reality is an ongoing accomplishment that emerges from efforts to create order and make retrospective sense of what occurs" (p. 634).

As one can imagine, shared and co-created curiosity, courage, and sensemaking are the basic pillars upon which to build a foundational and entrepreneurial culture and strong classroom community—our third desired outcome. As students play together, a culture of positive, communal learning can emerge in a manner that feels organic (even if designed!). In the students' minds, the fun is formative, useful, and worth pursuing. A classroom is just like any other organisation we may study in business; it is comprised of people with shared mental models (March, 1991). Because culture emerges from shared basic assumptions that create our mental model, norms begin to develop that guide how we think, do, and act (Schein, 2010). The shared culture around a class incorporating play experiences versus a standard lecture or even case-based course will produce dramatically different learning communities.

As noted previously, play theorists view the benefits of play across *all* stages of life, and there is empirical support that adult learning through play fosters community building because playful activities require dialogue, trust, sharing, coalition building, and overall vulnerability (Göncü & Perone, 2005; Gordon & Esbjörn-Hargens, 2007; Harris & Daley, 2008). A community does not exist without culture and is created through shared experience. Chavis and Lee (2015) offer us the most poignant definition of community as it relates to what we are working toward in our entrepreneurship classrooms:

> "Community is both a feeling and a set of relationships among people. Members of a community have a sense of trust, belonging, safety, and caring for each other. They have an individual and collective sense that they can, as part of that community, influence their environments and each other. That treasured feeling of community comes from shared experiences and a sense of—not necessarily the actual experience of—shared history." https://ssir.org/articles/entry/what_is_community_anyway#

A final student outcome in our model is one that happens naturally through play—immersion and fun, both of which are seen as a common denominator of educational play across all literatures and age cohorts. According to Csikszentmihalyi (1990), immersion is "when we act with total involvement" (p. 41), focused solely on the tasks at hand, not letting anything from the outside in. This state of "utter absorption" (Huizinga, 1944) is called *flow* and is often associated with play and creativity. Think artistic painter or video gamer or chess player! Flow yields a holistic sensation and feeling of "unified movement from one moment to the next, in which we feel in control of our actions, and in which there is little distinction between self and environment; between stimulus and response; or between past, present and future" (Csikszentmihalyi, 1990, p. 41). The concept of flow and immersion connects to McGonigal's work in *Reality is Broken* (2011), where she describes games as representing "[opportunities] to focus our energy, with relentless optimism, at something we're good at (or getting better at) and enjoy. Gamers don't want to game the system. Gamers want to play the game. They want to explore and learn and improve. They're volunteering for unnecessary hard work – and they genuinely care about the outcome of their effort" (p. 27).

Curiosity, courage, perspective, sensemaking, community, immersive and purposive learning, fun. Is this not what we want for our students? For us as educators? In our classrooms? If yes, it's time to play!

6 ESCALATION AND EXAMPLES OF PLAY IN AN ENTREPRENEURSHIP CLASSROOM

We recognise that it is far easier to write and talk about play than to design and execute play-based activities that deliver the sorts of outcomes we propose. Here, we offer four examples of play in our own entrepreneurship classrooms that fall at different points along our proposed continuum of play—demonstrating options that (1) involve open play and more structured games with rules, and (2) escalation from simple to complex. We recommend that instructors, in bringing play to their classroom, thoughtfully escalate from simpler to more complex over time—to ease adoption and manage the learning process (Fig. 2). In other words, if we start with more simple forms of play, educators and students become more comfortable with play over time—engaging with more sophisticated forms of play at later stages of a course. In each example below we offer

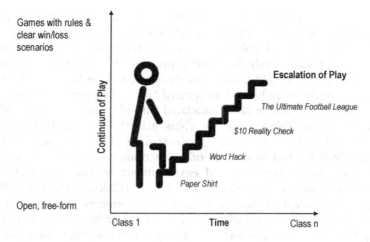

Fig. 2 Escalation of play

a description of the exercise, its purpose, and student responses. Though Lillard (2015) offered a comprehensive typology with six categories of play, we focus on symbolic, exploratory, and construction play as the most relevant to entrepreneurship education.

Symbolic Play and "The Paper Shirt" (from the Portfolio of Heidi Neck)

Students walk in on the first day of class. Blank pieces of coloured 8.5″ × 11″ paper sit on the front table. The professor says to students as they start to trickle in, "Take a piece of paper before you sit down." Some students eagerly grab a piece of paper, some question the relevance of the different colors, and the rest hesitantly walk to the table, smile and seem a little scared. It is the first day of a required MBA entrepreneurship course, a place where some can at last progress long held new venture concepts and others can learn the serious tools and frameworks to develop an entrepreneurial mindset. All 50 students have a blank piece of coloured paper, and class is about to begin.

"How entrepreneurial are you?" asks the professor. "On a scale from 1 to 10, with 10 being the most entrepreneurial and 1 being the least, what number do you give yourself?" By show of hands, the students share their numbers. A little levity is felt by the one "10" in the room – and big applause is offered to the sole "1" in the class. "This student is in the right place!" praises the professor. She notes that the scale is somewhat arbitrary because a "4" for one student may not hold the same weight as a "4" for another student. "So, I have a test for us all to test our entrepreneurial capacity." Now the coloured paper comes into play (pun intended!).

Through a series of steps, the professor facilitates the students in actively folding the paper so that the paper turns into a boat. Once all boats have been created, the professor leads the students in an interactive and immersive story. The students and their movement are critical to the story. 100% participation is required. The professor shares a story about a captain, crew, and boat sailing in an ocean. The students have to start moving their boat to simulate sailing in an ocean. As the story progresses, there is wind (students sound out wind), seagulls (crazy bird sounds), and waves that crash into the boat (students have to tear off a piece of the paper boat when a rogue wave crashes into the boat). After three big waves enter the story, the boat sinks (students spontaneously say "aww"). The professor concludes the story noting, "After the boat sank, search and rescue was on the water for days trying to find some evidence of the sunken boat. The only thing they could find was the captain's shirt." Students are then asked to unfold their boat. As the unfolding takes place, all of the paper boats have now become tshirts (due to the proper tearing of three different parts of the paper boats).

The first debrief question is: What does any of this have to do with entrepreneurship? Answers abound. Pivoting, taking risks, managing crises, creativity, don't go down with the ship, weathering storms are just some of the answers. The second debrief question is: Why am I doing this today in this class? The answers are beautiful. Building a community of trust, hands-on participation, if we can't handle feeling silly then can we really start something as serious as a business, action under uncertainty, play is important to learning, and yes, it's okay to play in this class. This was a good first day.

Exploratory Play and "The Word Hack" (from the Portfolio of Jeffrey Stamp)

The ability to play with and experiment with conceptual combinations of stimulus inputs or bisociation (Koestler, 1964) is a classic part of any creative aptitude. Musicians during an improv session combine various sounds and styles to create new music. Artists combine new colours and textures to create new art. Chefs combine new ingredients to create new tastes and textures in culinary creations.

In entrepreneurship education there is a push to create prototypes as a tool for experimentation and validate value creation (Linton & Klinton, 2019). An effective way to engage students in a playful use of bisociative thinking that has both novelty and utility with a prototype as output is the Word Hack exercise—an exercise in creating new hybrid words in the English language. English as a language has a very malleable structure, and there are hundreds of examples of hybrid words that are in common use, such as microscope (micro = small, scope = field of vision). The word hack exercise when utilised in a supportive creative classroom works amazingly well as a prototyping activity because creating new language sparks a natural intrinsic motivation to own what is created; is testable for social usefulness; has virtually no resource cost; and fits the utility and novelty criteria of a creative work (Stamp, 2016).

The word hack can be done individually or in groups (no more than 3). Have students bring to class some form of current, written news media. Whether as traditional print format or online, the first step is to scan the news for multisyllable words. The key is to not read the news, but to select by quick visual inspection approximately 20 eye-catching multisyllable words (the quickest way is to start at the bottom of the page and scan upwards) and list them on a separate sheet of paper. Next, examine the list of collected multisyllable words and draw a vertical line between the natural syllable splits in the words. In the final step, randomly select any two syllable fragments from different words and combine them together to create a new word.

While this exercise could be done in a brute force recombination of all the possible syllable combinations from a set of 20 words, the play aspect comes in from the random selection and recombination of visually and sound appealing combinations that spark new insights and meaning. This is an exercise in sharpening sensemaking skills. When a student forms an intriguing new word, they must also give the word a definition and supply a use for the word in a relevant sentence. For example, a group of students combined technology + disruptive = techruptive—a new technology that only disrupts the technology in place and not the user's experience.

The final component of the exercise is to test the newly created words in a real social context. For this, students test the words in any online social media of their choice. The goal of the test (aka experiment with prototype) is to evaluate reaction, reach, and potential re-use of their new prototype words. This social validation activity provides evidence that the playing Word Hack yielded utility and built their creative confidence. For example, a group of students combined fiction + sensational = fictisational—a politician whose ideas for change are absolutely ridiculous. This new word is not found on a Google search and was their unique invention that achieved hundreds of likes to meme posts online during an election year!

Exploratory Play and "The $10 Reality Check" (from the Portfolio of Doan Winkel)

Students arrive for their first class to a pre-determined location (on or off campus) that has plenty of shops and foot traffic. Each group of 4 receives ten $1 bills from the professor, and receive simple instructions: "You have 30 minutes to make as much money as you can, legally. Whichever team makes the most profit, keeps all the money from all the groups; winner takes all! Be back in the classroom in 35 minutes." Most students pause in disbelief, trying to process the ambiguity and unique experience into which they have been thrust. Eventually, the groups burst to life with rapid-fire discussion of ideas, resources, locations and tasks. This is the first experience in an Introduction to Entrepreneurship undergraduate course. Students quickly realise this course will be something different, something real, and something very experiential.

Students pursue one of a variety of activities to generate revenue. Some buy and resell a product (e.g. water, cookies, items from their dorm). Some choose a service-oriented model of undertaking tasks for their fellow students or for the local community (e.g. return books to library, tutoring, moving an office). One group may pursue a more high risk investment model where they ask for an "investment" from their peers (mostly friends) to win the challenge and promise a quick and high rate of return. The variety of business models are limited only by the students' imagination and time, but given they will be in shock, the professor should expect students to make fairly "easy" choices.

As teams arrive in the classroom, the professor notes on the board the profit made by each group, collects their money and distributes all the money to the team that generated the most profit. The debrief that fills the remainder of the class period has two levels. First is a discussion of tactics, with questions such as "How did you arrive at decisions?", "How did the ambiguity feel?", "How did you identify a market need?", and "How did you identify and connect with customers?" The professor then turns to a deeper reflective discussion with questions such as "Who is your customer? (Did you clearly identify them?)", "How would your experience have changed if you considered a problem that customers actually need solved?" and "Are there any ethical concerns associated with the decisions you made?".

The $10 Reality Check exercise gives students the opportunity to experience entrepreneurship first hand and to reflect on the consequences of their decisions. The exercise facilitates learning by providing a common experience for additional learning and reflection throughout the semester. The professor can quickly and easily assess the skills (or skills deficits) of the participants which gives them a baseline for learning throughout the semester. The exercise provides a reference for entrepreneurship in multiple contexts which creates value as a reference point that continues throughout the semester.

Construction Play and the "Ultimate Football League" (from the Portfolio of Elissa Grossman)

As students settle in to their seats, all but their writing implements set aside for the ensuing several hours, they are welcomed by the Professor. "It's that time of year," she says, "when the Managers in the Ultimate Football League assemble their teams for the Ultimate Bowl, a one-of-a-kind football competition with eight teams and only <u>one</u> winner. That's right. It's time for what you never knew existed before: the Ultimate Bowl Draft – or, as the sports pundits like to say, the Rough Draft. And, this year, YOU, yes YOU, have been appointed Manager!" The professor then outlines each Manager's goals—to (1) negotiate and trade with other Managers; (2) form a Joint Venture with one other; (3) field a high-scoring Team (using the People and Money at their disposal, based on Rules they will learn over time); and (4) win the Ultimate Bowl.

The professor proceeds to distribute briefing folders, each student receiving a *different* (but partially duplicative) set of cards in total, including Rule cards, People cards, Money cards, and one Joint Venture card. The players are told that, after a period of time in which to prepare their approach, they will be allowed to roam the room in an effort to learn the various rules for assembling the best football Team possible, with "best" defined as a group of People with the best qualities relative to other Teams, taking into account all of the provisions on the Rule cards (whether or not the students know them or not). The students are further told that each of them has a Rule card that someone else has, and each has a Rule card that is held only by them. What they are not told is arguably more relevant than what is shared; they do not know, as the draft begins, how many People cards exist or how many each player has, how much Money is available to each player, or how many Rules there are. The game thus begins with preparation focused on how to acquire information from competitive others against a backdrop of dynamic uncertainty—a challenge and context highly aligned with those faced by new venture founders.

Over the course of the ensuing class session, students play a version of what is known as a "haggle game," a complex card game introduced in Sid Sackson's *Gamut of Games* (1969) and well known to serious (non-academic) players. A game of resource needs identification, acquisition, and management, the haggle game is particularly well-suited to entrepreneurship education, allowing students to navigate issues of team creation (students may need to partner with unknown others to do well), trust versus uncertainty (i.e. students must rely on competing peers to secure information that may or may not be accurate), and forced operation within a system of unknown rules (students must grapple with the reality of informal rules that are institutionally known, but not codified).

7 THE FUTURE OF PLAY IN ENTREPRENEURSHIP EDUCATION

The complexity of play in tertiary education is complex and multifaceted. This is due in part to our reference of play for adult learners, which has theoretical roots in childhood play but is fundamentally different from an input and output perspective. Furthermore, play in entrepreneurship education is both underutilised and underappreciated, which is somewhat perplexing given the many voices suggesting that entrepreneurship is the most experiential, applied, and practiced-based of all the business disciplines (c.f. Barr et al., 2009; Nabi et al., 2017; Pittaway & Cope, 2007). The lack of play in entrepreneurship education is further confounded by the outcomes highlighted in this chapter. We have suggested that incorporating play experiences and playfulness can lead to student curiosity, courage, perspective building, sensemaking, community, immersive learning with purpose, and fun. So, if there is a future for play in entrepreneurship education, it must be destigmatised. The *perceived* lack of professionalism and productivity associated with play at tertiary levels is a misnomer. Play in entrepreneurship education, if well-designed, are serious, complex, and intense experiences that can lead to transformational learning and development of the entrepreneurial mindset we all seem to be chasing.

We have not given much attention to video games and gaming in this chapter. Our intention was to focus on the spectrum of play representing a continuum ranging from open, free-form activities (at one end) to structured interactions with clear win-loss conditions (at the other end). Video gaming is a form of play that certainly sits on the spectrum and it deserves attention not for what the video game is but who the players are. The generation of students we are teaching today, whether undergraduate or graduate, have grown up playing video games—and continue to play them. Though we are not promoting the use of Minecraft or Grand Theft Auto (the top selling video games of all time), we offer a few interesting facts related to gaming. First, it takes 50–100 hours to master a video game (Pink, 2006)—this is the amount of face time we have with students in a given semester. Those who play video games regularly, play for an average of 13 hours per week (McGonigal, 2011). 38% of all video gamers are between the ages of 18 and 34 years old and 26% are 35–54 years old (Clement, 2021a). Further, there is a misperception that only men play video games, but in reality 41% of gamers are women (Clement, 2021b). Our point is not to advocate for video games; rather, we simply want to highlight that our students are *playing* a lot of games and they need the same level of engagement, immersion, and focus in their learning activities that are taking place on our campuses, in our classroom, and on our Zoom sessions. Why can't entrepreneurship education be more fun? More playful?

In this chapter we have offered a model based on a philosophy of play (Fig. 1) designed to help entrepreneurship educators better design and facilitate play experiences. The guiding principles related to construction, use of physical activity, purposive and meaningful content, and connection to students' authentic selves lead to more robust and creative learning experiences. The benefits of play in childhood development and learning are undeniable and empirically proven. If we agree that learning does not stop after childhood and that entrepreneurship requires lifelong learning, then we should not fear using play in our classrooms. Furthermore, higher education is falling behind even corporate learning—the next level of education many of our students receive. Corporate trainers more commonly use visuals, multimedia techniques, props, music and other play-oriented tools and unconventional methods than college educators (Kumar & Lightner, 2007). As we end this chapter, we ask you, the reader, to think about all of the words that come to mind when you think about play in entrepreneurship education. We suspect words like immersion, ambiguity, uncertainty, creative, uncontrollable, win-loss scenarios, interactive, risk, experimenting, figuring it out, taking action, learning as you go, imagination, freedom, rules, no rules, and fun may be on your list. Are these not also words we associate with entrepreneurship education? It is time to play. Game on!

REFERENCES

Abt, C. C. (1987). *Serious games*. University Press of America.
Barr, S. H., Baker, T. E. D., Markham, S. K., & Kingon, A. I. (2009). Bridging the valley of death: Lessons learned from 14 years of commercialization of technology education. *Academy of management learning & education, 8*(3), 370-388.
Bettelheim, B. (1972). Play and education. *The School Review, 81*(1), 1–13.
Breckler, J., & Azzam, A. (2011). The basic science learning station: An innovative kinesthetic learning approach in one medical school. *Medical Science Educator, 19*(3), 72–79.
Brown, S., & Vaughn, C. (2009). *Play: How it shapes the brain, opens the imagination, and invigorates the soul*. Penguin Books.
Bruner, J. (1983). *In search of mind*. Harper.
Burghardt, G. M. (2010). Defining and recognizing play. In P. Nathan & A. D. Pellegrini (Eds.), *The Oxford handbook of the development of play*. Oxford University Press.
Burriss, K. G., & Tsao, L. L. (2002). Review of research: How much do we know about the importance of play in child development? *Childhood Education, 78*(4), 230–233.
Cadotte, E. (2014). The use of simulations in entrepreneurship education: Opportunities, challenges and outcomes. In *Annals of entrepreneurship education and pedagogy–2014*. Edward Elgar Publishing.
Chavis, D. M., and Lee, K. (2015, May 12). What is community anyway? *Stanford Social Innovation Review*. Retrieved from https://ssir.org/articles/entry/what_is_community_anyway

Clement, J. (2021a). U.S. video gaming audiences 2020, by age group. *Statista*. Accessed online at https://www.statista.com/statistics/189582/age-of-us-video-game-players-since-2010/

Clement, J. (2021b). U.S. video gaming audiences 2006–2020, by gender. *Statista*. Accessed online at https://www.statista.com/statistics/232383/gender-split-of-us-computer-and-video-gamers/

Courpasson, D., & Younes, D. (2018). Double or quits: Understanding the links between secrecy and creativity in a project development process. *Organization Studies, 39*(2–3), 271–295.

Csikszentmihalyi, M. (1990). *Flow: The psychology of optimal experience*. Harper & Row.

Damani, B., & Ghura, A. S. (2021). Innovative approaches to entrepreneurship education at FLAME University in India. In H. M. Neck & Y. Liu (Eds.), *Innovation in global entrepreneurship education: Teaching entrepreneurship in practice* (pp. 138–149). Edward Elgar Publishing.

Diamond, A., Barnett, S., Thomas, J., & Munro, S. (2007). Preschool program improves cognitive control. *Science, 318*, 1387–1388.

Forbes, L. K. (2021). The process of play in learning in higher education: A phenomenological study. *Journal of Teaching and Learning, 15*(1), 57–73.

Fox, J., Pittaway, L., & Uzuegbunam, I. (2018). Simulations in entrepreneurship education: Serious games and learning through play. *Entrepreneurship Education and Pedagogy, 1*(1), 61–89.

Göncü, A., & Perone, A. (2005). Pretend play as a life-span activity. *Topoi, 24*(2), 137–147.

Gordon, G., & Esbjörn-Hargens, S. (2007). Are we having fun yet? An exploration of the transformative power of play. *Journal of Humanistic Psychology, 47*(2), 198–222.

Green, P. G. (2011). The emergence of the serious games industry: To play or not to play. In C. Henry & A. de Bruin (Eds.), *Entrepreneurship and the creative economy: Process, practice and policy* (pp. 148–168). Edward Elgar Publishing.

Groos, K. (1916). *The play of man*. D. Appleton and Company.

Grossman, E., & Means, T. (2014). From tablet to stylus to table and stylus: An almost 6,000 year revolution in technology for teaching and learning. In M. Morris (Ed.), *Annals of entrepreneurship education and pedagogy* (pp. 44–59). Edward Elgar Publishing.

Hadida, A. L. (2013). Let your hands do the thinking! *Strategic Direction, 29*(2), 3–5.

Harris, P. J., & Daley, J. (2008). Exploring the contribution of play to social capital in institutional adult learning settings. *Australian Journal of Adult Learning, 48*(1), 50–70.

Harrison, R. T., & Leitch, C. M. (2005). Entrepreneurial learning: Researching the intersection between learning and entrepreneurial context. *Entrepreneurship Theory & Practice, 29*(4), 351–371.

Hart, J. D. (2018). *Classroom exercises for entrepreneurship: A cross-disciplinary approach.* Edward Elgar Publishing.

Hjorth, D., Strati, A., Dodd, S. D., & Weik, E. (2018). Organizational creativity, play and entrepreneurship: Introduction and framing. *Organization Studies, 39*(2–3), 155–168.

Huizinga, J. (1944). *Homo Ludens: A study of the play-element in culture.* The Beacon Press.

Hyson, M., Copple, C., & Jones, J. (2006). Early childhood development and education. Child psychology in practice. In K. A. Renninger & I. Sigel (Eds.), *Handbook of child psychology* (Vol. 4, pp. 3–47). Wiley.

James, A., & Nerantzi, C. (2019). *The power of play in higher education.* Palgrave Macmillan.

Jones, C. (2019). A signature pedagogy for entrepreneurship education. *Journal of Small Business and Enterprise Development, 26*(2), 243–254.

Karpov, Y. V. (2005). *The Neo-Vygotskian approach to child development.* Cambridge University Press.

Kassean, H., Vanevenhoven, J., Liguori, E., & Winkel, D. E. (2015). Entrepreneurship education: A need for reflection, real-world experience, and action. *International Journal of Entrepreneurial Behavior & Research, 21,* 690–708.

Koestler, A. (1964). *The act of creation: A study of the conscious and unconscious processes of humor, scientific discovery and art.* London: Hutchinson & Co.

Kraus, R. (1971). *Recreation and leisure in modern society.* Appleton-Century-Crofts.

Kristiansen, P., & Rasmussen, R. (2014). *Building a better business using the Lego serious play method.* Wiley.

Kumar, R., & Lightner, R. (2007). Games as an interactive classroom technique: Perceptions of corporate trainers, college instructors and students. *International Journal of Teaching and Learning in Higher Education, 19*(1), 53–63.

Lillard, A. S. (2015). The development of play. *Handbook of child psychology and developmental science* (pp. 1–44). Wiley.

Lillard, A. S. (2017). Why do the children (pretend) play? *Trends in Cognitive Sciences, 21*(11), 826–834.

Linton, G., & Klinton, M. (2019). University entrepreneurship education: A design thinking approach to learning. *Journal of Innovation and Entrepreneurship, 8*(1), 1–11.

March, J. G. (1991). Exploration and exploitation in organizational learning. *Organization Science, 2*(1), 71–87.

Marcon, R. (2002). Moving up the grades: Relationship between preschool model and later school success. *Early Childhood Research & Practice, 4*, 517–530.

McGonigal, J. (2011). *Reality is broken: Why games make us better and how they can change the world*. Penguin.

Melamed, L. (1987). The role of play in adult learning. In D. Boud & V. Griffin (Eds.), *Appreciating adults learning: From the learner's perspective* (pp. 13–24). Kogan Page.

Mezirow, J. (1997). Transformative learning: Theory to practice. *New Directions for Adult and Continuing Education, 1997*(74), 5–12.

Mukesh, H. V., Pillai, K. R., & Mamman, J. (2020). Action-embedded pedagogy in entrepreneurship education: An experimental enquiry. *Studies in Higher Education, 45*(8), 1679–1693.

Mullins, J. W. (2007). Discovering "Unk-Unks." *MIT Sloan Management Review, 48*(4), 17.

Nabi, G., Liñán, F., Fayolle, A., Krueger, N., & Walmsley, A. (2017). The impact of entrepreneurship education in higher education: A systematic review and research agenda. *Academy of Management Learning & Education, 16*(2), 277-299.

Neck, H. M. (2010). Idea generation. In B. Bygrave & A. Zacharakis (Eds.), *Portable MBA in entrepreneurship* (pp. 27–52). Wiley.

Neck, H. M., Brush, C. G., & Greene, P. G. (2021). *Teaching entrepreneurship: A practice-based approach* (Vol. 2). Edward Elgar Publishing.

Neck, H. M., & Corbett, A. C. (2018). The scholarship of teaching and learning entrepreneurship. *Entrepreneurship Education and Pedagogy, 1*(1), 8–41.

Neck, H. M., & Greene, P. G. (2011). Entrepreneurship education: Known worlds and new frontiers. *Journal of Small Business Management, 49*(1), 55–70.

Neck, H. M., Greene, P. G., & Brush, C. G. (2014). *Teaching entrepreneurship: A practice-based approach*. Edward Elgar Publishing.

Pellegrini, A. D. (2013). Play. In P. D. Zelazo (Ed.), *The Oxford handbook of developmental psychology, Vol. 2. Self and other* (pp. 276–299). Oxford University Press.

Piaget, J. (1962). *Play, dreams, and imitation in childhood* (G. Gattegno & F. M. Hodgson, Trans.). Norton.

Pink, D. H. (2006). *A whole new mind: Why right-brainers will rule the future*. Penguin.

Pittaway, L., & Cope, J. (2007). Simulating entrepreneurial learning: Integrating experiential and collaborative approaches to learning. *Management Learning, 38*(2), 211–233.

Rasmussen, E., & Sørheim, R. (2006). Action-based entrepreneurship education. *Technovation, 26*(2), 185–194.

Robinson, K. (2011). *Out of our minds: Learning to be creative*. Capstone

Roos, J., & Victor, B. (2018). How it all began: The origins of LEGO® Serious Play®. *International Journal of Management and Applied Research, 5*(4), 326–343.

Rubin, K. H. (1982). Early play theories revisited: Contributions to contemporary research and theory. In D. J. Pepler & K. H. Rubin (Eds.), *The play of children: Current theory and research* (Vol. 6, pp. 4–14). Karger.

Russ, S. W., & Wallace, C. E. (2013). Pretend play and creative processes. *American Journal of Play, 6*(1), 136–148.

Sackson, S. (1969). *A gamut of games*. Random House.

Schein, E. H. (2010). *Organizational culture and leadership* (Vol. 2). John Wiley & Sons.

Shane, S. (2003). *A general theory of entrepreneurship: The individual-opportunity nexus*. Edward Elgar Publishing.

Stamp, J. A. (2016). What entrepreneurship educators do not understand about creativity and how to teach it. In M. Morris & E. Liquori (Eds.), *Annals of entrepreneurship education and pedagogy* (pp. 26–59). Edward Elgar Publishing.

Tawalbeh, M., Riedel, R., Dempsey, M., & Emanuel, C. (2018). *Lego® Serious Play® as a business innovation enabler*. Paper presentation at the *5th European Lean Educator Conference*. NUI Galway.

United Nations Human Rights. Office of the High Commissioner. (1989). *Convention on the rights of the child*. Accessed June 29, 2021 at https://www.ohchr.org/en/professionalinterest/pages/crc.aspx

Vygotsky, L. S. (1978). *Mind in society*. Harvard University Press.

Wagner, E. A. (2014). Using a kinesthetic learning strategy to engage nursing student thinking, enhance retention, and improve critical thinking. *Journal of Nursing Education, 53*(6), 348–351.

Ward, T. B. (2004). Cognition, creativity, and entrepreneurship. *Journal of Business Venturing, 19*, 173–188.

Weick, K. E. (1993). The collapse of sensemaking in organizations: The Mann Gulch disaster. *Administrative Science Quarterly, 38*(4), 628–652.

White, R., Hertz, G., & Moore, K. (2016). Competency based education in entrepreneurship: A call to action for the discipline In M. Morris & E. Liquori (Eds.), *Annals of entrepreneurship education and pedagogy* (pp. 127–147). Edward Elgar Publishing.

Wolfe, J., & Bruton, G. (1994). On the use of computerized simulations for entrepreneurship education. *Simulation & Gaming, 25*(3), 402–415.

Woolwine, S., Romp, C. R., & Jackson, B. (2019). Game on: Evaluating the impact of gamification in nursing orientation on motivation and knowledge retention. *Journal for Nurses in Professional Development, 35*(5), 255–260.

Yogman, M., Garner, A., Hutchinson, J., Hirsh-Pasek, K., Golinkoff, R. M., & Committee on Psychosocial Aspects of Child and Family Health. (2018). The power of play: A pediatric role in enhancing development in young children. *Pediatrics, 142*(3), 1–15.

Zenk, L., Hynek, N., Schreder, G., Zenk, A., Pausits, A., & Steiner, G. (2018). Designing innovation courses in higher education using LEGO® SERIOUS PLAY®. *International Journal of Management and Applied Research, 5*(4), 245–263.

Conceptualising the Entrepreneurship Education and Employability Nexus

Andreas Walmsley, *Carolin Decker-Lange, and Knut Lange*

1   Introduction

This chapter focuses on the idea that entrepreneurship education is in many ways synonymous with the development of students' employability. The proximity of entrepreneurship and employability is expressed, for example, in the UK Quality Assurance Agency's (2018) proposition that:

"Enterprise and Entrepreneurship Education provides interventions that are focused on supporting behaviours, attributes and competencies that are likely to have a significant impact on the individual student in terms of successful careers…" (Quality Assurance Agency, 2018: 2).

A. Walmsley (✉)
Plymouth Marjon University, Plymouth, UK
e-mail: awalmsley@marjon.ac.uk

C. Decker-Lange
The Open University, Milton Keynes, UK
e-mail: Carolin.Decker-Lange@open.ac.uk

K. Lange
Royal Holloway University of London, London, UK
e-mail: Knut.Lange@rhul.ac.uk

© The Author(s), under exclusive license to Springer Nature
Switzerland AG 2022
G. J. Larios-Hernandez et al. (eds.), *Theorising Undergraduate Entrepreneurship Education*,
https://doi.org/10.1007/978-3-030-87865-8_6

For many readers the existence of this strong relationship between EE, employability and careers will come as no surprise, and yet this should not detract from a critical examination of this relationship. Perhaps precisely because of the apparent strength of the relationship, to date critical examinations have remained relatively scarce. We also believe a further examination of the relationship is timely given the place both entrepreneurship and employability assume in current higher education discourse, notably in relation to the preparation of graduates for the world of work. In an increasingly market-driven HE sector (Brown & Carasso, 2013), where policymakers expect a return on investment in education, employability has turned into an imperative (Tomlinson & Nghia, 2020) and is an indicator of educational value upon which universities are judged (Ustav & Venesaar, 2018). For example, in the UK graduates' employment outcomes are measured which feed into HEI rankings. Understanding the extent to which EE does in fact sit comfortably with the employability agenda, or at least how it relates to the employability agenda, is the subject matter of our conceptual review.

Although much of the literature and contextual focus in this chapter relates to the UK, we suggest the broader themes we discuss also relate to the delivery of entrepreneurship education across the globe: a focus on graduate employability, the expansion of higher education and entrepreneurship education, and ultimately the relationship between entrepreneurship and employability are issues that are certainly not unique to the UK.

2   Entrepreneurship Education

The rapid expansion of EE has been likened to an explosion by Morris and Liguori (2016). Not only has EE expanded quantitatively, i.e. in terms of provision, its remit has also broadened. "The aims of entrepreneurship education have been extending beyond business creation and management skills to students' preparation for work and life" (Ustav & Venesaar, 2018, p. 674). For example, Neergaard et al. (2020) identify multiple outcomes of EE in the literature, among them creativity, innovation, social and environmental concerns, as well as versatile skills, such as team building and design thinking. This presents a challenge to the researcher because it is difficult to operationalise what is amorphous. Researchers and educators have been trying to define the 'what', the 'why' the 'how' the 'for whom' and 'for which results' of EE for some time now (e.g.

Fayolle & Gailly, 2008) and this quest continues today (e.g. Fayolle et al., 2016). We acknowledge therefore that an attempt at clarifying the relationship between EE and employability will struggle to an extent with this 'fuzziness'.

The most fundamental distinction in the focus of EE is that between enterprise and entrepreneurship education (the previously-cited QAA study uses both terms and clearly distinguishes between them). Entrepreneurship education focuses on the processes and tasks associated with starting a new venture, becoming self-employed or growing a part of an established organisation. Enterprise education is more broadly understood as the development of enterprising behaviours and the capabilities and skills needed to adapt to changing circumstances in a flexible market economy (Jones & Iredale, 2007; Quality Assurance Agency, 2018). Historically, enterprise education may have developed out of entrepreneurship education [in Hynes' (1996) paper, for example, entrepreneurship education was very much about business start-up, with the consideration of relevance being extended to non-business students, but no mention being made of enterprise in a broader sense], today the calls for entrepreneurship education to be extended beyond business start-up are frequently made (Lackeus, 2018; Young, 2014).

While we agree with the view that EE can set itself apart from general business management programmes in its business start-up focus (Neck & Corbett, 2018), even with a start-up orientation EE can be seen to develop a common set of skills, attributes and competencies (Neergaard et al., 2020; Ustav & Venesaar, 2018). In fact, today, EE frequently includes enterprise too (Quality Assurance Agency, 2018). With regard to skills/competency development it is difficult to distinguish between enterprise and entrepreneurship outcomes. This is evidenced for example in Rae's (2007) list of enterprise skills which might be as useful in a start-up scenario as they would in an employment setting:

- initiative;
- problem solving;
- identifying and working on opportunities;
- leadership;
- acting resourcefully; and
- responding to challenges.

If we compare this to the UK's National Council for Graduate Entrepreneurship's (NCGE) suggestion to embed entrepreneurship education because to 'add value' graduates need to have "the entrepreneurial skills that enable them to seize and exploit opportunities, solve issues and problems, generate and communicate ideas, and make a difference in their communities" (NESTA et al., 2008: 6) we can see that there is substantial overlap with Rae's (2007) list of enterprise skills. Enterprise skills in this broader sense could be said, in a nutshell, to revolve around the development of an 'opportunity identification logic' (Lackeus, 2018). Regarded through an entrepreneurial mindset lens (Scheepers et al., 2018), we suggest there is little that distinguishes enterprise from entrepreneurship education outcomes. The only notable distinction is where those attributes might subsequently be employed, either for oneself in setting up a business, or for another as an employee, suggesting that they can be applied in diverse contexts, such as new or existing commercial ventures, charities, non-governmental organisations, public and voluntary sector organisations and social enterprises (Quality Assurance Agency, 2018).

To illustrate this point further, an extensive set of entrepreneurial competencies were outlined by Bacigalupo et al. (2016) in their EU-funded and widely referenced report that aimed to build a bridge between the worlds of education and work. The Entrepreneurship Competency Framework, commonly referred to as EntreComp, comprises three competence areas: 'Ideas and opportunities', 'Resources' and 'Into action'. The reason for this segmentation is because entrepreneurship competence was defined as the ability to transform ideas and opportunities into action by mobilising resources. Each of the three areas is made up of five competences, resulting in fifteen competences in total. Given the very comprehensive nature of the EntreComp framework it has widespread applicability, certainly beyond solely business start-up. The potential downside is that it could be difficult to distinguish the numerous competencies from generic skills (or competences) and hence generic employability competences.

In sum, entrepreneurship education has expanded and is being promoted beyond its original focus on business start-up to students on a wide range of programmes. The competences (or skills, attributes) EE develops are deemed beneficial in a wide range of scenarios. Lists of specific enterprise skills have been offered (e.g. Bacigalupo et al., 2016; Rae, 2007) but at their heart lies what we, with reference to Shane and Venkataraman (2000), describe as the ability to identify, evaluate and exploit opportunities, or what Lackeus (2018) terms an 'opportunity logic'.

3 Employability and a Changing World of Work

Employability is a contested concept. It has been variously defined (Forrier & Sels, 2003; Small et al., 2018), but the difficulties related to the concept are not solely about definitional details. Employability is a laden concept, one that strikes at the heart of the nature of the modern university and its place in society, being itself part of wider discourses surrounding the nature of knowledge in society and knowledge's contribution to economic development. This is directly referred to in Bacigalupo et al.'s (2016) EntreComp framework where the harnessing of the individual's entrepreneurial capacity is to prepare them for the 'knowledge-based society'.

Data from OECD countries indicate that the proportion of individuals with tertiary education grew from 26% in 2000 to 45% in 2019 (OECD, 2020).[1] This expansion of higher education is driven by notions of knowledge societies characteristic of post-industrial capitalism (Bell, 1973; Drucker, 1993). As Becker (2002) suggested, we are living in an 'Age of Human Capital' which explains policymakers' interest in expanding higher education to strengthen a nation's human capital base (O'Donovan, 2020). Although the relationship between the expansion of higher education and economic growth is recognised as being complex and growth in the former does not necessarily lead to growth in the latter (Brown & Lauder, 2006; Wolf, 2002) this has not led to a reduction of those participating in HE globally. HE understood here as strengthening a nation's human capital base has direct implications for employability. Creating employable graduates who can contribute to a nation's competitiveness is one of the key functions of HE in the knowledge society.

Viewed through the lens of policymakers, public sector investment in HE requires a return, which includes creating employable graduates (Tomlinson & Nghia, 2020). Here concerns have been raised about levels of graduate-level employment, specifically whether the increase in

[1] 25–34 year-olds, % in same age group.

graduate-level jobs has kept pace with the HE expansion (Battu et al., 1999; Brown & Lauder, 2006). This, as we discuss in greater detail below, relates directly to entrepreneurship because if proportionately fewer graduates are finding jobs with traditional graduate recruiters, typically large firms, then employment in SMEs (Gibb, 1996; Jones & Iredale, 2014), joining a family business and engaging in transgenerational entrepreneurship (Jaskiewicz et al., 2015), and even self-employment (Jones et al., 2017) is set to increase. Certainly this view was very much in evidence at the turn of the Millennium (Elias & Purcell, 2004; Holden & Jameson, 2002), and yet given the ongoing growth in HE participation the issue is likely to be true today also. Today it is understood that many graduates will not end up working for large corporations (Dhaliwal, 2017), and that they will not have linear careers within one organisation (Jones et al., 2017; Kornelakis & Petrakaki, 2020). However, fears of many graduates being overeducated for roles they end up working in persist (see, for example, the UK's Office for National Statistics, 2019).

Because policymakers' desire to ensure returns from investment in HE are realised, universities in the UK need to provide metrics on graduate outcomes (e.g. economic activity, salaries and occupational classifications). Pressure to 'produce' employable graduates also comes from prospective recruiters and graduates themselves and so universities have written the development of employability into their strategies (Kornelakis & Petrakaki, 2020; Small et al., 2018). This typically results in sets of skills or attributes that graduates should have developed that help them gain employment as well as contribute to organisational performance once employed. The frequently-used definition of employability provided by Yorke (2006: 4) captures this clearly: "A set of achievements – skills, understandings and personal attributes – that make graduates more likely to gain employment and be successful in their chosen occupations, which benefit themselves, the workforce, the community, and the economy".

Moving from an acknowledgement that, from an employer-centric perspective, employability requires certain skills and attributes (Fugate et al., 2021) has, inevitably, resulted in lists of what these attributes should be. An example of such is provided by the Confederation of British Industry who worked with the National Union of Students to determine the following: self-management, team working, problem solving, communication, application of numeracy, application of IT, and business and customer awareness (CBI, 2017). It would go beyond the scope of this chapter to explore similarities in universities' employability strategies, or indeed review the plethora of studies of employers' claimed skills needs, but it suffices to recognise that in the current environment employability is certainly 'writ large' in UK HEIs (Kornelakis & Petrakaki, 2020; Small et al., 2018).

Employability can also be understood from the perspective of the individual student, rather than from employers, policymakers or HEIs. Employability from the perspective of the individual (i.e. an employee-centric perspective) would include understanding one's own career interests and to find fulfilling work (Fugate et al., 2021). Work is a major activity in most working-age adults' lives. It provides livelihoods and also, for most people, offers a critical psychological function and a sense of identity (see, for example, Grint, 1991). Being employable might therefore be regarded as a key attribute of modern citizenship as it "is perceived as the way the individual can contribute to society, thus becoming an active citizen" (Mikelatou & Arvanitis, 2018: 501). It's converse, being unemployed and potentially even being designated unemployable is attached with stigma. Here it is important to recognise that employability and employment outcomes are a function of more than just graduate skills and attributes. Tomlinson and Nghia (2020) provide a list of 'capitals' (e.g. human, social, cultural and identity capital) that will influence employment outcomes, and structural factors (i.e. labour market circumstances) will also determine employment outcomes. As Rae (2007: 607) suggests, employability and employment outcomes may therefore go beyond solely knowledge, skills and attributes.

As the meaning of work and careers continues to change so does the nature of employability. Greater uncertainty surrounding careers has been captured in concepts such as the Protean career (Hall, 1996) or the Boundaryless career (Arthur & Rousseau, 1996). Hall (1996) describes the demise of the traditional psychological contract between employer and employee and the death of the organisational career. In its place, the twenty-first-century career "will be protean, a career that is driven by the person, not the organization, and that will be reinvented by the person from time to time, as the person and the environment change" (Hall, 1996: 8). The concept of the boundaryless career, while drawing on different meanings (Sullivan & Arthur, 2006) still has at its core the idea of "independence from, rather than dependence on, traditional organizational career arrangements" (Arthur & Rousseau, 1996: 6). There is greater flux in modern careers, and greater onus on the individual to manage their careers—this could reflect a broader loosening of ties in modern societies described in a number of key texts (Bauman, 2000; Beck, 1992; Giddens, 1991) and in fact contributes to them (Sennett, 1998). Rather than focusing on employment, employability may therefore be understood today as a form of employment security (Fugate et al., 2021).

A further driver of change in the careers landscape that supports the idea of non-linear, fluid careers, is the rapid pace of technological development, especially developments in artificial intelligence (AI). The implications of AI for work in the twenty-first century (and beyond) are still strongly debated (Bootle, 2018). Some predictions are dramatic in terms of the impact on employment (e.g. Ford, 2015; Frey & Osborne, 2017; Tegmark, 2017), others are more sanguine (Nedelkoska & Quintini, 2018). What is clear is that technological developments and especially developments in AI will change the nature of work, especially if it brings about a change in the kind of jobs that exist and how these are undertaken. Taken together, continued expansion of HE, a weakening of the psychological contract and rapid technological developments will result in even more fluid, less stable careers.

This leads to our final point, or development, in the world of work with implications for employability. Generation theory (Mannheim, 1952) has been used to explain the varying attitudes to work and careers of different generational cohorts. We recognise the danger in over-emphasising generation as an explanatory variable for an individual's work values (Schröder, 2018), and yet it is worth reflecting on how today's graduates understand the world of work. Whereas it could be argued that the weakening of the psychological contract began with employers who were reacting with layoffs in the 1990s to poor economic circumstances, it has been claimed by some that for Generation Z (those born between the Millennium and today) there is a realisation that careers will unfold in a variety of organisations and roles. According to a report by the Lovell Corporation (2017: 6): "They are a fiery generation, determined to pursue their passions and chart their own career paths". Generation Z has also been described as 'independent and entrepreneurial' in a Deloitte report although the report suggests in contrast to Millennials, Generation Z would like to realise entrepreneurial opportunities in the safety of stable employment. 'Stability' also ranked highly in another study of 1,753 business students in the US but likewise results indicated a recognition that careers will be flexible and non-linear (Maloni et al., 2019). Notions such as autonomy, opportunity identification, dealing with ambiguity and resilience frequently associated with entrepreneurship and arguably relevant in a fluid career environment might align with career values associated with Generation Z. If this is the case, then attempting to develop such attributes via EE should be supported.

4   The Entrepreneurship-Employability Nexus

Employability has attracted a substantial amount of attention from scholars in different disciplines but with limited cross-fertilisation (Fugate et al., 2021). The same lack of cross-fertilisation could be said to exist between entrepreneurship and employability. We suggest that despite wider recognition of the existence of a relationship between entrepreneurship and employability, the relationship between the two concepts is more complex than typically acknowledged. As was outlined above, employability is a laden term, but its contested nature has scarcely found its way into discussions of the relationship between entrepreneurship and employability where the two are assumed to sit comfortably together.

In fact, in some instances the apparent proximity of the two concepts has led to them being used interchangeably (Sewell & Pool, 2010). The close relationship between the two concepts goes back some time with Tate and Thompson (1994) setting enterprise skills on a par with vocational skills. Despite admittedly strong ties, there are grounds to contest the notion that the two concepts sit together unproblematically. If one adopts a narrow definition of entrepreneurship, i.e. in the business start-up sense, entrepreneurship and employability have very different foci. Unlike the employee who is by definition employed by someone else and therefore accountable to the employer, entrepreneurship relates to the individual who is their own boss, accountable in an employment sense only to themselves. Thus, employability is about preparing the individual, and in our case the undergraduate student, for the employ of someone else (Forrier & Sels, 2003). At the heart of EE is preparation of the individual for venture creation (Neck & Corbett, 2018). This is not a trivial point, because it would mean that rather than the three-dimensional 'employee-employer-society/economy' framework underpinning employability (Fugate et al., 2021), to which we would also add the HEI in our context, entrepreneurship would more appropriately be framed by an 'entrepreneur-society/economy' framework. Many of the issues that engage employability scholars such as the role of the psychological contract or remuneration would not apply to entrepreneurship.

A further consideration that in theory moves employability and entrepreneurship apart is EE's focus on developing autonomy (Bacigalupo et al., 2016; van Gelderen, 2010). Although entrepreneurs will have varying degrees of need for autonomy (Shepherd & Patzelt, 2018) autonomy is recognised as driver of entrepreneurship (Shane et al., 2003; van Gelderen & Jansen, 2006), and has been included in some models of employability (Sewell & Pool, 2010). However, there will be a limit to the extent to which autonomy is allowed to unfold within an employment situation, which is precisely why for some, the desire 'to do one's own thing' leads to entrepreneurship and may even lead to 'entrepreneurship addiction' (Spivack & McKelvie, 2018). This desire is likely particularly pronounced when entrepreneurship education prompts students to think that everyone should launch a business or if it reflects an overemphasis on venture creation leading to limited understanding of how to apply entrepreneurial skills in non-start-up environments (Bandera et al., 2021). While this point is speculative, it is worth considering at least the extent to which employability skills (or attributes) are always aligned with entrepreneurial attributes. There will be situations where too much autonomy is not desired by employers. On the point of autonomy, we should also consider that employment outcomes are in part at least determined by structural (labour market) factors. In a slack labour market the aspiring graduate employee may find themselves pushed into entrepreneurship out of necessity (Nabi et al., 2013).

On the whole however, despite these differences, there are strong connections between both concepts especially given that entrepreneurship education has moved beyond solely business start-up (as evidenced in the distinction between enterprise and entrepreneurship education discussed above). Even based on narrow definitions of entrepreneurship there are overlaps in terms of skills development: it is clear that those skills/competences helpful for starting a new venture are likely to be of use in a general business setting, or indeed more broadly in life (Neck & Corbett, 2018). For instance, they may prepare graduates for being change makers in established organisations (Neergaard et al., 2020), managing SMEs (Curtis et al., 2020; Gibb, 1996) or joining their family's business (Jaskiewicz et al., 2015). We also suggest a third aspect relating to the changing nature of work and meaning of employability which binds the two concepts of entrepreneurship and employability tightly together.

A comparison of skills that are deemed critical to both entrepreneurship and employability indicates substantial overlap. In fact, looking at the Entrecomp framework and its fifteen entrepreneurship competences many of them would directly relate to employability skills as desired by employers. For some of these competences there appears to be no distinction in terms of suitability for entrepreneurship or for employability: 'motivation and persistence', 'taking the initiative' and 'ability to work with others' would all be regarded as generic competences that would apply in many employment settings. It could be argued that some of the identified entrepreneurial competences (e.g. creativity or coping with ambiguity, uncertainty and risk) would only apply in specific employment settings, and yet drawing a clear division between competences that are suitable only in one domain and not in the other would be a futile undertaking. This interpretation is supported by Rae (2007: 611) who describes enterprise skills as "the skills, knowledge and attributes needed to apply creative ideas and innovations to practical solutions". While not all forms of employment will need high levels of enterprise skills thus defined, many will. So, we can see that enterprise skills/competencies could be regarded as a sub-set of a broader set of employability skills/competencies. The extent to which enterprise skills are required in a particular job will depend on the nature of the job, just as the extent to which specific employability skills will apply to entrepreneurship will depend on broad or narrow definitions of entrepreneurship. On the whole, there is substantial overlap.

In addition to acknowledgement of the overlap, if not complete equivalence between the two terms, of interest is how developments in the world of work are shaping the relationship between entrepreneurship and employability. Technological advancements and the increasing digitalisation of operations create new opportunities for entrepreneurship, on the one hand; they affect the availability and content of jobs and require new forms of work and mobility across organisations and industries, on the other hand (Kornelakis & Petrakaki, 2020; Mikelatou & Arvanitis, 2018). An emphasis on the development of entrepreneurial attributes for all, not just business and entrepreneurship students, is based on the dynamic nature of the business environment. In such an environment there is a benefit to employers of employing individuals who demonstrate entrepreneurial competencies. Consequently, EE is being promoted beyond its traditional focus on undergraduate business/economics students (Lackeus, 2018; NESTA et al., 2008;

Williams, 2019). This is further demonstrated in the UK Government-commissioned 'Young Report' (Young, 2014), which argued for the inclusion of EE in all disciplines and all levels of education. In fact, Gibb (2002: 234) recognised this need for greater levels of entrepreneur-ship in all spheres of life when he wrote entrepreneurial behaviour would be required by, for example, "priests, doctors, teachers, policemen, pensioners and community workers and, indeed, potentially everyone in the community". Understood thus, entrepreneurship is encroaching upon the domain of employability with entrepreneurship skills/competencies finding greater recognition in those skills employees need today.

A dynamic, uncertain business environment may be interpreted as part of broader fluidity in modern lives (Bauman, 2000; Beck, 1992). This fluidity applies also to the world of work and therefore also employability. This fluidity requires entrepreneurial attributes. Not only are enterprise skills, e.g. Rae (2007) good for employers, they apply also to the indi-vidual in their attempts to navigate the fast-moving waters of the world of work. The shift from a focus on employment to a focus on employability (Fugate et al., 2021) will favour those able to identify, evaluate and exploit opportunities (Shane & Venkataraman, 2000) in the labour market, including business start-up. The idea that graduates need to be more self-reliant also aligns with entrepreneurship education's focus on autonomy (van Gelderen, 2010) and the role of self-efficacy beliefs in entrepreneur-ship (Boyd & Vozikis, 1994; Chen et al., 1998). The first sentence in William's (2019) report on engaging students in EE demonstrates this dual connection between entrepreneurship and employability:

"Entrepreneurship education has grown in recent years. In part, this is due to debates regarding the employability of graduates, with enterprise and entrepreneurship being seen as a key route to securing future jobs, either by the graduates creating jobs themselves or applying entrepreneurial skills to employment opportunities" (Williams, 2019: 4).

EE may then help the graduate both to secure employment and to add value to the organisation once employed.

5   Conclusion

Having reviewed the relationship between entrepreneurship and employ-ability we propose three dimensions that characterise it: business start-up, intrapreneurship and career development. Here we summarise these dimensions whereby it is acknowledged that the categories themselves are related (the development for business start-up and associated skills will also be relevant for intrapreneurship, for example).

1. a business start-up (entrepreneurship) dimension

Because of the ongoing expansion in particular of tertiary education, entrepreneurship education will play an important role in preparing graduates for self-employment and also for employment in other contexts, such as SMEs, family businesses, non-governmental organisations, the public sector or social enterprises. An emphasis on entrepreneurship here relates also to the role SMEs, and particularly entrepreneurial ventures, can play in driving forward economic growth and development. In the UK current measures of graduate outcomes appear to favour employment, rather than business start-up. This is an ongoing issue whose persistence could be explored further (e.g. should non-traditional career paths be set on a par with employment outcomes upon which universities are assessed?).

2. an intrapreneurship (enterprise) dimension

Fundamentally, entrepreneurship education develops employability skills/competences although not all entrepreneurship skills/competences will be equally useful in all employability situations. Given the progressively dynamic business environment, driven in part by rapid technological development, enterprise skills, especially an 'opportunity logic' (Lackeus, 2018) are likely to be increasingly in demand by employers.

3. a career developmental ('life skills') dimension.

Entrepreneurship education supports career development in particular in relation to navigating a turbulent world of work. Where long-term careers with one organisation are increasingly rare, where the idea of having multiple careers is no longer regarded as extraordinary, entrepreneurship education can prepare the individual for this type of labour market. As Fugate et al. (2021) argue, employability is moving towards the notion of maintaining one's employability rather than having employment.

There are some potential contradictions between entrepreneurship and employability, rarely acknowledged, which support the rationale for the distinctions made above. Entrepreneurship has an empowering function, one that focuses on developing in an individual a sense of autonomy. Much of the emphasis in current employability discourses is about meeting the needs of employers, and employers tend to desire employees who will 'fit in'. While in theory autonomy, creativity and questioning the status quo may be beneficial to business, it is not clear whether all employers are happy to accept an empowered employee who furthermore seeks to push for greater autonomy. In addition to this, entrepreneurship education may contribute to dynamics that are changing the nature of careers specifically the erosion of long-term careers within one organisation. It is possible employers too are more attuned today to temporary employment contracts and are thus less likely to expect loyalty, but for employers who are expecting loyalty and long-term commitment then entrepreneurship education may not be operating entirely in their favour. Perhaps the key thing to acknowledge on the part of (prospective) graduates is that employment outcomes are not simply a function of one's individual skills and attributes but include a wider range of capitals (Tomlinson & Nghia, 2020). Here entrepreneurship education can play a key role in ensuring these capitals are developed and which will place the graduate in a strong position, irrespective of whether employment or self-employment is the desired outcome.

References

Arthur, M., & Rousseau, D. M. (1996). *The boundaryless career: A new employment principle for a new organizational era*. Oxford University Press.

Bacigalupo, M., Kampylis, P., Punie, Y., & Van den Brande, G. (2016). *Entre-Comp: The entrepreneurship competence framework*. European Commission.

Bandera, C., Santos, S. C., & Liguori, E. W. (2021). The dark side of entrepreneurship eduction: A delphi study on dangers and unintended consequences. *Entrepreneurship Education & Pedagogy, 4*(4), 609–636. https://doi.org/10.1177/2515127420944592.

Battu, H., Belfield, C. R., & Sloane, P. J. (1999). Overeducation among graduates: A cohort view. *Education Economics, 7*(1), 21–38.

Bauman, Z. (2000). *Liquid modernity*. Polity Press.

Beck, U. (1992). *Risk society: Towards a new modernity*. Sage.

Becker, G. (2002). The age of human capital In E. P. Lazear (Ed.), *Education in the twenty-first century* (pp. 3–8). Hoover Institution Press.

Bell, D. (1973). *The coming of post-indsutrial society: A venture in social forecasting*. Basic Books.

Bootle, R. (2018). *The AI economy: Work, wealth and welfare in the robot age.* Nicholas Brealey.

Boyd, N., & Vozikis, G. (1994). The influence of self-efficacy on the development of entrepreneurial intentions and actions. *Entrepreneurship Theory and Practice, 94*(18), 63–77.

Brown, P., & Lauder, H. (2006). Globalisation, knowledge and the myth of the magnet economy. *Globalisation, Societies and Education, 4*(1), 25–57.

Brown, R., & Carasso, H. (2013). *Everything for sale?* Routledge.

CBI. (2017). *Helping the UK thrive: CBI/Peason education and skills survey 2017.* Confederation of British Industry.

Chen, C. C., Greene, P., & Crick, A. (1998). Does entrepreneurial self-efficacy distinguish entrepreneurs from managers? *Journal of Business Venturing, 13*(4), 295–316.

Curtis, V., Moon, R., & Penaluna, A. (2020, in press). Active entrepreneurship education and the impact on approaches to learning: Mixed methods evidence from a six-year study into one entrepreneurship educator's classroom. *Industry and Higher Education.*

Dhaliwal, S. (2017). *The millennial millionaire: How young entrepreneurs turn dreams into business.* Palgrave.

Drucker, P. (1993). *Post-capitalist society.* Butterworth-Heinemann.

Elias, P., & Purcell, K. (2004). *Is mass higher education working? Evidence from the labour market experiences of recent graduates* (National Institute Economic Review No 190).

Fayolle, A., & Gailly, B. (2008). From craft to science: Teaching models and learning processes in entrepreneurship education. *Journal of European Industrial Training, 32*(7), 569–593.

Fayolle, A., Verzat, C., & Wapshott, R. (2016). In quest of legitimacy: The theoretical and methodological foundations of entrepreneurship education research. *International Small Business Journal, 34*(7), 895–904.

Ford, M. (2015). *The rise of the robots: Technology and the threat of mass unemployment.* Oneworld.

Forrier, A., & Sels, L. (2003). The concept employability: A complex mosaic. *International Journal of Human Resources Development and Management, 3*(2), 102–124.

Frey, C. B., & Osborne, M. A. (2017). The future of employment: How susceptible are jobs to computerisation? *Techological Forecasting and Social Change, 114,* 254–280.

Fugate, M., van der Heijden, B., de Vos, A., Forrier, A., & de Cuyper, N. (2021). Is what's past prologue? A review and agenda for contemporary employability research. *Academy of Management Annals, 15*(1), 266–298.

Gibb, A. A. (1996). Entrepreneurship and small business management: Can we afford to neglect them in the twenty-first century business school? *British Journal of Management, 7*(4), 309–321.

Gibb, A. (2002). In pursuit of a new 'enterprise' and 'entrepreneurship' paradigm for learning: Creative destruction, new values, new ways of doing things and new combinations of knowledge. *International Journal of Management Reviews, 4*(3), 233–269.

Giddens, A. (1991). *Modernity and self-identity: Self and society in the late modern age.* Polity Press.

Grint, K. (1991). *The sociology of work: An introduction.* Polity Press.

Hall, D. T. (1996). Protean careers of the 21st century. *Academy of Management Executive, 10*(4), 8–16.

Holden, R., & Jameson, S. (2002). Employing graduates in SMEs: Towards a research agenda. *Journal of Small Business and Enterprise Development, 9*(3), 271–284.

Hynes, B. (1996). Entrepreneurship education and training—Introducing entrepreneurship into non-business disciplines. *Journal of European Industrial Training, 20*(8), 10–17.

Jaskiewicz, P., Combs, J., & Rau, S. (2015). Entrepreneurial legacy: Toward a theory of how some family firms nurture transgenerational entrepreneurship. *Journal of Business Venturing, 30*(1), 29–49.

Jones, B., & Iredale, N. (2007). Viewpoint: Enterprise education as pedagogy. *Education & Training, 52*(1), 7–19.

Jones, B., & Iredale, N. (2014). Enterprise and entrepreneurship education: Towards a comparative analysis. *Journal of Enterprising Communities: People and Places in the Global Economy, 8*(1), 34–50.

Jones, P., Pickernell, D., Fisher, R., & Netana, C. (2017). A tale of two universities: Graduates perceived value of entrepreneurship education. *Education+ Training, 59*(7/8), 689–705.

Kornelakis, A., & Petrakaki, D. (2020). Embedding employability skills in UK higher education: Between digitalization and marketization. *Industry and Higher Education, 34*(5), 290–297.

Lackeus, M. (2018). Making enterprise education more relevant through mission creep In G. Mulholland & J. Turner (Eds.), *Enterprising education in UK higher education: Challenges for theory and practice.* Routledge.

Lovell Corporation. (2017). *The change generation^{TM} report: How millennials and generation Z are redefining work 2017.* Lovell Corporation.

Maloni, M., Hiatt, M. S., & Campbell, S. (2019). Understanding the work values of Gen Z business students. *The International Journal of Management Education, 17*(3), 100320.

Mannheim, K. (1952). *The problem of generations: Essays on the sociology of knowledge.* Routledge.

Mikelatou, A., & Arvanitis, E. (2018). Social inclusion and active citizenship under the prism of neoliberalism: A critical analysis of the European Union's discourse of lifelong learning. *Educational Philosophy and Theory, 50*(5), 499–509.

Morris, M. H., & Liguori, E. (2016). Preface: Teaching reason and the unreasonable. In M. H. Morris, & E. Ligouri (Eds.), *Annals of entrepreneurship education and pedagogy* (xiv–xxii). Edward Elgar Publishing.

Nabi, G., Walmsley, A., & Holden, R. (2013). Pushed or pulled? Exploring the factors underpinning graduate start-ups and non-start-ups. *Journal of Education and Work, 10*(1), 1–26.

Neck, H., & Corbett, A. (2018). The scholarship of teaching and learning entrepreneurship. *Entrepreneurship Education and Pedagogy, 1*(1), 8–41.

Nedelkoska, L., & Quintini, G. (2018). *Automation, skills use and training* (Social, employment and migration Working Papers 202). OECD.

Neergaard, H., Gartner, W. B., Hytti, U., Politis, D., & Rae, D. (2020). Editorial: Filling in the blanks: "Black boxes" in enterprise/entrepreneurship education. *International Journal of Entrepreneurial Behaviour and Research, 26*(5), 817–828.

NESTA, NCGE, & CIHE. (2008). *Developing entrepreneurial graduates: Putting entrepreneurship at the centre of higher education* (p. 40). NESTA, NCGE, CIHE.

O'Donovan, N. (2020). From knowledge economy to automation anxiety: A growth regime in crisis? *New Political Economy, 25*(2), 248–266.

OECD. (2020). *Education at a glance.* OECD.

Office for National Statistics. (2019). *One in three graduates overeducated for their current role.* ONS.

Quality Assurance Agency. (2018). *Enterprise and entrepreneurship education: Guidance for UK higher education providers* (p. 33). The Quality Assurance Agency for Higher Education.

Rae, D. (2007). Connecting enterprise and graduate employability: Challenges to the higher education culture and curriculum? *Education + Training, 49*(8), 605–619.

Scheepers, M. J. d. V., Barnes, R., Clements, M., & Stubbs, A. J. (2018). Preparing future-ready graduates through experiential entrepreneurship. *Education + Training, 60*(4), 303–317.

Schröder, M. (2018). Der Generationenmythos. *Kölner Zeitschrift Für Soziologie Und Sozialpsychologie, 70*(3), 469–494.

Sennett, R. (1998). *The corrosion of character: The personal consequences of work in the new capitalism.* W.W. Norton & Company.

Sewell, P., & Pool, L. D. (2010). Moving from conceptual ambiguity to operational clarity: Employability, enterprise and entrepreneurship in higher education. *Education & Training, 52*(1), 89–94.

Shane, S., Locke, E. A., & Collins, C. J. (2003). Entrepreneurial motivation. *Human Resource Management Review, 13*(2), 257–279.

Shane, S., & Venkataraman, S. (2000). The promise of entrepreneurship as a field of research. *Academy of Management Review, 25*(1), 217–226.

Shepherd, D., & Patzelt, H. (2018). *Entrepreneurial cognition: Exploring the mindset of entrepreneurs*. Palgrave Macmillan.

Small, L., Shacklock, K., & Marchant, T. (2018). Employability: A contemporary review for higher education stakeholders. *Journal of Vocational Education and Training, 70*(1), 148–166.

Spivack, A. J., & McKelvie, A. (2018). Entrepreneurship addiction: Shedding light on the manifestaion of the dark side in work-behavior patterns. *Academy of Management Perspectives, 32*(3), 358–378.

Sullivan, S. E., & Arthur, M. (2006). The evolution of the boundaryless career concept: Examining physical and psychological mobility. *Journal of Vocational Behavior, 69*(1), 19–29.

Tate, A., & Thompson, J. (1994). The application of enterprise skills in the workplace. In S. Haselgrove (Ed.), *The student experience* (pp. 127–140). The Society for Research into Higher Education and Open University Press.

Tegmark, M. (2017). *Life 3.0. being human in the age of Artificial Intelligence*. Random House.

Tomlinson, M., & Nghia, T. (2020). An overview of the current policy and conceptual landscape of graduate employability. In N. Tran, T. Pham, M. Tomlinson, K. Medica, & C. Thompson (Eds.), *Developing and utilizing employability capitals: Graduates' strategies across labour markets* (pp. 1–17). Routledge.

Ustav, S., & Venesaar, U. (2018). Bridging metacompetencies and entrepreneurship education. *Education & Training, 60*(7), 674–695.

van Gelderen, M. (2010). Autonomy as the guiding aim of entrepreneurship education. *Education & Training, 52*(8/9), 710–721.

van Gelderen, M., & Jansen, P. (2006). Autonomy as a start-up motive. *Journal of Small Business and Enterprise Development, 13*(1), 23–32.

Williams, N. (2019). *Engaging students in entrepreneurship education: Thoughts on the present context and future challenges*. Advance HE.

Wolf, A. (2002). *Does education matter?* Penguin.

Yorke, M. (2006). Employability in higher education: What it is—What it is not. In E. HEA (Ed.), *Learning and employability series one* (p. 22). The Higher Education Academy.

Young, D. L. (2014). *Enterprise for all: The relevance of enterprise in education* (p. 48).

Dual Learning Space in Undergraduate Entrepreneurship Education: A Framework Proposal

Guillermo J. Larios-Hernandez and *Itzel Lopez-Castro*

1 INTRODUCTION

Entrepreneurship Education (EE) continues to be one of the fastest growing topics in the university curricula, and scholars still attempt to establish ontological boundaries to the definition and implications of EE, affecting the educational principles that guide the design of courses and programmes (Gabrielsson et al., 2020). Though a variety of educational areas of expertise have contributed to the development of EE (Hägg & Kurczewska, 2021), there is a wide debate about the benefits of EE, along with suitable teaching and learning methods. One measure of EE effectiveness that has been widely accepted in the academic literature is related to indicators of Entrepreneurial Intentions (EI) (Gabrielsson et al., 2020), accepting that EI would expectedly trigger entrepreneurial action.

G. J. Larios-Hernandez (✉) · I. Lopez-Castro
Universidad Anáhuac, Mexico, Mexico
e-mail: guillermo.lariosh@anahuac.mx

I. Lopez-Castro
e-mail: itzel.lopez@anahuac.mx

© The Author(s), under exclusive license to Springer Nature
Switzerland AG 2022
G. J. Larios-Hernandez et al. (eds.), *Theorising Undergraduate Entrepreneurship Education*,
https://doi.org/10.1007/978-3-030-87865-8_7

This approach originates from the Theory of Planned Behaviour (TPB), which postulates that intentions affect conducts and attitudes (Ajzen, 1991; Bandura, 1977, 1982), and EI, in particular, is activated by students' self-efficacy (Drnovšek et al., 2010; Entrialgo & Iglesias, 2016; Fernández-Pérez et al., 2019; McGee et al., 2009; Sánchez, 2011). However, and contrary to this view, Ismail et al. (2018) find that self-efficacy and EI demonstrate a moderate, indirect or null relationship. Additionally, psychological limitations of young students make EI an outcome of EE that turns out misleading; Gielnik et al. (2018) have found that, while the young tend to demonstrate higher levels of EI after identifying opportunities, entrepreneurial action belongs to mature adults. In other words, whereas entrepreneurial intention characterises formative years, actual entrepreneurial pursuit is more likely in adulthood.

Therefore, if motivation for entrepreneurial intention (but not action) is more likely among the young, considering the perceptual differences in the gap between young and older generations (Gielnik et al., 2018), we must necessarily pose a question as to what type of benefits should be expected from Undergraduate Entrepreneurship Education (UEE). Van Praag (2003) finds that new venture creation is correlated with the existence of previous entrepreneurial experience in similar initiatives, whereas Higher Education (HE) students stand out by varied levels of inexperience. Similarly, Gielnik et al. (2018) find that advancements in education might have an opposite effect on entrepreneurship when there is no prior entrepreneurial experience. These findings make EE particularly problematic for HE, challenging the pertinence of entrepreneurship instruction among young people, especially when traditional HE in business tends to be causal, linear and predictable (Neck & Greene, 2011), which stands in contrast with the uncertainty and serendipity that characterise entrepreneurship.

However, this interpretation can be myopic in that it ignores the benefits and the broader perspective of entrepreneurship. Beyond the process of new venture creation, entrepreneurial value exists in a variety of forms, whose interpretation determines how EE is to be developed in HE institutions. The type of EE model adopted by a particular HE institution is contingent on the definition of entrepreneurship that such an organisation decides to embrace, outlining which competencies are contextually relevant: either to start up a new company or to encourage a mindset that can serve in a broader context (Lilleväli & Täks, 2017). While the first approach appears to take hold in the USA, the latter approach is more prominent in the European continent (Bacigalupo et al., 2016; Gibb, 2008; Rasmussen et al., 2015).

A solution can be found in the objectives that sustain EE, namely, the development of entrepreneurial competencies (Lackéus, 2015; Tittel & Terzidis, 2020), whose significance is connected to HE students' evolving generational characteristics, i.e. their nascent life experience, emerging identity and aspirations, which set them apart from other student cohorts. This reality should inform educators about the best learning approaches that harmonise with these students' developmental requirements. However, many educators tend to disregard the suitability of their instructional methods to the stage of development among HE students (Hägg & Kurczewska, 2021), a problem particularly relevant in UEE, suggesting the need for a reflexive exercise aimed at matching age-related qualities to the stages in the entrepreneurship development process (Gielnik et al., 2018).

To help address this challenge, this chapter conceptualises UEE as a progression of didactical methods and experiences that develop in a dual learning space environment, emphasising the value of mentorship in facilitating divergent and convergent thinking processes among HE students, who are distinguished by an emerging adulthood (EA) stage. The following section portrays EA as a life stage in which certain entrepreneurial competences are to be realised, which can be attained through the practice of entrepreneurship. Section 3 elaborates on the meaning of experiential learning in the context of UEE and EA, leading to the conceptualisation of the learning space as a construct that blurs the line between a classroom and real-life environment. After this discussion, Sect. 4 emphasises the role of mentorship in learning spaces, which has to be acknowledged as a necessary subjective contribution to help students navigate their learning space. Drawing from experiential learning space and mentorship, Sect. 5 introduces the Dual Entrepreneurship Learning Space (DELS) framework proposal, followed by the chapter conclusion.

2 Higher Education and Entrepreneurial Competencies

EE scholars have paid little attention to the characteristics of young people in Higher Education (HE) (Hägg & Kurczewska, 2021), who endure mental and emotional wants that embed them in a transitional stage between teenage years and full adulthood. Arnett (2000) has termed this development stage the Emerging Adulthood (EA), which is a mutable cultural construct made implicit in the enlargement of the adolescence life stage relative to the process of continued identity exploration that results from HE engagement. To a certain extent, HE triggers the EA condition among the young (Arnett, 2000).

Emerging adults are self-focused, involved in a broader range of activities, devoid of social roles. Therefore, they may take higher risks and embrace exploration and intensive experimentation to discover their place and identity in life and work (Arnett, 2000; Swanson, 2016). Before reaching adult life, emerging adults tend to make uncritical decisions, which are strongly influenced by external relations, internalising their meaning-making methods, according to the social situations in which they participate (Magolda & Taylor, 2015). Additionally, HE students have little knowledge of the immediate applications of their coursework and give priority to course performance over learning (Dachner & Polin, 2016). In the same way, they resolve meaning following an iterative dynamic that swings between internal definition and external reliance when facing new experiences (Magolda & Taylor, 2015). On this account, considering the diversity of learners' contexts, psychological characteristics, ambitions, identities and varied levels of proficiency, the manner in which entrepreneurial competences materialise for HE students is a topic of much needed research. Generally speaking, a competency involves both cognitive and non-cognitive abilities for successful task execution (Weinert, 2001), whereas entrepreneurial competencies imply the devotion of such skills and attitudes to realise entrepreneurial activities that lead to new value creation (Lackéus, 2015).

Preparatory scholarly research has meant to recognise and classify such competencies (Tittel & Terzidis, 2020), with the stage of advancement (Bacigalupo et al., 2016; Bozward & Rogers-Draycott, 2017), contexts (Man, 2001; Man et al., 2002; Schallenkamp & Smith, 2008; Mitchelmore & Rowley, 2013) and success factors (Bird, 1995) being some of the typical approaches. There are multiple entrepreneurial competencies already identified by the scholarly literature, such as action orientation, creativity, integrity and ethics knowledge, technical skills, self-efficacy, self-knowledge and learning skills, social skills, perseverance, tolerance of ambiguity (Bacigalupo et al., 2016; Lackéus, 2015; Tittel & Terzidis, 2020), among others.

However, the sole identification and classification of entrepreneurial competencies offers an incomplete outlook on the pertinence of certain techniques for the effectiveness of EE, especially among EA. Comparatively, other research viewpoints converge on the purposive identification of the necessary skills, attitudes and competencies that breed what is usually known as the Entrepreneurial Mindset (EM), which differentiates the outcomes of entrepreneurship from the advancement of the entrepreneurial thinking (Komarkova et al., 2015), while appreciating the required levels of entrepreneurial cognition (Lackéus, 2015). Though EE is primarily focused on the development of the mindset as well as the abilities and practice for new venture creation, its implications are profound in that these capabilities are useful across a variety of organisational types and careers (Neck & Corbett, 2018).

Hence, competencies should be chosen according to students' maturity level and their cognitive development, factors that are forerunners and predictors of future competencies (Obschonka et al., 2017) and whose interactions facilitate the advancement of further proficiencies (RezaeiZadeh et al., 2017). According to Lackéus (2015), UEE necessarily combines knowledge, skills and attitudes, expanding on previous EE stages, and evolves into a business orientation as the student progresses into postgraduate education. For instance, encouraging inexperienced students to be creative and generate problem-solving ideas is probably more valuable than teaching them how to monetise opportunities (Swayne et al., 2019), which involves critical thinking as a relevant HE competence to achieve self-authorship (Magolda & Taylor, 2015).

Nonetheless, it is the practice of entrepreneurship (new venture creation) that fosters an EM, given that new venture creation is what (in part) defines EE as an academic discipline (Neck & Corbett, 2018). Therefore, UEE should embrace both new venture creation and the development of an EM, namely, the narrower and broader perspectives of EE (Lackéus, 2015), whose timely application would lead to the development of divergent and convergent thinking among HE students (Neck et al., 2014), i.e. combined processes of practice and analytical reasoning that originate in experiential learning spaces.

3   The Experiential Learning Space in UEE

Herrington and Oliver (2000) criticise the traditional HE approach to abstract and decontextualised education delivered by teachers, encouraging a type of learning that originates in authentic interactions with "experts". Though this viewpoint appears to degrade the role of the academic educator, whose expertise is considered less valuable than that of practitioners in the field, it has its merits in that it emphasises the importance of realistic experience. However, it fails to recognise the character of education and its relationship with the necessary knowledge structures that affect judgement. Neck and Greene (2011) demystify the statement of many practitioner-led EE programmes, such as bootcamps and non-university incubators whose focus on personality profiling leads them to claim that entrepreneurship cannot be taught but only experienced in the real world. In said programmes, the authors emphasise a portfolio of techniques to practice entrepreneurship in order to create value. In other words, practitioners and academic programmes need to adapt each other's complementary qualities: while practitioners ought to go beyond personality heroes and successful new ventures by considering techniques for the development of a value creation mindset, decision-making skills and other cognitive attributes (such as experience analysis, reflection and problem-solving), academics are required to incorporate in their teaching experiential methods real-life interactions, ideation and opportunity discovery (Günzel-Jensen & Robinson, 2017; Neck & Greene, 2011), an approach deeply embedded in customer development or Lean Startup methodologies (Blank, 2013; Ries, 2012).

Hence, learning must develop as a social process that invites students to participate in groups of practitioners, who engage such groups in practical activities, where they gain new capabilities and identity (Bonnette & Crowley, 2020). The embeddedness of learners in realistic situations implicates collaborative activities that grant access to role-model experts, coaching, knowledge co-creation, self-reflection and learning evaluation (Herrington & Oliver, 2000). Such a practice-oriented approach, involving real-life experiential activities, idea generation, opportunity identification and self-knowledge, combines with management sciences in order to fulfil the ends of EE, namely, effectual learning from such experiences, innovation skills and exploitation of the opportunity (Günzel-Jensen & Robinson, 2017; Scott et al., 2016), which, ultimately, facilitate the acquisition of an entrepreneurial mindset among HE students.

EE has evolved from situating learning based on the types of entrepreneurship to emphasising the learner as the centre of the EE process and, though the field still struggles to make a connection to learning and education theories (Gabrielsson et al., 2020), some of them have influenced teaching methods, which have been useful in reinforcing the experiential learning approach that characterises EE nowadays (Bell &

Bell, 2020). In this sense, experiential learning stands out as the most popular instructive approach to EE (Kolb & Kolb, 2005), which allows students to bridge the gap that exists between knowledge acquisition and contextual application, leading to the construction of actionable learning (Miles et al., 2017). Experiential learning must include tangible experiences, self-reflection, conceptual abstraction and active experimentation, involving students in activities such as consulting projects or start-up initiatives (Dachner & Polin, 2016). According to Neck and Corbett (2018), the dominion of pedagogical approaches to EE represents an important barrier to practice-based learning, contending that andragogy methods should take precedence over pedagogy in that EE involves guidance and real-life experience in connection to students' individualities. The application of andragogy is flexible and context-dependent (Dachner & Polin, 2016), whose principles expose HE students to self-fulfilment, cooperative relations, shared responsibility in project groups, experiential learning activities and guidance to learn from meaningful experiences (Neck & Corbett, 2018).

On the other hand, reflective critical thinking and prior experience are prerequisites to succeed in self-determined modes of learning, which put into question the effectiveness of experiential learning among immature and unexperienced EA (Hägg & Kurczewska, 2021). However, emerging adults build identity through experiential learning, considering that EA consists of inexpert students who tend to generate news ideas based on their experiences as consumers (Swayne et al., 2019)—i.e. user innovation (Von Hippel, 2005). Additionally, each HE student has varied levels of maturity: while a student may be totally self-directed in one activity, she may be dependent on others regarding a different type of experience, stressing the need for variability in teaching methods in EE (Neck & Corbett, 2018). Hence, knowledge should be contextually learned, with the setting being either an actual work environment or its virtual substitute (Herrington & Oliver, 2000).

In that regard, Kolb and Kolb (2005) coined the term learning space, defined as a construct that relates the learners' character to the institutional setting, determining students' behaviour. As a subjective experience in a social environment, the learning space cannot be constrained by the boundaries of a physical classroom in that it results from collective involvement in specific activities, recognising the social nature of learning. Some EE scholars have embraced this principle to propose alternative constructs such as authentic learning (Bonnette & Crowley,

2020; Herrington & Oliver, 2000) and real-life environment (Neck & Corbett, 2018). Hence, since EE contexts can vary significantly, learning can occur within the teaching space as well as beyond such a structured milieu, clouding the line between classroom and real-life settings (Hägg & Kurczewska, 2021).

4 Guiding HE Students Through Learning Spaces

Real-world applications increase motivation in HE students (Swayne et al., 2019) and, considering that entrepreneurial success depends on both experience and practice, students should be encouraged to test out their hypotheses beyond the classroom (Blank et al., 2014). However, successful experiential groundwork requires a continuous learning facilitation activity, which relies on pedagogy principles to convey the necessary knowledge to have HE students complete those activities that help them acquire new skills, particularly among inexperienced undergraduates (Hägg & Kurczewska, 2021). In other words, EE requires mentorship or guidance.

Mentorship is relevant when students have a hard time to act with independence and empathy (Dachner & Polin, 2016), in that mentorship boosts learning by challenging entrepreneurial assumptions and delivering guidance that helps students appreciate reality (Miles et al., 2017), including the experience of failure (Dobson et al., 2021). The level of guidance in EE can fluctuate between structured instructions (cognitive approach) comprising project-based collaborative learning, self-regulated experiential learning, and self-directed projects (constructivist experiential learning), depending on students' characteristics, as part of a continuum between teaching and learning, that is aimed at evolving from external to internal motivation to learn (Hägg & Kurczewska, 2021). The culmination of this continuum can be found in the fulfilment of the andragogical assumptions at the end of HE, namely, self-concept, intrinsic motivation, proclivity, discernment and readiness to learn, and work experience (Dachner & Polin, 2016). Expressly, as emerging adults gain such skills, assistantship can be reduced, transferring more responsibility to the student (Dachner & Polin, 2016). Additionally, mentorship support is needed to validate learners' knowledge position, recognising their prevailing experience to construct mutual meaning, while emphasising autonomy and connection (Baxter Magolda, 2004). Accordingly, students' readiness and commitment to learn are instrumental in determining the role of the educator in terms of support and direction (Neck & Corbett, 2018).

However, mentoring is a human factor, which is influenced by the mentor's level of expertise, standards and subjective discernment about students' EE challenges (Henry, 2020). To put it another way, the educator's contribution to UEE is unique, in that, in the learning space, she guides her students through the following patterns that originate in her personal involvement with her own past and present learning space—e.g. specific entrepreneurial ecosystems (Guercini, 2012). Hence, contextual qualities and heuristics that educators acquire along with their real-life setting would have an impact on students' divergent and convergent thinking processes that develop in their corresponding learning space. Such uniqueness would need to be supported and channelled intentionally, according to the UEE institutional programme, and required competencies would need to be attained.

5   A Framework Proposal for UEE

The concept of experiential learning has been overly applied by entrepreneurship programmes in that activities so diverse such as a group discussion about life problems, blogging, opinion surveys or real customer interviews are all lumped together. Although the academic literature communicates experiential learning as an approach that involves real-life experiences, it fails to account in what way specific experiences are valuable to the student entrepreneur; that is, the type of experiential learning whose actions turn out appropriate for the level of cognition that a particular HE student cohort is expected to achieve.

The type of approximation to reality influences cognition, posing a problem of degree in the application of experiential learning. As exhibited by Neck et al. (2014), distinctive theoretical approaches to experimentation and corresponding student actions implicate unique learning outcomes, such as knowledge construction from a process of social negotiation and assessment (problem-based learning), scholarship from the interpretation and synthesis of incomplete information (evidence-based learning) or learning from perceptions and debate about an enacted reality (sensemaking). The highest levels of cognition (deep learning) are reached when conceptual comprehension and critical thinking derive from adaptive experiences that relate to students' intrinsic motivations

(Bain, 2004). Hence, it would be reasonable to expect that the closer HE students' experience is to real-life setting, the higher the level of cognition is, if learners manage to critically understand such experiences, whereby mentorship and guidance become instrumental, especially among HE students. As posed by Bell and Bell (2020, p. 992), "the combination of reflection-in-action with reflection-on-action provides a deeper understanding of the potential value and role of reflection in experiential learning". From this perspective, HE institutional setting blends with the real-life environment, which seems to suggest an interaction of two types of learning spaces for UEE: one that enhances experience like a real business, and another that facilitates analysis and reflection. These precepts have been included in the framework proposal shown in Fig. 1, which has been named Dual Entrepreneurship Learning Space (DELS).

DELS departs from the convergence of two different types of inter-related learning spaces: one led by the educator (e.g. classrooms, collaborative spaces, virtual classes, etc.) and the reality that lies beyond the university walls (emulating a business-like real-life scenario), which jointly build a type of dual learning space environment. A properly equipped educator-led location would allow for the improvement of knowledge, technical and learning skills, and other competencies such as creativity, which are exercised through the combination of both traditional and dynamic methods, including collaborative learning, gamification, role playing, project-based learning (PBL), master class, among others. Likewise, students' experience out of the university arranges for business-like experiential learning, including the development of skills and attitudes such as action orientation, perseverance, social skills, self-efficacy, self-knowledge, tolerance of ambiguity, among others, in correspondence with the need for exploration, experimentation, search for meaning and self-reflexion that characterise EA. In this business-like learning space, students still work on the class subject, but specific activities go beyond the walls of the university and into the real life, embedding students in experiences with real would-be customers. This space entails challenges for educators, who must plan for goal-directed out-of-the-university activities related to the attainment of entrepreneurial competencies, in which learners need to be self-directed and demonstrate collaborative skills with classmates. Additionally, the combination of self-directed methods and a diversity of activities in a real social environment would allow HE students to have a deeper understanding of the direct applications of EE.

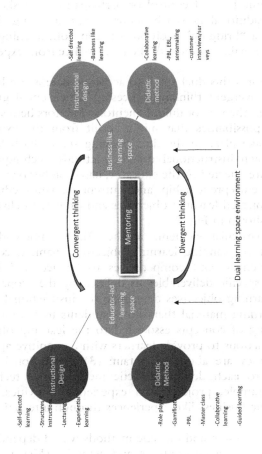

Fig. 1 Dual Entrepreneurship Learning Space (DELS) Framework

The role of an educator is fundamental in this model: on the one hand, she must mediate between teaching methods and the level of guidance to be provided, according to the maturity stage that students have attained in a particular activity and the learning space that is required. On the other hand, the educator ought to acknowledge that the business-like space cannot grant the same level of control or participation that she would usually expect in traditional or synchronous classes, implying that she would need to play a "bridging" position between both learning spaces to enable students to make the most of their experience from experiential learning.

Effectiveness requires this dual space to accommodate a combination of divergent and convergent thinking processes, which entail guidance from the educators in the role of unique mentors. Mentors help students assimilate learning possibilities that might result from the experience and activities that take place in the dual learning space. Each learning space involves its own instructional design, methods, techniques and assessments, which are selected by the educator, based on her own subjective experience in entrepreneurship and entrepreneurship education, according to the projected learning objectives and expected deliverables. This preparation is shown in Fig. 2.

The design of particular elements in the DELS framework must necessarily depart from planning learning objectives, namely, cognitive and emotional objectives, and competencies to be acquired by HE students as well as specific deliverables as defined by the scope of the EE programme. Learning objectives determine the instructional design: (1) self-directed learning material that allows students to have a fundamental understanding of concepts associated to the learning objective; (2) structured instructions to provide learners with a cognitive approach to the experience they are about to obtain; (3) a traditional lecture format. According to each design, didactic methods and techniques are selected, for example, project-based experiential activities, group collaboration, realistic business-like experiences through interaction with potential clients, etc.

These instructional design and didactic methods would depend of the educator's ability to aggregate contents and activities (Henry, 2020), according to the objectives and deliverables indicated by a particular UEE programme, whose definition sets the boundaries of the learning space in which students would experience EE. Educators would abide by such boundaries, guiding HE students in their business-like EE learning

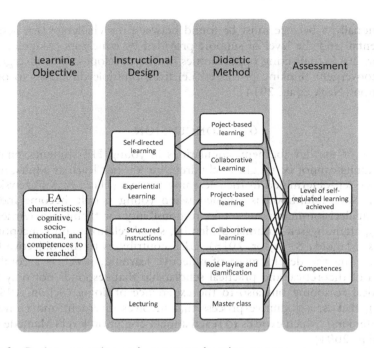

Fig. 2 Design, execution and assessment learning process

process. Continuous mentoring that adapts to HE students' characteristics in terms of internal definition skills vs. external reliance becomes instrumental, as this is the flexibility required by EA. The design of each activity must necessarily involve assessment of EE outcomes, prompting continuous improvement.

Based on the previous discussion, course activities should be designed according to the level of self-concept advancement among HE students, including opportunities for self-reflection and excitement, grounding information analysis on students' present life and work experiences—part-time jobs, faith organisations, sport teams, volunteering, etc.—but should also induce them to gain richer experience through trial and error (Dachner & Polin, 2016), which should include in their design a realistic learning experience such as that offered by immersive entrepreneurship programmes (e.g. incubators and accelerator) (Miles et al., 2017).

Additionally, a balance must be found between the challenge that activities entail and the level of support provided by educators (Magolda & Taylor, 2015), delivering opportunities for the development of divergent and convergent thinking processes, i.e. from multiple directions to one direction (Neck et al., 2014).

6 Conclusion

In view of the development singularities in young HE students, emergent adults cannot be taught as children, but do not learn as adults, nor are they self-determined in their learning process (Hägg & Kurczewska, 2021). Such adulthood is attained when young people become independent decision-makers who take responsibility for themselves (Arnett, 2000), attaining self-authorship identity, social relations and conceptual beliefs (Magolda & Taylor, 2015). UEE contributes to this objective by encouraging the development of reflective learning, which is a combination of theoretical and practical scholarship that responds not only to analytical reasoning but also to the experience of doing (Schön, 1983, 1987), that is, a cognitive process that involves divergent and convergent thinking, which evolves to reach a meta-cognition level (Mamede & Schmidt, 2004).

The framework presented in the previous section has been implemented in the HE institution where the authors of this chapter declare their affiliation, aiming to lead students to such reflective learning in that it purports to encourage a dynamic interaction between educator-led and business-like learning spaces, facilitating thoughtful realistic experiences in HE students. This iterative process piggybacks on the educator's expertise and values to derive meaning among undergraduates who are subject to developmental requirements that characterise EA.

Acknowledgement This project would not have been possible without the support of Universidad Anáhuac México.

References

Ajzen, I. (1991). The theory of planned behavior. *Organizational Behavior and Human Decision Processes, 50*(2), 179–211. https://psycnet.apa.org/doi/10.1016/0749-5978(91)90020-T

Arnett, J. (2000). Emerging adulthood: A theory of development from the late teens through the twenties. *American Psychologist*, *55*(5), 469–480. https://psycnet.apa.org/doi/10.1037/0003-066X.55.5.469

Bacigalupo, M., Kampylis, P., Punie, Y., & Van de Brande, G. (2016). *Entre-Comp: The entrepreneurship competence framework*. Publication Office of the European Union. https://ec.europa.eu/jrc/en/publication/eur-scientific-and-technical-research-reports/entrecomp-entrepreneurship-competence-framework

Bain, K. (2004). *What the best college teachers do*. Harvard University Press.

Bandura, A. (1977). Self-efficacy: Toward a unifying theory of behavioral change. *Psychological Review*, *84*(2), 191–215. https://psycnet.apa.org/doi/10.1037/0033-295X.84.2.191

Bandura, A. (1982). Self- efficacy mechanism in human agency. *American Psychologist*, *37*(2), 122–147. https://psycnet.apa.org/doi/10.1037/0003-066X.37.2.122

Baxter Magolda, M. B. (2004). Learning partnerships model: A framework for promoting self-authorship. In M. B. Baxter Magolda & P. M. King (Eds.), *Learning partnerships: Theory and models of practice to educate for self-authorship* (Vol. 1). Stylus Publishing.

Bell, R., & Bell, H. (2020). Applying educational theory to develop a framework to support the delivery of experiential entrepreneurship education. *Journal of Small Business and Enterprise Development*, *27*(6), 987–1004. https://doi.org/10.1108/JSBED-01-2020-0012

Bird, B. (1995). Towards a theory of entrepreneurial competency. *Advances in Entrepreneurship, Firm Emergence and Growth*, *2*(1), 51–72.

Blank, S. (2013, May). Why the lean start up changes everything. *Harvard Business Review*, 63–72.

Blank, S., Engel, J., & Hornthal, J. (2014). *Lean LaunchPad: Evidence-based entrepreneurship educators guide* (6th ed.). VentureWell.

Bonnette, R. N., & Crowley, K. (2020). Legitimate peripheral participation in a makerspace for emancipated emerging adults. *Emerging Adulthood*, *8*(2), 144–158. https://doi.org/10.1177%2F2167696818785328

Bozward, D., & Rogers-Draycott, M. (2017, August 31–September 1). Developing a staged competency based approach to enterprise creation. Paper presented at *International conference for entrepreneurship, innovation and regional development*, Thessaloniki (Greece).

Dachner, A. M., & Polin, B. (2016). A systematic approach to educating the emerging adult learner in undergraduate management courses. *Journal of Management Education*, *40*(2), 121–151. https://doi.org/10.1177%2F1052562915613589

Dobson, J., Castro, Y., Dobson, L., & Moros, A. (2021). Success through failure: Towards a problem-based approach to entrepreneurship. *Entrepreneurship Education and Pedagogy, 4*(3), 225–260. https://doi.org/10.1177/251 5127419884132

Drnovšek, M., Wincent, J., & Cardon, M. S. (2010). Entrepreneurial self-efficacy and business start-up: Developing a multi-dimensional definition. *International Journal of Entrepreneurial Behavior & Research, 16*(4), 329–348. https://doi.org/10.1016/j.jvb.2018.05.012

Entrialgo, M., & Iglesias, V. (2016). The moderating role of entrepreneurship education on the antecedents of entrepreneurial intention. *International Entrepreneurship and Management Journal, 12*(4), 1209–1232. https://doi.org/10.1007/s11365-016-0389-4

Fernández-Pérez, V., Montes-Merino, A., Rodríguez-Ariza, L., & Alonso-García, P. (2019). Emotional competencies and cognitive antecedents in shaping student's entrepreneurial intention: The moderating role of entrepreneurship education. *International Entrepreneurship and Management Journal, 15*(1), 281–305. https://doi.org/10.1007/s11365-017-0438-7

Gabrielsson, J., Hägg, G., Landström, H., & Politis, D. (2020). Connecting the past with the present: The development of research on pedagogy in entrepreneurial education. *Education + Training, 62*(9), 1061–1086. https://doi.org/10.1108/ET-11-2019-0265

Gibb, A. (2008). Entrepreneurship and enterprise education in schools and colleges: Insights from UK. *International Journal of Entrepreneurship Education, 6*(2), 101–144.

Gielnik, M., Zacher, H., & Wang, M. (2018). Age in the entrepreneurial process: The role of future time perspective and prior entrepreneurial experience. *Journal of Applied Psychology, 103*(10), 1067–1085. https://psycnet.apa.org/doi/10.1037/apl0000322

Guercini, S. (2012). New approaches to heuristic processes and entrepreneurial cognition of the market. *Journal of Research in Marketing and Entrepreneurship, 14*(2), 199–213. https://doi.org/10.1108/14715201211271410

Günzel-Jensen, F., & Robinson, S. (2017). Effectuation in the undergraduate classroom: Three barriers to entrepreneurial learning. *Education + Training, 59*(7/8), 780–796. https://doi.org/10.1108/ET-03-2016-0049

Hägg, G., & Kurczewska, A. (2021). Towards a learning philosophy based on experience in entrepreneurship education. *Entrepreneurship Education and Pedagogy, 4*(1), 4–29. https://doi.org/10.1177/2515127419840607

Henry, C. (2020). Reconceptualizing the role of the future entrepreneurship educator: An exploration of the content challenge. *Entrepreneurship & Regional Development, 32*(9–10), 657–676. https://doi.org/10.1080/089 85626.2020.1737416

Herrington, J., & Oliver, R. (2000). An instructional design framework for authentic learning environments. *ETR&D, 48,* 23–48. https://doi.org/10.1007/BF02319856

Ismail, A. B. T., Sawang, S., & Zolin, R. (2018). Entrepreneurship education pedagogy: Teacher-student-centred paradox. *Education and Training, 60*(2), 168–184. https://doi.org/10.1108/ET-07-2017-0106

Kolb, A., & Kolb, B. (2005). Learning styles and learning spaces: Enhancing experiential learning in higher education. *Academy of Management Learning and Education, 4*(2), 193–212. https://doi.org/10.5465/amle.2005.17268566

Komarkova, I., Gagliardi, D., Conrads, J. & Collado, A. (2015). Entrepreneurship competence: An overview of existing concepts, policies and initiatives. In M. Bacigalupo, P. Kampylis, Y. Punie, & G. Van de Brande (2016), *EntreComp: The entrepreneurship competence framework.* Publication Office of the European Union. https://ec.europa.eu/jrc/en/publication/entrepreneurship-competence-overview-existing-concepts-policies-and-initiatives-final-report

Lackéus, M. (2015). *Entrepreneurship in education: What, when, why, how.* OECD. https://www.oecd.org/cfe/leed/BGP_Entrepreneurship-in-Education.pdf

Lilleväli, U., & Täks, M. (2017). Competence models as a tool for conceptualizing the systematic process of entrepreneurship competence development. *Education Research International, 2017*(5160863), 1–16. https://doi.org/10.1155/2017/5160863

Magolda, M. B., & Taylor, K. B. (2015). *Developing self-authorship in college to navigate emerging adulthood.* Wiley Online.

Mamede, S., & Schmidt, H. G. (2004). The structure of reflective practice in medicine. *Medical Education, 38*(12), 1302–1308. https://doi.org/10.1111/j.1365-2929.2004.01917.x

Man, T. W. Y. (2001). *Entrepreneurial competencies and the performance of small and medium enterprises in the Hong Kong services sector.* Hong Kong Polytechnic University.

Man, T. W. Y., Lau, T., & Chan, K. F. (2002). The competitiveness of small and medium enterprises: A conceptualization with focus on entrepreneurial competencies. *Journal of Business Venturing, 17*(2), 123–142. https://doi.org/10.1016/S0883-9026(00)00058-6

McGee, J. E., Peterson, M., Mueller, S. L., & Sequeira, J. M. (2009). Entrepreneurial self-efficacy: Refining the measure. *Entrepreneurship Theory and Practice, 33*(4), 965–988. https://doi.org/10.1111%2Fj.1540-6520.2009.00304.x

Miles, M. P., de Vries, H., Harrison, G., Bliemel, M., de Klerk, S., & Kasouf, C. J. (2017). Accelerators as authentic training experiences for nascent entrepreneurs, *Education + Training, 59*(7/8), 811–824. https://doi.org/10.1108/ET-01-2017-0007

Mitchelmore, S., & Rowley, J. (2013). Entrepreneurial competencies of women entrepreneurs pursuing business growth. *Journal of Small Business and Enterprise Development, 20*(1), 125–142. https://doi.org/10.1108/14626001311298448

Neck, H. M., & Corbett, A. C. (2018). The scholarship of teaching and learning entrepreneurship. *Entrepreneurship Education and Pedagogy, 1*(1), 8–41. https://doi.org/10.1177/2515127417737286

Neck, M. N., & Greene, P. G. (2011). Entrepreneurship education: Known worlds and new frontiers. *Journal of Small Business Management, 49*(1), 55–70. https://doi.org/10.1111/j.1540-627X.2010.00314.x

Neck, M. N., Greene, P. G., & Brush, C. (2014). *Teaching entrepreneurship: A practice based-approach*. Edward Elgar.

Obschonka, M., Hakkarainen, K., Lonka, K., & Salmela-Aro, K. (2017). Entrepreneurship as a twenty-first century skill: Entrepreneurial alertness and intention in the transition to adulthood. *Small Business Economics, 48*, 487–501. https://doi.org/10.1007/s11187-016-9798-6

Rasmussen, A., Moberg, K., & Revsbech, C. (2015). *A taxonomy of entrepreneurship education: Perspectives on goals, teaching and evaluation*. The Danish Foundation for Entrepreneurship.

RezaeiZadeh, M., Hogan, M., O'Reilly, J., Cunningham, J., & Murphy, E. (2017). Core entrepreneurial competencies and their interdependencies: Insights from a study of Irish and Iranian entrepreneurs, university students and academics. *International Entrepreneurship and Management Journal, 13*, 35–73. https://doi.org/10.1007/s11365-016-0390-y

Ries, E. (2012). *El Método Lean Startup*. Grupo Planeta.

Sánchez, J. C. (2011). University training for entrepreneurial competencies: Its impact on intention of venture creation. *International Entrepreneurship and Management Journal, 7*, 239–254. https://doi.org/10.1007/s11365-010-0156-x

Schallenkamp, K., & Smith, W. L. (2008). Entrepreneurial skills assessment: The perspective of SBDC directors. *International Journal of Management and Enterprise Development, 5*(1), 18–29.

Schön, D. (1983). *The reflective practitioner*. Basic Books.

Schön, D. (1987). *Education the reflective practitioner*. Jossey-Bass.

Scott, J. M., Penaluna, A., and Thompson, J. L. (2016). A critical perspective on learning outcomes and the effectiveness of experiential approaches in entrepreneurship education: Do we innovate or implement? *Education + Training, 58* (1), 82–93. https://doi.org/10.1108/ET-06-2014-0063

Swanson, J. A. (2016). Trends in literature about emerging adulthood: Review of empirical studies. *Emerging Adulthood, 4*(6), 391–402. https://doi.org/10.1177/2167696816630468

Swayne, N., Selznick, B., McCarthy, S., & Fisher, K. A. (2019). Uncoupling innovation and entrepreneurship to improve undergraduate education. *Journal of Small Business and Enterprise Development, 26*(6/7), 783–796. https://doi.org/10.1108/JSBED-04-2019-0122

Tittel, A., & Terzidis, O. (2020). Entrepreneurial competences revised: Developing a consolidated and categorized list of entrepreneurial competences. *Entrepreneurship Education, 3,* 1–35. https://doi.org/10.1007/s41959-019-00021-4

Van Praag, M. (2003). Business survival and success of young small business owners. *Small Business Economics, 21,* 1–17. https://doi.org/10.1023/A:1024453200297

Von Hippel, E. (2005). *Democratizing innovation.* MIT Press.

Weinert, F. (2001). Competencies and key competencies: Educational perspective. In N. J. Smelser & P. B. Baltes (Eds.), *International encyclopedia of the social and behavioural sciences* (Vol. 4, pp. 2433–2436). Elsevier.

Impacting the Mindset of the Undergraduate

What Do We Talk About When We Talk About Entrepreneurial Mindset Training?

Lucrezia Casulli

1 Introduction

Entrepreneurial mindset is much talked about by business owners, policy-makers and entrepreneurship educators alike. But what are we referring to when we talk about entrepreneurial mindset (EM)? What entrepreneurial mindset training is relevant but missing in Undergraduate Entrepreneurial Education? How can we extend entrepreneurial mindset training?

In this chapter, I offer a critically discursive answer to these questions followed by setting-out a pedagogical approach to entrepreneurial mindset training.

I argue that extant definitions of entrepreneurial mindset as applied to entrepreneurial education are too narrowly defined, focusing primarily on venture idea generation and early-stage venturing. I propose moving to an understanding of mindset that aligns with extant scholarly appreciation

---

L. Casulli (✉)
Hunter Centre for Entrepreneurship, University of Strathclyde Business School, Glasgow, Scotland, UK
e-mail: Lucrezia.Casulli@strath.ac.uk

© The Author(s), under exclusive license to Springer Nature Switzerland AG 2022
G. J. Larios-Hernandez et al. (eds.), *Theorising Undergraduate Entrepreneurship Education*,
https://doi.org/10.1007/978-3-030-87865-8_8

of entrepreneurship as a journey requiring sustained effort over time and in the face of ups and downs (e.g. McMullen & Dimov, 2013).

I propose that such an approach to EM training is important in Undergraduate Entrepreneurial Education because students may not necessarily emerge from secondary education with the cognitive skills to sustain their entrepreneurial efforts over time and in the face of adversity as well as successes.

Following this, I suggest that EM training should prepare students for grappling with uncertainty and ambiguity, and associated setbacks, mistakes and failures (Peschl et al., 2021). Whilst the latter require the development of *individual level* mindsets, *interpersonal level* mindsets such as empathy and open mindedness are also key to persuade investors, understand customers and balance one's own visions with feedback from the environment.

2 To *What* Are We Referring When We Talk About Entrepreneurial Mindset (EM)?

Entrepreneurial mindset has become something of a buzzword in recent times, used by policymakers, business owners and researchers alike. The term "entrepreneurial mindset" has been used loosely to describe entrepreneurial intentions (Pfeifer et al., 2016), a set of attitudes and approaches to tackling entrepreneurial tasks (e.g. McGrath & MacMillan, 2000); as a set of specific skills such as the ability to spot opportunities and exploit them (McMullen & Kier, 2016); and the capacity to bear uncertainty (Ireland et al., 2003).

In an attempt to unravel the different and often vague uses of the word *entrepreneurial mindset*, Kuratko et al. (2020) identify three overarching meanings for the use of entrepreneurial mindset in the literature: the entrepreneurial thinking/cognition aspect, the entrepreneurial behaviour aspect (behaviours conducive to entrepreneurship) and the entrepreneurial emotion aspect (what entrepreneurs feel).

In this chapter, I seek to position the notion of entrepreneurial mindset firmly in the cognitive sphere and as an antecedent to behaviour (e.g. Krueger & Carsrud, 1993). The reader may find that the emotional component of mindset is not addressed directly in the chapter. This is because, whilst our thinking cannot easily be decoupled from emotions (i.e. we are more likely to have negative thoughts when we are sad and vice versa), the focus of the chapter is on training students to engage their "rational" brain, whilst acknowledging the role of their emotional (or less "rational") brain.

Entrepreneurial mindset is therefore treated here as a cognitive phenomenon (how someone thinks) which in turn influences the behavioural phenomenon (what someone does). Cognitive-behavioural models in entrepreneurship, such as the theory of planned behaviour (Krueger & Carsrud, 1993), suggest that behaviours can be explained by underlying cognitions (either conscious or unconscious). Conversely, a shift in behaviour is harder to achieve without a change in the cognitive pathways that underpin action (Bogdan et al., 2004).

Recently, early evidence has suggested that cognitive competences development in entrepreneurship students result in shifting behaviours (Burnett et al., 2020). Whilst the application of these interventions may be new in the setting of higher education and entrepreneurship, cognitive intervention has successfully demonstrated shifts in the behaviours of school pupils for the past fifteen years (Savvides & Bond, 2021). By implication, if we are seeking to foster behaviours conducive to entrepreneurial activity, we may start by developing the cognitive competencies that underpin those behaviours. This leads to the questions of what a cognitive lens to entrepreneurial mindset may be.

Extant definitions of entrepreneurial mindset have mixed cognition with the related but distinct area of psychological traits (e.g. Naumann, 2017). Thus, it is important to keep in mind that cognition is distinct from personality constructs such as traits (Burnett et al., 2020). Cognition is focused on thinking processes (assessments, judgements, decisions, coding and decoding of information) rather than on fixed personality traits (e.g. *the big five*—Burnett et al., 2020). The fundamental distinction between cognition and traits is that the former can be developed through intervention, whereas the latter tend to be much more stable throughout a person's adult life (Conley, 1985; Roberts & DelVecchio, 2000).

In this sense, a cognitive lens to entrepreneurial mindset more usefully aligns with the notion of entrepreneurship as something that can be taught, rather than an innate skill. It also aligns with research concluding that entrepreneurs cannot be defined by a set of distinctive characteristics that sets them apart from non-entrepreneurs (Gartner, 1988; Greenberger & Sexton, 1988; Ramoglou et al., 2020). Rather, extant approaches suggest that it is *how entrepreneurs think* that matters (Mitchell et al., 2002), thus giving rise to the cognitive lens to entrepreneurship.

140   L. CASULLI

The cognitive lens in entrepreneurship has shifted the focus from *who an entrepreneur is* to *how an entrepreneur thinks* (e.g. Baron, 2004; Mitchell et al., 2007). This lens has produced a significant and robust body of literature on the cognitive perspective to entrepreneurial mindset (Shepherd & Patzelt, 2018). Thus far, the focus of this work has been on how entrepreneurs think differently than other people. To make this more relevant and applicable to entrepreneurial education, I suggest that we flip this notion on its head and focus on what individuals (including students) can do to think in ways that are conducive to entrepreneurial, value-adding behaviour.

In the light of the above and in line with the focus of this chapter on undergraduate entrepreneurial education, I define **entrepreneurial mindset training** as:

Cognitive Competence Development Which Draws on Psychological Intervention and is Intended to Elicit Behaviours Conducive to Entrepreneurial Activity.

3   How Can Entrepreneurial Mindset Training Complement Existing Undergraduate Entrepreneurial Education?

The entrepreneurial education curriculum often includes classes and activities centring on venture idea generation and associated new venture modelling (e.g. Osterwalder & Pigneur, 2010). The creativity and idea generation component in particular is arguably a cognitive competence (Ward, 2004) and is essential in entrepreneurship education at all levels. However, the focus on creativity and venture ideation alone places a large emphasis on the early stage of the entrepreneurial process, neglecting the longer-term journey.

Increasingly, research has emphasised that it is not until individuals act on their ideas that they discover what their real options are (McMullen & Dimov, 2013; Sarasvathy, 2001). This literature places emphasis on entrepreneurship as practice and on entrepreneurial action rather than the idea. It suggests that viable entrepreneurial ventures are ultimately a function of engaging with others and the environment over time. This requires individuals to grapple with a journey laden with uncertainty (McMullen & Dimov, 2013), as the person has to deal with unexpected as well as with partially known scenarios.

Mindsets for grappling with uncertainty and ambiguity have long been a neglected component in undergraduate entrepreneurial education. More recently, some programmes are filling this gap (e.g. Arpiainen & Kurczewska, 2017; Peschl et al., 2021). However, the focus inherently remains on early-stage venturing, since start-ups emerging during undergraduate education can only be supervised for a few, initial years whilst they are in university incubators.

The capacity to grapple with uncertainty is likely to be needed particularly by undergraduate students coming from schooling systems constrained by sets of rules and procedures for measuring attainment (Dehler & Welsh, 2014). These rules apply equally to the teachers in these systems, who are incentivised to "coach" students on passing assessments. Consequently, students learn there are set parameters for performing well in an educational setting. They also learn that there is an established set of criteria against which they will be evaluated. This is possible in educational settings because both the means and the ends for evaluating students are knowable and known upfront. Whilst setting evaluation criteria is a fair way to measure attainment in the schooling system, this may create a way of thinking that is not geared up to cognise under conditions of uncertainty, where both the means and the ends cannot be fully known upfront, as in the entrepreneurial process (Packard et al., 2017). Consequently, students often struggle with uncertainty and ambiguity. They may look to identify the "right way" or the established protocol, both of which run counter to the unchartered territory that truly innovative ventures are required to travel.

On a related but distinct note from the above, university training programmes have traditionally focused on positive images of entrepreneurship by proposing aspirational models of entrepreneurs and entrepreneurial ventures (e.g. Warren, 2005). These individuals seem to never doubt themselves nor carry fear, which contradicts what research on entrepreneurial fear of failure has shown (Cacciotti et al., 2016). There seems to be a disconnect between the models we present in the classrooms and the experiences of struggle of the majority of entrepreneurial journeys (McMullen & Dimov, 2013). Whilst it is important to inspire students through models of ultimate success, we should also prepare them with a realistic expectation of the "downs" of the entrepreneurial process associated with disappointments, false starts and returns to the drawing board. They should develop a critical appreciation of the doubts and fears that more often than not characterise the entrepreneurial process, even for those who eventually succeed (Minniti & Bygrave, 2001). For undergraduate entrepreneurial education, this means that student mindset training should include training on how to deal with setbacks, mistakes and failures in the entrepreneurial process (Funken et al., 2020). This will be particularly important for students coming from schooling systems where a failure is considered final rather than from schooling systems promoting a mindset that sees failure as a learning opportunity (Glerum et al., 2020). In entrepreneurship, setbacks and failures are not necessarily final. In fact, they are commonplace enough that they should be expected and students should be trained to embrace them and learn from them (e.g. Cope, 2011).

Lastly, entrepreneurial mindset training should seek to build student cognitive competencies on self-reflection. Undergraduate students may not necessarily be trained in self-reflection. School curricula globally have traditionally tended to place stronger emphasis on hard skills, such as maths, literacy or even physical education and arts. Less widespread in curricula are reflective-based competencies such as self-awareness and self-reflection. Yet, research has increasingly shown that reflectiveness and self-awareness empower individuals to harness their strengths and become cognisant of their weaknesses, ultimately leading to personal and professional success (Gottfredson, 2020).

Self-awareness is a highly desirable soft skill for undergraduate students, as it enables them to become aware of their existing thinking patters (i.e. metacognition) and the extent to which those may promote or hinder their entrepreneurial mindset and associated behaviour (Ustav & Venesaar, 2018).

The self-reflective, inside-out pedagogical approach advocated in this chapter represents a clear departure from extant approaches to teaching mindset through the medium of student entrepreneurial experiences (e.g. Arpiainen & Kurczewska, 2017; Peschl et al., 2021). The latter activities involve creativity for problem solving and opportunity identification, framing solutions and business modelling, pitching to potential stakeholders, simulated ambiguity in the entrepreneurial endeavour, etc. (Peschl et al., 2021). Whilst those approaches are useful to engage in real-life issues as they manifest in the entrepreneurial context, they may have limited external validity for students. That is, students are unlikely to experience the same thoughts and the full range and intensity of emotions that they would in a real-business situation with the associated high stakes attached (e.g. failings with real cognitive and affective consequences rather than projects intended to gain class credits). Put differently, it is not always possible to replicate the full cognitive and affective impact of the entrepreneurial experience through entrepreneurial activities in the higher education settings.

To complement these limitations of entrepreneurial projects, the pedagogical approach proposed here is focused on reflections on students' lived experiences. Those lived experiences should be of situations requiring acting under conditions of ambiguity and facing adversity, regardless of them taking place in an entrepreneurial setting or other. The core criterion is that those experiences should be impactful enough in the person's life to be salient and vivid in their psyche (e.g. Cope & Watts, 2000). In turn, reflecting on those experiences though developing self-awareness allows for self-development (e.g. MacKay et al., 2020).

In summary, I propose that the **content** of Entrepreneurial Mindset Education should complement training on creativity and early venturing with the cognitive skills required to engage effectively with the entrepreneurial journey over time and through ups and downs.

In terms of **approach** to Entrepreneurial Mindset Education, I propose a reflective practice approach to the cognitive competencies development of students, focused on metacognition and self-awareness development. This approach focuses on the student's reflection and appraisal of impactful life experiences and the mindsets emerging from such experiences. Awareness development is the starting point for cognitive competence development. This reflective approach is intended to complement, not replace, extant business venturing experience approaches to developing an entrepreneurial mindset.

In the remainder of this chapter, I propose an extension of the syllabus for entrepreneurial mindset training that builds on the complementary components to existing syllabi in undergraduate entrepreneurial education programmes and I offer suggestions for pedagogical tools that draw on a self-reflective approach (e.g. MacKay et al, 2020).

4 How Can We Extend Entrepreneurial Mindset Training?

The conclusion from the discussion above is that entrepreneurial mindset training should aim to build cognitive (as well as affective) competencies for dealing with the venturing journey in its entirety, beyond the initial idea and beyond the aspirational images of entrepreneurial success.

It was mentioned earlier in the chapter that entrepreneurs face uncertainty, ambiguity and risk throughout the journey and that they need to develop cognitive competencies enabling them to grapple with such uncertainty. This begs the question: *what mindsets are conducive to grappling with uncertainty?*

I suggest that mindsets conductive to grappling with uncertainty and ambiguity can be categorised into *personal level mindsets* and *interpersonal level mindsets* (Fig. 1).

Personal level mindsets may be developed to grapple with mistakes and setbacks. Setbacks are difficult to avoid during the entrepreneurial process because the behavioural path taken in the pursuit of novel ideas is an unchartered one that is often navigated through trial and error (Lindholm-Dahlstrand et al., 2019). In turn, responses to mistakes and setbacks require the development of different mindsets, depending on whether the *errors are clearly discernible because the causes are known* or whether the *causes of the setbacks are unclear and subject to individual interpretation*.

Interpersonal level mindsets may be developed to effectively engage with other stakeholders in the entrepreneurial process. Those may include fellow founding team members, employees, prospective customers or investors. For the sake of parsimony, I propose that there are two broad mindsets to be developed at an interpersonal level. The first is

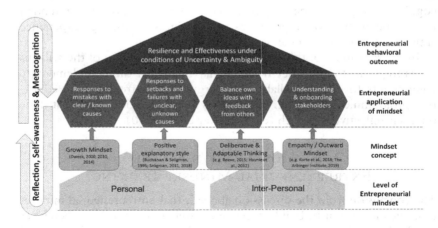

Fig. 1 Mindsets and applications underpinning entrepreneurial behaviour

a deliberative mindset needed to balance one's own vision and ideas with information (e.g. feedback) from others and from the environment. In such circumstances, entrepreneurs need to strike a balance between persevering with their own ideas and be open to feedback from others, which may run counter to the entrepreneur's thoughts (Holland & Shepherd, 2013). The second is an *Empathetic* (or *Outward) Mindset*, which is needed to build teams, on-board investors and serve prospective customers.

5 Individual Level Mindsets to Grapple with Mistakes, Setbacks and Failures

The entrepreneurial literature suggests that it is desirable for entrepreneurs to engage with mistakes and failures and learn from them (Cope, 2005, 2011). Engaging with and learning from mistakes is, in itself, a behaviour that stems from a particular mindset. Research in the area of competence motivation and self-theories (Dweck, 2000; Elliot & Dweck, 2013) has shown that those who believe that they can improve on their abilities through effort are more likely to learn from mistakes, whereas those who believe that their abilities are fixed are unlikely to engage and learn from mistakes.

The work of Carol Dweck has usefully highlighted that many students come to believe that they must be "talented" and that, if they have to try hard, they are probably not talented enough or smart enough (Dweck, 2010). Thus, when students join undergraduate degree programmes, they may already come with self-theories about their stance in relation to prospective academic achievements. By addressing this *fixed mindset* early on in undergraduate entrepreneurial education, students are more likely to develop a *growth mindset*. The latter encourages students to engage with their own mistakes as opportunities for growth and improvement and is conducive to resilience, which is a desirable behaviour at all stages of the entrepreneurial process (Burnett et al., 2020).

Burnett and colleagues propose an entrepreneurial growth mindset intervention through an adaptation of the assessment tool developed by Carol Dweck (Burnett et al., 2020). This tool presents students with multiple choice questions intended to ascertain the degree to which they exhibit a fixed or growth mindset in relation to entrepreneurship. Because this intervention starts with the student's own self-assessment, it aligns with the inside-out, reflective approach argued for earlier in the chapter.

A further extension to this intervention which has proven effective in my entrepreneurial mindset teaching is to combine self-assessment with journaling. Following Dweck's self-assessment, students are encouraged to keep a journal of their behavioural responses to everyday setbacks and mistakes and are invited to analyse those along the fixed-growth mindset continuum to identify the self-theories at the core of such behaviours. In a further reflection exercise, they are invited to also identify the root causes of their growth or fixed mindset by recollecting critical experiences that have shaped their core beliefs to date. Finally, students are also invited to consider how they experience their mindset as they interact with others.

Through these exercises, students become aware of their thinking surrounding mistakes and how that thinking, in turn, affects behaviour. They discover, for example, that when they feel uncomfortable with mistakes, they are more likely to hide them, run away from them and stop trying. They come to reflect that their self-worth is contingent on being "perfect" and not making mistakes, often because of the implicit messages received through their upbringing. On the flipside, those who are comfortable with mistakes often attach their self-worth on constant improvement and are less concerned with what others think of their mistakes. Individuals who do not see mistakes as defining them are also much more tolerant of the mistakes of others, thus creating environments conducive to openness and learning (e.g. Dweck, 2014; Syed, 2015).

The thinking style discussed above focuses on facing mistakes, setbacks and failures for which the cause can be tracked down. That is, the source of the error can be identified and the error corrected. This is because most of the work on growth mindset has focused on disciplinary settings such as maths and sciences, in which there are often right and wrong solutions to problems. Namely, the ends are known (the right answer) and any deviation from the correct ends can be identified and the error attributed to the student. However, in entrepreneurial settings some setbacks may be the consequence of complex interactions and not have a clear root cause, leaving space for idiosyncratic sensemaking of the setback and failure (Cardon et al., 2011) or heuristic judgements. Other setbacks, problems or outright disasters may be beyond human control. The COVID-19 pandemic is such an example. In such cases, a thinking style conducive to resilient behaviour may not be developed solely through growth mindset intervention. Other interventions are needed to prepare students to grapple with setbacks for which the causes or outcomes are unknown or unknowable.

Scholars from the emerging field of positive psychology (Peterson & Steen, 2002) have suggested that a resilient behavioural response depends whether or not the person has an optimistic or a pessimistic explanatory style. Put simply, those who have a positive pattern of thinking are more likely to be resilient and those who have a pessimistic thinking pattern are less likely to exhibit resilient behaviour.

The notion of optimism is not new in entrepreneurship. Early academic literature listed optimism as a trait of the entrepreneur (e.g. Chell, 1986). Whilst there is some evidence of individual disposition for optimism in entrepreneurship (Crane & Crane, 2007), work stemming from Penn State University suggests that optimism as a thinking pattern is learnable and that this acquired optimistic thinking is the foundation of resilient behaviour (Gillham et al., 2013; Seligman, 2011). The work of Seligman and colleagues offers evidence that whether or not the person decides to bounce back depends on how they make sense of events which, in turn, informs what they may expect to happen in the future (Buchanan & Seligman, 1995). The framework for this explanatory style features three dimensions: *permanence*, *pervasiveness* and *personalisation* (Seligman, 2018).

> *Permanence* is the temporal dimension of a positive explanatory style. Those who master an optimistic explanatory style come to view the causes of bad events as temporary, whilst believe that causes of good events can be permanent.
> *Pervasiveness* is the spatial dimension of a positive explanatory style. Those who master an optimistic explanatory style come to view the causes of bad events as limited to a specific sphere of life, whilst they believe that the causes of good events can be universal.
> *Personalisation* is the personal responsibility dimension of an optimistic explanatory style, whereby bad events are attributed to external forces and good events to one's own doing.[1]

This approach promotes a shift in thinking by reframing how students explain setbacks in the absence of clear causation. The itemisation of this frameworks by the three constituent dimensions of optimistic thinking

---

[1] It is worth noting that Seligman does not mean to encourage externalisation of responsibility. Rather, studies show that individuals with a pessimistic explanatory style tent to err on the side of blaming themselves for bad events regardless of evidence.

allows for a detailed analysis of current explanatory style and for reframing such thinking. Similarly to growth mindset, intervention on explanatory style starts with a self-assessment test (in Seligman, 2018), through which students become aware of their (often unconscious) optimistic or pessimistic thinking patterns. Students are then encouraged to engage in journaling their thinking and expectations surrounding events that bear a direct impact on their professional lives. For example, during the COVID-19 pandemic, entrepreneurship students have been encouraged to reflect on how they expect events to unfold and the likely impact of those events on their business venturing plans post-graduation. The aim of the intervention is to develop self-awareness of the explanatory style currently in use and coach students on reframing their thinking as well as taking notice of the behavioural changes that may follow.

In summary, preparing students for grappling with mistakes and setbacks through a growth mindset (Dweck, 2000, 2010, 2014) is useful when the causes of those mistakes are clearly knowable and known. Conversely, preparing students for setbacks and failures in the entrepreneurial process through a positive explanatory style (Seligman, 2018) is useful when the courses of setbacks are unclear, complex or unknown (Fig. 1).

6 INTERPERSONAL LEVEL MINDSETS TO ENGAGE WITH STAKEHOLDERS IN THE ENTREPRENEURIAL PROCESS

Entrepreneurs have long been characterised in popular culture as lone heroes who feel strongly about their venturing ideas and don't stop in the face of any obstacle or criticism (Warren, 2005). Indeed, images of visionary entrepreneurs such as Jeff Bezos and Elon Musk continue to fuel the entrepreneurship theme on media entertainment, with students benchmarking their entrepreneurial potential against these hyper stylised models (Swail et al., 2014).

However, increasingly in the academic sphere there is a recognition that entrepreneurs do not and cannot accomplish venture goals single-handedly. Interaction with the environment is essential for entrepreneurs because it allows for the gathering of new resources and new ideas (Sarasvathy, 2001). Often, entrepreneurs work in teams coming from different backgrounds and with different knowledge basis and thinking styles. This calls for preparing entrepreneurship students to engage fruitfully with others in the environment in order to turn entrepreneurial ideas into sustainable ventures. For instance, rather than simply persevering with their own ideas regardless of setbacks, entrepreneurs are increasingly required to strike a balance between maintaining a vision and being open to input from others (e.g. information, opinions, feedback), which may run counter to the entrepreneur's own ideas (Holland & Shepherd, 2013). Entrepreneurship scholars put the ability to take environmental feedback on board at the very core of the definition of entrepreneurial resilience (Holland & Shepherd, 2013).

This calls for the development of an *Open (Deliberative) mindset,* which may be defined as *a thinking style that recognised the transient and incomplete nature of information held by the individual at any point in time, thus making them open to external inputs and to shifts in thinking* (the author, based on Reeve, 2014; Haynie et al., 2012).

Developing an open mindset not only requires the individual to be able to adapt their thinking as they integrate new information (Haynie et al., 2012), they must also believe that changing one's mind is not a sign of non-committal posture but a sign of intellectual humility (Spiegel, 2012). This runs against traditional academic research on entrepreneurial thinking and judgement, which often reports of overconfident entrepreneurs making swift judgements based on intuition (Mitchell et al., 2005) and heuristics (Busenitz & Barney, 1997). Whilst potentially useful for speeding-up decision processes and acting fast to capitalise on opportunities, this thinking style may also result in incomplete analysis and biased decisions.

Thus, entrepreneurial mindset training should convey that the image of the intuitive and overconfident entrepreneur needs to be tempered with the appreciation that there are likely to be blind spots in entrepreneurial thinking. Open mindset training may start with student self-reflections and self-appraisal on the following (the author, adapted from Gottfredson, 2020):

- How do we react when we have our ideas challenged? Are we open to it (open mindset) or do we get defensive (closed mindset)?
- What motivates us most: the pursuit of the truth (open mindset) or having our current ideas confirmed (closed mindset)?
- Do we debate to learn (open mindset) or to prove our points (closed mindset)?
- Do we prefer interactions with those who challenge us (open mindset) or those who agree with us (closed mindset)?

- When interacting with others, do we ask more questions (open mindset) or we offer more statements (closed mindset)?

It is recognised that deliberative versus implemental mindset is a continuum along which each individual sits, rather than a binary measure. It is also recognised that our responses to the questions above may change depending on the momentary state of our mind. However, the point is that developing an awareness of when and why we adopt an open or closed mindset is a first important step in mindset shift.

A deliberative mindset alone may not suffice to fully and effectively engage with and gain feedback from the environment. Recently, scholars have emphasised the importance of being able develop empathy as a mindset in order to understand others in the entrepreneurial process (Korte et al., 2018; Packard & Burnham, 2021). This is particularly important when entrepreneurs have to anticipate the needs and wants of others through offerings that were not previously available (Packard & Burnham, 2021). Also, stakeholders may not volunteer their views, needs and wants to the entrepreneur in the form of codified, explicit information for consideration. Finally, feedback from customers, employees or boards of investors may be subtle and come in the form of behaviours to decipher. Empathy has been found to be beneficial to entrepreneurs as it allows them to put themselves in the shoes of customers, investors and employees, to understand what they may need and thus be best placed in engaging productively with their input (Korte et al., 2018). More broadly, the ability to consider the needs and wants of others has been put forward as a win–win approach in today's business world (The Arbinger Institute, 2019).

Whilst empathy has both cognitive and affective components (Korte et al., 2018), it has been suggested that empathy in entrepreneurship should be developed as a cognitive competence rather than an affective one. Specifically, Packard and Burnham (2021) propose a model of vicarious mental simulation whereby the individual uses their deliberate rational thinking, along with information, in order to understand what others think and feel.

Developing empathy in undergraduate students has been identified as a priority, because there is evidence to suggest that students do not believe that empathy is a valuable skill in today's business environment. This is because the aggressive and Darwinian portrayal of business in the twentieth century has created the impression that in order to succeed in business, one must adopt a zero-sum attitude (Holt & Marques, 2012).

Thus, I propose that the first step in developing empathy in undergraduate entrepreneurship students should be to demonstrate the power of empathy as a win–win, non-zero-sum approach to doing business (The Arbinger Institute, 2019).

Self-assessment may follow (Zhou et al., 2003), in order for the student to appraise their empathy levels before intervention. The act of intervention itself has proven effective in improving student empathy both emotionally and cognitively (Stehlíková & Valihorová, 2016) using established instruments by Davis (2018).

To summarise, in order for students to engage effectively in the entrepreneurial process, they need to develop the ability to be open and receptive to inputs from the environment and respond accordingly. Preparing students for being open to inputs through a deliberative and adaptive thinking style (e.g. Haynie et al., 2012; Reeve, 2014) is useful when they need to balance their own ideas with ideas, feedback and information from others and the environment. On the other hand, developing empathy and an Outward Mindset (The Arbinger Institute, 2019) is useful to understand and respond to the often unspoken and uncodified needs of stakeholders at different points of the entrepreneurial process (e.g. Korte et al., 2018; Packard & Burnham, 2021; Fig. 1).

To conclude, this chapter has highlighted the need to extend undergraduate entrepreneurship education to include cognitive competencies training that enables students to navigate the uncertain entrepreneurial process beyond the early ideation phase. The author has proposed drawing on entrepreneurial cognition literature as well as self-theories psychology and positive psychology in order to design a novel entrepreneurial mindset syllabus.

It has been argued that entrepreneurial mindset training should develop both personal and interpersonal level entrepreneurship-related mindsets in undergraduate students. The development of these mindsets is intended for grappling effectively with situations often encountered in the post-ideation stage of business venturing and for which students emerging from secondary education may not yet be equipped.

At the *individual level*, students need to be coached on confronting mistakes and learning from them whenever possible, as those are sometimes unavoidable in the entrepreneurial process. Also, given that the root cause of setbacks and adverse events in entrepreneurship cannot always be known, it has been proposed that it is important to coach students on developing a positive explanatory style. This is particularly important to sustain students' resilience even when they are facing misfortunes through no fault of their own.

Interpersonally, it has been highlighted that entrepreneurship undergraduate students should be fostered in developing empathy in order to be receptive to the needs and wants of stakeholders in the entrepreneurial process, such as prospective customers, investors and employees. Another interpersonal component of entrepreneurial mindset highlighted in the chapter is that of open mindedness, modelled on the notion of deliberative reasoning. That is, students should be encouraged to constantly seek input from others and look for what they do not yet know rather than focus on what they already know. This will help them avoid overconfidence in their existing knowledge and views, given that overconfidence can be detrimental when making judgements under uncertainty in the entrepreneurial process. Remaining actively open to inputs from others and from the environment is likely to promote robust testing of ideas and prototypes so as to avoid poor judgement and costly mistakes.

The ultimate goal of developing those mindsets, both personal and interpersonal, is to behave in ways that are conducive to entrepreneurial resilience and effectiveness long after the students have left higher education.

The proposed conceptual model of entrepreneurial mindset training will require development and refinement over time. In this sense, the model is put forward more as a starting point for consideration rather than as a tool ready for use. Future work should consider context-specific applications of the notions presented here, including (but not limited to) cultural and institutional contexts. The author also invites entrepreneurship educators worldwide to critique and extend the notions presented in this chapter, so that we can collectively move towards a cognitive competence development approach to entrepreneurial mindset.

REFERENCES

Arpiainen, R. L., & Kurczewska, A. (2017). Learning risk-taking and coping with uncertainty through experiential, team-based entrepreneurship education. *Industry and Higher Education, 31*(3), 143–155.

Baron, R. A. (2004). The cognitive perspective: A valuable tool for answering entrepreneurship's basic "why" questions. *Journal of Business Venturing, 19*(2), 221–239.

Bogdan, D., Christian, G., Volker, B., Gerhard, S., Ulrich, B., & Arne, M. (2004). Neuroplasticity: Changes in grey matter induced by training. *Nature, 427*(6972), 311–312.

Buchanan, G. M., & Seligman, M. E. (1995). Afterword: The future of the field. *Explanatory style*, 247–252.

Burnette, J. L., Pollack, J. M., Forsyth, R. B., Hoyt, C. L., Babij, A. D., Thomas, F. N., & Coy, A. E. (2020). A growth mindset intervention: Enhancing students' entrepreneurial self-efficacy and career development. *Entrepreneurship Theory and Practice, 44*(5), 878–908.

Busenitz, L. W., & Barney, J. B. (1997). Differences between entrepreneurs and managers in large organizations: Biases and heuristics in strategic decision-making. *Journal of Business Venturing, 12*(1), 9–30.

Cacciotti, G., Hayton, J. C., Mitchell, J. R., & Giazitzoglu, A. (2016). A reconceptualization of fear of failure in entrepreneurship. *Journal of Business Venturing, 31*(3), 302–325.

Cardon, M. S., Stevens, C. E., & Potter, D. R. (2011). Misfortunes or mistakes? Cultural sensemaking of entrepreneurial failure. *Journal of Business Venturing, 26*(1), 79–92.

Chell, E. (1986). The entrepreneurial personality: A review and some theoretical developments. *The Survival of the Small Firm, 1*, 102–119.

Conley, J. J. (1985). Longitudinal stability of personality traits: A multi-trait–multimethod multioccasion analysis. *Journal of Personality and Social Psychology, 49*(5), 1266.

Cope, J. (2005). Toward a dynamic learning perspective of entrepreneurship. *Entrepreneurship Theory and Practice, 29*(4), 373–397.

Cope, J. (2011). Entrepreneurial learning from failure: An interpretative phenomenological analysis. *Journal of Business Venturing, 26*(6), 604–623.

Cope, J., & Watts, G. (2000). Learning by doing—An exploration of experience, critical incidents and reflection in entrepreneurial learning. *International Journal of Entrepreneurial Behavior & Research*.

Crane, F. G., & Crane, E. C. (2007). Dispositional optimism and entrepreneurial success. *The Psychologist-Manager Journal, 10*(1), 13–25.

Davis, M. H. (2018). *Empathy: A social psychological approach*. Routledge.

Dehler, G. E., & Welsh, M. A. (2014). Against spoon-feeding. For learning. Reflections on students' claims to knowledge. *Journal of Management Education, 38*(6), 875–893.

Dweck, C. S. (2000). *Self-theories: Their role in motivation, personality, and development* (Essays in social psychology). Psychology Press.

Dweck, C. S. (2010). Even geniuses work hard. *Educational Leadership, 68*(1), 16–20.

Dweck, C. S. (2014). Talent: How companies can profit from a "growth mindset." *Harvard Business Review, 92*(11), 7.

Elliot, A. J., & Dweck, C. S. (Eds.). (2013). *Handbook of competence and motivation*. Guilford Publications.

Funken, R., Gielnik, M. M., & Foo, M.-D. (2020). How can problems be turned into something good? The role of entrepreneurial learning and error mastery orientation. *Entrepreneurship Theory and Practice, 44*(2), 315–338.

Gartner, W. B. (1988). "Who is an entrepreneur?" is the wrong question. *American Journal of Small Business, 12*(4), 11–32.

Gilham, J. E., Abenavoli, R. M., Brunwasser, S. M., Linkins, M., Reivich, K. J., & Seligman, M. E. P. (2013). Resilience education. In I. Boniwell, S. A. David, & A. C. Ayers (Eds.), *Oxford handbook of happiness*. Oxford University Press.

Glerum, J., Loyens, S. M. M, & Rikers, R. M. J. P. (2020). Mind your mindset. An empirical study of mindset in secondary vocational education and training. *Educational Studies, 46*(3), 273–281.

Gottfredson, R. (2020). *Success mindsets: Your keys to unlocking greater success in your life, work, & leadership*. Morgan James Publishing.

Greenberger, D. B., & Sexton, D. L. (1988). An interactive model of new venture creation. *Journal of Small Business Management, 26*(3), 1–7.

Haynie, J. M., Shepherd, D. A., & Patzelt, H. (2012). Cognitive adaptability and an entrepreneurial task: The role of metacognitive ability and feedback. *Entrepreneurship Theory and Practice, 36*(2), 237–265.

Holland, D. V., & Shepherd, D. A. (2013). Deciding to persist: Adversity, values, and entrepreneurs' decision policies. *Entrepreneurship Theory and Practice, 37*(2), 331–358.

Holt, S., & Marques, J. (2012). Empathy in leadership: Appropriate or misplaced? An empirical study on a topic that is asking for attention. *Journal of Business Ethics, 105*(1), 95–105.

Ireland, R. D., Hitt, M. A., & Sirmon, D. G. (2003). A model of strategic entrepreneurship: The construct and its dimensions. *Journal of Management, 29*(6), 963–989.

Korte, R., Smith, K. A., & Li, C. Q. (2018). The role of empathy in entrepreneurship: A core competency of the entrepreneurial mindset. *Advances in Engineering Education, 7*(1), n1.

Krueger, N. F., & Carsrud, A. L. (1993). Entrepreneurial intentions: Applying the theory of planned behaviour. *Entrepreneurship & Regional Development, 5*(4), 315–330.

Kuratko, D. F., Fisher, G., & Audretsch, D. B. (2020). Unraveling the entrepreneurial mindset. *Small Business Economics*, 1–11.

Lindholm-Dahlstrand, Å., Andersson, M., & Carlsson, B. (2019). Entrepreneurial experimentation: A key function in systems of innovation. *Small Business Economics, 53*(3), 591–610.

MacKay, B., Arevuo, M., Meadows, M., & Mackay, D. (2020). *Strategy: Theory, practice.* Oxford University Press.

McGrath, R. G., & MacMillan, I. C. (2000). *The entrepreneurial mindset: Strategies for continuously creating opportunity in an age of uncertainty* (Vol. 284). Harvard Business Press.

McMullen, J. S., & Dimov, D. (2013). Time and the entrepreneurial journey: The problems and promise of studying entrepreneurship as a process. *Journal of Management Studies, 50*(8), 1481–1512.

McMullen, J. S., & Kier, A. S. (2016). Trapped by the entrepreneurial mindset: Opportunity seeking and escalation of commitment in the Mount Everest disaster. *Journal of Business Venturing, 31*(6), 663–686.

Minniti, M., & Bygrave, W. (2001). A dynamic model of entrepreneurial learning. *Entrepreneurship Theory and Practice, 25*(3), 5–16.

Mitchell, J. R., Friga, P. N., & Mitchell, R. K. (2005). Untangling the intuition mess: Intuition as a construct in entrepreneurship research. *Entrepreneurship Theory and Practice, 29*(6), 653–679.

Mitchell, R. K., Busenitz, L. W., Bird, B., Marie Gaglio, C., McMullen, J. S., Morse, E. A., & Smith, J. B. (2007). The central question in entrepreneurial cognition research 2007. *Entrepreneurship Theory and Practice, 31*(1), 1–27.

Mitchell, R. K., Busenitz, L. W., Lant, T., McDougall, P. P., Morse, E. A., & Smith, J. B. (2002). Toward a theory of entrepreneurial cognition: Rethinking the people side of entrepreneurship research. *Entrepreneurship Theory and Practice, 27*(2), 93–104.

Naumann, C. (2017). Entrepreneurial mindset: A synthetic literature review. *Entrepreneurial Business and Economics Review, 5*(3), 149–172.

Osterwalder, A., & Pigneur, Y. (2010). Business model canvas. *Self-published. Last.*

Packard, M. D., & Burnham, T. A. (2021). Do we understand each other? Toward a simulated empathy theory for entrepreneurship. *Journal of Business Venturing, 36*(1).

Packard, M. D., Clark, B. B., & Klein, P. G. (2017). Uncertainty types and transitions in the entrepreneurial process. *Organization Science (Providence, R.I.), 28*(5), 840–856.

Peschl, H., Deng, C., & Larson, N. (2021). Entrepreneurial thinking: A signature pedagogy for an uncertain 21st century. *The International Journal of Management Education, 19*(1), 100427.

Peterson, C., & Steen, T. A. (2002). Optimistic explanatory style. *Handbook of Positive Psychology,* 244–256.

Pfeifer, S., Šarlija, N., & Zekić Sušac, M. (2016). Shaping the entrepreneurial mindset: Entrepreneurial intentions of business students in Croatia. *Journal of Small Business Management, 54*(1), 102–117.

156 L. CASULLI

Ramoglou, S., Gartner, W. B., & Tsang, E. W. (2020). "Who is an entrepreneur?" is (still) the wrong question. *Journal of Business Venturing Insights*, *13*, e00168.

Reeve, J. (2014). *Understanding motivation and emotion*. Wiley.

Roberts, B. W., & DelVecchio, W. F. (2000). The rank-order consistency of personality traits from childhood to old age: A quantitative review of longitudinal studies. *Psychological Bulletin*, *126*(1), 3.

Sarasvathy, S. D. (2001). Causation and effectuation: Toward a theoretical shift from economic inevitability to entrepreneurial contingency. *Academy of Management Review*, *26*(2), 243–263.

Savvides, H., & Bond, C. (2021). How does growth mindset inform interventions in primary schools? A systematic literature review. *Educational Psychology in Practice*, 1–16.

Seligman, M. E. (2011). Building resilience. *Harvard Business Review*, *89*(4), 100–106.

Seligman, M. E. (2018). *Learned optimism: How to change your mind and your life*. Vintage.

Shepherd, D. A., & Patzelt, H. (2018). *Entrepreneurial cognition: Exploring the mindset of entrepreneurs*. Springer Nature.

Spiegel, J. S. (2012). Open-mindedness and intellectual humility. *Theory and Research in Education*, *10*(1), 27–38.

Stehlíková, J., & Valihorová, M. (2016). Possibilities of targeted development of empathy in teachers' undergraduate training. *The New Educational Review*, *45*(3), 186–198.

Swail, J., Down, S., & Kautonen, T. (2014). Examining the effect of 'entretainment' as a cultural influence on entrepreneurial intentions. *International Small Business Journal*, *32*(8), 859–875.

Syed, M. (2015). *Black box thinking: The surprising truth about success*. Hachette UK.

The Arbinger Institute. (2019). *The outward mindset: How to change lives and transform organizations* (2nd ed.). Berrett-Koehler Publishers.

Ustav, S., & Venesaar, U. (2018). Bridging metacompetencies and entrepreneurship education. *Education & Training (london)*, *60*(7/8), 674–695.

Ward, T. B. (2004). Cognition, creativity, and entrepreneurship. *Journal of Business Venturing*, *19*(2), 173–188.

Warren, L. (2005). Images of entrepreneurship: Still searching for the hero? *The International Journal of Entrepreneurship and Innovation*, *6*(4), 221–229.

Zhou, Q., Valiente, C., & Eisenberg, N. (2003). Empathy and its measurement. In *Positive psychological assessment: A handbook of models and measures*. (pp. 269–284). American Psychological Association.

Supporting Students and Society: Underpinning Entrepreneurship Education with a Humanistic Philosophy

Robin Bell

1 THE ROLE OF PHILOSOPHY IN EDUCATION

There has been a rapid rise in entrepreneurship education programs' availability in the last two decades (Fayolle, 2013; Neck & Greene, 2011). To support effective entrepreneurship education, entrepreneurship teaching should be based on solid foundations, which are both theoretically and methodologically robust (Pittaway & Cope, 2007). However, it has been suggested that entrepreneurship educators are often not supported in developing their pedagogic practices (Lackéus et al., 2016; Neck & Corbett, 2018), despite previous research identifying that the pedagogical understanding and competence of educators influence the quality of teaching and learning in higher education (HE) (Kaynardağ, 2019). Many academics and higher education institutions (HEIs) still believe teaching undergraduates requires no formal educational training (Stewart, 2014). This has left some entrepreneurship educators having

R. Bell (✉)
Worcester Business School, University of Worcester, Worcester, UK
e-mail: r.bell@worc.ac.uk

© The Author(s), under exclusive license to Springer Nature Switzerland AG 2022
G. J. Larios-Hernandez et al. (eds.), *Theorising Undergraduate Entrepreneurship Education*,
https://doi.org/10.1007/978-3-030-87865-8_9

only received limited pedagogical training and support, and only a partial understanding of the educational theories and philosophies underpinning their practice (Bell, 2021). As entrepreneurship education is a discipline which is still developing and evolving, it has been suggested that the practice of entrepreneurship education has moved ahead of its scholarship (Morris & Liguori, 2016). Despite education scholarship and research having a long and established history, there remains a degree of separation between educational science literature and entrepreneurship education practice (Fayolle, 2013). Thus, the potential exists for educational science to be leveraged to inform entrepreneurship education practice.

It has been highlighted that educators bring their personal values and beliefs into the classroom, influencing what and how they teach (Peters, 1959; Zappe et al., 2013). Wraae and Walmsley (2020) emphasise that entrepreneurship educators can shape the entrepreneurship education landscape. One way of doing this is through the educational philosophy that the educator chooses to inform and underpin their teaching practice. The educational philosophy chosen shapes the educators' thinking, behaviour and action, based on a set of underpinning values and beliefs. It supports educators' understanding of what they are doing and for what purpose (Merriam, 1982). Whilst educators might not always be able to convey and verbalise their underpinning philosophy, they will have an underpinning philosophy directing and driving their practice (Darkenwald & Merriam, 1982), which will have implications on what they teach, how they teach it, how knowledge and experience are valued and what form of assessment will be adopted (Bell, 2021). Increased knowledge and comprehension of educational philosophies can help educators more effectively understand how and why they teach in a particular way (Hannon, 2006). For educators to maximise their teaching effectiveness, they should understand and grasp the philosophies and theories that underpin their practice (Bell & Bell, 2020), a circumstance that Fayolle et al. (2016) suggested is not always the case. However, it has been suggested that there is increasing awareness of the importance of educational theory underpinning entrepreneurial learning (Kakouris & Morselli, 2020). Bechard and Gregoire (2005) propose that for effective entrepreneurship education, educators need balance in both entrepreneurship and education principles and perspectives in their teaching methods.

Behaviourism and constructivism are commonly seen as opposing educational philosophies and are commonly used to underpin educational practice in HE (Bélanger, 2011). However, Jones (2019) suggests that there is no widely accepted concise philosophy of entrepreneurship education, and other scholars have suggested a range of philosophies and theories should be adopted to support successful entrepreneurship education (Bell & Bell, 2020; Ramsgaard, 2018; Robinson et al., 2016). This chapter explores and presents the case for a humanistic approach to be included within entrepreneurship education. The next section will briefly discuss the philosophies of behaviourism and constructivism and their key principles, before discussing the principles of humanism and the benefits it can provide to entrepreneurship education. The chapter will conclude by discussing how a humanism philosophy can be applied in the entrepreneurship education classroom.

2   BEHAVIOURISM AND CONSTRUCTIVISM

Behaviourism has often been coined as the philosophy which underpins traditional teaching, often in the form of lectures, where the students are passive receivers of knowledge. Within this paradigm, students are passive receivers in the didactic transmission of objectivist knowledge from the educator. From an objectivist standpoint, the knowledge taught and understood can be used and transferred into new situations. Within such a teaching approach, students bank knowledge presented to them by the educator (Freire, 2006). Such an approach can be devoid of context and offers only limited opportunity for students to apply their own context and experience to the learning. The educator delivers knowledge that they perceive as important for the learner to have, hoping that it will change their future behaviour. Therefore, the educator needs to manage, direct and predict students learning to ensure set objectives are achieved (Hannon, 2006). Behaviourism is commonly used to underpin entrepreneurship education, or at least elements of it, although its usefulness in isolation to prepare students for entrepreneurship is increasingly considered as ineffective (Gedeon, 2014). Whilst Wraae and Walmsley (2020) opined that there was widespread agreement amongst entrepreneurship educators that entrepreneurship education needs to be tied to practice, it has been highlighted that objectivist knowledge is still required to ensure students understand the course objectives (Béchard & Toulouse, 1998). It is essential for students to have a solid understanding of the basic theory and frameworks of entrepreneurship, to allow them to effectively learn from experience (Bell & Bell, 2020; Peltier & Scovotti, 2010).

It has been observed that entrepreneurship educators believe that it is important to teach students beyond just subject knowledge (Wraae & Walmsley, 2020). This is underpinned by an extensive body of research which has found experience to be valuable for developing students' entrepreneurial behaviours in a range of contexts. Such experiential approaches to learning can be underpinned by a constructivist educational philosophy, which posits knowledge lies in the individual and that learners should create their own meaning from knowledge in relation to their individual context and experience (Mueller & Anderson, 2014). Therefore, knowledge construction is an active and interpretive process, where meaning-making is dependent on past and present knowledge and experience (Merriam et al., 2007). Experiential learning methods have been proposed to be efficacious for entrepreneurship education as they support the development of entrepreneurial action by using situationally and context specific activities and experiences (Bell, 2015; Mueller & Anderson, 2014). As entrepreneurs face dynamic, ever-changing environments, experiential approaches help develop the skills entrepreneurs require in the fast-changing environments that entrepreneurs face (Balan & Metcalfe, 2012; Kyrö, 2015).

3 Humanism and Entrepreneurship Education

No consensus exists within the literature for a definition of humanistic education and what it entails, however, more consensus prevails as to what humanistic learning environments should focus on and include. Veugelers (2011) opines that a humanist educational approach should focus on the development of rationality, empowerment, autonomy, creativity, affections and a concern for humanity. Humanistic education should seek to develop the whole learner, including their intellectual, socioemotional and physical development (Aloni, 2002). Humanism places the learner's autonomy and dignity centrally within the learning process and therefore emphasise the learner's personal choice and commitment to their development through education (Billings & Halstead, 2019). Humanism resembles constructivism in that it focuses on active-learning and experience, which have been argued to be key to the development of entrepreneurs (Jones & Iredale, 2010). Both humanism and constructivism appreciate the subjectivity of knowledge and the need for it to be learnt in context, but humanism places greater emphasis on the development of the learner's integrative judgement and the acquiring of value-oriented skills. The tenets of humanism will now be considered, and an argument presented as to how they can be aligned to entrepreneurship education and the development of entrepreneurs and broader society.

A central tenet within humanism is compassion, which can be demonstrated through interaction with individuals and broader society. Increasingly, HEIs seek to positively influence the communities with which they engage and interact and seek to encourage and develop learners to act in a morally sustainable manner in their future graduate endeavours (Dierksmeier, 2020). The application of humanism to underpin entrepreneurship education teaching and learning can support the objectives of HEIs, by encouraging future entrepreneurs to think more holistically about their communities and stakeholders and the promotion of positive engagement and interactions with these groups. An increased focus in the entrepreneurship education classroom on the human side of economic agency and the creation of value through entrepreneurship could help frame entrepreneurship in a more sustainable and compassionate manner. Such an approach in the classroom supports the principle within humanism of promoting social development (Leach, 2018). There is increasing growth and recognition for the need for sustainable and humane entrepreneurship. It has been posited that humane entrepreneurship can drive sustainable wealth and job creation (Kim et al., 2018). Compassion is a value central to the concepts of humane entrepreneurship, social entrepreneurship and eco-preneurship, which are increasingly becoming prominent and important in society. Previous research has suggested that more socially focused entrepreneurs have different traits to traditional entrepreneurs (Smith et al., 2014) and thus entrepreneurship education would benefit from being tailored to support entrepreneurship education for social entrepreneurship. A humanistic approach and bringing compassion as a value into the entrepreneurship education classroom can help learners link the concepts to not only traditional entrepreneurial ventures, but to other more societal mission-focused ventures.

A critical movement is developing, which seeks to situate entrepreneurship education outside the neoliberal paradigm which is focused on the generation of profit (e.g., Berglund & Verduijn, 2018; Lackéus, 2017). The concept of entrepreneurship education being solely focused on profit

162   R. BELL

generation and maximisation does not always fit comfortably within HE and those educators who are commonly focused on social value and outcomes. This is particularly true in some contexts where a focus on venture creation and profit maximisation do not sit in harmony with educators and institutions' goals and objectives. Entrepreneurship education delivered by educators in other subject disciplines outside of business, in less capitalistic societies and schools, might be less comfortable promoting the neoliberal principles and profit maximisation commonly associated with entrepreneurship. The application of a humanistic philosophy to underpin and inform the delivery of entrepreneurship education in such contexts can provide a more relaxed and effective fit to the goals and objectives sought to be achieved through the teaching. Such an approach could help solve the bias within entrepreneurship education towards business activity rather than an educational pursuit for the learner, which has limited the applicability of entrepreneurship education to wider contexts (Ratten & Jones, 2020).

The increasing emphasis for entrepreneurship to consider its impact on local communities and moving beyond focusing solely on profit has led to the relationship between entrepreneurship education and neoliberalism and profit maximisation to be questioned. Underpinning entrepreneurship education with a humanistic philosophy can encourage the students to bring compassion and values into their entrepreneurial decision making and actions. Having considered how the axiological position and focus on compassion within humanism can be used to support and underpin entrepreneurship education, the focus of learning within a humanistic learning environment and how it can be leveraged to support effective entrepreneurship education will now be discussed.

The Focus of Learning Within Humanism

Using humanism refocuses how and what learners should learn. A humanistic underpinning promotes learning that develops attitudes and skills that will benefit society (Greenberg, 2015; Hesselbarth & Schaltegger, 2014; Schaltegger & Wagner, 2011). As argued by Laasch and Moosmayer (2015), humanism transitions learning from being of competences to for competence that can be used outside the classroom.

Within the humanism philosophical paradigm, educators seek to maximise the personal growth of the learner. Santos et al. (2019) viewed entrepreneurship education as potentially being emancipatory and empowering. Entrepreneurship education and entrepreneurialism have been found to support the growth and employability of students and graduates, and it has been suggested that there is good reason to link entrepreneurship with employability, career growth and development (Bell, 2016; Rae, 2007). The potential within entrepreneurship education to develop future entrepreneurs and support students' development and future careers is well aligned with the humanistic paradigm's desire to support the growth and future development of learners.

Learning within the humanistic philosophy is viewed as an act of fulfilment to achieve developmental needs and to support potential self-actualisation. Therefore, there is an assumption that learners are seeking self-actualisation through concentrating on their own personal development and growth (Elias & Merriam, 1995; Leach, 2018). Entrepreneurship education is provided across a range of levels using a variety of methods and practices. These can include teacher led pedagogic practices, andragogic self-directed learning practices and heutagogical approaches which encourage students to find their own challenges and questions to answer. A humanistic approach to entrepreneurship education fits neatly with a heutagogical approach to learning, where rather than being assigned tasks by the educator, students can seek out their own areas to explore, review and question in relation to their own interests. However, humanism can still be used to support and underpin more directed pedagogic and andragogic approaches, where the educator still leaves room for learners to have some say in the direction of their study and learning supported by the scaffolding provided in such approaches. In some contexts, the learner is likely to need a degree of scaffolding and direction to lay the foundation for entrepreneurship education. However, the focus of interest in terms of enterprise and entrepreneurship can still be left open. Even in introductory entrepreneurship education classes, the basic theory is often taught, whilst also providing room and opportunity for students to apply the theory by developing their own entrepreneurial ideas, allowing scope for students to direct their learning to some degree.

In order to support the development and self-actualisation of learners, humanism seeks to create liberating learning environments. Liberating learning environments can be a powerful motivator for student learning and can encourage and support social change (Rincón-Gallardo, 2019). A facet within effective entrepreneurship is innovation and the requirement to develop something of value, which is new and novel. Liberating learning environments can help achieve this by encouraging students to

164   R. BELL

think of, and develop, new ideas in a safe space. Creativity and innovation can be challenging concepts and skills to teach and instil within students. However, liberating learning environments can support the teaching of creativity and innovation by supporting students to break free from existing thinking, solutions and offerings already in the marketplace and develop their own new and novel ideas and solutions to problems. To achieve this, the educator acts as a facilitator encouraging students to solve problems within a liberating environment focused on development and change (Merriam et al., 2007).

Humanism encourages and promotes the learner to direct their own learning to maximise their own personal growth (Morris, 2019). It is posited that such a focus can support learners to learn how to learn, preparing them to effectively handle future challenges (Rogers, 1969). Such learning and skills have been identified as an essential resource for entrepreneurs (Ferreira, 2020). As there is no single entrepreneurial opportunity that will resonate with all potential entrepreneurs, students need to be given space and room to explore entrepreneurship related to their own experiences, abilities and context. Students need to follow their own interests and passion to find entrepreneurial opportunities that align with their individual context and abilities. Developing positive emotions within learning has been posited as being important to support the effective learning process (Lackéus, 2014; Loon & Bell, 2018). A humanistic learning environment can effectively support students to explore entrepreneurialism and entrepreneurial opportunities in relation to their development and individual context.

The above paragraphs have presented how humanism can be applied to inform an entrepreneurship education learning environment to support the development of entrepreneurial students. The next section will explore and put forward a case as to how a humanistic educational philosophy can support the development of skills essential for effective entrepreneurship.

The Potential for Humanistic Learning Environments to Develop Essential Entrepreneurial Skills

Learning approaches rooted in learning from experience, such as constructivism, have been posited as being particularly effective for entrepreneurship education (Kyrö, 2015). Whilst humanism similarly promotes learning through experience and doing, it has additional embedded values which support the development of skills useful for entrepreneurship.

Humanism seeks to develop autonomous learners, who are capable and enthusiastic to learn, to learn from their experiences. Within entrepreneurship there is a need to continue to learn and reflect from experiences. Such learning can help entrepreneurs develop and pivot their offerings in the face of developing markets and competition to be sustainable in the longer term. To develop effective and sustainable entrepreneurs, entrepreneurship education needs to ensure that it develops autonomous learners, who are willing and able to continue to learn independently.

Effective entrepreneurship requires ongoing decision making and risk management. Such skills can be supported in the entrepreneurship education classroom through the de-emphasis of knowledge and rote memorisation in favour of the development and acquisition of value-orientated skills and integrative judgements (Lester et al., 2005; Solberg et al., 1995). Learning within a humanistic environment seeks to encourage and promote integrative judgments, where learners bring together information from a range of sources and consider their value to underpin and support their decision making. Bringing a humanistic lens into decision making in the classroom or learning environment helps to bring morals and values into decisions and integrative judgements, rather than relying only on analytical specialisation.

It has been suggested that entrepreneurship is both an economic and social process, where both social interaction and networking play a prominent role (Korsgaard & Anderson, 2011). This is reinforced by scholars who have opined that effective entrepreneurship education should focus on learning from social processes and experiences (Rae, 2005). Humanism presents learning as being a relational activity, where the learner needs to engage with others to develop their knowledge and skills. Such a perspective is a shift away from learning which can be a socially isolated activity where the learner is focused on their own self-interest, to a more community-oriented view of learning (Dierksmeier, 2020). Learning in a humanistic environment can support students in developing their social skills and developing their networks, both of which can support effective entrepreneurship.

Entrepreneurship education literature stresses the importance of supporting learners' emotional well-being as entrepreneurial experiences frequently present stressful situations and potentially failure (Shepherd, 2004; Testa & Frascheri, 2015). Therefore, there is a need to develop resilient learners who can manage, learn and bounce back from entrepreneurial failure (Kauppinen et al., 2019). However, well-being and failure are rarely addressed and discussed in the entrepreneurship classroom, giving an unrealistic picture of entrepreneurship to students (Alvarado Valenzuela et al., 2020). Humanistic learning encourages educators to consider students current and future well-being, and the knowledge and skills they will need to ensure this. This could be effectively translated into the entrepreneurship education classroom by discussing and preparing students for potential stressful entrepreneurial situations and failure by engaging with emotion. Negative entrepreneurial experiences can be discussed in a humanistic learning environment, which creates a warm, accepting and non-threatening atmosphere, where positive and respectful interactions between peers can occur (Allender, 2001). It has been suggested that failure to prepare and support students for entrepreneurial failure adequately is a potential unspoken shortcoming of entrepreneurship education (Bandera et al., 2020).

Having discussed and explored how a humanistic entrepreneurship education classroom can offer a learning environment suitable for developing entrepreneurs, this chapter will now conclude by discussing how a humanistic approach can be used effectively in entrepreneurship education.

4 Applying Humanism in the Entrepreneurship Classroom

Entrepreneurship education requires a range of approaches based on a variety of philosophies and theories to support the successful delivery of entrepreneurship education (Bell & Bell, 2020; Ramsgaard, 2018; Robinson et al., 2016). Different philosophies support different types of learning which are required within entrepreneurship education. Traditional didactic teaching approaches can provide the basic factual knowledge, structural frameworks and instruction to undertake more progressive forms of active learning, which are particularly efficacious in entrepreneurship education.

Humanism, like constructivism, supports the development of subjective knowledge through active experience. This involves the educator moving away from a rigid curriculum, encouraging choice, allowing students to follow and engage in activities of interest, and learn through inquiry and challenge, to achieve the entrepreneurial skills they require within a humanistic learning environment. The role of the educator is to facilitate the wider development of the whole person within a liberating environment (Merriam et al., 2007) which requires them to facilitate the process in an empathetic, positive and supportive manner, in a safe and constructive environment.

Whilst the influence of humanism can, perhaps, be visualised most clearly in a heutagogical approach to teaching and learning, in a setting in which learners are largely autonomous and self-directed, it can also be introduced into androgogic/pedagogic approaches, alongside other philosophies to achieve different types of learning. Even within the more directed approaches to entrepreneurship education, students are commonly given space to generate their own ideas and business plans that can be directed towards solving social problems. Such approaches can reinforce students' creativity, empowerment and concern for others.

Humanism espouses the acquisition of value-orientated skills and the integrative judgements within learners. It incorporates personal acts of fulfilment that include engaging and working with the community. Humanistic approaches to education can incorporate these values. For example, value creation pedagogy is an approach that has been gaining traction in recent years and can be considered in terms of entrepreneurship as it is based on acting upon opportunities and ideas and transforming them into value for others (Lackéus, 2020). It focuses on value for others rather than neoliberal values and venture creation, which may make it more widely acceptable across disciplines (Lackéus et al., 2016). Importantly, it has the potential to encourage humanistic learning and behaviours including rationality, autonomy, empowerment, creativity and a concern for others. It can also provide an opportunity to work with a community to develop empathy and compassion skills to understand and solve a problem which, in the long term, may play a part in encouraging the development of social entrepreneurship. Such approaches have the potential to integrate more practical and active learning in more traditional educational contexts and where institutions and educators might be less focused on commercialism and profit (Bell, 2020). However, challenges have been identified around ensuring students can see the links between the development of value and entrepreneurship and innovation (Bell, 2020) and there is a need to ensure that the value created in the

168 R. BELL

classroom is driven by purpose, agency and capability and supported by cultured reflection (Jones et al., 2021).

In conclusion, Humanism seeks to move learning from a socially isolated activity to a more relational activity and from a perspective of individual self-interest to a more community orientated perspective (Dierksmeier, 2020). Whilst the integration of a humanistic approach to entrepreneurship education can be seen to be more complex, lacking structure and routine, and potentially more time consuming, the addition of humanistic values to entrepreneurship education can offer genuine benefits to both the individual learners and society alike and can support HEI's in meeting their organisational missions.

REFERENCES

Allender, J. (2001). *Teacher self: The practice of humanistic education*. Rowman & Littlefield.

Aloni, N. (2002). *Enhancing humanity: The philosophical foundations of humanistic education*. Kluwer Academic Press.

Balan, P., & Metcalfe, M. (2012). Identifying teaching methods that engage entrepreneurship students. *Education + Training, 54*(5), 368–384.

Bandera, C., Santos, S. C., & Liguori, E. W. (2020). The dark side of entrepreneurship education: A Delphi study on dangers and unintended consequences. *Entrepreneurship Education and Pedagogy*. https://doi.org/10.1177/2515127420944592

Bechard, J. P., & Gregoire, D. (2005). Entrepreneurship education research revisited: The case of higher education. *Academy of Management Learning and Education, 4*, 22–49.

Béchard, J.-P., & Toulouse, J.-M. (1998). Validation of a didactic model for the analysis of training objectives in entrepreneurship. *Journal of Business Venturing, 13*(4), 317–332.

Bélanger, P. (2011). *Theories in adult learning and education*. Barbara Budrich Publishers.

Bell, R. (2015). Developing the next generation of entrepreneurs: Giving students the opportunity to gain experience and thrive. *The International Journal of Management Education, 13*(1), 37–47.

Bell, R. (2016). Unpacking the link between entrepreneurialism and employability: An assessment of the relationship between entrepreneurial attitudes and likelihood of graduate employment in a professional field. *Education + Training, 58*(1), 2–17.

Bell, R. (2020). Developing entrepreneurial behaviours in the Chinese classroom through value creation pedagogy. *Innovations in Education and Teaching International*. https://doi.org/10.1080/14703297.2020.1793800

Bell, R. (2021). Underpinning the entrepreneurship educator's toolkit: Conceptualising the influence of educational philosophies and theory. *Entrepreneurship Education*. https://doi.org/10.1007/s41959-020-00042-4

Bell, R., & Bell, H. (2020). Applying educational theory to develop a framework to support the delivery of experiential entrepreneurship education. *Journal of Small Business and Enterprise Development, 27*(6), 987–1004.

Berglund, K., & Verduijn, K. (2018). *Revitalising entrepreneurship education: Adopting a critical approach in the classroom*. Routledge.

Billings, D., & Halstead, J. (2019). *Teaching in nursing: A guide for faculty*. Elsevier.

Darkenwald, G. G., & Merriam, S. B. (1982). *Adult education: Foundations of practice*. Harper & Row.

Dierksmeier, C. (2020). From Jensen to Jensen: Mechanistic management education or humanistic management learning? *Journal of Business Ethics, 166*(1), 73–87.

Elias, J. L., & Merriam, S. (1995). *Philosophical foundations of adult education*. Krieger Publishing.

Fayolle, A. (2013). Personal views on the future of entrepreneurship education. *Entrepreneurship & Regional Development, 25*(7–8), 692–701.

Fayolle, A., Verzat, C., & Wapshott, R. (2016). In quest of legitimacy: The theoretical and methodological foundations of entrepreneurship education research. *International Small Business Journal, 34*(7), 895–904.

Ferreira, C. C. (2020). Experiential learning theory and hybrid entrepreneurship: Factors influencing the transition to full-time entrepreneurship. *International Journal of Entrepreneurial Behavior & Research, 26*(8), 1845–1863.

Freire, P. (2006). Banking versus problem-solving models of education. In R. Curren (Ed.), *Philosophy of education: An anthology* (1 ed., pp. 68–75). Wiley-Blackwell.

Gedeon, S. (2014). Application of best practices in university entrepreneurship education: Designing a new MBA program. *European Journal of Training and Development, 38*(3), 231–253.

Greenberg, D. N. (2015). Globally responsible leadership: Managing according to the U.N. global compact. *Academy of Management Learning & Education, 14*(2), 297–299.

Hannon, P. (2006). Teaching Pigeons to Dance: Sense and meaning in entrepreneurship education. *Education + Training, 48*(5), 296–308.

Hesselbarth, C., & Schaltegger, S. (2014). Educating change agents for sustainability—Learnings from the first sustainability management Master of Business Administration. *Journal of Cleaner Production, 62*, 24–36.

Jones, B., & Iredale, N. (2010). Enterprise education as pedagogy. *Education + Training, 52*(1), 7–19.

Jones, C. (2019). A signature pedagogy for entrepreneurship education. *Journal of Small Business and Enterprise Development, 26*(2), 243–254.

Jones, C., Penaluna, K., & Penaluna, A. (2021). Value creation in entrepreneurial education: Towards a unified approach. *Education + Training, 63*(1), 101–113.

Kakouris, A., & Morselli, D. (2020). Addressing the pre/post-university pedagogy of entrepreneurship coherent with learning theories. In S. Sawang (Ed.), *Entrepreneurship education: A lifelong learning approach* (pp. 35–58). Springer.

Kauppinen, A., Paloniemi, K., & Juho, A. (2019). Failed firm founders' grief coping during mentoring: Learning as the single catalyst of their restarting performance narratives. *The International Journal of Management Education.* https://doi.org/10.1016/j.ijme.2019.02.008

Kaynardağ, A. Y. (2019). Pedagogy in HE: Does it matter? *Studies in Higher Education, 44*(1), 111–119.

Kim, K.-C., ElTarabishy, A., & Bae, Z.-T. (2018). Humane entrepreneurship: How focusing on people can drive a new era of wealth and quality job creation in a sustainable world. *Journal of Small Business Management, 56*(S1), 10–29.

Korsgaard, S., & Anderson, A. R. (2011). Enacting entrepreneurship as social value creation. *International Small Business Journal, 29*(2), 135–151.

Kyrö, P. (2015). The conceptual contribution of education to research on entrepreneurship education. *Entrepreneurship & Regional Development, 27*(9–10), 599–618.

Laasch, O., & Moosmayer, D. (2015). Competences for responsible management: A structured literature review. *CRME Working Paper, 1*(2).

Lackéus, M. (2014). An emotion based approach to assessing entrepreneurial education. *The International Journal of Management Education, 12*(3), 374–396.

Lackéus, M. (2017). Does entrepreneurial education trigger more or less neoliberalism in education? *Education + Training, 59*(6), 635–650.

Lackéus, M. (2020). Comparing the impact of three different experiential approaches to entrepreneurship in education. *International Journal of Entrepreneurial Behavior & Research, 26*(5), 937–971.

Lackéus, M., Lundqvist, M., & Middleton, K. W. (2016). Bridging the traditional-progressive education rift through entrepreneurship. *International Journal of Entrepreneurial Behavior & Research, 22*(6), 777–803.

Leach, N. (2018). Impactful learning environments: A humanistic approach to fostering adolescents' postindustrial social skills. *Journal of Humanistic Psychology.* https://doi.org/10.1177/0022167818779948

Lester, S. W., Tomkovick, C., Wells, T., Flunker, L., & Kickul, J. (2005). Does service-learning add value? Examining the perspectives of multiple stakeholders. *Academy of Management Learning & Education, 4*(3), 278–294.

Loon, M., & Bell, R. (2018). The moderating effects of emotions on cognitive skills. *Journal of Further and Higher Education, 42*(5), 694–707.

Merriam, S. (1982). Some thoughts on the relationship between theory and practice. In S. Merriam (Ed.), *Linking philosophy and practice: New directions for continuing education* (pp. 87–91). Jossey-Bass.

Merriam, S., Caffarella, R., & Baumgartner, L. (2007). *Learning in adulthood: A comprehensive guide.* Jossey-Bass.

Morris, M. H., & Liguori, E. (2016). Preface: Teaching reason and the unreasonable. In M. H. Morris & E. Liguori (Eds.), *Annals of Entrepreneurship Education and Pedagogy—2016* (pp. 14–22). Edward Elgar.

Morris, T. H. (2019). Self-directed learning: A fundamental competence in a rapidly changing world. *International Review of Education, 65*(4), 633–653.

Mueller, S., & Anderson, A. R. (2014). Understanding the entrepreneurial learning process and its impact on students' personal development: A European perspective. *The International Journal of Management Education, 12*(3), 500–511.

Neck, H., & Greene, P. (2011). Entrepreneurship education: Known worlds and new frontiers. *Journal of Small Business Management, 49*(1), 55–70.

Neck, H. M., & Corbett, A. C. (2018). The scholarship of teaching and learning entrepreneurship. *Entrepreneurship Education and Pedagogy, 1*(1), 8–41.

Peltier, J. W., & Scovotti, C. (2010). Enhancing entrepreneurial marketing education: The student perspective. *Journal of Small Business and Enterprise Development, 17*(4), 514–536.

Peters, R. S. (1959). *Authority, responsibility and education.* Allen and Unwin.

Pittaway, L., & Cope, J. (2007). Entrepreneurship education: A systematic review of the evidence. *International Small Business Journal, 25*(5), 479–510.

Rae, D. (2005). Entrepreneurial learning: A narrative-based conceptual model. *Journal of Small Business and Enterprise Development, 12*(3), 323–335.

Rae, D. (2007). Connecting enterprise and graduate employability: Challenges to the higher education culture and curriculum? *Education + Training, 49*(8/9), 605–619.

Ramsgaard, M. B. (2018). Experiential learning philosophies of enterprise and entrepreneurship education. In D. Hyams-Ssekasi & E. F. Caldwell (Eds.), *Experiential learning for entrepreneurship* (pp. 3–18). Palgrave Macmillan.

Ratten, V., & Jones, P. (2020). Entrepreneurship and management education: Exploring trends and gaps. *The International Journal of Management Education.* https://doi.org/10.1016/j.ijme.2020.100431

Rincón-Gallardo, S. (2019). *Liberating learning: Educational change as social movement.* Routledge.

Robinson, S., Neergaard, H., Tanggaard, L., & Krueger, N. F. (2016). New horizons in entrepreneurship education: From teacher-led to student-centered learning. *Education + Training, 58*(7/8), 661–683.

Rogers, C. (1969). *Freedom to learn.* Charles Merrill.

Santos, S. C., Neumeyer, X., & Morris, M. H. (2019). Entrepreneurship education in a poverty context: An empowerment perspective. *Journal of Small Business Management, 57*(S1), 6–32.

Schaltegger, S., & Wagner, M. (2011). Sustainable entrepreneurship and sustainability innovation: Categories and interactions. *Business Strategy and the Environment, 20*(4), 222–237.

Shepherd, D. A. (2004). Educating entrepreneurship students about emotion and learning from failure. *Academy of Management Learning & Education, 3*(3), 274–287.

Smith, R., Bell, R., & Watts, H. (2014). Personality trait differences between traditional and social entrepreneurs. *Social Enterprise Journal, 10*(3), 200–221.

Solberg, J., Strong, K. C., & McGuire, C. (1995). Living (not learning) ethics. *Journal of Business Ethics, 14*(1), 71–81.

Stewart, M. (2014). Making sense of a teaching programme for university academics: Exploring the longer-term effects. *Teaching and Teacher Education, 38*, 89–98.

Testa, S., & Frascheri, S. (2015). Learning by failing: What we can learn from un-successful entrepreneurship education. *The International Journal of Management Education, 13*(1), 11–22.

Valenzuela, J. F. A., Wakkee, I., Martens, J., & Grijsbach, P. (2020). Lessons from entrepreneurial failure through vicarious learning. *Journal of Small Business & Entrepreneurship.* https://doi.org/10.1080/08276331.2020.183 1839

Veugelers, W. (2011). Introduction. In W. Veugelers (Ed.), *Education and humanism: Linking autonomy and humanity* (pp. 1–7). Sense Publishers.

Wraae, B., & Walmsley, A. (2020). Behind the scenes: Spotlight on the entrepreneurship educator. *Education + Training, 62*(3), 255–270.

Zappe, S., Hochstedt, K., Kisenwether, E., & Shartrand, A. (2013). Teaching to innovate: Beliefs and perceptions of instructors who teach entrepreneurship to engineering students. *International Journal of Engineering Education, 29*(1), 45–62.

Success Through Failure: Towards a Problem-Based Approach to Entrepreneurship Education

John Alver Dobson and Lisa Dobson

1 Introduction

There is an accepted understanding that increasing entrepreneurship will spur economic growth and employment within academic, business, and policymaking communities (Wu & Gu, 2017). Unfortunately, business dynamism has been declining in the US (Decker et al., 2018) and has fallen by nearly 50% since the 1970s (Hathaway & Litan, 2014). During the same time frame there has been a dramatic increase in Entrepreneurship Education (EE) programmes in the US (Morris & Liguori, 2016). Over 600 universities have launched entrepreneurship centres or institutes (Morris et al., 2014). However, recent government calculations found increasing levels of EE has not resulted in increased levels of new venture creation. In fact, the opposite is happening. The rate of new venture

---

J. A. Dobson (✉)
Clark University, Worcester, MA, USA
e-mail: jdobson@clarku.edu

L. Dobson
DYME Institute, Worcester, MA, USA

© The Author(s), under exclusive license to Springer Nature Switzerland AG 2022
G. J. Larios-Hernandez et al. (eds.), *Theorising Undergraduate Entrepreneurship Education*,
https://doi.org/10.1007/978-3-030-87865-8_10

creation is at historic lows (Keating, 2016). Further, the survival rates of the businesses that were started have not improved (Bureau of Labour Statistics, 2016). Thus, growth in EE does not appear to have had a positive impact on the number of new ventures created nor on the survival rates of those that are started.

The lean start-up, business models, canvases, and writing business plans have become the default teaching methodology for EE across US. Unfortunately, this growth in programming has occurred without a universally accepted approach or pedagogy, leaving many gaps between research and practice of EE (Naia et al., 2015). More recently, researchers have been theorising about the impact of undergraduate EE on the development of student intention to become entrepreneurs.

The scope of the intention-impact gap is significant. Notably, today's students are much less entrepreneurial, measured through business creation and ownership, than Baby Boomers or Generation X were in their 20s (Campbell et al., 2017). This lack of entrepreneurial activity will have a long-term negative impact on economic growth, employment, and poverty reduction. Yet, many private sector organisations and public institutions continue to believe that EE is an effective tool in developing new entrepreneurs (Neck et al., 2014), with the goal of re-igniting entrepreneurial dynamism (Nabi et al., 2017).

Universities and colleges have made substantial efforts in the development of EE programming (Kamovich & Foss, 2017). There is significant momentum in higher education to create curricula on the belief that EE will create economic development and jobs (O'Connor, 2013). This has resulted in the development of curriculum in the form of minors, majors, master's, and PhD programmes in entrepreneurship. Additionally, co-curricular activities such as 'pitch nights', business model competitions, hack-a-thons, mentoring programmes, and internships have become the norm. The efforts to create an entrepreneurship workspace have included the establishment of maker spaces and collaborative spaces on campus. Despite these efforts, entrepreneurship continues to stagnate; a meta-analytic investigation reviewed 73 studies of 37,285 students and found no statistically significant impact of EE on entrepreneurial intention (Bae et al., 2014).

There continues to be disagreement about competencies and activities needed to build effective EE programming (Middleton & Donnellon, 2014). In the literature there is ontological confusion and methodological issues in how EE is taught (Wu & Gu, 2017). Further, minimal attention is paid to the impact of teaching approaches and methods on the development of entrepreneurs (Kamovich & Foss, 2017). Suggesting that there is a large gap between the growing supply of EE and our understanding of how best to approach teaching and learning (Morris, 2014). Additionally, Fayolle (2013) suggested EE should be reinforced with robust intellectual and conceptual underpinnings as well as sound reflection on practice and applications, instead of simply relying on 'taken for granted' (p. 692) methods. Why is the growth of EE creating more entrepreneur graduates and not more entrepreneurs? This is the emerging question. We believe that the answer lies in the pedagogical approaches used by educators.

From a pedagogical view, entrepreneurship terms, methods, content, and context vary widely (Wu & Gu, 2017). As a point of clarity for this exploratory research chapter, we will use the Harvard Business School definition of entrepreneurship: *the pursuit of opportunity beyond resources controlled* (Stevenson, 1983). This definition clarifies the separation of entrepreneurship from the practice of small business management. Entrepreneurship involves the development of opportunities. Entrepreneurship is not small business management, nor is it the purchasing of a franchise, nor the opening of a new business as a similar or replica of another. Rather, entrepreneurs use their own knowledge, skills, and abilities in developing something new with the anticipation that this novel idea will create and capture value in unexpected ways.

We propose a new, radical, yet straightforward approach to current EE's ineffectiveness. Namely, to abandon the current standards in favour of giving students autonomy in constructing their entrepreneurial knowledge. Our approach is based on learning theories of adult education that empower students to pursue their passions instead of hypothetically filling in boxes on canvases or non-sensical business plans.

This chapter is divided into four sections. After the introduction, section two will review the literature on EE. Section three will examine research on entrepreneurial learning by comparing process-based and problem-based approaches. In addition, we will present a novel learning approach for problem-based EE. Section four will be a discussion, followed by the conclusion.

2 LITERATURE REVIEW

We identified two primary approaches to EE: process-based and problem-based learning. Process-based learning is the most common approach to

EE; curriculum is focused on following a prescribed process of sequential steps in starting a business. It begins with developing an idea and ending with launching a business, in some cases selling that business, or a liquidation event. This approach is present in numerous leading textbooks (e.g. *Kuratko's Entrepreneurship Theory, Process,* and *Practice* [2005] or *Vesper & Gartner's New Venture Experience* [1997]). Learning outcomes in process-based courses focus on demonstrating knowledge of the various steps in the process, traits of entrepreneurs, understanding opportunity recognition, and knowledge of the various forms of venture funding, etc.

The second approach reviewed is problem-based learning (Svinicki & McKeachie, 2011), focused on identifying and solving real problems. This approach avoids pre-determined outcomes as well as best practices. This focus allows students to construct knowledge and, through experiential problem-based learning, develop and test novel solutions for real market problems.

After reviewing the literature, we argue that part of the failure of EE to develop entrepreneurs may be the reliance on pedagogical techniques focused on process-based learning approaches, which do not actually resemble how entrepreneurs learn to become entrepreneurs in real life. Further, these approaches do not resonate with today's students, who are different, in significant ways, then those of previous generations (Twenge, 2009). These differences have influenced higher education; the well-documented phenomenon of grade inflation is but one example. These students have a high sense of entitlement (Harvey & Martinko, 2009) and an inflated sense of efficacy, yet cannot cope with uncertainty or failure (Marston, 2010). Research found that they personally want to change the world (Johnson, 2015) but are paralysed by fear, they desire feedback, but more importantly peer feedback (Bye, 2018). Furthermore, their low levels of empathy (Grijalva & Zhang, 2016) and high levels of narcissism (Metz, 2014) helps explain their unwillingness to take ownership of the entrepreneurial process and why they are unwilling to actually spend the time in many of the menial tasks (Tulgan, 2009) required to become an entrepreneur.

This prior personality sketch suggests that today's students are incompatible with the required entrepreneurial *grit* that is necessary when facing adversity while working towards one's goals (Syed & Mueller, 2014). Moreover, a lack of empathy will make it difficult for students to understand their customers if they cannot connect with the experiences of others and with the broader community or world (Adler, 1927).

The entrepreneurial journey has so many ups and downs that *grit* appears to be a fundamental reason why some persist and others give up under the pressure of adversity and unpredictability (Syed & Mueller, 2014). Entrepreneurship Education should reflect mindfulness that today's student lacks grit, have an inflated sense of their abilities, are risk-averse, and are unable to cope with adversity. Critically, we believe that knowledge, skills, and abilities in the domains just listed are essential competencies of learning for success in entrepreneurship. Thus, if EE is to produce successful entrepreneurs, it may rest upon curricula that develop the abilities necessary to navigate the inherent ambiguity and uncertainty of the entrepreneurial marketplace.

Unfortunately, at a curricular level, EE is often taught through a process-based lens. In which students are exposed to and then tested on their ability to understand theory-laden curricula aligned with key elements of best practices (Morris, 2014). This approach presents entrepreneurship as a *linear* process and instructors are usually using discipline-specific models (Neck et al., 2014). Such activities include developing business plans, business models, reviewing case studies, creating five-year pro-forma income statements, developing marketing plans, operating within simulation systems with the intent on building the necessary management skills, and having students develop an understanding of the process needed to successfully launch and run a business.

Teaching process-based courses appears at first glance, theoretically, to be an obvious approach for EE since students are taught all elements of launching and running a successful business. However, real entrepreneurship functions as a messy phenomenon with uncertain outcomes along a variety of economic, political, social, and cultural dimensions over time (Nabi et al., 2017; Pittaway & Thorpe, 2012). Entrepreneurs develop innovations prior to and in anticipation of market acceptance. This approach runs counter to process-based learning, which relies heavily on the assumption of market acceptance and pre-determined outcomes, resulting in courses focused on the basic functions of management that overlook critical unpredictable aspects of the entrepreneurial process. Entrepreneurship is a non-linear process, and as such none of the learning activities within the process-based approaches can specify, in advance how it will map onto the real marketplace.

Researchers have noted that educators who rely on process-based approaches to EE are likely to be ineffective in creating entrepreneurs because entrepreneurship is a discipline of action in a real-world ecology of complex changes (Neck et al., 2014). Furthermore, these approaches, that focus on idealised hypothetical business plans and models, ignore constraints under which entrepreneurship functions. For instance, constraints such as resource scarcity, limited human capital, or missing technological know-how. Entrepreneurs must learn to overcome these constraints if they are to succeed.

Process-Based Learning

Consequently, process-based learning may inadvertently create distance between entrepreneurial students and their ideas, since it focuses attention on the things the entrepreneur lacks instead of the knowledge, skills, and abilities the entrepreneur brings to the idea. Moreover, an examination of the impact of EE indicates that in forming entrepreneurs there appears to be a lack of intended outcomes, instructional processes, and assessment criteria in process-based approaches (Nabi et al., 2017). These approaches, which focus on idealised hypothetical business plans and models, ignore constraints under which entrepreneurship functions, including resource scarcity, limited human capital, or missing technological know-how. Entrepreneurs must learn to overcome these constraints if they are to succeed.

Process-based courses focus teaching and learning on the steps of starting a new venture. A final deliverable of these courses is to submit a completed business plan. The process involves students forming a hypothetical founding team, conducting market analysis, outlining the operational plan, development of a marketing plan, creating pro-forma financial statements, and outlining the funding requirements for this venture. In summation, process-based courses use a teaching-centric perspective which relegates the student to passive learner (Morris, 2014; Nabi et al., 2017; Neck et al., 2014).

Problem-Based Learning

Conversely, problem-based learning focuses curricular attention on helping students learn how to solve real problems using a learner-centred approach. There are six generally accepted steps in problem-based learning (Svinicki & McKeachie, 2011). First, identify and analyse the problem. Second, determine prior knowledge of the underlying and related concepts to solve the problem. Third, identify and address knowledge gaps related to solving the problem. Fourth, outline and evaluate possible solutions and fifth, attempt to solve the problem; and sixth, report the findings.

Within problem-based learning, incidental preparation is critical to understanding entrepreneurial success since the entrepreneur incorporates their specific context into developing potential solutions to market problems. Here, the EE student determines what prior knowledge they possess to solve the market problem, while experiencing and learning about personal exposure to social, emotional, and financial risk involved in developing their idea (Cope & Watts, 2000). Additionally, Middleton and Donnellon (2014) noted 'few programs provide robust outcomes such as actual new ventures or entrepreneurial behavior in real contexts' (p. 1). While Kassean et al. (2015) argue EE should be defined by reflection, real-world experience, and action.

Entrepreneurship Process

The opportunity recognition process integral to entrepreneurship (Stevenson, 1983) focuses on the identification of qualities that make a good opportunity (Timmons & Spinelli, 2007). However, Singh (2001) questions the value of focusing on the identifications of opportunity qualities since this approach permits post hoc validation, offering little understanding of which conditions or opportunities are developed by entrepreneurs in the beginning. Overcoming this limitation, Lumpkin and Lichtenstein (2005) identify the need for the entrepreneur to effectively pursue the opportunity. Additionally, Sarasvathy (2009) suggests effectual thinking is required to help overcome the uncertainty of opportunity identification.

Opportunity recognition, sometimes called the 'Eureka' or 'Aha!' moment, often happens as individual are working or going about their daily lives (Rogers, 2014). This moment arises when the subconscious connects the dots to solve wicked problems. Once the novel patterns have been discerned, entrepreneurs successfully pursue these opportunities, relying on their personal and professional experiences, or incidental preparation (Wallas, 1926), distinct from formal deliberate learning (Singh et al., 1999). Therefore, incidental experiences form the bases of essential problem-solving skills in entrepreneurship.

We theorise that using a problem-based approach to EE, that eschews the creation of hypothetical businesses, plans, simulations, and case studies are more effective in developing entrepreneurs because the course is grounded in the learner's context and not hypotheticals. Faculty essentially meet students where they are and not where we want them to be and build entrepreneurial knowledge from there. Problem-based learning is student-centred, designed and structured with curriculum and co-curricular activities, that ensure students' gain concrete entrepreneurial experiences. The active nature of the experiential learning process provides an experience from which the learner can reflect and learn (Argyris & Schon, 1996). The reflective process allows students to interpret and understand their experiences so that new learning can occur (Moon, 2004). The problem-based course switched from focusing on 'what to learn' and instead taught students 'how to learn', building on self-directed, and ultimately creating self-determined learners (Hase & Kenyon, 2013).

The problem-based course follow Piaget's (1973) constructivist approach to teaching and learning in which entrepreneurial knowledge is actively constructed by the individual in a process of building on prior knowledge through concrete experiences. The learning environment is focused on creating opportunities for students to test their ideas in the real world outside the classroom and learn informally (Rogers, 2014). This intentional approach allows for collaboration among students as they develop solutions based on their current knowledge. It involves weekly student presentations on the current state of their ventures, which included student dialogue, interpretation, reflection, and collaboration. This process facilitated the development of an effective transactive memory system (Huang, 2009), which enables the entrepreneur to recognise their own missing expertise and identify people who can help them. Sharing their personal experiences with others in their network serves to increase knowledge sharing, empathy, and seeking member participation to help solve problems (Cope, 2005). The transactive memory system relies on learning by doing, learning from others, and working together, all key elements to the problem-based learning course. This approach aligns with Smilor's (1997) assessment of how entrepreneurs are exceptional learners from experiences with other entrepreneurs, customers, associates, employees, suppliers, and competitors. Finally, entrepreneurs learn from what worked and what did not work.

As the course progresses students rely on their previous experiences and those of their cohort to learn how to better evaluate various options. The students test their ideas, make lots of mistakes, but learn to overcome these failures with personal reflection, learning from other students, and working together as a cohort to help each other solve problems. This process is repeated throughout the semester. Students make iterations based on market feedback, peer input, and their reflective learning. Using a non-linear approach throughout the semester, the students purposefully build their entrepreneurial knowledge through learning from doing, from others, and from working together. This is similar to how Rae & Rae and Carswell (2000), Cope and Watts (2000), and Pittaway and Thorpe (2012) associate entrepreneurship as a learning journey.

3   ENTREPRENEURIAL LEARNING

Entrepreneurial opportunities are not identified nor pursued in an experiential vacuum, but rather are developed through action-learning from a culmination of an iterative process through real-life experiences (Gartner, 1985). Solomon and Matthews (2014) added that entrepreneurs pursue opportunities in their environment and context. We argue that an iterative non-linear problem-based methodology for EE is a direct mechanism by which students develop into entrepreneurs and actively engage with the world (Pittaway & Thorpe, 2012). A particularly well-stated critique by Hindle (2007) noted that in higher education, EE includes two different approaches: those that 'teach about it' and those that 'teach it' (p. 107). There is a growing consensus of the utility of a problem-based approach, and the need to develop more self-directed and self-determined students (QAA, 2018) through the exposure to concrete experiences.

Problem-based EE learning focuses on active student-centred learning requiring students to assume responsibility for exploring, adapting, and transitioning ideas with unknown outcomes (Kolb & Kolb, 2008). Entrepreneurship comes from finding practical solutions to problems based on what does and does not work (Cope, 2005; Smilor, 1997) and becomes a personal journey over time (McMullen & Dimov, 2013). This teaching approach relies on self-directed learning elements (Hartree, 1984; Merriam & Bierema, 2013) allowing for student autonomy. Students assume personal responsibility to become self-directed. Thus, they are no longer a passive recipient of knowledge. Once self-directed learning is practiced over time, entrepreneurs build agency, noted as critical in becoming a self-determined learner (Blaschke et al., 2016) (Table 1).

Table 1 Comparison between process-based and problem-based EE

	Process-based	Problem-based
Assumptions	Entrepreneurs start new ventures Courses teach the process of starting a new venture	Entrepreneurs solve (market) problems Learners should learn to solve real problems
Teaching methodology	Teacher-centred Theoretical lecturing Pre-determined exercises	Student-centred Concrete experiential learning No pre-determined outcomes
Role of student	Passive learner Follows a linear process to start a business or develop a business model Learns pre-determined deliverables	Active learner Self-directed learner constructs their non-linear journey of entrepreneurship and becomes self-determined in their learning Learns to be autonomous and develop agency through practicing creativity and innovation
Activities	Write a hypothetical Business Plan, conduct marketing analysis, assess financial feasibility, read case studies, and use simulations Taught aspects of management and leadership from theory	First, identify and analyse a real problem; second, determine prior knowledge of the underlying and related concepts to solve the problem; third, identify and address knowledge gaps related to solving the problem; fourth, outline and evaluate possible solutions; fifth, attempt to solve the problem; and sixth, report the findings Develop entrepreneurship tools and leadership skills in real time and practice
Learning outcomes	Learn about Entrepreneurship	Learn how to be an entrepreneur in practice
Assessments	Summative and formative assessments based on pre-determined best practices	Time spent working on and performance in their venture, self-reflection, journaling, incorporating feedback to improve their idea, iterating business idea, and demonstrating learning Building soft skills and hard skills

4   Discussion

Why isn't the growth of EE creating more entrepreneur graduates and not more entrepreneurs? This question emerged from a literature review that EE has had no positive impact on the development of entrepreneurs

(Bae et al., 2014). In the light of the significant financial and academic focus devoted to these programmes we believe that it is vitally important researchers understand why these programmes are not effective. This chapter identified how experiential learning and corresponding *success through failure* are key components of EE. Learning practices include: concrete experiences, experiencing failure, and developing grit and resilience by working through this failure. Relying on our experiences in teaching entrepreneurship through the process-based learning approach, on intuition from the researchers' own entrepreneurial experiences, and evidence from our previous research (Dobson et al., 2017, 2021), demonstrate that process-based approaches are not suitable for learning entrepreneurship in the real world (White & D'Souza, 2014).

This chapter connected research showing that today's students are risk-averse, avoid uncertainty, have high levels of self-efficacy, and are unable to cope with failure (Campbell et al., 2017). These traits are contrary to the inherent uncertainty embedded in entrepreneurial action. The specific tasks embedded in problem-based learning, namely related to the requirement of having students identify a real market problem and encouraging their attempts to solve it through concrete activities (Svinicki & McKeachie, 2011), expose students to personal and business failure as they attempt to figure out actual market need (Pittaway & Thorpe, 2012).

At the beginning of the problem-based course students experienced concrete actions that challenge the student's sense of self when faced with failure which initially caused attitudes towards entrepreneurship to decline (Dobson et al., 2017, 2021). However, throughout the semester the students worked through these failures in their cohort and began to develop grit and resilience, an important factor in entrepreneurial learning (Syed & Mueller, 2014), and they became more aware and self-directed in their learning (Hase & Kenyon, 2013). Over time, students experience successes in their ventures that served as catalysts to rebound, stimulate, and encourage entrepreneurial learning, attitudes, subjective norms, perceived behavioural control (PBC), and intention to be an entrepreneur.

In addition, as successes emerged, such as, a product or service modification to fit with the customer's need, this allowed students to overcome their fear of failure, notably prevalent in today's students (Twenge, 2009). Furthermore, developing real solutions often required that students work on menial tasks, which they are not predisposed to do (Tulgan, 2009), but which are essential to starting a business. Finally, to successfully develop solutions, students need to develop empathy (Grijalva & Zhang, 2016) for their customers. The literature noted that students of today are weak in these three areas. The problem-based class focused on solving real problems ensures learners encounter and strengthen skills in these areas.

The problem-based course allows exposure to mitigate personal risks, unpredictability, and especially to failures in the development of one's own idea; these are all aspects of entrepreneurship learning (Nabi et al., 2017). Part of the strategy in problem-based learning should be to remove the objective threat, i.e. the potential to 'fail' the course from experience of subjective failure, or if a student venture 'fails'. In other words, a failed business venture will not equate to a failed grade, provided the student reflectively learns from their experiences. This approach may increase students' intrinsic motivation to try novel solutions to market problems and to be more self-directed in their learning (Merriam & Bierema, 2013).

Students should be offered a safe environment to be challenged, strengthen awareness of agency to navigate concrete experiences, and view failure as an opportunity to learn. This is of interest, since peer recognition from feedback is something, younger generations crave (Bye, 2018). The class emphasised the students' ability to develop their business idea in search of gaining some level of market acceptance rather than the worry of a failed grade based on a successful first venture. Student progress and assessment is not based on a competition between students to see who can develop the best business, but rather each student is on a personal learning journey and supports each other.

The problem-based approach is in stark contrast to process-based learning in which students rely on 'best practices', theoretical assumptions, preconceived correct answers and methods to develop hypothetical business plans, business models, or complete coursework. Process-based approaches are contradictory to how entrepreneurs actually learn and behave (Pittaway & Thorpe, 2012). Inadvertently, by creating an idealised business plan and hypothetical business model, it focuses attention on what students lack and away from what they have, or the 'bird in hand' concept (Sarasvathy, 2009).

There is utility in problem-based teaching and learning methods for EE. Until students experience entrepreneurship, its value and application are abstract. After the struggle involved with initial entrepreneurial experiences, one may feel more equipped to approach entrepreneurial behaviour. This was evident by increases in perceived behavioural control in research in the US (Dobson et al., 2017) and internationally (Dobson et al., 2021).

Indeed, entrepreneurship is certainly not for everyone, and we believe that a problem-based approach in early levels of entrepreneurship curricula may be critical in helping students realise that they do not, in fact, want to pursue entrepreneurship as a career or at this time. However, our research demonstrates that problem-based EE increases PBC and intention of students compared to process-based courses. Thus, the concrete experiences in a problem-based course are critical to the developing of the necessary *grit* and resilience that will foster the next generation of entrepreneurs.

Here we reflect on our own implementation of a problem-based class. We have developed a number of problem-based courses with great utility. It is important to intentionally separate the grade from the success or failure of the business, allowing students to reconcile the time and effort expended with the importance of building a venture. Further, this approach allows students to take risks in testing ideas without worrying about how a mistake will impact their grade. Entrepreneurship is a messy process in which students make many incorrect assumptions about market demand. A challenge becomes how to assess student learning (Lackeus & Middleton, 2018). Students are assessed on their effort and time spent working on their venture, tactics and how they incorporated feedback (customer and peer) into improving their venture, and progress they have made in their learning journey. This includes reflection, journaling, iterating, and demonstrating both self-directed and self-determined learning. Creating this environment allows students to take bigger risks and effectively go through a process that we are calling 'success through failure'.

5 Conclusion

This paper explored the impact of problem-based and process-based learning on EE. The literature review offered both educational and entrepreneurial underpinnings for concrete problem-based learning in EE.

The process of becoming an entrepreneur is built on previous failures or what we are calling 'success through failure' since we argue that failure is an integral part of entrepreneurial development and thus, should be a part of EE. The entrepreneurship classroom followed Svinicki and McKeachie's (2011) six steps for problem-based learning that align with Kolb's (1984) concept of experiential learning through concrete experiences. Students are required to execute a business venture by developing and engaging their ideas into opportunities.

The growing body of literature suggests the moving away from a pedagogical approach to EE, and towards treating them like adults holds the most promise in actually developing entrepreneurs. Adult-learning requires that faculty abandon some control over the learning process embedded in pre-determined outcomes and 'best practice' in favour of allowing students to construct their own entrepreneurial knowledge. Thus, faculty must become comfortable with learner-centred or entrepreneurship-centred learning in order to create more entrepreneurs.

REFERENCES

Adler, H. M. (1927). The relation between psychiatry and the social sciences. *American Journal of Psychiatry, 83*(4), 661–669.

Argyris, C., & Schon, D. A. (1996). *Organizational learning II: A theory of action perspective.* Addison-Wesley.

Bae, T. J., Qian, S., Miao, C., & Fiet, J. O. (2014). The relationship between entrepreneurship education and entrepreneurial intentions: A meta-analytic review. *Entrepreneurship Theory and Practice, 38*(2), 217–254.

Blaschke, L. M., & Hase, S. (2016). Heutagogy: A holistic framework for creating twenty-first-century self-determined learners. In *The future of ubiquitous learning* (pp. 25–40). Springer.

Bureau of Labour Statistics. (2016). *Business employment dynamics: Entrepreneurship and the U.S. economy.* United States Department of Labor. https://www.bls.gov/bdm/entrepreneurship/bdm_chart3.htm

Bye, D. (2018). Beyond stereotypes: How to manage & motivate millennials. *HR Specialist, 16*(3), 7.

Campbell, S. M., Twenge, J. M., & Campbell, W. K. (2017). Fuzzy but useful constructs: Making sense of the differences between generations. *Work, Aging and Retirement, 3*(2), 130–139.

Cope, J. (2005). Toward a dynamic learning perspective of entrepreneurship. *Entrepreneurship Theory and Practice, 29*(4), 373–397.

Cope, J., & Watts, G. (2000). Learning by doing: An exploration of experience, critical incidents and reflection in entrepreneurial learning. *International Journal of Entrepreneurial Behavior & Research, 6*(3), 104–124.

Decker, R. A., Haltiwanger, J. C., Jarmin, R. S., & Miranda, J. (2018). *Changing business dynamism and productivity: Shocks vs. responsiveness.* Finance and Economics Discussion Series 2018–2007. Board of Governors of the Federal Reserve System. https://doi.org/10.17016/FEDS.2018.007

Dobson, J. A., Castro Nieto, Y., Dobson, L., & Moros Ochoa, A. (2021). Success through failure: Towards a problem-based approach to entrepreneurship. *Entrepreneurship Education and Pedagogy, 4*(3), 225–260. https://doi.org/10.1177/2515127419884132

Dobson, J. A., Jacobs, E., & Dobson, L. (2017). Toward an experiential approach to entrepreneurship education. *Journal of Higher Education Theory and Practice, 17*(3), 57–69.

Fayolle, A. (2013). Personal views on the future of entrepreneurship education. *Entrepreneurship & Regional Development, 25*(7–8), 692–701.

Garrison, D. R. (1997). Self-directed learning: Toward a comprehensive model. *Adult Education Quarterly, 48*(1), 18–33.

Gartner, W. B. (1985). A conceptual framework for describing the phenomenon of new venture creation. *Academy of Management Review, 10*(4), 696–706.

Grijalva, E., & Zhang, L. (2016). Narcissism and self-insight: A review and meta-analysis of narcissists' self-enhancement tendencies. *Personality and Social Psychology Bulletin, 42*(1), 3–24.

Hartree, A. (1984). Malcolm Knowles' theory of andragogy: A critique. *International Journal of Lifelong Education, 3*(3), 203–210.

Harvey, P., & Martinko, M. J. (2009). An empirical examination of the role of attributions in psychological entitlement and its outcomes. *Journal of Organizational Behavior: The International Journal of Industrial, Occupational and Organizational Psychology and Behavior, 30*(4), 459–476.

Hase, S., & Kenyon, C. (2013). The nature of learning. In S. Hase & C. Kenyon (Eds.), *Self-determined learning: Heutagogy in action* (pp. 19–35). Bloomsbury Academic.

Hathaway, I., & Litan, R. E. (2014). *Declining business dynamism in the United States: A look at states and metros.* Brookings Institution.

Hindle, K. (2007). Teaching entrepreneurship at university: From the wrong building to the right philosophy. In A. Fayolle (Ed.), *Handbook of research in entrepreneurship education* (Vol. 1, pp. 104–126). Edward Elgar Publishing.

Huang, C. C. (2009). Knowledge sharing and group cohesiveness on performance: An empirical study of technology R&D teams in Taiwan. *Technovation, 29*(11), 786–797.

Johnson, M. (2015). Stop talking about work/life balance. *Workforce Solutions Review, 6*(2), 4–7.

Kamovich, U., & Foss, L. (2017). In search of alignment: A review of impact studies in entrepreneurship education. *Education Research International.* https://doi.org/10.1155/2017/1450102

Kassean, H., Vanevenhoven, J., Liguori, E., & Winkel, D. E. (2015). Entrepreneurship education: A need for reflection, real-world experience and action. *International Journal of Entrepreneurial Behavior & Research.*

Keating, Raymond J. (2016). *Entrepreneurship in decline: Millions of missing businesses gap analysis #3*. Small Business & Entrepreneurship Council. https://sbecouncil.org/2016/08/04/gap-analysis-3-millions-of-missing-businesses/

Kolb, A. Y., & Kolb, D. A. (2008). Experiential learning theory: A dynamic, holistic approach to management learning. *Education and Development, 101*(20), 42–68.

Kolb, D. A. (1984). *Experiential learning: Experience as the source of learning and development*. Prentice-Hall International. https://pdfs.semanticscholar.org/f6ec/20a7a3150822140be7466353d0de572cc4bb.pdf

Lackéus, M., & Karen Williams M. (2018). Assessing experiential entrepreneurship education: Key insights from five methods in use at a venture creation programme. *Experiential learning for entrepreneurship* (pp. 19–49). Palgrave Macmillan.

Lumpkin, G. T., & Lichtenstein, B. B. (2005). The role of organizational learning in the opportunity—Recognition process. *Entrepreneurship Theory and Practice, 29*(4), 451–472.

Marston, C. (2010). *Motivating the "what's in it for me" workforce: Manage across the generational divide and increase profits*. John Wiley & Sons.

McMullen, J. S., & Dimov, D. (2013). Time and the entrepreneurial journey: The problems and promise of studying entrepreneurship as a process. *Journal of Management Studies, 50*(8), 1481–1512.

Merriam, S. B., & Bierema, L. L. (2013). *Adult learning: Linking theory and practice*. John Wiley & Sons.

Metz, A. (2014). Back to nature: The impact of nature relatedness on empathy and narcissism in the millennial generation. *Educational Specialist, 65*. https://commons.lib.jmu.edu/edspec201019/65

Middleton, K. W., & Donnellon, A. (2014). Personalizing entrepreneurial learning: A pedagogy for facilitating the know why. *Entrepreneurship Research Journal, 4*(2), 167–204.

Moon, J. A. (2004). *A handbook of reflective and experiential learning: Theory and practice*. Routledge.

Morris, M. (2014). Preface: Establishing moorings and foundations in entrepreneurial education. In M. H. Morris (Ed.), *Annals of entrepreneurship education and pedagogy–2014* (pp. xiii–xviii). Edward Elgar Publishing.

Morris, M. H., & Liguori, E. (Eds.). (2016). *Annals of entrepreneurship education and pedagogy–2016*. Edward Elgar Publishing.

Morris, N. M., Kuratko, D. F., & Pryor, C. G. (2014). Building blocks for the development of university-wide entrepreneurship. *Entrepreneurship Research Journal, 4*(1), 45–68.

Nabi, G., Liñán, F., Fayolle, A., Krueger, N., & Walmsley, A. (2017). The impact of entrepreneurship education in higher education: A systematic review and research agenda. *Academy of Management Learning & Education, 16*(2), 277–299.

Naia, A., Baptista, R., Januário, C., & Trigo, V. (2015). Entrepreneurship education literature in the 2000s. *Journal of Entrepreneurship Education, 18*(1), 111.

Neck, H., Greene, P., & Brush, C. (2014). Practice-based entrepreneurship education using actionable theory. In M. H. Morris (Ed.), *Annals of entrepreneurship education and pedagogy–2014* (pp. 3–20). Edward Elgar Publishing.

O'Connor, A. (2013). A conceptual framework for entrepreneurship education policy: Meeting government and economic purposes. *Journal of Business Venturing, 28*, 546–563.

Piaget, J. (1973). *To understand is to invent: The future of education.* Grossman publishers.

Pittaway, L., & Thorpe, R. (2012). A framework for entrepreneurial learning: A tribute to Jason Cope. *Entrepreneurship & Regional Development, 24*(9–10), 837–859.

QAA [Quality Assurance Agency for Higher Education]. (2018). *Enterprise and entrepreneurship education guidance for UK higher education providers.* http://www.qaa.ac.uk/en/Publications/Documents/Enterprise-and-entrpreneurship-education-2018.pdf

Rae, D., & Carswell, M. (2000). Using a life-story approach in researching entrepreneurial learning: The development of a conceptual model and its implications in the design of learning experiences. *Education and Training, 42*(4/5), 220–228.

Rogers, A. (2014). *The base of the iceberg: Informal learning and its impact on formal and non-formal learning.* Barbara Budrich Publishers.

Sarasvathy, S. D. (2009). *Effectuation: Elements of entrepreneurial expertise.* Edward Elgar Publishing.

Singh, R. P. (2001). A comment on developing the field of entrepreneurship through the study of opportunity recognition and exploitation. *Academy of Management Review, 26*(1), 10–12.

Singh, R. P., Hills, G. E., Lumpkin, G. T., & Hybels, R. C. (1999, August). The entrepreneurial opportunity recognition process: Examining the role of self-perceived alertness and social networks. In *Academy of management proceedings* (Vol. 1999, No. 1, pp. G1–G6). Briarcliff Manor, NY: Academy of Management.

Smilor, R. W. (1997). Entrepreneurship: Reflections on a subversive activity. *Journal of Business Venturing, 12*(5), 341–421. https://doi.org/10.1016/S0883-9026(97)00008-6

Solomon, G., & Matthews, C. (2014). The curricular confusion between entrepreneurship education and small business management: A qualitative analysis. In M. H. Morris (Ed.), *Annals of entrepreneurship education and pedagogy* (pp. 91–115). Edward Elgar Publishing.

Stevenson, H. H. (1983). *A perspective on entrepreneurship* (Vol. 13). Harvard Business School.

Svinicki, M., & McKeachie, W. J. (2011). *McKeachies's teaching tips*. Wadsworth Cengage Learning.

Syed, I., & Mueller, B. (2014). Finding the passion to persevere: An exploration of the mechanisms by which passion fuels entrepreneurial grit. *Frontiers of Entrepreneurship Research, 34*(6), 1. http://digitalknowledge.babson.edu/fer/vol34/iss6/1

Timmons, J. A., & Spinelli, S. (2007). *New venture creation: Entrepreneurship for the 21st century*. McGraw-Hill.

Tulgan, B. (2009). *Not everyone gets a trophy: How to manage generation y*. Jossey-Bass.

Twenge, J. M. (2009). Change over time in obedience: The jury's still out, but it might be decreasing. *American Psychology, 6*(1), 28–31.

Vesper, K. H., & Gartner, W. B. (1997). Measuring progress in entrepreneurship education. *Journal of Business Venturing, 12*(5), 403–421.

Wallas, G. (1926). *The art of thought*. Harcourt-Brace.

White, R., & D'Souza, R. (2014). Links between learning speed and opportunity recognition. In M. H. Morris (Ed.), *Annals of entrepreneurship education and pedagogy–2014* (pp. 21–43). Edward Elgar Publishing.

Wu, H., & Gu, J. (2017). Rethinking what is entrepreneurship education: A macro integrative perspective. *International Education Studies, 10*(6), 150.

Exploring the Professional Identity and Career Trajectories of Undergraduates on a Team-Based, Experiential Degree Programme

Lauren Davies, Berrbizne Urzelai, and Karolina Ozadowicz

1 ENTREPRENEURSHIP EDUCATION AND THE TEAM ACADEMY APPROACH

Entrepreneurship Education (EE) is a relatively new scholarly field and, according to Fayolle (2018), is rarely defined and conceptualised. There is a wide variety of approaches related to "how" to teach entrepreneurship and viewpoints of which approaches are superior abound (Hindle, 2007).

L. Davies (✉)
Team Entrepreneurship Programme, Faculty of Business & Law, University of the West of England, Bristol, England
e-mail: lauren.davies@uwe.ac.uk

B. Urzelai · K. Ozadowicz
University of the West of England, Bristol, England
e-mail: berrbizne2.urzelai@uwe.ac.uk

K. Ozadowicz
e-mail: karolina.ozadowicz@uwe.ac.uk

© The Author(s), under exclusive license to Springer Nature Switzerland AG 2022
G. J. Larios-Hernandez et al. (eds.), *Theorising Undergraduate Entrepreneurship Education*,
https://doi.org/10.1007/978-3-030-87865-8_11

Still, EE literature gives a lot of attention to student-centred methods, in which knowledge and content are defined by the students' needs and expectations, using such pedagogical methods as exploration, discussion and experimentation (Béchard & Gregoire, 2005).

Research in entrepreneurship education highlights that there are generally three types of courses: "about", "for" and "through" (Pittaway & Edwards, 2012). "About" courses typically teach theories about entrepreneurship, "for" courses focus on providing tools for completing specific tasks within entrepreneurship and "through" courses aim to move students through a process of entrepreneurial behaviour (Robinson et al., 2016). Pittaway and Edwards (2012) argue that "through" courses have the most potential to "produce" entrepreneurs, because they require students to mimic and simulate what entrepreneurs do.

An interesting example of EE delivery in an undergraduate context is that of the Team Academy model, pioneered in Finland during the 1990s. Today Team Academy-inspired degree programmes exist within higher education institutions spanning four continents and 16 countries (Akatemia, n.d.). Along with Northumbria University, the University of the West of England was the first in the UK to launch this degree programme in 2013, namely BA (Hons) Business: Team Entrepreneurship (referred to as Team Entrepreneurship hereafter).

The core principle of the Team Academy approach is that learning is team-based, self-managed and experiential. On Team Academy programmes, learners create and operate real enterprises and their learning is centred around their Team Company, a team of up to 20 fellow students that collaborate on projects and ventures and support each other's learning goals. Each Team Company is assigned a Team Coach, who supports learning through enquiry rather than instruction. Students are referred to as "Team Entrepreneurs" to emphasise the practice-led nature of the programme and to espouse the value of entrepreneurial mindset.

Within the Team Academy pedagogy, learners are required to engage in self-managed learning with support from others, namely peers within their Team Company and their Team Coach. This involves a form of negotiated learning in which Team Entrepreneurs are required to develop learning goals that align to their personal ambitions as well as the mission, vision and values of their Team Company, with regular feedback provided by their Team Coach and their peers.

2 Pedagogies That Support Entrepreneurial Learning

Within EE team-based pedagogies, experiential learning, and self-managed learning are often utilised to supporting entrepreneurial learning. While research highlights that most successful enterprises are founded by teams (Brüderl & Preisendörfer, 1998), undergraduate students often have pre-conceived notions of what it means to be entrepreneurial, often underpinned by stereotypes of entrepreneurs as charismatic individuals portrayed in the media (Warhuus et al., 2017). This viewpoint is supported by Gibb and Hannon (2006) who postulated that the association of entrepreneurship with high levels of innovation, scale and growth reinforce the "heroic" view of entrepreneurship as something difficult to attain and only for a select few. While entrepreneurship educators have started to recognise the value of students engaging in collaboration, and team formation is often included in the curriculum in entrepreneurship education programmes (Warhuus et al., 2017), there is surprisingly little research focused on the impact of team-based pedagogies within entrepreneurship education.

Considering business education more broadly, studies have explored the perceived benefits and challenges of a team-based pedagogy from students' perspectives (e.g. Schultz et al., 2010). Perceived benefits include the generation of increased ideas and stronger deliverables, owing to a wider range of perspectives and skillsets; improved learning, reduced workload and collective security, resulting in reduced anxiety and stress (Schultz et al., 2010). Students that favoured autonomous work highlighted key challenges in relation to team learning, including grade reciprocity; social loafing; schedule challenges and a disparity between "school teams" and "work teams", in which fellow students are viewed as "unreliable" and that levels of commitment and participation do not mirror those experienced in a work setting (Schultz et al., 2010).

The notion of a disparity between team learning within higher education and team working in an organisational context is interesting to consider. This poses questions regarding the authenticity of team-based learning within higher education. Lohmann et al. (2019, p. 458) argue that authentic team-based learning should include "authentic contexts and activities that require interaction and interdependence between team members to produce skills development and knowledge co-creation". They argue that business simulations can offer a learning environment that incorporates these elements. The approach offered on Team Academy arguably takes this a step further by transcending beyond team-learning via business simulations to a combination of team-based learning with authentic experiential learning within real ventures.

Experiential learning is prominent within EE and several studies have explored its efficacy. Taatila (2010) considers experiential learning to be the most effective method within entrepreneurship education because of the pragmatic and abductive, rather than deductive or inductive approach adopted. Numerous scholars (e.g. Mandel & Noyes, 2016) point towards experiential learning as effective learning where action is the primary source of learning and which requires students to intellectually and physically engage in the learning process and reflect on their experiences (Kolb, 1984). It departs from the traditional lecture-led passive learning, towards action-orientated, problem-solving and project-based learning (Jones & English, 2004). Heinonen and Poikkijoki (2006) found that this approach instils entrepreneurial skills and behaviours, while also broadening students' perspectives. Through "learning by doing" and reflecting on learning, it is argued that the student becomes more competent in crucial elements of entrepreneurship, such as recognising opportunities (Heinonen & Poikkijoki, 2006).

However, Scott et al. (2016) argue that there is little evidence that experiential learning is more effective than other approaches in entrepreneurship education. The authors postulate that much of the literature within entrepreneurship education highlights "good practice" within experiential approaches and that these are assumed to be more effective than "traditional" approaches, but the underlying philosophies behind such approaches are not built upon how effective they are. Moreover, the authors point to a lack of empirical evidence that such approaches are more effective at enabling students to achieve desired learning outcomes.

Entrepreneurial individuals also need to manage their own learning and understand their individual strengths and weaknesses. As Tseng (2013) argues, entrepreneurs are required to take ownership of their learning, continuously responding to changes in their personal contexts, thus self-managed learning can be seen as a key approach in meeting the complex demands associated with the changing world of work. Self-managed learning can be seen as synonymous with self-directed learning, defined by Brookfield (2009) as a learning process in which individuals take the initiative, with or without the help of others, in identifying their own learning needs, creating appropriate learning goals and devising suitable learning strategies to help them achieve their defined goals.

While the aforementioned studies have explored the impact of these pedagogies on entrepreneurial learning, few have considered the impact of integrating these approaches within one programme of study. The Team Academy pedagogy thus represents somewhat of a unique approach to EE delivery in terms of how these pedagogies are integrated.

3   Professional and Entrepreneurial Identity

Studies have shown that development of one's professional identity helps to enhance learning. Professional identity is defined by Tan et al. (2017, p. 1505) as "the self that has been developed with the commitment to perform competently and legitimately in the context of the profession, and its development can continue over the course of the individuals' careers".

It is argued that an individual that has developed a sense of professional identity can find meaning in their work and identify with their profession's guiding beliefs and values. For example, Jensen and Jetten (2016) found that students needed to develop their sense of professional identity in order to understand their intended profession and visualise themselves in this domain. This emphasises professional socialisation, the "social construction and internalisation of norms and values by the profession" (Ajjawi & Higgs 2008, p. 135), which occurs over time and requires a commitment to learning (Tomlinson & Jackson, 2019).

Donnellon et al. (2014) suggest that successful entrepreneurship education should consider incorporating the concept of self-identity (i.e. subjective views entrepreneurs hold about themselves as revealed through their narratives) into programme design. With a well-established link between learning and identity development (Wenger, 1998) there has been a growing emphasis on exploring how EE interlinks with identity creation (Heinonen et al., 2013; Matlay & Harmeling, 2011;.

Several studies explore the role of entrepreneurship education in the creation of the student entrepreneurial identity (e.g. Donnellon et al., 2014; Howorth et al., 2012; Matlay & Harmeling, 2011). As entrepreneurial identity has a direct impact on the outcomes of entrepreneurial actions, one of the priorities of EE could be to ensure such identity of entrepreneurs is established during the course of EE interventions (Matlay & Harmeling, 2011).

The work of Nielsen et al. (2017) provides a starting point for understanding the multiple identity processes involved in negotiating between the two identities of "student" and "entrepreneur". The authors posit a continuum from low ("student" or "entrepreneur") to high ("student" and "entrepreneur") identity plurality.

4 Methodology

This study adopted a mixed methodology encompassing four key stages.

Stage 1—Documentary Analysis of Final year Team Entrepreneurs' Learning Contract Assignments

The Learning Contract is an example of negotiated learning in which Team Entrepreneurs agree specific goals with their Team Company (including their Team Coach) and reflect on their long-term vision. In order to determine their vision, it is useful for learners to reflect on where they have been and where they are now, including key factors that have shaped their personal journeys and their values, beliefs and mindset. The Learning Contract is thus a rich source of data in relation to final year Team Entrepreneurs' reflections on their identity and career decision-making.

A total of 10 Learning Contracts were analysed out of 46 final year Team Entrepreneurs. Key themes were highlighted, and the data was used to inform the design and recruitment for the semi-structured interview with both graduates and final year Team Entrepreneurs.

Stage 2—Analysis of Destinations of Leavers of Higher Education Data for the Programme

This helped set the context for the study and enabled the researchers to understand the extent to which self-employment is taken as a graduate career path on the programme, compared to professional-level employed positions and other career choices.

Stage 3—Online Questionnaire with Graduates of the Team Entrepreneurship Programme

The questionnaire was distributed to all of the 172 graduates of the programme for which email contact information was available, resulting in completion by 43 graduates in total. The questionnaire explored graduates' current career situation and whether they identified with certain terms in relation to entrepreneurship (e.g. "entrepreneur", "intrapreneur", "entrepreneurial"). This highlighted key themes to explore in greater depth in the interviews.

Stage 4—Semi-Structured Interviews with Team Entrepreneurship Graduates and Final year Team Entrepreneurs

Interviews were conducted with seven graduates of the programme and two final year Team Entrepreneurs, allowing key themes identified in the questionnaire and Learning Contract analysis to be explored in greater depth.

Table 1, found in the Appendices, provides anonymous contextual information on all research participants, and a reference code is assigned to each individual which will be referenced when directly quoting participants.

5   FINDINGS

This section will summarise the professional and entrepreneurial identity, career decision-making and career trajectories of Team Entrepreneurs/Team Entrepreneurship graduates and the impact that the Team Academy pedagogy has on these aspects.

Professional and Entrepreneurial Identity

Our research has found that the self-perceived professional identity of Team Entrepreneurs/Team Entrepreneurship graduates varies considerably and it is not associated to one specific profession. Thus, how do Team Entrepreneurs develop their sense of professional identity in a programme where there is no pre-defined professional pathway? If we are to assume that the Team Entrepreneurship programme may support learners to become "entrepreneurial", for a wide range of career pathways including, but not limited to, self-employment, then it is pertinent to consider how entrepreneurial identities may be formed within entrepreneurship education programmes.

Values-Driven Identities

There is a strong sense of values-driven identity formation from the final-year and graduate Team Entrepreneurs. Several of the participants appear to have a strong sense of the values and beliefs that shape their identity, either as an entrepreneur or within their graduate career destinations/ambitions. This may relate to having a strong sense of who they are as an individual and what they desire from their chosen career, whether as an employee, an entrepreneur or both.

It appears that the strong focus on self-reflection within the programme, particularly prominent within the self-managed and experiential learning pedagogies, enables graduates to develop strong levels of self-awareness and a deep understanding of what drives them. Through directing their own learning according to their needs, Team Entrepreneurs learn how to reflect authentically on their strengths, weaknesses, ambitions and values. Furthermore, through experimenting with different types of projects and ventures, through experiential learning, and subsequently reflecting on the key learning that they have gained through their entrepreneurial actions, Team Entrepreneurs develop their reflective skills further and a strong level of self-awareness.

Engaging in experiential entrepreneurial learning also enables Team Entrepreneurs' to develop their entrepreneurial identity to a greater or lesser extent, or at least to develop some of the competencies associated with being entrepreneurial. This supports the viewpoint of Heinonen and Poikkijoki (2006) that through "learning by doing" and reflecting on learning, learners becomes more competent in elements of entrepreneurship, such as recognising opportunities.

It can be argued that, on Team Entrepreneurship, learning transcends beyond learning to recognise opportunities to learning how to create opportunities. This is, in part, driven by the self-managed pedagogy in which learners set their own goals and engage in their own initiated projects and ventures. Thus, we can see that the integration of self-managed and experiential learning pedagogies enables learners to develop high levels of entrepreneurial competencies and strong skills in self-reflection.

Self-Motivation

A key theme that emerges throughout the research is that of self-motivation being a key aspect of Team Entrepreneurs'/Team Entrepreneurship graduates' professional identity. Several interviewees describe themselves using phrases such as "driven" and "self-motivated". Again, this appears to be, in part, driven by the self-managed learning pedagogy. Our research finds that the extent to which Team Entrepreneurs' exhibit self-motivation varies, but that the self-managed pedagogy appears to be instrumental in developing this quality. This is highlighted in the quote below from a final year Team Entrepreneur:

> I know that it was kind of a shock at the beginning...like 'why do we have to run these training sessions?'...I'd say that that style of learning is a lot more beneficial. I mean, there are times when I feel like, you know, I would quite like to be more knowledgeable in something, but I recognise that I'd probably have to pick up a book on that and do some research into it, which means you have to be quite a motivated and driven individual, which is definitely something that I feel I'm slowly building up to being. (SSI008)

Team/Community Identity

While the research focused on Team Entrepreneurs'/graduates' individual professional identities, the strong focus on team-learning inevitably plays a significant role in their identity formation. Team dynamics emerge as a prominent theme across the research, including reflections on the skills developed through working as part of a team, such as coaching and leadership, as well as reflections on the challenges of balancing team and individual priorities.

While team dynamics can be a challenge, it appears that such challenges offer rich learning experiences for the Team Entrepreneurs. For example, one Team Entrepreneur reflects on his key learning from a team venture formed with some of the members of his Team Company:

> I learnt more from building [Business Name] than I had ever learnt in my entire life. I gained so much experience. But, it was destined to fall apart. In the end, we all had different values, which made it difficult to work together. (SSI0015)

Participants also reflect on the shared learning space, socialisation, community and team-learning element as a distinctive feature of the programme. This encompasses relationships built with team members and Team Coaches and creating a safe space to test their ideas.

> There is no community like the TE community. I say that because what you learn, how to work in a team, is so essential to how you should be in everyday life [...]. (SSI003)

> Being able to... test out those ideas on the course in what is quite a safe environment. That was a really great aspect of the course and real, you know, learning curve [...] One key factor that I personally think is great about the course is the integration between all the levels. So, like the fact that I would know Level 2 and Level 3 really well even though I was a first year was so valuable to me and my development. We're all in the same space where, you know, we're encouraged to share and communicate. (SSI004)

> Everyone can learn from everyone else and we spent a lot more time with each other so it becomes...like a family. (SSI006)

Such reflections mirror the phenomenon of "collective security" referred to by Schultz et al. (2010) in relation to the perceived benefits (from students' perspectives) of team-based learning within business education. Interestingly, while this "collective security" is viewed in high regard by the graduates interviewed, some reflected on the sense of being in "a bubble" during their time on the programme. In some cases, this leads to a juxtaposition between their experience on the programme and the realities of running a business and/or developing their career after graduating. The programme is intended to prepare graduates for their futures through a pedagogy focused on learning through real entrepreneurial projects and ventures, rather than case studies or simulations, so this is a surprising finding.

> I feel like sometimes when you're on TE you can have like a student bubble [...]. I'd say that in the environment of TE I would have considered myself an entrepreneur 100% but within the environment of like not having the financial backing of like student finance...I don't want to say in the real world but...when you're outside of that environment and you're in with all the other players...that's why I would say the money thing...I wouldn't call myself an entrepreneur until I'm fully paying myself. (SSI003)

EXPLORING THE PROFESSIONAL IDENTITY AND CAREER ...   201

> I think I've been able to know that I'm capable of certain things [since graduating], but also there's a lot of areas where I need to improve on, whereas on TE I think you probably think that you're better in a certain area than you are, either because you haven't really tried that area or just because you're in that bit of a bubble, where you probably think 'I will be all right'. Whereas when you're in real life business you know you are actually having to do something that you quickly find out on areas where you are not strong enough. (SSI004)

Entrepreneurial Identity

Related to the previous point, regarding the sense of being in "a bubble", there is a sense from some of the graduates that they considered their entrepreneurial skills and/or their sense of entrepreneurial identity to be stronger during their time on the programme, compared to their perspective now as a graduate, as illustrated by the previous two quotes. This leads on to an interesting theme that emerged from the interviews and questionnaires, that some participants seem to question their legitimacy as an entrepreneur and feel that they have to "earn" that title.

Interestingly, some of the participants expressed that they would not identify as an entrepreneur even though they had started their own venture. They argue that their ventures are at too early a stage to legitimately call themselves an "entrepreneur", thus suggesting that achieving a certain level of success and maturity within their venture would allow them to identify with that term. Some consider paying themselves a "decent" income from the business to be a measure of success, while others are less clear on what that measure of success looks like.

> All of my friends say 'you're an entrepreneur because you're doing this, you've done that', but I sometimes don't feel like one...I feel like I might be still at the early stages of starting something...I think that until I make it to a certain level of success...I can't earn that badge of entrepreneur, you know?. (SSI006)

This somewhat reinforces the viewpoints of Warhuus et al. (2017) and Gibb and Hannon (2006) regarding the stereotypical/"heroic" notion of an individual entrepreneur that many undergraduates hold. On a related note, an interesting discussion point in the interviews was around the duality of the "student" and "entrepreneur" identity, building on the work of Nielsen et al. (2017). Within the Team Entrepreneurship programme, learners are referred to as "Team Entrepreneurs" rather than students, but do they identify with this term? Do they consider themselves students rather than entrepreneurs, entrepreneurs rather than students or perhaps a combination of both?

The majority of interviewees highlighted that they considered themselves both a student and a Team Entrepreneur, reflecting that the environment outside of the programme, i.e. living a "typical student lifestyle" has an influence on this identity. One of the graduate interviewees expressed that he did not identify as a student, thus finding resonance with the "Team Entrepreneur" identity.

> I clearly remember saying 'I'm not a student, I'm a Team Entrepreneur. I'm here to start a business. I'm working three times as hard as the average student'. (SSI005)

While others highlighted that they identified as a student, while recognising the unique nature of the programme and the opportunities it affords.

> ...I've always felt like a student, but I felt like I've had more privileges than other students, essentially because we are treated like entrepreneurs. We are given those opportunities. So, there is kind of a balance and I think it's a good balance. (SSI008)

This suggests that the combination of self-managed and experiential learning pedagogies plays a key role in the formation of an entrepreneurial identity, in that learners value the independence to direct their own learning and the opportunities provided through a strong focus on experiential learning. The findings suggest that the different levels of integration of the different pedagogies (the "team", the "self" and the "doing") is key in the way the team entrepreneurs construct their own learning and entrepreneurial identity.

Career Decision-Making and Career Trajectories

Analysis of questionnaire data, and of the data captured through the Destinations of Leavers from Higher Education survey between 2015 and 2017, highlights that the Team Entrepreneurship programme has experienced a shift in graduate outcomes, with a larger percentage of graduates attaining graduate-level employment and fewer graduates starting their own business. Data from the cohort graduating in 2016 highlighted that 45% of the graduates completing the survey had started a business or become self-employed within six months of graduating, compared with only 21% within the 2017 graduating cohort. The data collected from the online questionnaire for this chapter highlights that 15% of graduate participants are self-employed as their main source of income.

The types of roles that Team Entrepreneurship graduates attain vary, but include graduate trainee roles, recruitment consultancy and business management roles, including sales and marketing management and office management. These roles appear largely similar to the destinations of graduates of a more traditional business management degree programme, which is surprising given the strong focus on entrepreneurial learning within the programme. While the programme does not espouse to equip learners solely with the skills required for creating their own ventures, one might expect graduates of the programme to attain roles requiring more of an "enterprising" approach, such as those within start-ups.

Our findings thus do not support the notion espoused by Pittaway and Edwards (2012) that "through" type entrepreneurship education courses have the most potential to "produce" entrepreneurs. We argue that focusing on "producing" entrepreneurs ignores the myriad of complexities in relation to the purpose of entrepreneurship education. Our findings thus support the views proposed by Penaluna et al. (2012) that the commonly employed metric of business start-up does not account for the full breadth of entrepreneurship education and of Neck et al. (2014) that the role of entrepreneurship educators is to "unleash the entrepreneurial spirit" of students to support them in navigating increasingly uncertain futures.

So, how does the Team Entrepreneurship pedagogy influence career decision-making? As was found when considering the impact on professional identity, the self-managed learning pedagogy appears to have a strong influence on Team Entrepreneurs' value formation, which influences their chosen career paths. Through navigating their own learning and reflecting on their interests, values and beliefs, Team Entrepreneurs seem to develop a strong desire to join/create values-driven organisations. For example, several participants have founded, or are in the process of founding social enterprises while others have found graduate employment within charitable organisations. Participants discuss the desire to "do good" in the world and to make a difference.

One of the graduate interviewees discusses his experience of joining an organisation whose values did not align with his own and his dissatisfaction with the organisational culture. He reflects that, upon this realisation, he created an adapted Learning Contract (an assessment utilised on the programme as a self-managed learning tool) to identify his long-term ambitions and drivers and this resulted in him successfully pursuing a career within the third sector.

Arguably, the team-learning pedagogy may indirectly influence graduates in their pursuit of values-driven career paths. The strong sense of community on Team Entrepreneurship appears to create a desire amongst graduates to work with like-minded people and in an organisation where the mission, vision and values align with one's own. Learning together in a team for three years, co-creating value and developing a shared sense of purpose within their Team Companies seems to instil a strong desire amongst Team Entrepreneurship graduates for belonging and collectivism within their chosen career.

The experiential learning pedagogy seems to play a significant role in influencing the career decision-making of Team Entrepreneurs and graduates. Participants discuss the benefits of experimenting with different types of projects and ventures, in a relatively safe environment, in helping them determine their chosen career path, which may or may not include venture creation. Such experimentation allows Team Entrepreneurs to reflect on their strengths and weaknesses, demonstrating strong levels of self-awareness, which also seems to have a positive impact when interviewing for graduate positions.

Finally, entrepreneurial ambitions are prevalent amongst some of the participants. For some, the Team Entrepreneurship programme seems to have re-affirmed their desire to create their own venture. In some cases this is driven by the negative motivation of not wishing to work for somebody else. The self-managed pedagogy perhaps heightens this independent mindset in some cases. Others seem to be driven by the positive motivation of wanting to create their own path, which again seems to be reinforced by the self-managed pedagogy whereby learners direct their own learning.

6 Conclusion

The Team Academy pedagogy enables learners to develop a values-driven professional identity and a strong sense of self-motivation, constructed through self-managed, experiential learning. The strong sense of community, instilled through team-learning, and of "a safe space to fail", supported by experiential learning, appear to be key elements of the programme that learners value and that support them in the formation of their professional and/or entrepreneurial identity. A consideration for the programme is how to ensure the "safe space" does not become a "bubble", which does not align with the reality faced upon graduation, i.e. how to ensure that experiential learning is truly authentic.

The self-managed and experiential learning pedagogies seem to have a noticeable influence on career decision-making through enabling learners to develop strong levels of self-awareness in terms of their strengths and weaknesses and their core values and beliefs. The team learning pedagogy seems to indirectly influence some Team Entrepreneurs in pursuing careers within the social enterprise and charitable sectors, driven by a desire to work towards a shared purpose.

While previous studies have considered the impact of team-learning, experiential learning and self-managed learning within an entrepreneurship education context, few have considered the impact of integrating these pedagogical approaches within one programme design, particularly in relation to the impact on professional identity and career decision-making. The study makes an important contribution to the field of entrepreneurship education by considering the impact of the unique Team Academy model of learning, through seeking to understand how the combination of pedagogical approaches influences learners in forming their sense of professional identity and in their career decision-making.

APPENDIX

Table 1 Research participants

Year of graduation	Age group	Gender	Employment status	Data collection	Reference code
2016	24–26	Male	Employed (full time)	Questionnaire	Q001
2016	24–26	Male	Self-employed	Questionnaire	Q002
2016	24–26	Make	Other, please specify	Questionnaire	Q003
2016	24–26	Female	Employed (full time)	Questionnaire	Q004
2016	24–26	Female	Employed (full time), Employed (part time), Self-employed	Questionnaire Interview	Q005
2016	24–26	Male	Employed (full time), Further study	Questionnaire	Q006
2016	24–26	Female	Employed (full time)	Questionnaire	Q007
2016	27–30	Male	Self-employed	Questionnaire	Q008
2017	24–26	Male	Employed (full time)	Questionnaire	Q009
2017	24–26	Male	Employed (full time)	Questionnaire	Q010
2017	24–26	Male	Employed (full time)	Questionnaire	Q011
2017	24–26	Male	Employed (full time)	Questionnaire	Q012
2017	24–26	Male	Employed (full time)	Questionnaire	Q013
2018	21–23	Female	Employed (full time), Self-employed	Questionnaire	Q014
2018	21–23	Male	Employed (full time)	Questionnaire	Q015
2018	24–26	Male	Employed (full time)	Questionnaire	Q016
2018	21–23	Male	Employed (full time)	Questionnaire	Q017
2018	24–26	Male	Employed (full time), Self-employed	Questionnaire	Q018

(continued)

Table 1 (continued)

Year of graduation	Age group	Gender	Employment status	Data collection	Reference code
2018	21–23	Male	Employed (full time)	Questionnaire	Q019
2018	24–26	Male	Employed (full time)	Questionnaire	Q020
2018	21–23	Male	Employed (full time)	Questionnaire	Q021
2019	21–23	Female	Further study	Questionnaire	Q022
2019	21–23	Female	Employed (full time)	Questionnaire	Q023
2020	21–23	Male	Employed (full time)	Questionnaire	Q024
2020	21–23	Male	Employed (full time)	Questionnaire	Q025
2020	24–26	Male	Self-employed	Questionnaire	Q026
2020	21–23	Male	Further study	Questionnaire	Q027
2020	21–23	Female	Self-employed	Questionnaire	Q028
2020	21–23	Male	Self-employed, Further study	Questionnaire	Q029
2020	21–23	Male	Self-employed, Further study	Questionnaire	Q030
2020	24–26	Male	Employed (part time)	Questionnaire	Q031
2020	21–23	Female	Employed (part time), Unemployed	Questionnaire	Q032
2020	21–23	Male	Employed (full time)	Questionnaire	Q033
2020	21–23	Male	Employed (full time)	Questionnaire	Q034
2020	24–26	Male	Employed (full time)	Questionnaire	Q035
2020	21–23	Male	Employed (full time)	Questionnaire	Q036
2016	24–26	Male	Self-employed	Questionnaire Interview	SSI001
2019	21–23	Male	Employed (full time)	Questionnaire Interview	SSI002
2019	24–26	Female	Self-employed	Questionnaire Interview	SSI003

(continued)

208 L. DAVIES ET AL.

Table 1 (continued)

Year of graduation	Age group	Gender	Employment status	Data collection	Reference code
2020	21–23	Male	Employed (part time), running business	Questionnaire Interview	SSI004
2018	24–26	Male	Self-employed	Questionnaire Interview	SSI005
2017	27–30	Male	Employed (full time), setting up business	Questionnaire Interview	SSI006
2020	24–26	Female	Employed (part time), setting up business	Questionnaire Interview	SSI007
2021	21–23	Female	Final year Team Entrepreneur	Questionnaire Interview Documentary analysis	SSI008
2021	21–23	Males	Final year Team Entrepreneur	Questionnaire Interview Documentary analysis	SSI009
2021	21–23	Male	Final year Team Entrepreneur	Documentary analysis	SSI0010
2021	21–23	Males	Final year Team Entrepreneur	Documentary analysis	SSI0011
2021	21–23	Male	Final year Team Entrepreneur	Documentary analysis	SSI0012
2021	21–23	Male	Final year Team Entrepreneur	Documentary analysis	SSI0013
2021	21–23	Male	Final year Team Entrepreneur	Documentary analysis	SSI0014
2021	21–23	Male	Final year Team Entrepreneur	Documentary analysis	SSI0015
2021	18–20	Male	Final year Team Entrepreneur	Documentary analysis	SSI0016
2021	18–20	Male	Final year Team Entrepreneur	Documentary analysis	SSI0017

Source Own Elaboration

REFERENCES

Ajjawi, R., & Higgs, J. (2008). Learning to reason: A journey of professional socialisation. *Advances in Health Sciences Education, 13*(2), 133–150.

Akatemia, (n.d.). *Team academy degrees—Akatemia*. Available at: https://aka temia.org.uk/team-academy-degrees/.

Béchard, J. P., & Grégoire, D. (2005). Entrepreneurship education research revisited: The case of higher education. *Academy of Management Learning & Education, 4*(1), 22–43.

Brookfield, S. (2009). Self-directed learning. In R. Maclean & D. Wilson (Eds), *International handbook of education for the changing world of work* (pp. 2615–2627). Springer.

Brüderl, J., & Preisendörfer, P. (1998). Network support and the success of newly founded business. *Small Business Economics, 10*(3), 213–225.

Donnellon, A., Ollila, S., & Middleton, K. W. (2014). Constructing entrepreneurial identity in entrepreneurship education. *The International Journal of Management Education, 12*(3), 490–499.

Fayolle, A. (Ed.). (2018). *A research agenda for entrepreneurship education*. Edward Elgar Publishing.

Gibb, A., & Hannon, P. (2006). Towards the entrepreneurial university? *International Journal of Entrepreneurship Education, 4*, 73–110.

Heinonen, J., Hytti, U., & Vuorinen, E. (2013). Intrapreneurial risk-taking in public healthcare: Challenging existing boundaries. In *Entrepreneurial business and society*. Edward Elgar Publishing.

Heinonen, J., & Poikkijoki, S. (2006). An entrepreneurial-directed approach to entrepreneurship education: Mission impossible? *Journal of Management Development, 25*(1), 80–94.

Hindle, K. (2007). Teaching entrepreneurship at university: From the wrong building to the right philosophy. *Handbook of Research in Entrepreneurship Education, 1*, 104–126.

Howorth, C., Smith, S. M., & Parkinson, C. (2012). Social learning and social entrepreneurship education. *Academy of Management Learning & Education, 11*(3), 371–389.

Jensen, D., & Jetten, J. (2016). The importance of developing students' academic and professional identities in higher education. *Journal of College Student Development, 57*(8), 1027–1042.

Jones, C., & English, J. (2004). A contemporary approach to entrepreneurship education. *Education and Training, 46*(8/9), 416–423.

Kolb, D. (1984). *Experiential learning: Experience as the source of learning and development*. Prentice-Hall.

Lohmann, G., Pratt, M. A., Benckendorff, P., Strickland, P., Reynolds, P., & Whitelaw, P. A. (2019). Online business simulations: Authentic teamwork, learning outcomes, and satisfaction. *Higher Education, 77*(3), 455–472.

Mandel, R., & Noyes, E. (2016). Survey of experiential entrepreneurship education offerings among top undergraduate entrepreneurship programs. *Education and Training, 58*(2), 164–178.

Matlay, H., & Harmeling, S. S. (2011). Re-storying an entrepreneurial identity: Education, experience and self-narrative. *Education and Training, 53*, 741–749.

Neck, H., Greene, P., & Brush, C. (2014). *Teaching entrepreneurship: A practice-based approach*. Edward Elgar Publishing Limited.

Nielsen, S. L., & Gartner, W. B. (2017). Am I a student and/or entrepreneur? Multiple identities in student entrepreneurship. *Education and Training, 59*(2), 135–154.

Penaluna, K., Penaluna, A., & Jones, C. (2012). The context of enterprise education: Insights into current practices. *Industry & Higher Education, 26*(3), 163–175.

Pittaway, L., & Cope, J. (2007). Entrepreneurship education: A systematic review of the evidence. *International Small Business Journal, 25*(5), 479–510.

Pittaway, L., & Edwards, C. (2012). Assessment: Examining practice in entrepreneurship education. *Education and Training, 54*, 778–800.

Robinson, S., Neergaard, H., Tanggaard, L., & Krueger, N. (2016). New horizons in entrepreneurship: From teacher-led to student-centered learning. *Education and Training, 58*(7/8), 661–683.

Schultz, J. L., Wilson, J. R., & Hess, K. C. (2010). Team-based classroom pedagogy reframed: The student perspective. *American Journal of Business Education, 3*(7), 17–24.

Scott, J., Penaluna, A., & Thompson, J. (2016). A critical perspective on learning outcomes and the effectiveness of experiential approaches in entrepreneurship education: Do we innovate or implement? *Education & Training, 58*(1), 82–93.

Taatila, V.P. (2010). Learning entrepreneurship in higher education. *Education+Training, 52*(1), 48–61.

Tan, C., Van der Molen, H., & Schmidt, H. (2017). A measure of professional identity development for professional education. *Studies in Higher Education, 42*(8), 1504–1519.

Tomlinson, M., & Jackson, D. (2019). Professional identity formation in contemporary higher education students. *Studies in Higher Education, 46*(4). https://doi.org/10.1080/03075079.2019.1659763.

Tseng, C. (2013). Connecting self-directed learning with entrepreneurial learning to entrepreneurial performance. *International Journal of Entrepreneurial Behaviour & Research, 19*(4), 425–446.

Warhuus, J. P., Tanggaard, L., Robinson, S., & Ernø, S. M. (2017). From I to We: Collaboration in entrepreneurship education and learning? *Education and Training, 59*(3), 234–249.

Wenger, E. (1998). Communities of practice: Learning as a social system. *Systems Thinker, 9*(5), 2–3.

Delivering Entrepreneurship Education for Would-Be and Existing Small Business Entrepreneurs

Peter Wyer, Seynam Kwakuvi-Zagbedeh, and Jonathan Nii Okai Welbeck

Chapter Contribution

If one accepts that a major task of educators in entrepreneurship is to equip students with knowledge and skills to survive in a fast and rapidly changing environment (Linton & Klinton, 2019), then such

---

P. Wyer (✉)
Institute of Continuing Education, University of Cambridge, Cambridge, UK

S. Kwakuvi-Zagbedeh
Bank of Ghana, Accra, Ghana

J. N. O. Welbeck
Founder & Director Enterprise Risk Management Institute,
University of Ghana, Accra, Ghana
e-mail: Jnowelbeck@ug.edu.gh

© The Author(s), under exclusive license to Springer Nature
Switzerland AG 2022
G. J. Larios-Hernandez et al. (eds.), *Theorising Undergraduate Entrepreneurship Education*,
https://doi.org/10.1007/978-3-030-87865-8_12

entrepreneurship education processes must be informed by robust understanding of just how enterprising individuals effectively cope with such change contexts.

This is particularly so in the case of nurturing entrepreneurial capabilities commensurate with small business development where problems associated with 'smallness of operation', organisational resource and ability constraints exacerbate the task of effective interface with the external environment. And where academia and the world of small business support continues to fall short in determining how best to help would-be and existing owner managers in this key task.

This chapter addresses that shortfall. Drawing upon our many years of in-depth case study and 'partnership working' action research within micro and small enterprises in developed, emerging and transitional economies, we demonstrate the potential application of personal construct theory (Kelly, 1955, 1977) in understanding entrepreneurial small business management and provision of entrepreneurship education which fosters that understanding and integral abilities.

Central to our thesis is how in-depth insight into what constitutes 'best small business strategic management practice' begins to make explicit the core body of managerial, organisational and learning skills and abilities that we as entrepreneurship educators should be fostering in both undergraduates and practising owner managers—and how it informs design and delivery modes of such education process.

We commence by making explicit the distinctiveness of small business and the unique problem-types they potentially face. Teasing out for special attention the key difficulty they face of relating to their uncertain external operating environment, we draw upon personal construct theory to demonstrate the highly complex strategic learning task they face. This chapter then proceeds with brief presentation of our own research findings of what constitutes best small business strategic learning and development practice.

We then consider the finer detail of the key parameters of personal construct theory (PCT) as robust foundation for proffering of how a more concerted utilisation of PCT can effectively inform design and delivery of entrepreneurship education for undergraduate students.

1 Distinctiveness of Small Business

Our ongoing research interfaces and partnership working with small businesses (Smallbone & Wyer, 2012; Wyer, 1990; Wyer & Bowman, 2019; Wyer & Smallbone, 1999; Wyer et al., 2010) continues to highlight their distinctiveness vis-à-vis large well-resourced companies and the need for those involved in their support to recognise, understand and respond to that distinctiveness.

Our work orients around micro enterprises and small businesses and as a classification approximation is guided by the EU defined employee base whereby micro enterprises are deemed those organisations employing up to 9 workers and small businesses are those with a staff base of between 10 and 50 workers (EU, 2015).

Integral to our co-working with micro and small enterprises is the progressive reinforcement of understanding of the distinctiveness of such businesses and use of that understanding in both training and consultancy support. Crucially, that 'distinctiveness understanding' informs our conceptualisation of small business entrepreneurship and entrepreneurship education.

While smallness of operation confers possible benefits such as ease of decision-making, fast responsiveness or functioning as a close-knit social unit, such advantages are *not absolute*—rather they are potential benefits that have to be worked for and earned.

The early works of Gibb (1983, 1990, 1997) and Wyer (1990—ongoing) highlight how the distinguishing features of small businesses have their origins in owner manager and size-related characteristics and may culminate in unique problem-types. For example, owner manager attitudes, values, preferences and abilities can impact beneficially or in constraining manner on the development of his or her enterprise.

Potential size-related constraints can impact all functional areas of activity. Ability to access reasonable cost working and developmental capital is frequently restricted by lack of collateral or profit history—with banks perceiving smaller enterprises as high risk (Irwin & Scott, 2010). The early works of Curran (1988) highlighted key staffing issues: small businesses frequently face a marginal labour market whereby inability to match large company wage levels or career path can leave small firm owner managers attracting less experienced, qualified or committed workforce. Thereby encountering problems such as persistent lateness, low quality and productivity levels or leaving without notice.

Crucially, inability to cope with the vagaries of the external environment is a predominant size-related difficulty (Gibb, 1983) and major impediment to small business survival and development (Kwakuvi-Zagbedeh, 2019).

2 Use of Personal Construct Theory in Understanding and Supporting Small Business

The Highly Complex Nature of Small Business Strategic Learning

Integral to our work is the use of PCT to make explicit the complexity of the small business strategic learning task and unfold robust insight into how more entrepreneurial small businesses cope with that complexity and learn in practice. This understanding in turn helps shape the provision of entrepreneurship education.

Our use of a version of Personal Construct Theory (PCT: Kelly, 1955) as drive motor to our small enterprise case study and action research has facilitated conceptualisation of the high-level complexity of the small business strategic learning task in coping with what is effectively an unpredictable external operating environment. And of just how entrepreneurial owner managers do in every-day practice learn about and act upon such operating contexts.

For Stacey (1990, 1993), the contemporary external environment is not only highly uncertain, businesses are predominantly facing open-ended change situations that are unknowable and unpredictable in terms of timing and consequences—essentially unplannable and requiring high-level management capability to identify and learn about such change.

In brief, PCT views an individual as a kind of 'inquiring scientist' ('man the scientist') who when faced with a change situation creates his or her own personal theories or mental models to try to understand that situation and guide his/her behaviour in dealing with that situation.

We as individuals, having formulated our own personal theory or hypothesis as to what appears to be happening and of how we should behave in order to deal with that situation, then test out our personal theory by putting it into action. If our behaviour produces the outcome we have anticipated, our personal theory is confirmed as valid. We have confidence in the theory and will use it again in the future if a similar change situation arises. In such circumstances, we merely undertake *'simple'* learning—using an existing personal construct more or less in its current form, with only marginal adjustment to fit the encountered similar circumstances.

However, when a change situation that an individual faces is new to her, of a nature never before experienced, her existing personal constructs will be inadequate. In such cases, he or she is faced with a difficult learning task of surfacing and challenging the assumptions upon which the personal construct is based. This is a highly '*complex*' learning task— it requires her to attempt to improve her constructs by altering them to better inform her behaviour and actions or developing a totally new personal construct.

Thus, extrapolating this conceptualisation to the small business development context, to effectively '*complex*' learn owner managers have to:

- Surface underlying assumptions that underpin their existing personal constructs.
- Reflect on those assumptions.
- Consider those assumptions vis-à-vis insight being offered by alternative personal constructs and worldviews held by others (in dialogue; observation; reading and so on).
- Challenge their own existing personal construct assumptions.
- 'Try on for size' the world views of others to 'see if there is anything in it for me' (Beck, 1980).
- Test out in action their own newly developing personal construct for confidence-build and confirmation of practical usefulness.

Moreover, there are potential barriers or constraints that can hinder or constrain the owner manager's adjustment or enhancements of his or her personal constructs. Constraints which may be self- and/or externally imposed, including: holding fixed attitudes, selective focusing on limited issues or embracing frozen meanings where, for example, an individual lacks understanding of the issue under consideration, feels need for more information or dislikes being pushed beyond his comfort zone.

Clearly, if we can lift the lid on the current 'black box of hazy understanding' of how more entrepreneurial owner managers of successfully developing small businesses undertake such complex learning then we can be more robustly guided in the design and delivery of support provision for would-be and existing growth-seeking small enterprise entrepreneurs.

Within the following section, we begin to delve into that black box.

Effective Strategic Control in Entrepreneurial Small Businesses—Our Research Findings

Our ongoing case study investigations of and 'partnership working' with micro and small enterprises reveals insight into the management approaches and learning actions within growth-achieving small businesses that over time are successfully coping with their unpredictable operating contexts through effective forms of strategic control.

The key characteristics of effective small business strategic management embrace the following:

- The same three elements of strategic control as found integral to traditional rational planning modes of management are apparent. Thus, Discovery-Choice-Action management activities are evident in small business strategic management—but not as a tidy sequential step-process.
- Discovery of understanding of the external environment is predominantly from learning interactions and activities with key informants on the boundaries of the small firm's activities—such as from owner manager or key workforce learning conversations with suppliers, customers, potential customers, distributors and even competitors.
- Long-term written plans are rarely found as a guide to development and action.
- Instead, owner managers have a mentally held framework of understanding of the business's existing core markets, products and processes activities and the key relevant impacting parts of the external environment—and a flexible 'preferred end' which, given current understanding of the external environment, the owner manager feels the business should be striving towards.
- Such a mentally held framework does represent a form of long-term planning frame—an owner manager 'meaningful picture' of the business in its environment and its preferred direction of travel given current understanding (his personal constructs of the business and its parts).
- As such, the 'meaningful picture' is used as a 'learning focus'—a mental focal frame to focus ongoing strategic learning.
- Focus is on a 'slice' or 'slices' of the operating environment. Comprehensive external analysis is constrained by resource and management deficiencies, and by the unpredictable nature of the

environment—thus, attention often shifts from one issue to another as situations develop.

- Formal search for information does take place, but insight is often built out of opportunistic interaction or accidental encounter with key informants—both owner manager and key workforce exploit daily interfaces with external stakeholders as 'learning sources'.
- Interface with key informants often builds into deep dialogical learning interactions whereby an owner manager (and more able workers) 'tries on for size' the personal constructs (worldviews) of the informant and uses this to challenge his/her own existing personal constructs (worldviews).
- Integral to the learning is an owner manager's willingness to adjust parts of the core activity and/or the 'preferred end' if current learning activities so suggest: the learning process often requires 'try out' or experiment to facilitate full understanding of the change event under investigation.
- Intuitive judgements appear to frequently take the place of rational perspective and logical reasoning.
- In PCT terms, the owner manager is responding not to the actual stimuli of a change event he faces, but to his or her idiosyncratic interpretation of that event.

A 'discovery', 'choice' and 'action' strategic control process is thus in place: but not as linear, sequential process based upon logical reasoning. For example, discovery process may be embedded in experimental action (messier than a tidy step-process; iterative to-ing and fro-ing rather than linear).

Given this 'best practice' insight, we now proceed to consider the potential for creative embrace of personal construct theory alongside this understanding of the distinctive managerial and entrepreneurial learning activities of successfully developing small businesses in underpinning entrepreneurship education provision.

3   DRAWING ON THE PARAMETERS OF PCT TO FACILITATE ENTREPRENEURSHIP EDUCATION

Personal Construct Theory in Finer Detail

We have seen in the previous sections how PCT helps us understand the complexity of the small business strategic learning task and also aids our understanding of the learning activities and actions which make up the complex learning in successfully growing small enterprises.

A robust combination understanding of PCT and of how small businesses learn has key implications for design and delivery of entrepreneurship education provision. This section examines the key tenets of personal construct theory in more detail as further underpinning to consideration of a PCT-informed approach to entrepreneurship education. The proposition here is that PCT offers a rigorous theory-base for explaining an individual's learning and development process.

The Finer Detail of the Key Parameters of Kelly's (1955) Theory

- As outlined in Sect. 2, central to PCT is Kelly's (1955) positioning of man (or woman) as a kind of 'scientist' (man the scientist) who *makes sense of his world by building a personal theory of it*. These personal theories form the basis of subsequent actions and anticipations (Harri-Augstein et al., 1995). Thus, the personal theory guides the individual's anticipations: 'if I do x then I expect y to be the outcome'.
- It is his or her past experiences and positions and responsibilities in life that contribute to the formation of his/her individual personal constructs—and she uses her personal constructs as *a pair of spectacles or a lens* through which to view and deal with unfolding change situations that arise and confront him.
- Thus, for Kelly, we as individuals experience the world through the lens of our personal constructs. These constructs are used to predict and anticipate events, which in turn determines our behaviours, feelings and thoughts.
- Like a 'scientist', a layperson, ordinary man-in-the-street seeks to predict, and thus control, the course of events. The constructs that she formulates are intended to aid her in her predictive efforts.

- Crucially, in a constantly changing world man is *incapable of effecting an absolute construction of the environment that he is trying to understand* and thus has to be content with making a series of successive approximations. All of his *present interpretations of his world are open to revision or replacement* in the light of his testing them out in practice.
- In adopting this stance, Kelly created a philosophical standpoint of constructive alternativism which propounds that all occurring events or situations lend themselves to multiple interpretations. In effect, we as individuals are free to produce our own idiosyncratic interpretations of unfolding events or reflect back on our experiences and view them from a different perspective.
- Thus, for Kelly, an individual has the potential to hold his previous experiences open to the possibility of fresh construction; the opportunity to seek alternative perspectives and interpretations of a given change event and *use these as 'lenses' to put facts and insight together in more productive combinations.* He has opportunity to be more imaginative in unfolding alternative constructions and thus in providing more rigorous practical grounds for more effective anticipation and prediction.
- However, while we as individuals are natural predictors in our approach to coping with new change situations, this does not mean that we are all good at it. Or that we are all able and willing to persevere at predicting and anticipating the future by revising our constructs (our lenses). *'People (learners) are often not very skilled as scientists and their models of their world are often implicitly held in almost total non-awareness. Such models become impossible to revise and individuals become very impoverished as a result. This inhibits their growth'* (Harri-Augstein et al., 1995, p. 7).
- Crucially, in a small business development context, owner managers are in, PCT terms, natural predictors—but in a predominantly unpredictable external operating environment. Thus, like a scientist, the progressive and successful owner manager will, in order to achieve sustained growth, need to ably develop and test out his personal constructs in practice to determine their validity and build confidence in the adequacy and appropriateness of the personal construct. And, given the unknowability of his external environment, experiment and 'try out' activity will be key part of that development process. In short, he will need to become 'man the good scientist'.

4 Implications for Entrepreneurship Education Provision

Our parallel use of Personal Construct Theory as drive motor in our research and business support relationships with growth-achieving small businesses is facilitating build-up of enhanced understanding of best small enterprise strategic learning practices. This in turn provides rich informing insight with regard to approach to entrepreneurship education provision.

Resilient Learning Capability at the Fore: At the core of our research findings is the way that growth-achieving small businesses faced with an essentially unpredictable operating environment predominantly 'learn their enterprises along'. A key source of competitive advantage derives from the evermore effective and resilient learning capability of the owner manager. Fostering such entrepreneurial learning capability within students should thus be at the fore of entrepreneurship education provision.

PCT is a key vehicle for facilitating student understanding of how they themselves learn and thus of how they can progressively improve their learning capability. Students need to constantly enhance 'learning to learn' capability and become that ever more effective and resilient learner which epitomises small enterprise development success. If they do not understand how they learn, how can they improve their learning capabilities and become better learners?

Kelly does not refer to learning at all within his development and explanation of PCT, instead giving emphasis to bringing about changes in personal constructs over time. Proponents of PCT suggest that this is because the process of learning is so ubiquitous within the totality of an individual's personal construing activities.

Making Learning Process Explicit: Thus, for us, 'learning and development' can be viewed as a construing and re-construing process: an individual's progressive reflecting on existing personal constructs, surfacing underlying assumptions, challenging those assumptions; and 'trying on for size' the perspectives of others. Adjusting or replacing own existing personal constructs with this new 'try on for size' insight—and testing out the newly forming personal construct by 'try out' or experiment actions (*'my construct is informing me that if I behave like this, X will be the likely outcome'*).

Making explicit such learning and development process to students at the outset of entrepreneurship education provision provides them with working frame of reference with regard to what learning involves and what is required of them in their plight to become ever more capable and effective learners.

Entrepreneurship Education Process as Joint Enterprise: Integral to the above is a parallel consideration of what a PCT-informed approach to entrepreneurship education involves from an 'action' standpoint from both the educator and the student perspective. Use of PCT tells us that a key dimension of effective entrepreneurship education or owner management development is helping the student or owner manager to 'simple' and 'complex' learn. Entrepreneurship education provision should thus involve the educator in helping would-be and existing small enterprise owner managers reflect on adequacy of existing constructs—not merely assuming need for new personal constructs; and then, where appropriate, to develop new personal constructs.

Thus, the fostering of both simple learning (single loop learning—or personal construct 'definition' in Kelly's PCT terms) and complex learning (double loop learning—or personal construct 'extension' in PCT terms) are equally significant. As entrepreneurship educators, our starting point with an individual student is thus that 'definition' (slight adjustment to existing constructs) is just as valuable a part of the owner manager/student learning process as more complex 'extension'. In short, our role is to help the student see the validity and utility of current personal constructs as well as to foster ability to complex learn. Effectively, help the individual learner stand outside himself and see himself from a new perspective in terms of relevance or shortfall of his current personal constructs in a given situation and provide opportunity to, where necessary, develop new constructs and alternative perspectives. For Beck (1980), the ongoing enhancement of simple and complex learning as a whole (definition and extension) represents a process of 'learning to learn'.

With regard to learning facilitation, PCT is giving emphasis to the 'active participant' role of student as learner, in both classroom and other learning contexts. Contrary to some ongoing cognitive theorising of student as passive recipient of information and perspectives presented by the teacher, Kelly's underpinning philosophical foundations of constructive alternativism would suggest teacher–learner in some form of action oriented 'partnership working'. An enabling of learner reflection on own existing perspectives, robust consideration of those offered by the teacher and identification of potential for construction of new meanings. From the teacher's standpoint, such 'partnership working' requires facilitation of dialogue or development activities to surface learner understanding and start-point perspectives of focal issues being 'taught'; and to determine appropriateness and relevance of the materials under consideration with regard to enhancement, refinement or replacement of learner current constructs.

Informed by PCT, enhancing student capacity to learn thus becomes central to the entrepreneurship education process. With PCT making explicit the kinds of barriers which can constrain individual learning and development and prompt for us as entrepreneurship education providers to help student awareness and challenge of fixed mind set patterns of thought and ingrained feelings and perceptions that influence their behaviour and actions.

Eliciting Personal Meaning: The early work of Harri-Augstein, et al. (1995) gave focus to the potential for development of reflective and meaning-eliciting tools to systematically foster learner awareness of 'personal meanings' and to show how these personal meanings are constructed and used to influence actions. Such tools can allow learners to stand outside themselves and see themselves from a new perspective.

For Harri-Augstein et al., a key role of the educator and trainer is developing an individual's capacity to learn through experience—on the job and in daily life. Here, they proffer how the educator fostering of 'learning conversations' with a learner can facilitate his or her nurturing towards 'Self Organised Learning'. Individuals can then progressively learn to develop the conversational skills for themselves. Thus, fostering ability and propensity to converse with oneself as well as with other key information and knowledge holders and explore the possible relationships between experience and action. This requires developing a frame of reference of how personal meanings, needs and purposes lead to anticipations and actions; and how the results of actions feedback and lead to revised or new meanings. Integral to such an approach is Harri-Augstein, et al.'s perception of how learning as a process of self-organisation is a key vehicle for living and working on the edge of chaos.

Nurturing Entrepreneurial Learning: In a small business development context, such conversational learning capability is prevalent in more entrepreneurial owner managers. Layering in our case study and action research findings, demonstrates how both design and delivery of entrepreneurship education needs to embrace understanding of how entrepreneurial learning in growth-achieving small businesses differs from other forms of learning. And thus reflect the creative ways in which innovative owner managers undertake the personal construing/re-construing learning and development process in the uncertain operating environment.

Our successful owner managers are, through entrepreneurial learning, inventing and reinventing models of the reality of their enterprises and their organisational life to help them understand what is going on and where development opportunity may exist. Some may periodically use formal training inputs or specialists and experts but all seek out the less formal support input of others as a resource for learning, predominantly milking insight and understanding from key informants on the boundaries of their enterprise's activities. Thus, suppliers, agents, distributors, customers and competitors as a 'resource' for the 'learning conversation' and as key part of their personal construing/re-construing process.

Crucially, integral to the central focus on enhancement of student capacity to learn through experience, is opportunity to embrace student exposure to 'best small business entrepreneurial learning practice'. A fostering of understanding of, and abilities and behaviours relating to, the different entrepreneurial learning activities that progressive owner managers undertake in challenging and enhancing their current personal constructs in given situations and the development of new constructs to cope with unfolding change.

Thus, the entrepreneurship education process would embrace the nurturing of entrepreneurial learning capability using innovative teaching–learning vehicles both in classroom and in live business context learning environments. With focus upon how more capable and progressive owner managers engage in *distinctive entrepreneurial learning activities* involving *simple learning* to reinforce existing personal constructs and *complex learning* to create and develop new personal constructs. This includes:

- Learning in context (in the internal and external business contexts).
- Treating learning as a social process involving multiple actors.
- Dialogical learning from internal workforce.

- Dialogical learning from external key informants and expert/knowledgeable individuals.
- 'Trying on for size' the perspectives and world views of others.
- Learning by doing.
- Learning by problem solving.
- Learning by opportunity seeking.
- Learning from mistakes.
- Learning by observation.
- Learning by copying.
- Learning by experiment and 'try out'.
- Learning by telling one's story to others—and responding to feedback.

PCT Informing Creativity and Innovation: Finally, deserving here of specific focus are two behavioural and ability areas that are core to small business entrepreneurship: opportunity identification and discovery; and owner manager creativity and innovation. PCT offers rich guidance on both.

Discovery or revealing of niche opportunity is pivotal to entrepreneurship and integral to the sustained development of the growth-achieving small enterprises within our studies. But our use of PCT shows that owner manager undertaking of entrepreneurial learning activities such as those listed above facilitates build-up of understanding of slices of the firm's external environment and creative interpretation of change situations. Frequently, the more entrepreneurial owner manager is transcending mere identification of discovery of latent opportunity to *co-create* parts of his operating environment and create business development opportunity. Application of PCT thus guides us as entrepreneurship educators towards fostering student understanding of and behaviours surrounding personal idiosyncratic and creative interpretation of events and situations with which we are faced. In PCT terms, we respond not to the stimuli of an unfolding change event, but to our own personal interpretation of that stimuli.

On the issues of creativity and innovation, PCT offers similarly robust guidance. Integral to Kelly's development of PCT are the processes of 'loose' and 'tight' personal constructing. 'Loose construction sets the stage for creative thinking. This loosening releases facts long taken as self-evident from their conceptual moorings. Once so freed, they may be seen in new aspects hitherto unsuspected and the creative cycle my get under way' (Kelly, 1955; Wyer et al., 2010, p. 21). Thus, for an individual to be creative or create something new, he or she has to surface, address and challenge the assumptions upon which his existing personal construct is based. She has to loosen her constructions and produce alternatives.

Moreover, for creativity to effectively feed into innovative small business development, the creative individual must be capable of moving his loose construing forward. Fransella (2003) emphasises that the creative person must have the ability to move from loosened to tightened construing. The person who uses loose constructions never gets out of the stage of mumbling to himself. He must get round to testing out that construction. Those locked into loose construing find it very difficult to come to any firm conclusions.

It is such owner manager ability to loosen current personal constructions, create and follow up on potential alternatives and subsequently tighten those constructions and subject them to experimental testing that distinguishes the more entrepreneurial small business owner managers with whom we work and support (Wyer & Bowman, 2019; Wyer et al., 2010).

PCT thus offers clear guiding frames of reference for fostering entrepreneurial opportunity creation abilities, creativity and innovation capability as pivotal to entrepreneurship provision.

In the following section, we provide example of the kinds of meaning-eliciting tools used in our own entrepreneurship programmes.

5 Example Reflective and Meaning-Eliciting Tools

Following Harri-Augstein, et al.'s lead, as key part of our provision we develop 'meaning-eliciting tools' to help our learners see the validity and limitations of their existing personal constructs in given situations under consideration. Thus, meaning-eliciting tools to foster and heighten awareness of personal meanings and help the learner challenge rigid thought patterns and perceptions.

Indicative of the meaning-eliciting tools used are integration of our own and literature-based business models and concepts—as alternative 'frames of reference' for students/owner managers to 'try on for size'. Examples include:

- *Innovative Small Business Strategic Management Model*

The model is developed to provide alternative perspectives on how successful growth-achieving owner managers understand and manage their often-hostile external environment.

It is derived from our own research (as outlined in Sect. 2 above) and the grounding of existing strategic management theory and knowledge base in understanding of the distinctiveness of small business.

The approach uses the traditional rational long-term planning model as base frame of reference and offers alternative perspectives for the learner to 'try on for size'—as vehicle to reflect upon and challenge own existing personal constructs and perspectives.

The model demonstrates how best small business strategic management is a predominantly learning-oriented strategy formation process (learning school of strategic management thought)), but significantly underpinned as a mental process (cognitive school of strategic management thought) and visionary process (entrepreneurial school of strategic management thought).

Figure 1 provides indicative snapshot of our modelling which we continue to progressively refine in the light of our experiences of its application in our entrepreneurship research, consultancy and teaching contexts (Wyer & Baldwin, 2022, forthcoming).

- *Conceptualisation of the Small Business as Potential Learning Organisation*

We are progressively developing a robust meaning-eliciting tool through integration of our own research and the Learning Organisation knowledge base (Wyer & Bowman, 2019; Wyer & Mason, 1998; Wyer et al., 2000).

It uses key areas of traditional organisational behaviour knowledge as base frame of reference.

The tool offers key dimensions of best practice small business entrepreneurial learning activities in their identification and understanding of unexpected external change situations. Embracing:

- The pivotal and hub positioned role of the owner manager.

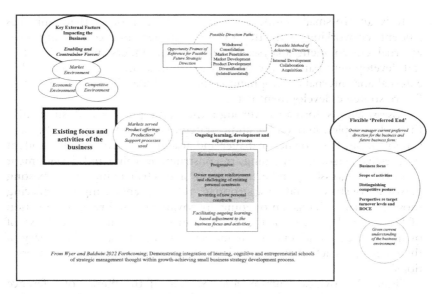

Fig. 1 Small Business Strategic Planning and Development Frame

- Owner manager entrepreneurial learning activities—and use of more able staff as learning nodes in supporting key areas of strategic learning.
- How individual strands of learning are creatively yoked by the owner manager into potential new innovative business development activity (such as new market niche opportunity).
- The key role of experiment and 'try out' in practice of the newly emerging understanding of the potential business development opportunity (that is, the owner manager testing of newly developing personal construct of opportunity).

- *Use of Live Practising Small Businesses as Learning and Assessment Vehicles*

This meaning-eliciting vehicle involves student undertaking over time of a strategic development audit of a growth-achieving micro or small enterprise.

It is an 'In-small business-context' learning process that embraces student co-working with the owner manager and conducting own external environment analysis to build-up of understanding of historical development path of the business, current strategic position and key external and internal development context, and identification of potential future strategic development path.

Assessment is formative through the audit process and summative through completion of end of audit strategic consultancy report. Ongoing support input from owner manager and academic coach facilitate student progressive personal construing/re-construing learning and development process—progressively reflecting upon and challenging own existing personal constructs and as appropriate refining, enhancing or replacing those constructs. Thus, an ongoing approximation and re-approximation of 'meaningful picture' of the business in its environment—and use of owner manager, academic coach and key informants on the boundary of the enterprise's activities as complementary sources of'learning conversations'.

Figure 2 provides diagrammatic example of the frames of reference that we are developing in facilitating the fostering of student learning from the small business practice interface. Not least in the nurturing of student 'reflexivity capacity'. Thereby encouraging student continuous examination of self and the research and project relationship with the owner manager—including making explicit the forms of 'conceptual baggage' he or she may be carrying (personal constructs that may be embedded with academic theory or conceptualization, personal assumptions and current theories-in-use). Here, we are emphasising reflexivity as the bedrock assumption of personal construct theory (Fransella & Dalton, 2000) and how in a qualitative investigation and learning context 'reflexivity' embraces the capacity of learners and researchers to reflect upon their actions and values during a project, whether in producing data or writing accounts (Feighery, 2006).

While not scientifically evaluated as to efficacy, some 20 years of development and application of such learning facilitation tools has helped enhanced student learning as evidenced in production of high-level student performance and module pass rates; and by insight and recommendations within student consultancy reports adopted by participant practicing small businesses. Students have regularly progressed onto further entrepreneurship study at both Masters and PhD levels and/or own enterprise start up.

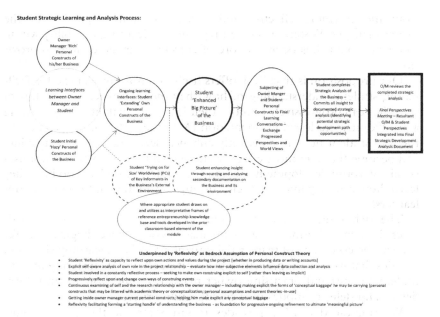

Fig. 2 Personal construct theory-based action learning and development path (Co-driven—Student and Owner Manager)

6 Conclusion

The underlying premise of this chapter is that a major task of educators in entrepreneurship is to equip students, particularly today's undergraduates, with knowledge and skills to survive in a fast and rapidly changing environment (both within business and in daily life). With this effectively achieved by an entrepreneurship education process informed by robust understanding of just how enterprising individuals effectively cope with such change contexts.

We have suggested that creative application of a version of Personal Construct Theory can help make explicit the high-level complexity of the small business strategic learning task and underpin the unfolding of understanding of best small business entrepreneurial learning practice in micro and small enterprises who successfully undertake that complex task.

Our own research confirms that a key source of small business competitive advantage in highly uncertain operating environments derives from the evermore effective and resilient learning capability of the owner manager. Fostering such entrepreneurial learning capability within students should thus be at the fore of entrepreneurship education provision.

Our proposition is that PCT offers itself as innovative vehicle for facilitating student understanding of how they themselves learn and thus of how they can progressively improve their learning capability. Propounding a significant meta-learning orientation (Maudsley, 1979), we position to the fore student need to constantly enhance 'learning to learn' capability and become that ever more effective and resilient learner which epitomises small enterprise development success. If they do not understand how they learn, how can they improve their learning capabilities and become better learners?

The rich insight revealed by our own research as to what constitutes 'best small business strategic management practice' begins to make explicit the core body of managerial, organisational and learning skills and abilities that we as entrepreneurship educators should be fostering in both undergraduates and practising owner managers—and how it can inform design and delivery modes of such education process.

We suggest that PCT provides robust steer for the entrepreneurship educator with regard to the key role of facilitating student personal construing-based simple and complex learning capability, potential barriers to that learning and opportunity for development and application of innovative reflective and meaning-eliciting tools and vehicles to more effectively assist that student learning process. A steer that, in its totality, posits entrepreneurship education as a 'joint enterprise' transcending teacher as mere knowledge provider and student as passive recipient of information into a predominantly action and activity oriented experiential learning process.

Prominent therein is opportunity for encouraging of a discovery approach to learning: bringing out the student as inquiring man ('man the good scientist'). Engaging him or her in formal and informal research activities and inquiry and in learning interactions with live practicing small enterprises and the wider business environment and community. Thereby providing opportunity for development of creative thinking, proactivity, creativity and innovativeness capabilities.

REFERENCES

Beck, J. E. (1980). Changing a manager's construction of reality: The perspective of personal construct theory on the process of management education. In J. E. Beck & C. Cox (Eds.), *Advances in management education*. Wiley.

Curran, J. (1988). Training and research strategies for small firms. *Journal of General Management, 13*(3), 24–37.

EU. (2015). *User guide to the SME Definition*. Publications Office of the European Union.

Feighery, W. (2006). Reflexivity and tourism Research: Telling an(other) story. *Current Issues in Tourism, 9*(3), 269–282.

Fransella, F. (2003). *Creativity Cycle*. Retrieved on 23 May 2009 www.pcp-net. org/encycloedia/create.cycle

Fransella, F., & Dalton, P. (2000). *Personal construct counselling in action*. Sage.

Gibb, A. A. (1983). The small business challenge to management education. *Journal of European Industrial Training., 7*(5), 3–41.

Gibb, A. A. (1990). *In search of quality in small firms policy research in the 1990s*. Paper presented to the 13th UK Small Firms Policy and Research Conference, Harrogate.

Gibb, A. A. (1997). Small firms training and competitiveness: Building upon the small business as a learning organisation. *International Small Business Journal, 15*(3), 13–29.

Harri-Augstein, S., & Webb, I. M. (1995). *Learning to change*. McGraw-Hill.

Irwin, D., & Scott, J. M. (2010). Barriers faced by SMEs in raising bank finance. *International Journal of Entrepreneurial Behavior and Research, 16*(3), 245–259.

Kelly, G. (1955). *The psychology of personal construct theory*. Norton.

Kelly, G. (1977). The psychology of the unknown. In D. Bannister (Ed.), *New perspectives in personal construct theory* (pp. 1–20). Academic Press.

Kwakuvi-Zagbedeh, S. (2019). *An Examination of the Key Factors and Issues which Underpin and Facilitate Small Business Success within Ghana* (Unpublished PhD thesis). University of Wales.

Linton, G., & Klinton, M. (2019). University Entrepreneurship Education: a design thinking approach. *Journal of Innovation and Entrepreneurship, 8*, Article number 3.

Maudsley, D. B. (1979). *A theory of meta-learning and principles of facilitation: An organismic perspective*. University of Toronto.

Smallbone, D., & Wyer, P. (2012). Growth and development in small firm. In S. Carter & D. Evans (Eds.), *Enterprise and small business: Principles, practice and policy* (3rd ed.). Pearson Education.

Stacey, R. D. (1990). *Dynamic strategic management for the 1990s: Balancing opportunism and business planning*. Kogan Page.

Stacey, R. D. (1993). *Strategic management and organisational dynamics.* Pitman.

Wyer, P. (1990). *The effects of varying forms and degrees of government intervention upon the effective competitiveness of UK small business* (Unpublished PhD thesis). University of Aston.

Wyer, P., & Baldwin, J. (2022, Forthcoming). *The Reality of Small Business Strategic Management.* Grosvenor House Publishing.

Wyer, P., & Bowman, S. (2019). The Potential to nurture small business toward learning organisation form. In A. Ortenbald (Ed.), *The Oxford handbook of the learning organisation.* Oxford University Press.

Wyer, P., Donohoe, S., & Matthews, P. (2010). Fostering strategic learning capability to enhance creativity in small service businesses. *Service Business: An International Journal.*

Wyer, P., & Mason, J. (1998). An organisational learning perspective to enhancing understanding of people management in small businesses. *International Journal of Entrepreneurial Behaviour and Research, 4*(2), 112–128.

Wyer, P., Mason, P., & Theodorakopoulos, N. (2000). An examination of the concept of the learning organisation within the context of small business development. *International Journal of Entrepreneurial Behaviour and Research, 6*(4), 239–259.

Wyer, P., & Smallbone, D. (1999). Export activity in SMEs: A framework for strategic analysis. *Journal of Academy of Business Administration, 4*(2), 9–24.

Pedagogy and Andragogy, a Shared Approach to Education in Entrepreneurship for Students in Higher Education

Glorimar Santini-Hernández

1 Introduction

Throughout history, adaptation has always been decisive for survival. Civilizations have risen and fallen, unable to transition by embracing change. Although the pursuit of power and the living urge are powerful motivators, survival of the fittest redefines the paradigms of how to succeed. In the globalised world of the twenty-first century, higher education is no stranger to adaptation. As the dwindling younger generations (Keshner, 2019) have forced a change in the fabric of education, pedagogy and andragogy increasingly coexist within the academic ecosystem to better serve the population.

Traditionally, the higher education newcomer used to be the high school graduate, and the occasional adult, who would blend into the population. Today's reality presents a different scenario. Higher education has adapted to serve a diverse population in which the emerging adult

---

G. Santini-Hernández (✉)
EDP University of Puerto Rico, San Juan, Puerto Rico, USA
e-mail: gsantini@edpuniversity.edu

© The Author(s), under exclusive license to Springer Nature Switzerland AG 2022
G. J. Larios-Hernandez et al. (eds.), *Theorising Undergraduate Entrepreneurship Education*,
https://doi.org/10.1007/978-3-030-87865-8_13

(Arnett, 2000) and the adult (29+) coexist and collaborate within the same academic context. The population has changed, and newcomers are defined as "the young, adults and life-time learners" (De Jonghe, 2014, p. 66).

The diversity among higher education participants is extensive to education in entrepreneurship. This population, encompassing the non-adolescent, the not-yet adults (Hägg & Kurczewska, 2020; Salvatore, 2018), and the adults, translates into a sundry of educational and life experiences brought forth by students into the classroom (De Jonghe, 2014; Lemoine et al., 2017). Hägg and Kurczewska (2018) utilise the concept of emergent adulthood, to describe the student entrepreneur, and a phase of identity exploration, which calls for the creative use of teaching and learning methods. This phase bridges adolescence and adulthood by providing learning experiences that support more elevated forms of thinking (Arnett, 2000). In this context, pedagogy and andragogy combine to deliver the higher education newcomer, and the student entrepreneur, with the tools to grow into the experience and to flow from essential knowledge acquisition into a more critical and assertive decision-making process (Béchard & Grégoire, 2005; Hägg & Kurczewska, 2018, 2020). Through practical applications, entrepreneurship education promotes engagement into "entrepreneurial action" (Kouakou et al., 2019, p. 117) throughout the higher education experience.

This chapter conceptualises the shared approach of teaching a mixed profile in entrepreneurship education as a journey that enables essential knowledge acquisition and subsequent incremental progression to attain competency. The first section focuses on profiling the student entrepreneur in higher education. The following section discusses the principles and roles of pedagogy and andragogy in teaching entrepreneurship to the mixed profile. The discussion goes on to elaborate on the process and strategies implemented to teach entrepreneurship. The final section proposes that, while each journey is personal and unique, active learning, experiential learning and mentoring coexist and revolve around the mindset becoming triggers behind the progressions towards competency building. To that end, the strategic approaches used by the educator promote exploration and induce disposition to exposure, observation and experimentation. The encouragement to learn by doing (Dewey, 1938) eases the learner into mobilising beyond the basics and real-life scenarios for a hands-on knowledge acquisition.

2 Profiling of the Student Entrepreneur in Higher Education

Higher education has adapted to serve a heterogeneous population, which extends to entrepreneurship education. The literature on entrepreneurship refers to the elusive nature of pinpointing specific personality traits within this population (Gartner, 1988). Although some proposals, like the Big-5 model, have attempted to frame the entrepreneur with descriptors such as openness to experience, conscientiousness, extraversion, agreeableness and neuroticism, there is no blueprint for predicting the personality types and behavioural patterns of the entrepreneur (Kerr et al., 2017).

Nonetheless, beyond the ambiguity of the entrepreneur's profile, the concept has been defined, and the extant literature provides multiple interpretations. For Schumpeter (1951), the entrepreneur is an innovator of services, products or technology, while Bruyat and Julien (2001) refer to a risk-taker who creates new value and pursues profits. Jones and English (2004) describe an individual with the insight to recognise opportunities and the self-esteem, knowledge and skills to act on them. However, while referring to a desirable result of the academic journey, none of these definitions address who is the student entrepreneur in higher education.

According to Hägg and Kurczewska (2018), the student entrepreneur is an emerging adult who lacks theoretical knowledge in entrepreneurship and most likely lacks relevant business experiences. The emergent adult, which refers to an age range of 18–29, along with adult newcomers (29+), and their diversified backgrounds (De Jonghe, 2014; Lemoine et al., 2017), presuppose different levels of basic knowledge, skillsets, maturity, motivation, prior learning and learning readiness (Arnett, 2000; Hidayat, 2018). This assessment regarding the population is critical, as it shapes the experience within the classroom.

The complexities of educating the student entrepreneur of the twenty-first century become apparent as De Jonghe (2014) and Lemoine et al. (2017) highlight the added value of a diverse population, while Hägg and Kurczewska (2020) warn about the limitations of pedagogy and andragogy to address the different learning processes required. Adding on, Hidayat (2018) recognises the maturity level to be particularly significant on the learning disposition, while Bandura (2006) states that the student entrepreneur connects with the social surroundings chooses social commitments, and self-directs towards the desired outcomes. The result is a mixed profile of heterogeneous formation influenced by family, culture and everyday commitment to a social ecosystem that runs parallel to the academic experience. And still, whether on-site or online, this population requires an educational approach through which content production, pertinence and applicability to real-life scenarios may serve and nurture the academic journey. Teaching this population requires creativity (Gimmon, 2014) and requires multiple strategies to ensure common ground for all participants (Allan et al., 2009). The following section will elaborate on the shared approach to teach entrepreneurship in higher education.

3   A Shared Approach: Pedagogy and Andragogy in Entrepreneurship Education

It has been established that entrepreneurship education faces the challenge of teaching a heterogeneous profile in entrepreneurship courses (von Graevenitz et al., 2010). The quest for the right way to educate relies on a shared approach to accommodate the differing backgrounds and levels of knowledge. Consequently, pedagogy and andragogy coexist and aim to awaken creativity, inspire and motivate into action, and provoke results-driven engagement in entrepreneurship education (Hägg & Kurczewska, 2018, 2020). In this context, the educator and the student pilot the experience to transition from basic knowledge into more profound critical thinking opportunities and practice scenarios. While the end goal is the same, navigating the teaching/learning process relies on the creative use of educational methodologies and strategies ensuring the proper acquisition of essential knowledge and the subsequent layers in complexity up to the competency (Gimmon, 2014; Heinonen & Poikkijoki, 2006). The fluidity of the process should enable and motivate the student towards competency development and subsequent expertise (Jones et al., 2019).

Pedagogy is considered an educational practice to teach subject matter from an information-based and teacher-based perspective (Hägg & Kurczewska, 2018; Jones et al., 2019). In it, the educator designs the instruction and procedures to communicate the desired contents. As part of the shared approach, the higher education newcomer benefits from pedagogical methods to attain instructional clarity (Blaich et al., 2016; Gibb, 2002; Hägg & Kurczewska, 2018).

Andragogy, on the other hand, refers to a learner-centred approach (McNally et al., 2019) led by motivation, perceived pertinence and applicability to real life. As opposed to pedagogy, the andragogic perspective, presupposes "a process of active inquiry, not passive reception of transmitted content" (Knowles, 1990, p. 27). The Andragogy in Practice Model, as outlined by Knowles et al. (2005), identifies the "six core learning andragogic principles" (p. 149), which are: need to know, self-concept, experience, readiness to learn, orientation to learning and motivation to learn. In this regard, Béchard and Toulouse (1991) reflect on how the students' learning approach changes as they mature and take ownership over the learning experience. In this context, the educator becomes an enabler, not a feeder.

Pedagogy and andragogy have transitioned to become more participative and dynamic (Bonwell & Eison, 1991), and their interplay (Garnett & O'Beirne, 2013; Hägg & Kurczewska, 2018) provides the medium to acquire entrepreneurial knowledge, skills and judgmental abilities (Arnett, 2000; Hägg, 2017 as cited by Hägg & Kurczewska, 2018). Beyond the construction and proper understanding of foundational knowledge, the educational process progresses into elevated analysis and contextualization and more involved intuitive experiences. The result is an empowered individual who combines academic knowledge, an evolving critical thinking capacity, and confidence to venture into practical experiences. This person is autonomous to make decisions and face the consequences accordingly (Knowles, 1980a, 1980b).

In terms of the academic experience, the student entrepreneur in higher education benefits from multiple efforts and resources. The information-based perspective or pedagogic approach (Jones et al., 2019) enables knowledge construction and combines with the student-centred approach or andragogy (Knowles, 1990), to nurture the growing capacity of deciding what to do with the knowledge acquired. As the student matures, the andragogic assumptions (Knowles, 1984) shape the empowerment and the attitude moving forward. Heinonen and Poikkijoki (2006) support this notion by alerting to the fact that the "budding entrepreneur needs not only knowledge (science), but also new ways of thinking, new kinds of skills and new modes of behaviour (arts)" (p. 84). Although the continuum between pedagogy and andragogy (Hägg & Kurczewska, 2018) is highly contextual, a shared approach relying on both perspectives supports knowledge acquisition, active participation and ownership over the learning experience in entrepreneurship (Gibb, 1993, 1996, 2002; Heinonen & Poikkijoki, 2006).

4 THE PROCESS OF TEACHING ENTREPRENEURSHIP IN HIGHER EDUCATION

The process of teaching entrepreneurship in higher education entails serving a mixed profile, inclusive of the emergent adult (18–29) and adults (29+). Regardless of the diversified motivational and involvement levels (Arnett, 2000; De Jonghe, 2014; Hidayat, 2018; Lemoine et al., 2017), the process starts by approaching the need to provide essential instruction through academic courses with educational objectives. Subsequent deepening and subject matter exploration should continue to provoke more complex forms of thinking. Combined with the exposure to academic content, the use of active and experiential learning methodologies, access to mentoring and mindset development become significant components in this educational effort throughout higher education.

The process of teaching entrepreneurship relies on the combination of pedagogic and andragogic strategies to accommodate the diversified needs within the population. Although the combination of methodologies and strategies depend on theoretical knowledge acquisition and validation through practical experience (Neck et al., 2017), student-led instructional practices in entrepreneurship education echo andragogy (Robinson et al., 2016), and align with the hands-on approach of learning to do by doing (Brown, 2003; Dewey, 1938; Hannum & McCombs, 2007; Jonassen, 1991; Kolb & Kolb, 2017). As entrepreneurship is built on the premise of thought and action (Neck et al., 2017), playing, empathising, creating, experimenting and reflecting (Bonwell & Eison, 1991; Neck et al., 2017) are identified as best practices to promote a creative and exciting classroom. Teaching entrepreneurship in this environment enriches academic formation, encourages conceptual connections and boosts the skill acquisition process (Dreyfus, 2004). On the latter, exposure to deliberate practice (Ericsson et al., 1993) enables skill development, and students go through the stages of novice, advanced beginner, competent, proficient and expert (Dreyfus, 2004). In response to the student's progression and advancement, knowledge materialises into execution. Therefore, action-oriented methods are effective to guide the student entrepreneur through the transition from novice to competent and into an iterative flux between pedagogy and andragogy.

Because entrepreneurship is highly contextual, the claim of a precise methodology to teach it would be misleading. Nevertheless, educators favour active learning strategies to provide context and to make concepts graspable. Active learning compensates for the lack of real-life experience and promotes involvement (Bonwell & Eison, 1991). Regardless of the age group, the evidence supports the notion "that active learning enhances learning of course content in comparison to more conventional learning approaches" (Caruth, 2015, p. 47). Some popular strategies used to pursue active learning are Cooperative Learning (Jareño et al., 2014) Simulation and Gamification (Taylor et al., 2012; Wood & Reiners, 2014), Storytelling (Borgoff, 2018), Problem-Based Learning (Bethell & Morgan, 2011; Gurpinar et al., 2011), Flipped Classroom (Hernández & Pérez, 2015), Design Thinking (Tu et al., 2018), Critical Thinking Based Learning, (Bahr, 2010), Competency Based Learning (Voorhees, 2001), Service Learning (Bielefeldt, 2011) and Adventure Education (Dana, 2017). Other initiatives observed in entrepreneurship education are the implementation of co-teaching, the creation of co-working spaces, and the establishment of incubators and accelerators to nurture the academic experience.

The process of entrepreneurship education also capitalises on experiential learning. Popular among entrepreneurship educators, compatible to andragogy and effective in teaching to develop an entrepreneurship mentality (Kolb & Kolb, 2017), experiential learning (Kozlinska, 2011; Lackéus et al., 2016; Mandel & Noyes, 2016; Vanevenhoven & Liguori, 2013) constitutes an important resource to ascertain knowledge acquisition through real-life scenarios. It benefits from self-motivation, maturity and prior learning acquired, and the integration of engaging activities that trigger active involvement.

Experiential learning, or learning from experience, applies to "all levels of human society from the individual, to the group, to organizations, and to society as a whole" (Kolb & Kolb, 2017, p. 11). It starts with exploration, initial decision-making, and eventually, enduring choices (Hägg & Kurczewska, 2018). Neck et al. (2017) state that students cannot be involved spectators but deliberate practitioners through experiential and vicarious learning. Activities like laboratory experiments, discussions, problem-solving cases, simulation exercises, and field experiences focus on action and practice, as a way to learn by experience (Johannisson, 2011; Knowles, 1980b, Mandel & Noyes, 2016; Scott et al., 2016). Living through experiences shapes beliefs (Kolb & Kolb, 2017).

Consequently, providing real-life set-ups to provoke new concept development through association and experience makes experiential learning a significant platform and an enabler for innovation.

While active and experiential learning invoke and provoke deeper understanding through "active inquiry, not passive reception of transmitted content" (Knowles, 1990, p. 27), the evolving mindset shapes entrepreneurial intentions, sharpens opportunity identification and defines the role to be played as involved participants (Neck et al., 2017). Described as the capability of identifying opportunities, and understanding how the entrepreneurial action affects the economic and the social system (Kouakou et al., 2019), the mindset can be developed by addressing contents related to resilience, innovativeness, tolerance to uncertainty, entrepreneurial intentions, value creation and risk-aversion, among others (Krueger, 2015). The mindset may or may not be used for commercial gain, as desirable projects may be directed towards social, cultural and academic endeavours. So, the applicability of knowledge supports empowerment and favours self-commitment, as the student entrepreneur willingly "learns and transforms the experience" (Kolb, 1984, p. 38) into a useful reference.

Alongside active and experiential learning, mentorship nurtures the educational process by providing role models in addition to the skill enhancing scenarios (Gimmon, 2014). Mentoring implies contextualization of theory through practice and guidance based on the students' needs, interests and level of cognition (Gimmon, 2014). It may require differentiated learning strategies to facilitate skill development, intrinsic motivation and opportunity recognition (Detienne & Chandler, 2004; Hägg & Kurczewska, 2020; Honig, 2004).

The diversity of roles (Kent et al., 2003) adopted by mentors attest to their resourcefulness in nurturing the student entrepreneur and impacting the entrepreneurial activity (Honig, 2004). Each mentor–mentee relationship is unique, and its relevance stems from the challenges faced and the strategies used to manoeuvre towards individualised interpretation and knowledge acquisition. Thus, whether to achieve foundational cognitive development or guidance through self-directed approaches in the presence of deeper understanding, every scenario aims to support the progression towards the andragogic assumptions and into transforming experience into permanent learning (Hägg & Kurczewska, 2020; Politis, 2005).

As the need for education in entrepreneurship has never been greater (Blencher et al., 2006; Raposo & do Paço, 2011), newcomers to higher education view knowledge acquisition as a means to an end (De Jonghe, 2014; Wrenn & Wrenn, 2009). Therefore, pertinent scenarios and engaging opportunities become fundamental to connect with students (Senior et al., 2018). Linking knowledge with the needs identified enables meaningful changes and ties academia with society. Through mentorship and co-participation, social interactions translate into involvement with the community, motivation and personal growth (Gimmon, 2014). At the core, social exposure shapes belief, propels the maturation process and promotes a shifts to focus on personally chosen commitments (Bandura, 2006) for social and personal advancement. In sum, provision of essential knowledge relying on active and experiential learning, on shaping the mindset and on mentoring, allows for a layered yet dynamic process of teaching entrepreneurship in higher education.

5   A Framework for the Dual Approach in Entrepreneurship Education

Already described as a non-linear path, this section provides a framework to depict entrepreneurship education as a multi-level journey, inclusive of pedagogy, andragogy and the interactions in-between. Even though, the oversimplified descriptions of the dual approach in education often places pedagogy and andragogy as the extremes of a linear effort, the movement within is highly contextual and layered. As students enter higher education with heterogeneous backgrounds and abilities, interactivity among activities and strategies have become a constant within the journey.

The proposal for the dual approach on entrepreneurship education, named The Pedagogy-Andragogy Shared Approach Model for Entrepreneurship Education, shown in Fig. 1, conceptualizes pedagogy and andragogy as coexisting educational journey's components. The triangular shape on the right side, broader at the bottom and slimmer at the top, represents the pedagogic approach, which refers to the essential information and knowledge dictation required in any learning process. The figure in the left, slimmer at the bottom and broader at the top, represents the andragogic approach and incremental instructional growth (Knowles et al., 2005) along the trajectory. As a whole, the diagram's composition points to equally significant sides and to triangular figures exhibiting inverse proportionality and complementarity.

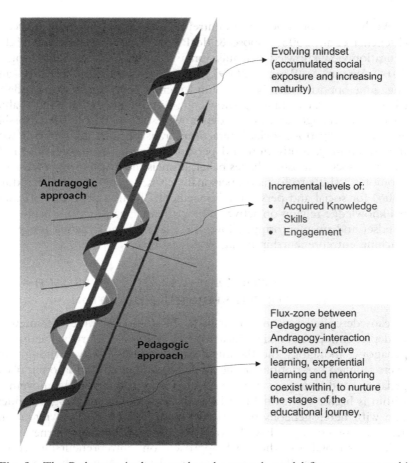

Fig. 1 The Pedagogy-Andragogy shared approach model for entrepreneurship education

It is key to clarify that the slimming of the right side does not imply the disappearance of pedagogy, just as the slimmer left side does not mean the non-existence of andragogy. In turn, the model proposes that both approaches fluidly coexist as required throughout the journey. From a practical perspective, the process will always require information-based pedagogical strategies to attend to specific instances. Yet, as the student journey progresses, these instances should be scantier and short-lived due to acquired knowledge and increased autonomy.

The ascending spiral, located between andragogy and pedagogy represents a progressive accumulation of life-shaping events. Although the higher education newcomer requires foundational knowledge, the diversified profile within this population implies various understanding levels and differentiated movements along the educational journey. Along the highly contextual journey, the student can self-assess and choose to iterate the process at any given point, to ensure proper understanding before moving on to more complex set-ups. The model also depicts the spiral revolving around the mindset and increased socialisation, while knowledge, engagement and skills escalate.

This spiral is positioned within the flux-zone where pedagogy and andragogy meet and complement each other while providing for the student's needs. The flux-zone is the ever-present in-between zone, where educational strategies associated to active learning, experiential learning and mentoring pave the way to further the academic journey. Knowledge and experience combine to promote an increased sense of ownership, personal growth, growing confidence and maturity. Furthermore, the combination serves to ease the student towards incursions into social set-ups, handling feedback from real-life stakeholders, and making "enduring choices" (Hägg & Kurczewska, 2018, p. 3).

A clarifying note regarding the model presented is that it does not refer to the concept of odigogy proposed by Hägg and Kurczewska (2020). Odigogy relates to a guided teaching/learning approach for emerging adults in higher education, which addresses individual proficiency levels, student–teacher content co-creation, tailored instructional design and constant guidance throughout the academic journey. The Pedagogy-Andragogy Shared Approach Model for Entrepreneurship Education shows the flux-zone as a place for interactivity where experience and modelling influence the mindset by way of knowledge contextualization and skill-testing. However, the model does not address the specifics of tailoring the academic journey according to individual proficiency levels or the shared responsibility of teacher–student instructional design co-creation.

The case of Diana (pseudonym) (G. Rodriguez, personal communication, June 18, 2021) serves to illustrate the applicability of the model proposed. Diana is a 21-years-old, fourth-year undergraduate biology student enrolled in an accredited higher education institution in the.

Caribbean. At age 19, she identified a need and an opportunity for a business venture. Although she was already a second-year student, her incursion into a different academic field proved highly intimidating.

Having no previous knowledge on the subject, she enrolled in an introductory entrepreneurship course at her institution. The course's learning product required her to prepare a business plan, and it seemed daunting. She felt unprepared. Therefore, her journey as an entrepreneurship student started with basic knowledge dictation (information-based approach) to become comfortable with the terminology, concepts and course contents. Although the educator applied active learning strategies, the highly structured constructs of the course and program, did not allow for content tailoring and personalised guidance beyond the required feedback within the class. Diana decided to take a second course, during which she started to feel more at ease with the subject matter. Her sense of empowerment and engagement escalated during the course as her business idea became the group project's focus.

Although there was no formal accompaniment, the interactivity among the group and the feedback received provided enough guidance to complete the project. The team created a prototype which she evolved, on her own, into the webpage for her online shop. Parallel to launching her business, *Godly Closets*, she adopted a hands-on attitude, recognised additional need and identified training opportunities through external sources. Feeling more mature and confident, she enrolled in her third course on entrepreneurship, and accessed mentorship. The course professor provided said mentorship as part of the class. Although Diana does not have an official mentor, the bond created with her professor transcended the classroom, and occasional counselling is still ongoing. Currently, her business is in operation.

This case shows how the shared approach supplied Diana with cumulative life-shaping events, starting with the teacher-led acquisition of essential knowledge and the occasional need to revert to that approach, followed by growing instructional clarity and increased skills and engagement. Along the way, Diana revisited concepts and iterated as required to advance and achieve her goals. Going back to review before pushing forward became an ongoing exercise, along with active engagement and setting herself within real-life scenarios. The disposition to learn, receive feedback, launch her web shop, and to continue her journey, attest to the evolving mindset and increased maturity characteristic of the andragogic assumptions in adult education. Although each journey is unique, the model proposed illustrates how entrepreneurship education benefits from the pedagogy–andragogy binomial and the interactivity in-between.

6 CONCLUSION

As higher education and entrepreneurship education have adapted to serve the incoming population, the interplay among pedagogy, andragogy, and the interactions in-between, have given way to a layered journey for education in entrepreneurship. The student population, inclusive of the emergent adults and adults alike, navigates the experience capitalising from a diversified array of educational strategies, practical set-ups and mentoring.

To that effect, this chapter discussed the higher education newcomer's profile and ways in which the process mobilises towards competency development. It also gave additional attention to the practice of teaching entrepreneurship by relying on active learning, experiential learning, mindset development and mentoring. The case study presented provided a reference to show how the proposed model applies to students in entrepreneurship education. It also showcased the flux-zone as the area where both approaches benefit from interactivity among diverse educational strategies. As a collective, these components nurture the student entrepreneur and enrich the experience resulting in increased maturity and independent decision-making based on defined beliefs, identity and social relations (Baxter Magolda, 2008; McNally et al., 2019).

As learning is not a spectator sport (Chickering & Gamson, 1987), it takes effort, and education in entrepreneurship relies on fostering the entrepreneurial intention to accomplish results. Yet, regardless of the efforts to offer pertinent curricula, real-life scenarios and guidance, the process itself is highly individual and contextual. Moreover, even though a basic configuration of the educational journey in entrepreneurship has been described, there is no specific method to determine, with surgical precision, what works for each individual.

Nonetheless, regardless of the age group, students converge in the search of a pathway towards economic independence, wealth (De Jonghe, 2014; Wrenn & Wrenn, 2009) and personal achievement through an education that makes sense. Entrepreneurship education is a journey with a purpose: to shape individuals who can identify opportunities and foresee possibilities that the world has to offer (Kouakou et al., 2019; Reed &

Stoltz, 2011). The call to action aims to transcend by bridging the theory into practice and taking academia into the real world.

REFERENCES

Allan, J., Clarke, K., & Jopling, M. (2009). Effective teaching in higher education: Perceptions of first year undergraduate students. *International Journal of Teaching and Learning in Higher Education, 21*(3), 362–372.

Arnett, J. J. (2000). Emerging adulthood: A theory of development from the late teens through the twenties. *American Psychologist, 55*(5), 469–480.

Bahr, N. (2010). Thinking critically about critical thinking in higher education. *International Journal for the Scholarship of Teaching and Learning, 4*(2). Recovered from https://doi.org/10.20429/ijsotl.2010.040209

Bandura, A. (2006). Towards a psychology of human agency. *Perspectives on Psychological Science, 1*(2), 164–180.

Baxter Magolda, M. B. (2008). Three elements of self-authorship. *Journal of College Student Development, 49*(4), 269–284. https://doi.org/10.1353/csd.0.0016

Bechard, J. P., & Toulouse, J. M. (1991). Entrepreneurship and education: Viewpoint from education. *Journal of Small Business & Entrepreneurship, 9*(1), 3–13.

Béchard, J. P., & Grégoire, D. (2005). Entrepreneurship education research revisited: The case of higher education. *Academy of Management Learning and Education, 4*(1), 22–43.

Bethell, S., & Morgan, K. (2011). Problem-based and experiential learning: Engaging students in an undergraduate physical education module. *The Journal of Hospitality Leisure Sport and Tourism, 10*(1), 128–134. https://doi.org/10.3794/johlste.101.365

Bielefeldt, A. R. (2011). Incorporating a sustainability module into first-year courses for civil and environmental engineering students. *Journal of Professional Issues in Engineering Education and Practice, 137*(2), 78–85.

Blencher, P., Dreisler, P., & Kjeldsen, J. (2006). Entrepreneurship education at university level—Contextual challenges. *TUTWPE, 151*, 43–62.

Bonwell, C. C., & Eison, J. A. (1991). *Active learning:Creating excitement in the classroom.* ERIC Clearinghouse on Higher Education. George Washington University.

Blaich, C., Wise, K., Pascarella, E., & Josipa Roksa, J. (2016). Instructional clarity and organization: It's not new or fancy, but it matters. *Change: The Magazine of Higher Learning, 48*(4), 6–13. https://doi.org/10.1080/00091383.2016.1198142

Borghoff, B. (2018). Entrepreneurial Storytelling as Narrative Practice in Project—and Organizational Development, Findings of a narrative—and discourse analytical case study in Switzerland. In E. Innerhofer, H. Pechlaner & E. Borin (Eds.), *Entrepreneurship in culture and creative industries, perspectives from companies and regions (FGF Studies in Small Business and Entrepreneurship)*. Wiesbaden: Springer.

Brown, K. L. (2003). From teacher-centered to learner-centered curriculum: Improving learning in diverse classrooms. *Education, 124*(1), 49.

Bruyat, C., & Julien, P. (2001). Defining the field of research in entrepreneurship. *Journal of Business Venturing, 16*(2), 165–180.

Caruth, G. (2015, Janauary). Online education, active learning and andragogy: an approach for student engagement. *GLOKALde, 1*(4). ISSN2148-7278

Chickering, A. W., & Gamson, Z. F. (1987). Seven principles for good practice. *AAHE. Bulletin, 39*(7), 3–7.

Dana, B. (2017). The educational impact of implementation the education through adventure discipline in physical education and sports academic curriculum. *Physical Education of Students*. University of Medicine and Pharmacy of Targu Mures. https://doi.org/10.15561/20755279.2017.0302

De Jonghe, A. (2014, August). *Strategies in traditional higher education: Lessons from a newcomer?* University of Southampton Faculty of Law, Arts & Social Sciences School of Management. Thesis for the degree of Doctor of Philosophy.

Detienne, D., & Chandler, G. (2004). Opportunity identification and its role in the entrepreneurial classroom: A pedagogical approach and empirical test. *Academy of Management Learning and Education, 3*(3), 242–257.

Dewey, J. (1938). *Experience and education*. The Macmillan Company.

Dreyfus, S. E. (2004). The five stage model of adult skill acquisition. *Bulletin of Science Technology and Society, 24*(3), 177–181. https://doi.org/10.1177/0270467604264992

Ericsson, K., Krampe, R., & Tesch-Römer, C. (1993). The role of deliberate practice in the acquisition of expert performance. *Psychological Review, 100*(3), 363–406.

Garnett, F., & O'Beirne, R. (2013). Putting heutagogy into learning. In S. Hase & C. Kenyon (Eds.), *Self- determined learning: Heutagogy in action* (pp. 131–143). Bloomsbury Publishing Plc.

Gartner, W. B. (1988). Who is an entrepreneur? Is the wrong question. *American Journal of Small Business, 12*(4), 11–32.

Gibb, A. A. (1993). The enterprise culture and education. understanding enterprise education and its links with small business, entrepreneurship and wider educational goals. *International Small Business Journal, 11*(3), 11–34.

Gibb, A. A. (1996). Entrepreneurship and small business management: Can we afford to neglect them in the twenty-first century business school? *British Journal of Management, 7*, 309–21.

Gibb, A. A. (2002). In pursuit of a new enterprise and entrepreneurship paradigm for learning: Creative destruction, new values, new ways of doing things and new combinations of knowledge. *International Journal of Management Review, 4*(3), 233–269.

Gimmon, E. (2014). Mentoring as a practical training in higher education of entrepreneurship. *Education + Training, 56*(8/9), 814–825.

Gurpinar, E., Bati, H., & Tetik, C. (2011). Learning styles of medical students change in relation to time. *Advances in Physiological Education, 35*(3), 304–311. https://doi.org/10.1152/advan.00047.2011

Hägg, G., & Kurczewska, A. (2018). Who is the student entrepreneur? Understanding the emergent adult through the pedagogy and andragogy interplay. *Journal of Small Business Management, 00*(00), 1–18. https://doi.org/10.1111/jsbm.12496

Hägg, G., & Kurczewska, A. (2020). Towards a learning philosophy based on experience in entrepreneurship education. *Entrepreneurship Education and Pedagogy, 3*(2), 129–153.

Hannum, W., & McCombs, B. (2007). Enhancing distance learning for today's youth with learner-centered principles. *Educational Technology, 48*(3), 11–21.

Heinonen, J., & Poikkijoki, S. (2006). An entrepreneurial-directed approach to entrepreneurship education: Mission impossible? *Journal of Management Development, 25*(1), 80–94. https://doi.org/10.1108/02621710610637981

Hernández Nanclares, N., & Pérez Rodríguez, M. (2015). Students' satisfaction with a blended instructional design: The potential of "flipped classroom" in higher education. *Journal of Interactive Media in Education, 2016*(1), 4, 1–12. https://doi.org/10.5334/jime.397

Hidayat, D. (2018). Social entrepreneurship andragogy-based for community empowerment. *SHS Web of Conferences, 42*, 00102. https://doi.org/10.1051/shsconf/20184200102

Honig, B. (2004). Entrepreneurship education: Toward a model of contingency-based business Planning. *Academy of Management Learning and Education, 3*(3), 258–273.

Jareño, F., Jiménez-Moreno, J., & Lagos, G. (2014). Cooperative learning in higher education: Differences in the perception of the contribution to the group. *Universities and Knowledge Society Journal, 11*(2), 70–84. https://doi.org/10.7238/rusc.v11i2.1936

Johannisson, B. (2011). Towards a practice theory of entrepreneuring. *Small Business Economics, 36*(2), 135–150.

Jonassen, D. H. (1991). Objectivism versus constructivism: Do we need a new philosophical paradigm? *Educational Technology Research and Development, 39*(3), 5–14.

Jones, C. & English, J. (2004). A contemporary approach to entrepreneurship education. *Education + Training, 46*(8/9), 416–423.

Jones. C., Penaluna, K., & Penaluna, A. (2019). The promise of andragogy, heutagogy, and academagogy to enterprise and entrepreneurship education pedagogy. *Education + Training, 6*(9), 1170–1186.

Kent, T., Dennis, C. & Tanton, S. (2003). An evaluation of mentoring for SME retailers. *International Journal of Retail & Distribution Management, 31*(8), 440–448.

Kerr, S., Kerr, W., & Xu, T. (2017). *Personality traits of entrepreneurs: A Review of recent literature personality traits of entrepreneurs: A review of recent literature.* Harvard Business School. Recovered from https://www.hbs.edu/ris/Publication%20Files/18-047_b0074a64-5428-479b-8c83-16f2a0e97eb6.pdf

Keshner, A. (2019). The upshot on the continuing decline in the fertility rate. *Market Watch.* Recovered from https://www.marketwatch.com/story/americas-declining-birth-rate-foreshadows-some-tough-financial-times-ahead-2019-05-15

Knowles, M. S. (1980a). *The modern practice of adult education: From pedagogy to andragogy* (2nd ed.). Cambridge Books.

Knowles, M. S. (1980b). *The modern practice of adult education: Andragogy versus pedagogy—Revised and updated.* Cambridge and The Adult Education Company.

Knowles, M. S. (1984). *Andragogy in action: Applying principles of adult learning.* Jossey-Bass.

Knowles, M. S. (1990). *The adult learner: A neglected species* (4th ed.). Gulf Publishing Company.

Knowles, M. S., Holton, E., & Swanson, R. (2005). *The adult learner: A neglected species* (6th ed.). Elsevier Butterworth-Heinemann.

Kolb, D. (1984). *Experiential learning, experience as the source of learning and development.* Prentice Hall.

Kolb, A., & Kolb, D. (2017). Experiential learning theory as a guide for experiential educators in higher education. *Experiential Learning & Teaching in Higher Education, 1*(1), 7–44.

Kouakou, K., Li, C., Akolgo, I., & Tchamekwen, A. (2019). Evolution view of entrepreneurial mindset theory. *International Journal of Business and Social Science, 10*(6), 116–129. https://doi.org/10.30845/ijbss.v10n6p13

Kozlinska, I. (2011). Contemporary approaches to entrepreneurship education. *Journal of Business Management, 4*(1), 205–220.

Krueger, N. (2015). Entrepreneurial education in practice: Part 1-The entrepreneurial mindset. *Entrepreneurship 360.* Recovered from https://www.oecd.org/cfe/leed/Entrepreneurial-Education-Practice-pt1.pdf

Lackéus, M., Lundqvist, M., & Middleton, K. (2016). Bridging the traditional—Progressive education rift through entrepreneurship. *International Journal of Entrepreneurial Behavior & Research, 22*(6), 777–803.

Lemoine, P., Jenkins, W., & Richardson, M. (2017). Global higher education: Development and implications. *Journal of Education and Development, 1*(1), 58–71.

Mandel, R., & Noyes, E. (2016). Survey of experiential entrepreneurship education offerings among top undergraduate entrepreneurship programs. *Education + Training, 58*(2), 164–178.

McNally, J., Piperopoulos, P., Welsh, D., Mengel, T., Tantawy, M., & Papageorgiadis, N. (2019). From pedagogy to andragogy: Assessing the impact of social entrepreneurship course Syllabi on the millennial learner. *Journal of Small Business Management.* https://doi.org/10.1080/00472778.2019.1677059

Neck, H., Greene, P., & Brush, C. (2017). *Teaching entrepreneurship, a practice-based approach.* Edward Elgar Publishing Inc.

Politis, D. (2005). The process of entrepreneurial learning: A conceptual framework. *Entrepreneurship: Theory and Practice, 29*(4), 399–424.

Raposo, M., & do Paço, A. (2011). Entrepreneurship education: Relationship between education and entrepreneurial activity. *Psicothema, 23*(3), 453–457.

Reed, J., & Stoltz, P. G. (2011). *Put your mindset to work.* Penguin UK.

Rodriguez, G. (2021, June 18). *Personal Interview* (Phone interview).

Robinson, S., Neergaard, H., Tanggaard, L., & Krueger, N. (2016). New horizons in entrepreneurship: From teacher-led to student-centered learning. *Education + Training, 58*(7/8), 661–683.

Salvatore, C. (2018). Introduction to emerging adulthood. *Sex, crime, drugs, and just plain stupid behaviors* (pp.1–7). Palgrave McMillan. DOI: https://doi.org/10.1007/978-3-319-72766-0_1

Schumpeter, J. A. (1951). *Essays: On entrepreneurs, innovations, business cycles, and the evolution of capitalism.* Transaction Books.

Scott, J. M., Penaluna, A., & Thompson, J. (2016). A critical perspective on learning outcomes and the effectiveness of experiential approaches in entrepreneurship education: Do we innovate or implement? *Education + Training, 58*(1), 82–93.

Senior, C., Fung, D., Howard, C., & Senior, R. (2018). What is the role for effective pedagogy in contemporary higher education? *Frontiers in Psychology, 9*, 1299. https://doi.org/10.3389/fpsyg.2018.01299

Taylor, A., Backlund, P., & Niklasson, L. (2012). *The Coaching Cycle. Simulation & Gaming, 43*(5), 648–672. https://doi.org/10.1177/1046878112439442

Tu, J., Liu, L., & Wu, K. (2018). Study on the learning effectiveness of Stanford sesign thinking in integrated design education. *Sustainability, 10*, 2649.

Vanevenhoven, J. & Liguori, E. (2013). The impact of entrepreneurship education: Introducing the entrepreneurship education project. *Journal of Small Business Management , 51*(3), 315–328.

von Graevenitz, G., Harhoff, D., & Weber, R. (2010). The effects of entrepreneurship education. *Journal of Economic Behavior and Organization, 76*(1), 90–112.

Voorhees, R. (2001). Competency-based learning models: A necessary future. *New Directions for Institutional Research, 110*, 5–13.

Wood, L. & Reiners, T. (2014). *Gamification encyclopedia of information science and technology* (3rd ed.). Information Science Reference. https://doi.org/10.4018/978-1-4666-5888-2.ch297

Wrenn, J., & Wrenn, B. (2009). Enhancing learning by integrating theory and practice. *International Journal of Teaching and Learning in Higher Education, 21*(2), 258–265.

Ecosystem experiences in UEE

Innovative Educators: The State of Undergraduate Entrepreneurship Education in the United States

Sara L. Cochran

1 INTRODUCTION

Entrepreneurship education is a relatively new discipline in the history of higher education. It has been lauded the fastest growing discipline in the history of higher education (Kauffman Foundation, n.d.). Despite all the progress, we are still dealing with legitimacy today. As Charles Matthews, editor of the *2021 Annals of Entrepreneurship Education and Pedagogy* described,

"I know of no other academic (or non-academic for that matter) discipline that has allowed itself to be so abused and ultimately hijacked by others when it comes to what the discipline actually is. As a result, the word "entrepreneurship" continually suffers a definitional crisis, which in turn, systematically obscures the core element of entrepreneurship education, and all that it encompasses" (Matthews et al., 2021, xvii).

S. L. Cochran (✉)
Indiana University, Bloomington, IN, USA
e-mail: Cochran9@iu.edu

© The Author(s), under exclusive license to Springer Nature Switzerland AG 2022
G. J. Larios-Hernandez et al. (eds.), *Theorising Undergraduate Entrepreneurship Education*,
https://doi.org/10.1007/978-3-030-87865-8_14

Yet, in spite of this crisis, entrepreneurship education around the world is thriving. Because it is a worldwide phenomenon, educators around the world rely on one another to learn best practices, conduct research and understand the best ways to educate students. The United States (U.S.) is just one country which has experienced this growth, and this chapter will explore the innovative curricular and co-curricular initiatives taking place in the United States as evidenced by recent publications of the United States Association for Small Business and Entrepreneurship (USASBE).

USASBE is "an inclusive community advancing entrepreneurship education through bold teaching, scholarship, and practice" (United States Association for Small Business and Entrepreneurship, n.d.). While membership is open to anyone from any country, the majority of the members are entrepreneurship educators from the United States. USASBE holds a conference each year in January, offers year-round programming, and oversees scholarly publications including the *Annals of Entrepreneurship Education and Pedagogy (Annals)* and the journal of *Entrepreneurship Education and Pedagogy (EE&P)* whose sister journal is *Entrepreneurship Theory and Practice (ETP)*. This chapter will focus on evidence from items published in the *Annals, EE&P* and *ETP*.

With existing knowledge of entrepreneurship education research as well as these publications, along with a cursory review of the articles, a priori themes were developed to be representative of the overall trends in the research. The articles were first evaluated against the location and date published criteria described below. The articles which met these criteria were systematically reviewed while seeking information related to the a priori themes. Because of the large amount of data within multiple of the themes, the data was then further categorised into sub-themes that emerged from the data.

The articles more fully reviewed for this study were those which explore programs, students or issues related to undergraduate entrepreneurship education within the United States, were written by authors representing U.S. institutions, and were published from December 2018 through April 2021. It should be noted that the *Annals* editions were dated 2018 and 2021, but were made available to the USASBE community in January 2019 and January 2021, respectively. Therefore, the time period covered in this chapter is effectively 2019 and 2020. This chapter is not meant to be an exhaustive literature review, but rather provides highlights of educational initiatives and innovations, both curricular and co-curricular, in the United States.

2 Curricular Programs

Alabduljader, Ramani and Solomon (2018) found that entrepreneurship programs at four-year institutions are primarily housed within business schools with the most popular program choice of students to be a minor in entrepreneurship. However, much of the research shows schools to have majors, minors, and certificates. The publications reviewed feature model programs, award-winning programs, as well as other programs of interest, providing educators a variety of types of institutions and programs from which to derive best practices.

Highlighted Programs

American University Center for Innovation was named a top twenty entrepreneurship centre in April 2017 by the Association to Advance Collegiate Schools of Business (AACSB) and in October 2017 as an "Oasis of Excellence" by the American Council of Trustees and Alumni (ACTA). The program includes an entrepreneurship minor for non-business students, entrepreneurship specialisation for business students, as well as programs for graduate students. The curriculum emphasises experiential learning with unique offerings such as social entrepreneurship courses with an included travel stay in Bergen, Norway and a FedTech commercialization course partnering students with cutting-edge inventions from the U.S. Federal lab system (Terjesen & Li, 2018).

North Carolina State University was recognised in 2017 by USASBE as Outstanding Emerging Entrepreneurship Program for the E-Clinic, a hands-on practicum. In order to prepare undergraduate students to work in the E-Clinic, students take courses designed to teach opportunity analysis and creation, new venture planning, and finance and accounting for entrepreneurs. During the E-Clinic practicum, students work with clients in a "teaching hospital" model in that the clients are the patients, and the students provide services under the direction of "attending physicians" or experienced professors (Pollack et al., 2018).

Grove City College has been recognised in rankings in Forbes, U.S. News & World Report, Money, Business Insider and The Princeton Review. Grove City College offers a major and several minors in entrepreneurship. The major includes courses in internet entrepreneurship, social innovation, social enterprise, social entrepreneurship and high-tech entrepreneurship. Additionally, corporate partnerships have been leveraged to offer specialised courses such as corporate healthcare innovation and supply chain management where the students work on projects for companies (English, 2018).

Miami University employs a practice-based model in that students are immersed in experience throughout their entrepreneurship major coursework by having at least five real-world, real-time entrepreneurial experiences ranging from a Start-up Weekend or a client analytics project, or a semester-long immersion experience across the country or abroad. There are various specific courses to provide these opportunities, such as the Altman internship experience where students spend the summer working with high growth companies. Additionally, the accelerator launch course provides students an opportunity to work on their start-up in a top-ranked accelerator for credit and the semester immersion in San Francisco places students in internships in high growth companies. Miami University is unique in that it is one of the few top 25 entrepreneurship programs that does not offer a graduate program and simply focuses on undergraduate education (Smith & Holcomb, 2018).

Florida State University's (FSU) Jim Moran College (JMC) of Entrepreneurship was recognised as the 2019 USASBE Model Emerging Program and additionally by the Global Consortium of Entrepreneurship Centers for Exceptional Activities in Entrepreneurship across Disciplines in 2019. The JMC offers a Bachelor of Science in entrepreneurship with majors in commercial entrepreneurship, social entrepreneurship and retail entrepreneurship. Each student who earns a major in entrepreneurship must complete an internship and is strongly encouraged to have an international experience. Additionally, the JMC partners collaborate with various colleges and majors across campus to offer minors in entrepreneurship. The curriculum offers case study learning as well as hands-on applications (Fiorito & Plant, 2021).

The University of Missouri Kansas City (UMKC) Regnier Institute offers a major emphasis and minor and special courses with other disciplines (Hornsby et al., 2021). The Regnier Institute has taken a cross-campus approach through which an entrepreneurship professor partners with a discipline-specific area professor to develop a course in entrepreneurship focused on a specific discipline as part of a general education requirement. Courses developed include Biological Innovation and Entrepreneurship, Innovation and the Aging Population (a partnership with the nursing program) and Arts Entrepreneurship: The Music Business in Different Cultures and Industries. Since the launch of these courses, enrolment in business courses by non-business majors has gone from 15 to 26 per cent, thereby exposing more non-business students to entrepreneurship concepts (Mendes et al., 2021). Additionally, the Regnier Institute offers the Entrepreneurship Scholars (E-Scholars) program for early-stage entrepreneurs to take their business ideas from concept to reality through a program for which they can earn up to six hours towards their major or minor (Hornsby et al., 2021).

Courses

These previously mentioned programs, as well as numerous other programs around the United States, are teaching an innovative curriculum with unique courses, exercises and cases. The most popular forms of pedagogical strategies in the entrepreneurship classroom are discussions, creation of business plans, case studies and guest speakers (Alabduljader et al., 2018).

When looking at programs across the country Alabduljader et al. (2018) found that the most popular course in entrepreneurship programs is simply called "Entrepreneurship" (Alabduljader et al., 2018). While many schools offer courses in entrepreneurship, introduction to entrepreneurship, or the entrepreneurial mindset, there are several other courses being offered. Some innovative courses highlighted in the recent literature are included here.

The Creator Pedagogy at Georgetown University is an undergraduate course that teaches about entrepreneurship through authorship. Through the semester-long course, students learn the publishing process and publish a book that can "demonstrate their competency, credibility and expertise in a field" (PAGE) and long-term gives students necessary skills to launch successful ventures (Reid & Koester, 2018).

Barber, Harris, and Paynter (2021) describe a program through which service learning is used to increase the impact of student consulting projects in rural communities. The program includes grant-funded internships after two consulting-based courses.

California State University provides an experiential entrepreneurship opportunity through which students are placed in paid jobs with local small businesses (Woods & Burley, 2021). Similarly, the University of California Santa Cruz quickly developed the GetVirtual Local Business Assistance course to assist local businesses during the COVID-19 pandemic. This course was a community partnership to connect local industry experts and mentors with students and the City of Santa Cruz economic development program to assist local brick-and-mortar businesses to go virtual rapidly (Miljkovic & D'Intino, 2021).

Utah State University's Small Enterprise Education and Development (SEED) Program provides students an opportunity to spend 12 weeks in a developing country teaching entrepreneurs fundamental business. The program is open to students from any major and includes a consulting course before the travel experience (Holland & Glauser, 2021).

Grove City College offers a course in corporate healthcare innovation where students work with a corporate partner to develop and pitch business models to solve problems in the healthcare industry (English, 2018).

Miami University offers the Accelerator Launch Course where students attend class in an accelerator program at The Brandery accelerator in Cincinnati, OH. The program is taught by entrepreneurs and investors and facilitated by Miami University faculty. At the conclusion of the program, the students pitch in a Demo Day with judges (Smith & Holcomb, 2018).

Exercises

While many universities, like those featured above, offer unique innovative courses, these and other educators are using a number of exercises, learning innovations and cases to teach entrepreneurship theories and principles, as well as help students develop an entrepreneurial mindset. There have long been innovative exercises to teach basic entrepreneurial principles, many which are still highly regarded and used today. In order to expand the topics covered, educators have developed the below exercises.

Storytelling. Story telling by having a classmate tell your story (Hart, 2018). Entrepreneurs frequently need to tell their story and express their vision for solving a problem for customers to journalists, investors, donors, prospective employees, partners and even customers. Recognising this, Hart (2018) describes an exercise during which students tell their life stories to a classmate and learn to craft a person brand through stories.

Design thinking. Zane and Zimbroff (2021) describe a human centred design exercise for ideation and brainstorming building something from supplies brought into the classroom (Zane & Zimbroff, 2021). Meanwhile to teach serving customers and hidden assumptions, Winkel et al. (2021) describe an exercise to design a toothbrush.

Gender and Diversity. Solomon and Solomon (2021) describe an exercise that encourages diversity using personality tests. To enable classroom-based conversations about bias in the domain of entrepreneurship, Michaelis et al. (2018) present a learning innovation which explores gender bias in venture funding.

Minimum viable products (MVP) and Scaling. Through Hart's (2021) exercise, students design a minimum viable product and scale up and scale back as the need arises. Winkle, Wilcox and Teckchandri (2021) use an MVP exercise through which students work in teams to develop a landing page and video to gather information from prospective customers in just 60 min.

Finance. Tonhozi de Oliveira and Peak's (2021) exercise helps students strengthen skills in the areas of basic pricing and pricing strategy and learn how to use market research to make such decisions.

Use of Films. Solomon (2018) uses George A, Romero's 1968 *Night of the Living Dead* as a metaphor for entrepreneurship, finding it full of metaphors for topics such as competition, opportunity recognition, group dynamics, strategy and leadership (Solomon, 2018). Meanwhile, Vanevenhoven et al. (2021) use the film *Door to Door* because of its numerous learning points on topics such as perseverance, persistence, passion, and community and relationship building.

Cases

Family business. *Continuing the legacy at Nordic Lodge: Succession planning at an iconic family-owned restaurant* covers family business and succession planning (Graham & Mischel, 2019).

Social entrepreneurship. Balachandra and Stoddard's (2019) *Rahama Wright and Shea Yeleen* covers topics on social entrepreneurship, women's entrepreneurship, start-ups in Africa, impact investing and non-profit versus for-profit organisation. Narapareddy and Berte's (2019)

Entrepreneurship in a non-profit healthcare organisation highlights non-profit entrepreneurship, social entrepreneurship, non-profit management and new venture feasibility.

Technology entrepreneurship. *Entrepreneurship in the digital era: Creating your own online business* teaches about digital entrepreneurship, creativity and innovation and technology entrepreneurship (Finkle & Olsen, 2019). Mancha et al. (2019) *LBRY, Inc: Scaling and monetizing a blockchain start-up* covers blockchain and digital platform.

Entrepreneurial strategy. Craig et al. (2019) *The impact of climate and weather on a small tourism business: A SWOT case study* covers topics of climate change, weather and SWOT analysis. While *Pokey O's: Determining the location and future structure of a dessert food truck* covers the industry life cycle and supplier threat (Artz et al., 2020).

Marketing. Anderson et al. (2019) *Pepper Place Farmers' Market and the need for research and strategy* covers marketing strategy and market research. Specific to the pricing strategy is *Do not leave your pricing strategy hanging: The Elevate Hammock Company* (Walker et al., 2019).

Finance and investment. *Breathometer: Shut down by the Federal Trade Commission* focuses on due diligence, investors, board of directors and startup success (Miller et al., 2020). While Noyes and Mandel's (2020) *Wefunder: Leading the growth of a new industry* focuses on crowdfunding, equity crowdfunding, opportunity creation, regulatory entrepreneurship, crowdfunding law, industry creation and entrepreneurial finance.

Training Faculty

In addition to training students, Rowan University has developed a faculty certificate program to train faculty to train students. This program begins with a one-day boot-camp prior to the beginning of the fall semester and is followed by five sessions throughout the academic year. The program is designed for faculty outside of the business school to develop an entrepreneurial mindset and integrate such into their existing class content. Additionally, it provides an opportunity for faculty to develop relationships with entrepreneurially—minded faculty from other disciplines (Bodnar et al., 2018). Similarly, Iona College Hynes Institute offers the Hynes Faculty Fellowship Program for faculty across campus to develop and implement entrepreneurial learning innovations within courses in their disciplines (Winkler et al., 2021).

3 Co-curricular Programs

In addition to the great work being done in entrepreneurship classrooms in the United States, programs are offering co-curricular opportunities to enhance the student experience and entrepreneurial learning. Outside the classroom, the most popular co-curricular opportunities for students include business plan competitions, entrepreneurship clubs and pitch competitions (Alabduljader et al., 2018) and programs offer these as well as many other innovative opportunities for students to apply their classroom learnings. Some unique and noteworthy offerings published about recently include these below.

Technology Commercialisation. Eastern Washington University's (EWU) Technology Commercialisation Academy (TCA) is an eight-week summer program for students to develop working commercialization plans based on patented technologies. The EWU's Centre for Entrepreneurship partners with local research universities to procure access to patented technologies and leads the students through sessions to understand the program and work on their ventures (Teague & Liu, 2021).

Student Consulting. Bear Studies is an undergraduate student-run consulting and design firm which employs student fellows who freelance for local start-ups and small businesses in business, design and technology services. It was developed by students, is managed by students, and, because of great success, is being developed on additional university campuses (Delaney et al., 2019).

Incubator and Co-Working. American University's Center for Innovation offers the AUCI Incubator which helps students build successful ventures, access mentors and gain access to funding (Terjesen & Li, 2018). Grove City College offers the VentureLab for students to work with coaches and mentors as they build their ventures (English, 2018). FSU's JMC offers the Greenhouse student business incubator through the InNOLEvation Center for Student Engagement (Fiorito & Plant, 2021). The Georgetown Entrepreneurship Initiative offers the Summer

Launch Incubator where students receive coaching and a stipend so they can focus on their ventures full-time (Reid, 2021). Iona College's Hynes Institute provides a collaborative workspace for students to work with fellow students, mentors and faculty as they develop their ideas (Winkler et al., 2021).

Study Abroad. Grove City College offers the GCC-Oniris Engineer + Entrepreneurship Collaboration through which students can combine their engineering and entrepreneurship expertise to address real-world engineering problems in Nantes, France (English, 2018).

Living Learning Community. FSU's JMC has an Entrepreneurship and Innovation Learning Community where first-year students live together in a residence hall with speakers, coursework and shadowing opportunities (Fiorito & Plant, 2021).

Investing Apprenticeship. The Georgetown Entrepreneurship Initiative Venture Fellows Program is an eight- to twelve-month apprenticeship within a local venture capital firm for students to work alongside active investors (Reid, 2021).

Accelerator and Competition. The Iona Hynes Institutes Iona Innovation Challenge is a two-month program for students to work on their ideas culminating in a competition where students compete for $6,000 in prizes (Winkler et al., 2021). The Regnier Institute at UMKC offers the Regnier Venture Creation Challenge for students from all across the region to pitch their business model and compete for $75,000 in total prizes (Hornsby et al., 2021). The Georgetown University Entrepreneurship Initiative also offers a competition called Bark Tank through during which eight selected teams pitch for $100,000 in prize money for their ventures (Reid, 2021).

4 Outcomes

Scholars have long worked to understand the outcomes and impact of an entrepreneurship education and in this review, there were contributions to this body of research.

Lee, Kreiser, Wrede and Kogelen (2018) surveyed entrepreneurship students to understand their development of capabilities related to networking skills, self-confidence and proactiveness. The study found that students' entrepreneurship capabilities had a significant correlation with entrepreneurial intentions, family background and GPA. Additionally, the study indicated that students' entrepreneurial capabilities are further cultivated the longer they are in school.

Similarly, undergraduate engineering students have been found to have an increased self-efficacy after taking an entrepreneurship course in all areas tested including searching, planning, marshalling, implementing people, and implementing finance. The strongest increased self-efficacy was in planning followed closely by finance (Shekhar et al., 2018).

In an experimental design, Burnette et al. (2020) randomly assigned students in an introduction to entrepreneurship course to either a growth mindset intervention or a knowledge-based control. Those students in the growth mindset group reported greater entrepreneurial self-efficacy on their main class project as well as increased academic and career interests in entrepreneurship. However, the intervention did not impact their performance on a classroom assignment.

When looking at the combination of curricular and co-curricular programs, Chandler and Broberg (2019) found that in a new venture competition judged on a ten-page business plan, teams with entrepreneurship students scored higher than those with no entrepreneurship students.

Shekhar, Huang-Saad and Libarkin (2018) studied undergraduate students in a co-curricular, five-month social entrepreneurship program in the United States and found them to have an increased self-efficacy after participating in the program. While they showed an increased self-efficacy in all areas: searching, planning, marshalling, implementing people, and implementing finance, the largest increases were for the marshalling and searching construct.

Cochran (2021) explored the role of gender in entrepreneurship education by studying women students' experiences in an undergraduate entrepreneurship program. The study found that women students are superwomen, similar to the dictionary definition of the word. These women successful and performed very well in the men-dominated area in that they were very responsible and coped successfully with multiple demands including schoolwork. They worked hard in school and were highly responsible.

5 Conclusion

This chapter has provided an overview of the latest initiatives and innovations in undergraduate entrepreneurship education in the United States as presented in three leading entrepreneurship publications: *Annals of Entrepreneurship Education and Pedagogy*, *Entrepreneurship Education and Pedagogy* (EE&P) and its sister journal *Entrepreneurship Theory and Practice (ETP)*. This snapshot of recent trends shows that these innovations have included curricular changes from entire classes, exercises and cases, to co-curricular innovations such as programs, internships and study abroad opportunities. In order to understand the impact of entrepreneurship education and these innovations, scholars continue to research the field. Because entrepreneurship education has been lauded the fastest growing discipline in the history of higher education (Kauffman Foundation, n.d.), it is not surprising that the field continues to constantly innovate. While it is a relatively new discipline, it has had a strong hold for more than 30 years (Kauffman Foundation, n.d.). Because of this, there are standard theories, methods, principles and concepts being taught. But, by the very nature of the discipline, educators continue to innovate and act in entrepreneurial ways.

Anecdotally, these trends are consistent with what can be observed on entrepreneurship education by researching program websites, attending USASBE and other similar conferences, and visiting with colleagues from around the country and world. Because of the very nature of the discipline, entrepreneurship educators are constantly innovating programs and courses. The COVID-19 pandemic has caused educators to be even more innovative (McMurtrie, 2021), while the United States has seen an overwhelming surge in entrepreneurial activity (Ahuja, 2021) and a call for entrepreneurs to address the world's ailments (Miller, 2020). Entrepreneurship education was already changing, and these events are exacerbating this trend. Given these trends and current events, it is anticipated that the future will bring a continued rise and presence of entrepreneurship programs, more experiential opportunities in and out of the classroom, and a rise in the number of programs and initiatives using entrepreneurship to approach the world's wicked problems.

REFERENCES

Ahuja, M. (2021, June 17). Covid's entrepreneur explosion. *Forbes*. http://www.forbes.com

Alabduljader, N., Ramani, R. S., & Solomon, G. T. (2018). Entrepreneurship education: A qualitative review of U.S. curricula for steady and high growth potential ventures. In C. Matthews & E. Liguori (Eds.), *Annals of entrepreneurship education and pedagogy 2018*. Edward Elgar.

Anderson, R., Walls, S., Junggren, G., & Gerdts, N. (2019). Pepper Place Farmers' Market and the need for research and strategy. *Entrepreneurship Education and Pedagogy, 2*(4), 363–367.

Artz, K., Reed, M. M., & Laurie, J. (2020). Pokey O's: Determining the location and future structure of a dessert food truck. *Entrepreneurship Education & Pedagogy, 3*(2), 195–207.

Balachandra, L., & Stoddard, D. (2019). Rahama Wright and Shea Yeleen. *Entrepreneurship Education and Pedagogy, 2*(1), 43–57.

Barber III, D., Harris, M., & Paynter, S. (2021). A model to increase the impact of student consulting projects in rural communities. In C. Matthews & E. Liguori (Eds.), *Annals of entrepreneurship education and pedagogy 2021*. Edward Elgar.

Bodnar, C., Byrd, K., & Ross, L. (2018). Capacity building for innovation and entrepreneurship on campus through a faculty certificate program. In C. Matthews & E. Liguori (Eds.), *Annals of entrepreneurship education and pedagogy 2018*. Edward Elgar.

Burnette, J. L., Pollack, J. M., Forsyth, R. B., Hoyt, C. L., Babij, A. D., Thomas, F. D., & Coy, A. E. (2020). A growth mindset intervention: Enhancing students' entrepreneurial self-efficacy and career development. *Entrepreneurship Theory and Practice, 44*(5), 878–908.

Chandler, G. N., & Broberg, J. C. (2019). Using a new venture competition to provide external assessment of a university entrepreneurship program. *Entrepreneurship Education and Pedagogy, 2*(2), 96–122.

Cochran, S. L. (2021). Donning their capes: Women entrepreneurship students emerge as superwomen. In C. Matthews & E. Liguori (Eds.), *Annals of entrepreneurship education and pedagogy 2021*. Edward Elgar.

Craig, C. A., Sayers, E. P., Feng, S., & Kinghorn, B. (2019). The impact of climate and weather on a small tourism business: A wSWOT case study. *Entrepreneurship Education and Pedagogy, 2*(3), 255–266.

Delaney, P. G., Harrington, K., & Toker, E. (2019). Undergraduate student-run business development services firms: A new educational opportunity and growth alternative for small and medium enterprises. *Entrepreneurship Education and Pedagogy, 2*(2), 171–187.

English, Y. J. (2018). Entrepreneurship at Grove City College. In C. Matthews & E. Liguori (Eds.), *Annals of entrepreneurship education and pedagogy 2018*. Edward Elgar.

Fiorito, D., & Plant, W. (2021). Florida State University Jim Moran College of entrepreneurship. In C. Matthews & E. Liguori (Eds.), *Annals of entrepreneurship education and pedagogy 2021*. Edward Elgar.

Finkle, T. A., & Olsen, T. (2019). Entrepreneurship in the digital era: Creating your own online business. *Entrepreneurship Education and Pedagogy, 2*(2), 133–150.

Graham, E., & Mischel, L. (2019). Continuing the legacy at Nordic lodge: Succession planning at an iconic family-owned restaurant. *Entrepreneurship Education and Pedagogy, 2*(3), 245–254.

Hart, J. (2018). Have a classmate tell your story. In C. & E. Liguori (Eds.), *Annals of entrepreneurship education and pedagogy 2018*. Edward Elgar.

Hart, J. (2021). Scale up, scale back: An experiential exercise in scaling. In C. Matthews & E. Liguori (Eds.), *Annals of entrepreneurship education and pedagogy 2021*. Edward Elgar.

Holland, D. & Glauser, M. (2021). The small enterprise education and development program. In C. Matthews & E. Liguori (Eds.), *Annals of entrepreneurship education and pedagogy 2021*. Edward Elgar.

Hornsby, J., Mendes, A, & Heise, A. (2021). University of Missouri-Kansas City Regnier Institute. In C. Matthews & E. Liguori (Eds.), *Annals of entrepreneurship education and pedagogy 2021*. Edward Elgar.

Kauffman Foundation. (n.d.). *Entrepreneurship in American higher education*. A report from the Kauffman Panel on Entrepreneurship Curriculum in Higher Education.

Lee, Y., Kreiser, P. Wrede, A. H. & Kogelen, S. (2018). Examining the role of university education in influencing the development of students' entrepreneurship capabilities. In C. Matthews & E. Liguori (Eds.), *Annals of entrepreneurship education and pedagogy 2018*. Edward Elgar.

Matthews, C. H., Liguori, E. W., & Santos, S. C. (2021). Preface: Entrepreneurship education—What is it we need to know? In. C. Matthews & E. Liguori (Eds.), *Annals of entrepreneurship education and pedagogy 2021*. Edward Elgar.

Mancha, R., Gordon, S., & Stoddard, D. (2019). LBRY, Inc.: Scaling and monetizing a blockchain startup. *Entrepreneurship education and pedagogy, 2*(3), 267–280.

McMurtrie, B. (2021, April 1). Teaching: Find insights to improve teaching and learning across your campus. *The chronicle for higher education*. http://www.chronicle.com

Mendes, A, Hornsby, J. & Heise, A. (2021). Cross-campus entrepreneurship through a general education strategy. In C. Matthews & E. Liguori (Eds.), *Annals of entrepreneurship education and pedagogy 2021*. Edward Elgar.

Miljkovic, N., & D'Intino, R. (2021). Rapidly responding to the COVID-19 pandemic impact on small businesses: The getvirtual local business assistance course at the University of California Santa Cruz. In C. Matthews & E. Liguori (Eds.), *Annals of entrepreneurship education and pedagogy 2021*. Edward Elgar.

Miller, L. (2020, June 18). How entrepreneurs can solve the world's biggest problems. *Entrepreneur*. http://www.entrepreneur.com

Miller, M. C., Jackson, L., & Campbell, N. (2020). Breathometer: Shut down by the Federal Trade Commission. *Entrepreneurship Education & Pedagogy, 3*(4), 364–370.

Narapareddy, V., & Berte, E. (2019). Entrepreneurship in a non-profit healthcare organization. *Entrepreneurship education and pedagogy, 2*(2), 123–132.

Noyes, E. & Mandel, R. (2020). Wefunder: Leading the growth of a new industry. *Entrepreneurship Education & Pedagogy, 3*(2), 182–194.

Pollack, J. M., Barr, S. H., Michaelis, T. L., Ward, M. K., Carr, J. C, Sheats, L., & Gonzalez, G. (2018). Entrepreneurship at North Carolina University. In C. Matthews & E. Liguori (Eds.), *Annals of entrepreneurship education and pedagogy 2018*. Edward Elgar.

Reid, J. (2021). The Georgetown University entrepreneurship initiative. In C. Matthews & E. Liguori (Eds.), *Annals of entrepreneurship education and pedagogy 2021*. Edward Elgar.

Reid, J. & Koester, E. (2018). The creator pedagogy" Learning about entrepreneurship through authorship. In C. Matthews & E. Liguori (Eds.), *Annals of entrepreneurship education and pedagogy 2018*. Edward Elgar.

Shekhar, P., Huang-Saad, A., & Libarkin, J. (2018). Examining differences in students' entrepreneurship self-efficacy in curricular and co-curricular entrepreneurship education programs. In C. Matthews & E. Liguori (Eds.), *Annals of entrepreneurship education and pedagogy 2018*. Edward Elgar.

Smith, B. R. & Holcomb, T. R. (2018). Innovation on and beyond campus: Entrepreneurship at Miami University. In C. Matthews & E. Liguori (Eds.), *Annals of entrepreneurship education and pedagogy 2018*. Edward Elgar.

Solomon, S. (2018). *Night of the Living Dean* as a metaphor for entrepreneurship In C. Matthews & E. Liguori (Eds.), *Annals of entrepreneurship education and pedagogy 2018*. Edward Elgar.

Solomon, S. & Solomon, Jr., O. (2021). *Are you the one?* A game for encouraging diversity. In C. Matthews & E. Liguori (Eds.), *Annals of entrepreneurship education and pedagogy 2021*. Edward Elgar.

Teague, B. & Liu, T. (2021). The technology commercialization academy: Fueling student startups. In C. Matthews & E. Liguori (Eds.), *Annals of entrepreneurship education and pedagogy 2021*. Edward Elgar.

Terjesen, S. & Li, H. (2018). Model program: American University Center for Innovation. In C. Matthews & E. Liguori (Eds.) *Annals of Entrepreneurship Education and Pedagogy 2018*. Northampton, MA: Edward Elgar.

Tonhozi de Oliveira, P., & Peake, W. (2021). Entrepreneurship finance over coffee. In C. Matthews & E. Liguori (Eds.), *Annals of entrepreneurship education and pedagogy 2021*. Edward Elgar.

United States Association for Small Business and Entrepreneurship. (n.d.). *Mission Statement*. http://www.usasbe.org

Vanevenhoven, J., Bendickson, J., Liguori, E. W., & Bunoza, A. (2021). Film as an experiential medium: Entrepreneurship education through *Door to Door*. In C. Matthews & E. Liguori (Eds.), *Annals of entrepreneurship education and pedagogy 2021*. Edward Elgar.

Walker, D., Walls, S., Junggren, G., & Gerdts, N. (2019). Do not leave your pricing strategy hanging. *Entrepreneurship Education & Pedagogy, 2*(4), 368–378.

Winkel, D., Wilcox, J., & Mammano, F. (2021). Assume less, observe more: The toothbrush design challenge. In C. Matthews & E. Liguori (Eds.), *Annals of entrepreneurship education and pedagogy 2021*. Edward Elgar.

Winkler, C., Pacheco-Jorge, L., & Monzon, J. B. (2021). Iona College Hynes Institute for entrepreneurship and innovation. In C. Matthews & E. Liguori (Eds.), *Annals of entrepreneurship education and pedagogy 2021*. Edward Elgar.

Woods, J., & Burley, P. M. W. (2021). A learning-by-doing approach to entrepreneurship education, student job creation and new venture incubation. In C. Matthews & E. Liguori (Eds.), *Annals of entrepreneurship education and pedagogy 2021*. Edward Elgar.

Zane, L. & Zimbroff, A. (2021). Ideation techniques and applications to entrepreneurship. In C. Matthews & E. Liguori (Eds.), *Annals of entrepreneurship education and pedagogy 2021*. Edward Elgar.

Ecosystem Engagement in Entrepreneurship Education: A View from Sri Lanka

Nilusha Gallage, Richard Laferriere, and Christopher Selvarajah

1 INTRODUCTION

Despite the rapid growth of entrepreneurship education among universities around the world (Rauch & Hulsink, 2015), university-based entrepreneurship ecosystems (U-BEEs) is still evolving as a concept, including their definition (Hsieh & Kelley, 2020). Within the current understanding, stakeholders (i.e. actors) are fundamental in the U-BEE as they create a conducive environment for students aspiring for an entrepreneurial career. These stakeholders are the human and social elements of ecosystems that create engagement and dynamism (Johnson

---

N. Gallage (✉) · R. Laferriere · C. Selvarajah
School of Business, Law and Entrepreneurship, Swinburne University of Technology, Melbourne, VIC, Australia
e-mail: ngallage@swin.edu.au

R. Laferriere
e-mail: rlaferriere@swin.edu.au

C. Selvarajah
e-mail: cselvarajah@swin.edu.au

© The Author(s), under exclusive license to Springer Nature Switzerland AG 2022
G. J. Larios-Hernandez et al. (eds.), *Theorising Undergraduate Entrepreneurship Education*,
https://doi.org/10.1007/978-3-030-87865-8_15

et al., 2019). Successful ecosystems can foster entrepreneurial intention to become an entrepreneur among undergraduate students; nurture their ability to create start-ups with growth potential; connect budding student entrepreneurs to stakeholders while developing their entrepreneurial knowledge and competencies. Thus, stakeholder engagement within the ecosystem contributes towards undergraduate entrepreneurial transformation.

Although stakeholders are a key component of U-BEEs, limited attention has been given to stakeholders and their collaboration in entrepreneurship education (Bischoff et al., 2018). Universities creating shared value combined with stakeholders have been studied previously in other disciplines (Karwowska, 2019) but not extensively within an ecosystem setting. Further, stakeholders and their engagement have received less attention with only a few studies exploring stakeholders in U-BEEs. Therefore, it is unclear how universities can engage stakeholders in their ecosystem for entrepreneurship education. Thus, in this chapter, an opportunity emerges to understand and establish new knowledge on the stakeholders' moderator role in influencing the entrepreneurial behaviour of undergraduates.

By investigating ecosystem engagement in entrepreneurship education, this chapter improves current knowledge of stakeholder engagement in higher education. The study advances U-BEE theory through three theoretical contributions including the addition of parents as a new stakeholder to U-BEEs and provides the scope for building a broader view of the concept. Another contribution of this chapter is the insights on ecosystem engagement in U-BEE factors; entrepreneurship curriculum, pedagogy, and assessments within the context of Sri Lanka, a developing country. These U-BEE factors are discussed in conjunction to theory of planned behaviour. We have also proposed recommendations as practical guidance for higher education providers to co-create their U-BEE, thus recognising key actors and fostering the engagement of multiple stakeholders in the ecosystem for the pursuit of undergraduate entrepreneurial education.

2 Where Did It Begin?

Traditionally, universities were known for the provision of education producing highly skilled graduates and specialised talent (Bramwell & Wolfe, 2008) in the role of shaping a nation's community and society

(Redford & Fayolle, 2014). More recently, entrepreneurial universities are undertaking the third mission[1] by contributing to an entrepreneurially engaged economy and society (Etzkowitz, 2011). To promote entrepreneurship nationally, universities are advancing education in entrepreneurship and thus, entrepreneurship education has experienced exponential growth in recent years (Bischoff et al., 2018; Rauch & Hulsink, 2015). Scholars have conceptualised a university's environment as an entrepreneurial ecosystem (Fetters et al., 2010) and creating a university-based entrepreneurship ecosystem is a significant element of an entrepreneurial university. This ecosystem of entrepreneurial universities plays a vital role in developing more and/or better student entrepreneurs with greater entrepreneurial knowledge and competencies (Martin et al., 2013). Through the impetus of entrepreneurial universities, U-BEEs gained momentum among academics, researchers and policymakers (Brush Candida, 2014).

While entrepreneurial ecosystem was described as '*a set of individual components...*' (Isenberg, 2010, p. 43) the concept is further defined as '*a set of interdependent actors and factors coordinated in such a way that they enable productive entrepreneurship within a particular territory*' (Stam, 2015, p. 1765). In the extension from entrepreneurial ecosystems to U-BEEs, U-BEE include a combination of actors and factors associated with entrepreneurship education, co-curricular, research, support and commercialization (Brush Candida, 2014; Miller & Acs, 2017; O'Brien et al., 2019; Rice et al., 2014). Entrepreneurship is a complex process that relies on the numerous stakeholders socially embedded in the environment (Neck et al., 2004) and entrepreneurial ecosystems involve multiple stakeholders and processes in various contexts (Isenberg, 2010). For this study, we undertake a stakeholder view of entrepreneurship education in U-BEEs of a developing country.

U-BEEs are co-created by consolidated efforts undertaken by universities to nurture and sustain entrepreneurial communities, in particular nascent entrepreneurs among students (Rice et al., 2014). Universities' provision of these efforts in the ecosystem actively contributes to enhancing students' career intentions of becoming an entrepreneur, commercialization of knowledge and new private businesses for the economy (Ho et al., 2010). Such efforts of ecosystems can also ease

---

[1] Third mission refers to the third role beyond teaching and research that centers on the contribution for economic and social development.

the process of market testing, market-entry and networking with external actors (Belitski & Heron, 2016). While the benefits can be common, U-BEEs are unique when compared to each university and geographic context as scholarly work argues that these ecosystems do not follow a one-size fits all approach (Ricci et al., 2019). The multi-stakeholder environment includes stakeholders who may facilitate or hinder entrepreneurship education and the development of new ventures (Belitski & Heron, 2016). This establishes the significance of exploring context-specific stakeholders within U-BEEs.

3 What Is Known?

As every U-BEE is distinct, each ecosystem consists of a set of actors and factors unique to the university (Miller & Acs, 2017; O'Brien et al., 2019; Rice et al., 2014). Although scholars emphasise the importance of stakeholder engagement, universities lack a broader understanding of stakeholder collaboration in entrepreneurship education and their ecosystems (Bischoff et al., 2018). When managing stakeholder engagement in U-BEEs, universities need to be mindful that it is a progressive process that can be planned and phased (Redford & Fayolle, 2014). By embedding key stakeholders into the ecosystem and engaging them effectively, universities can sustain entrepreneurial activity within their U-BEE and contribute to their region and country. In the below section, we establish the variety of stakeholders, types of relationships, levels of involvement, roles of stakeholders, points of engagement and methods of collaboration from U-BEE literature.

Variety of Stakeholders

Stakeholders are classified using various criteria in related entrepreneurial literature. From the inception of U-BEEs, a combination of internal and external stakeholders is evident among U-BEEs. In higher education, the internal stakeholders are the students, faculty, staff, administrators and sometimes the government depending on the country and higher education structure. Emerging studies emphasise how connections with various external actors shape the U-BEE's development and the significance of managing these external actors to increase entrepreneurial activity (Alvedalen & Boschma, 2017; Link & Sarala, 2019). For instance, Babson College (US) receives external funding for its ecosystem operations and these funds secured from various sources outside the university are a key success factor (Hancock, 2011). Entrepreneurs and corporates are the most common external stakeholders engaged in sharing the practical essence of entrepreneurship and complementing the academic views (Bischoff et al., 2018). Students intending to become entrepreneurs or alumni creating a start-up value this practical knowledge and are influenced by the external environment as much as the university's ecosystem (Hayter et al., 2017). The interactions and interconnectedness among various stakeholders may result in a truly entrepreneurial learning experience for students and highlight the dynamic nature of entrepreneurial activity within the ecosystem (Wright et al., 2017). This draws on the importance of the variety of stakeholders within the U-BEE, especially external stakeholders from the broader entrepreneurial ecosystem (Wright et al., 2017).

Type of Relationships

An entrepreneurial university becomes a relationship builder that creates a configuration of stakeholders through its relationships and these relationships are likely to change throughout the university's life cycle (Redford & Fayolle, 2014). Different stakeholders within the university such as management, faculty, and students and external stakeholders at local, regional and national levels share synergies in the ecosystem. These relationships are networks of various stakeholders from the university and its external domain (Belitski & Heron, 2016). In a successful ecosystem, some relationships can be internal to internal (faculty and student), external to internal (entrepreneur and student) and external to external (alumni to investor) (Powell & Walsh, 2018). While stable relationships can be critical in the flow of entrepreneurship education (Bischoff et al., 2018), creating a balance in synergies between these stakeholders is complex (Leydesdorff, 2000).

Levels of Involvement

Levels of stakeholder involvement and interaction vary from high to low among universities and stakeholder groups (Bischoff et al., 2018). Perceptions and interests held by stakeholders influence their involvement and contribution to entrepreneurship education and its outcomes in higher education (Matlay, 2009). Therefore, the involvement of stakeholders must be mutually beneficial and self-sustaining where the ecosystem works together with shared efforts in stimulating entrepreneurial ventures (Wadee & Padayachee, 2017). Such involvement can be geographically constrained creating a boundary and making it difficult for stakeholders to effectively engage (Acs et al., 2014). The dynamics of the environment affect the ecosystem and its outcomes; however, the involvement of stakeholders significantly impacts each other and factors of the ecosystem (Godley et al., 2019).

Roles of Stakeholders

Entrepreneurial universities play a prominent role in economic development and social transformation in a nation (Leydesdorff, 2000). In U-BEE studies stakeholders play roles related to leadership (Rice et al., 2014), engagement with the wider communities (Morris & Kuratko, 2013), support as intermediary or innovation agents for incubators and technology transfer offices (Rothaermel et al., 2007), resources providers (Belitski, 2019). Within entrepreneurial ecosystems literature, stakeholders contribute by sharing knowledge (Bischoff et al., 2018) and entrepreneurial insights (Godley et al., 2019) while connecting with other stakeholders (Spigel, 2017). The interplay of stakeholders and their engagement in entrepreneurial universities have extended the roles of stakeholders such as researchers being a support system, developing transferrable skills and contributing to active teaching/learning for students (Clauss et al., 2018). In the case of each U-BEE, all stakeholders have their roles (Galvão et al., 2020) to create an entrepreneurial experience and not just entrepreneurship education (Belitski & Heron, 2016).

Points of Engagement

U-BEEs appeal to collective action from engaged stakeholders instilling entrepreneurial knowledge and competencies among aspirants and promoting networking among students (Redford & Fayolle, 2014). In addition to stakeholders from the university, engaging external stakeholders in providing and promoting entrepreneurship education is deemed necessary (Bischoff et al., 2018). Internal and external stakeholders are involved in educational factors such as curriculum and co-curriculum design and activities within the U-BEE (Belitski & Heron, 2016; Brush Candida, 2014). Increasing initiatives are taken by universities to collaborate with industry and entrepreneurs to support teaching/learning (Secundo et al., 2019). Co-curricular activities such as mentoring, start-up competitions and entrepreneurial presentations can be conducted along with external stakeholders, thus, extending beyond the internal staff (Ferrandiz et al., 2018). Stakeholders may engage in other factors of the U-BEEs for research, support services and/or commercialization.

Methods of Collaboration

Collaborations with and among stakeholders are essential for the U-BEE (Rice et al., 2014) and methods of collaboration in entrepreneurship education are developing. One method of collaboration is where internal and external stakeholders are connected as networks and these networks combine and share knowledge, experiences and resources for an entrepreneurial future (Galvão et al., 2020). Growing ecosystem engagement through a stakeholder network can be an iterative process through trial and error to increase means and decrease constraints to/on stakeholders (Yi & Uyarra, 2018). Another method of collaboration is public and private partnerships between universities and stakeholders for mutually beneficial services while building successful U-BEEs (Guerrero et al., 2016). These networks and partnerships enable learning by connecting academic content and real-world experiences, mentoring and coaching to provide students with feedback and participation in events to exchange knowledge and network (Bischoff et al., 2018).

Stakeholders interconnect and interact by collaborating in various engagement points of U-BEEs to foster entrepreneurship education. Despite managing stakeholders not being a new concept, understanding the variety of stakeholders, their roles, and possibilities for collaboration is critical in developing a well-connected and productive U-BEE (Brush Candida, 2014). The next section is an overview of the context in which empirical investigation was conducted for this study.

4   WHERE IS THE CONTEXT?

Governments around the world benchmark and attempt to replicate characteristics of entrepreneurial ecosystems proven to be successful in other countries into their development plans and policies (Hruskova & Mason, 2020). However, such successful environments are impossible to recreate in the context of entrepreneurship education and ecosystems as successful U-BEEs are context-dependent embracing local conditions and characteristics (Spigel, 2016). The concept U-BEEs began in the United States (Kirby, 2004) and is commonly investigated in the geographic context of developed countries and high-income economies. With the paucity of graduate entrepreneurship-related studies in developing countries (Nabi & Liñán, 2011) and the current century coined as the 'Asian century' (Walmsley, 2018), we extend the research to Sri Lanka, a lower-middle-income country in the Asian continent (The World Bank, 2021). Examining how U-BEEs are emerging in developing countries such as Sri Lanka provides an opportunity to see how the ecosystem evolves uniquely in geographically dispersed contexts.

Sri Lanka faces national challenges including youth unemployment and underemployment. A steady increase in unemployment among youth was recorded from 18.1% in 2013 to 21.02% in 2019 (Ministry of Sustainable Development, 2018). A quarter of its total youth population was identified as disengaged meaning they are neither in education, training or employment (Ministry of Sustainable Development, 2018). Within the South Asian context, Sri Lanka suffers from the highest rate of youth unemployment indicating underutilised human capital (Jayathilake, 2020).

Along with 192 other nations, Sri Lanka is committed to achieving sustainable development by providing quality education and supporting economic growth under the Sustainable Development Goals (United Nations, 2020). The 2030 agenda for sustainable development encourages entrepreneurship as an effective measure to alleviate economic and social challenges (The World Bank, 2021). Further, scholars postulate that entrepreneurship can help nations recover after the COVID-19 pandemic (Maritz et al., 2020). With the impetus of change from outside, universities and higher education institutes in Sri Lanka and around the world are now facing a greater responsibility to contribute to economic and social development through their entrepreneurship ecosystems.

For this study, we undertook qualitative research to explore broad views from stakeholders while gaining a deep understanding of U-BEEs in Sri Lanka. To investigate ecosystem engagement in entrepreneurship education, thirty online interviews were conducted among five stakeholder groups of U-BEEs. Perceptions and experiences from academics/educators, mentors, alumni from private higher education institutes, and entrepreneurs and incubator organisations located in

Colombo, Sri Lanka are included in this empirical study. Thematically analyzed data led to the below section on academic and practical insights relating to current practices, gaps and opportunities in stakeholder engagement within U-BEEs in Sri Lanka.

5 What Did Stakeholders Say?

In this study, a set of diverse stakeholders including academics, mentors, alumni entrepreneurs, expert entrepreneurs and representatives from incubators shared their perceptions on ecosystem engagement in entrepreneurship education. Below is an exclusive discussion of closely related higher education elements; curriculum, pedagogy and assessment based on stakeholders and their ecosystem engagement in entrepreneurship education. These factors are frequently included in U-BEEs (Brush Candida, 2014; Miller & Acs, 2017; O'Brien et al., 2019; Rice et al., 2014) and this study explores context-specific insights in a developing country.

Entrepreneurship Curriculum

Curriculum refers to a course and its content based on a syllabus organized by a discipline or concentration for a degree (Brush Candida, 2014). Currently, the undergraduate degrees in entrepreneurship are minimal and only a few private higher education institutes offer entrepreneurship as a major course in Sri Lanka. Some entrepreneurs and mentors/coaches argue that more institutes should offer a major in entrepreneurship and minors by identifying specific undergraduate groups. For instance, in Sri Lanka, it is common for the younger generation to join parents in the family business resulting in family entrepreneurs. Such family business-oriented parents seek suitable entrepreneurship education for their children. However, the majority of offered Business degrees are limited to Business Management and Business Administration. These courses only cover a minimal extent of entrepreneurship within the degree. For example, by including one module such as 'Entrepreneurship Essentials' covering the fundamentals on entrepreneurship or a view of entrepreneurship through 'Entrepreneurial Marketing'. Thus it became evident that curriculum development lacked external influences such as parents of students. Although parents have been identified as an influence on student's entrepreneurial intention (Webber et al., 2020) and parents are not currently recognized within the U-BEE. Thus, it appears that there is a disengagement between these institutes and their broader environment where the U-BEE requires to address the students' needs and other key stakeholders such as parents.

Adapting Pedagogical Practices

At present, entrepreneurship units are largely taught by entrepreneurship or management qualified academics with no or limited entrepreneurship experience among investigated institutes. On the contrary, external stakeholders perceive that facilitating entrepreneurship education should be the task of entrepreneurship-experienced academics combined with practitioners such as start-up founders and entrepreneurs. For instance, curriculum content can be delivered by in-campus entrepreneurship experienced faculty while tutorials consisting of learning activities are conducted by practitioners such as alumni entrepreneurs. This combination of academics and practitioners creates a unique learning experience relevant for entrepreneurship. Moreover, when learning entrepreneurship, the facilitator's passion and charisma play an essential role, and this may not happen through an individual who does not possess entrepreneurial background. Further, institutes in Sri Lanka are mainly connected with large companies and these companies may not be the most suitable for facilitating entrepreneurship. This is because the experiences and insights of start-up founders and entrepreneurs are more recent and relevant to knowledge transfers in entrepreneurship education. Therefore, involving alumni, who have successfully become entrepreneurs or failed, offers richer learning experience and interconnects the U-BEE better with practitioners.

Assessment and Evaluations

Assessments of entrepreneurial units are mainly in the form of written reports, reflections and activities such as an idea pitch or role play. The strong belief among entrepreneurs and incubation representatives is that assessments require to be practical as much as the other educational factors. Students should have access and interactions with real-world entrepreneurs or potential customers through assessments. A suggestion was that students should have work placements as assessments. Such an opportunity involves placing students with start-ups and Small and Medium Entreprises (SMEs) where students work a certain number of hours or days, gain experience and report back at the end of a semester. Such experience as part of an assessment may help students to find solutions for real business problems and challenges that start-ups face. However, there was no evidence of such assessments for undergraduates among investigated institutes. The challenge may stem from the norm that Sri Lanka does not foster a working culture among undergraduates and such assessments are uncommon within the employment structure. While assessments are evaluated by academics, stakeholders indicate that students will benefit from evaluations and feedback by practitioners such as entrepreneurs, in addition to academics. Work assessment could extend to the degree where the entrepreneur can evaluate the student on observed entrepreneurial traits and characteristics such as leadership, team working, risk-taking, problem-solving, innovation and creativity. Such assessments not only create the opportunity for students to showcase their talent and ideas to an external audience but also receive feedback from entrepreneurs. Assessments beyond academic-based evaluations will provide students a more practical review of their performance.

An evolving U-BEE is illustrated in Fig. 1 that fits and frames the findings from this study. Drawing from the above current practices, gaps and opportunities, the understanding is that private higher education institutes need to strengthen their U-BEE through stakeholder engagement. Despite stakeholders being involved to some extent such as ad-hoc guest lectures by entrepreneurs and corporates, when improving or developing ecosystems, universities must identify key stakeholders and engage relevant stakeholders to support the U-BEE.

6 WHERE TO FROM HERE?

Leading from the above literature and investigation, the cornerstone of this empirical study is new insights that lead to theoretical contributions on entrepreneurship education and ecosystems for undergraduates. The following discusses suggestions to offer the practical contribution for higher education providers of similar context.

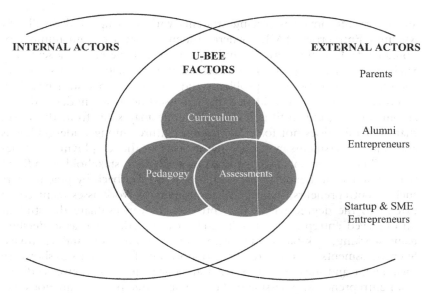

Fig. 1 External stakeholders contributing to U-BEE factors

Theoretical Contribution

In an entrepreneurship education context, it is essential to discover the crucial and relevant stakeholder groups. When deciding on the various stakeholders, it is significant to determine the importance and prospective contribution of each stakeholder (Redford & Fayolle, 2014). Even though literature showcases stakeholders with different interests involved in facilitating entrepreneurship (Galvão et al., 2020), stakeholder collaboration has limited attention in entrepreneurship education (Bischoff et al., 2018) and context-specific stakeholders-based studies from developing countries are uncommon.

Through this exploratory empirical study, parents and entrepreneurs emerged as crucial external stakeholders that may engage and strengthen the U-BEE in the context of a developing country. Given this, the contribution to theory is three-fold and these contributions are discussed with the U-BEE factor, point of engagement, and Azjen's (1991) theory of planned behaviour (Refer Table 1) in the following paragraphs. Theory of planned behaviour is common within U-BEE literature and is widely

ECOSYSTEM ENGAGEMENT IN ENTREPRENEURSHIP ... 283

Table 1 Actors engagement in U-BEE factors

Stakeholder (i.e. actor)	U-BEE factors	Point of engagement	Link to theory of planned behaviour
Parents of Students	Curriculum	Courses	Subjective norms
Entrepreneurs (Alumni)	Pedagogy	Tutorials	Perceived behavioural control
Entrepreneurs (Start-ups or SMEs)	Assessment	Work placements	Attitude towards behaviour

applied by U-BEE frameworks which focus on entrepreneurship intention as an outcome.

Literature asserts that parental entrepreneurship is the most prominent factor that influences a student's career choice and increases the probability of children following an entrepreneurial career (Lindquist et al., 2015). While entrepreneurial family culture is widely accepted and parental influence on student's entrepreneurial intention is investigated (Webber et al., 2020), to our knowledge U-BEE studies have not included parents as an external stakeholder within empirical and conceptual U-BEEs. Our first contribution to theory is the recognition of a new stakeholder 'parents' to the U-BEE framework as an external actor.

Discussions with multiple stakeholders of ecosystems divulged the parental influence on student's choice of education and intended career. From a theoretical perspective, specifically theory of planned behaviour, this influence relates to subjective norms where the student holds a belief that parents prefer the child to enrol in a specific degree (such as a major in entrepreneurship or small business) and join the family business as work in intended behaviour. The strong parental influence may come from their education and experience which conditions the children's career choices over time based on parents' life experiences (Webber et al., 2020). In Sri Lanka, the cultural norm is such that parents are highly involved in children's' lives, even during adulthood decisions (Dissanayake, 2020). Moreover, parents heavily support children, which makes education and career-related decisions more family-based and less of an individual preference (Dissanayake, 2020). This impact emphasises a positive association between parents and students significant for U-BEEs.

Entrepreneurs are common in U-BEEs and are recognized as a primary stakeholder supporting to identify opportunity, offer confidence about the business idea and create a start-up (Spigel & Harrison, 2017), however, this study divulges how their role can be enhanced within the U-BEE. For example, alumni who became entrepreneurs are known to serve universities as mentors, investors or donors, and they are also involved in teaching as visiting faculty (Powell & Walsh, 2018). As the second contribution to U-BEE theory, this study suggests the inclusion of alumni as educators in the role of conducting tutorials within pedagogy.

As U-BEEs promote 'entrepreneurship', stakeholders argue that naturally, the ecosystem should involve more entrepreneurs, such as alumni entrepreneurs, youth who have scaled up businesses from start-ups, and second-generation entrepreneurs in family businesses. Engaging entrepreneurs, such as alumni in pedagogy, for example conducting tutorials, can affect the student's perception of his ability to perform a given behaviour (i.e. becoming an entrepreneur following undergraduate education). Through the lens of the theory of planned behaviour, this association refers to perceived behavioural control leading to entrepreneurial intention. This may encourage or impede an entrepreneurial related career intention; however, such an alumni entrepreneur in the role of a facilitator raises awareness through shared experiences and may improve student's confidence through the entrepreneur's personality. If students are interested in entrepreneurship and perceive they can become an entrepreneur, alumni may even become a role model for an aspiring undergraduate. Outside of the classroom setting, alumni may become mentors and coaches extending the established relationship. Such relationships between stakeholders improve the co-creation of U-BEE by which students receive entrepreneurship education most effectively.

In terms of assessment, the association between work placements and graduate entrepreneurship was investigated and found to be beneficial (Jones & Jones, 2014) however work placements do not appear among U-BEE models developed until now. Student's perceptions establish that learnings, experience and networks from work placements drive the idea, intention and confidence to set up one's start-up (Donald et al., 2018). Our third contribution to theory is the addition of work placements as part of assessments in U-BEEs, in collaboration with start-ups and SMEs.

Entrepreneurs express their belief in the importance of 'hands-on' experience for future graduate entrepreneurs and their willingness to get involved with higher education providers on a more regular and long-term arrangement. This creates an opportunity for students to participate in work placements as an assessment within an entrepreneurship-related study unit. Entrepreneurs of start-ups and SMEs can assign work or tasks to students, which is aligned to their learning outcomes. The practical experience gained at a new or developing venture can impact the student's attitude towards behaviour in the setting of the theory of planned behaviour. From the outcomes, such as assessment feedback and student's performance in this real-life experience, the student may develop a favourable or unfavourable evaluation of the entrepreneurial behaviour that leads to an intention on an entrepreneurial career. The right blend of actors and factors can strengthen the U-BEE from within facilitating entrepreneurial intention among students.

Practical Contribution

The practical contribution is the context-specific insights provided by this empirical study, which could be tested and extended for developing countries. Findings reveal that a variety of stakeholders such as parents and entrepreneurs should be acknowledged and embraced to the U-BEE by higher education providers, forming a range of internal to external relationships. Ecosystem stakeholders may be involved at a low, moderate or high level according to their diverse roles that include influencing, knowledge/experience sharing and mentoring/coaching. Stakeholders may engage with the U-BEE through factors being curriculum, pedagogy and assessments. For this, higher education providers need to identify stakeholders and create suitable opportunities for them to engage. It may become beneficial for higher education providers to have collaborative strategies in place (1) to develop curriculum recognising parental influence on student's choice of study and career, (2) to build its alumni network creating a talent pool for facilitating tutorials and (3) to partner with start-ups and SMEs for work placements. We contend that this study presented an important practical contribution by advocating to connect and collaborate with external stakeholders (including parents, alumni entrepreneurs, start-up and SME entrepreneurs) with U-BEEs for entrepreneurship education.

7   CONCLUSION

U-BEE is a collective action and coordinated collaboration by universities and other stakeholders (Wright et al., 2017), yet stakeholders have received less attention in the context of entrepreneurship education (Bischoff et al., 2018). Our focus in this chapter was to give an opportunity to stakeholders and hear these voices from a developing country, which relies on entrepreneurs and entrepreneurship for post-pandemic recovery and sustainable development. This chapter investigated how to improve ecosystem engagement in entrepreneurship education by examining current practices, gaps and opportunities in stakeholder collaboration. Findings indicate that stakeholder involvement is rather low and weak whereas all stakeholders highlight the importance of stakeholder engagement in U-BEEs. Further, the study highlighted the key role played by parents in student's education and shaping entrepreneurial intention. There is an opportunity for alumni, start-ups and SME entrepreneurs to join forces with universities in what has predominately remained internal—pedagogy and assessments, through networks and partnerships. These contribute to theory and practice where far too little is established on U-BEEs regarding the context-specific stakeholders and their engagement within the ecosystem.

Future research could build on the findings of this chapter where stakeholders such as parents, alumni, entrepreneurs, start-ups and SMEs are empirically investigated within a respective U-BEE. Based on these results, a U-BEE comprising context-dependent actors and factors could be established. Although the investigation of this study is based on Sri Lanka, these findings may be of relevance for other developing countries that share many of the same characteristics of Sri Lanka such as the importance of parents/family and the continuation of family-owned businesses. Further, an investigation can examine the impediments within the U-BEE to improve ecosystem engagement. While developed countries such as the United States and the UK led research and development of U-BEEs, there could be insights for developing countries, giving them a late-mover advantage. Scholars can investigate the comparison of U-BEE co-creation in developed versus developing countries involving the dynamics such as sociocultural influences. Finally, scholarly work on U-BEE may continue extending into the wider community of urban/regional/national entrepreneurial ecosystem.

REFERENCES

Ács, Z. J., Autio, E., & Szerb, L. (2014). National Systems of Entrepreneurship: Measurement issues and policy implications. *Research Policy, 43*(3), 476–494.

Ajzen, I. (1991). The theory of planned behavior. *Organizational Behavior and Human Decision Processes, 50*(2), 179–211.

Alvedalen, J., & Boschma, R. (2017). A critical review of entrepreneurial ecosystems research: Towards a future research agenda. *European Planning Studies, 25*(6), 887–903.

Belitski, M. (2019). Entrepreneurship ecosystems in higher education. In *Innovate higher education to enhance graduate employability: Rethinking the possibilities* (p. 20). Taylor & Francis Group.

Belitski, M., & Heron, K. (2016). Expanding entrepreneurship education ecosystems. *Journal of Management Development, 36*(2), 163–177.

Bischoff, K., Volkmann, C., & Audretsch, D. (2018). Stakeholder collaboration in entrepreneurship education: An analysis of the entrepreneurial ecosystems of European higher educational institutions. *The Journal of Technology Transfer, 43*(1), 20–46.

Bramwell, A., & Wolfe, D. A. (2008). Universities and regional economic development: The entrepreneurial University of Waterloo. *Research Policy, 37*(8), 1175–1187.

Brush Candida, G. (2014). Exploring the concept of an entrepreneurship education ecosystem. In *Innovative pathways for university entrepreneurship in the 21st century* (Vol. 24, pp. 25–39): Emerald Group Publishing Limited.

Clauss, T., Moussa, A., & Kesting, T. (2018). Entrepreneurial university: A stakeholder-based conceptualisation of the current state and an agenda for future research. *International Journal of Technology Management, 77*(1/2/3).

Dissanayake, M. (2020). *Explaining Mismatch between Labor Supply and Demand in Sri Lanka.* http://documents1.worldbank.org/curated/en/601981591360828247/pdf/Explaining-Mismatch-Between-Labor-Supply-and-Demand-in-Sri-Lanka-Youth-and-Gender-Qualitative-Study.pdf

Donald, W. E., Ashleigh, M. J., & Baruch, Y. (2018). Students' perceptions of education and employability. *Career Development International, 23*(5), 513–540.

Etzkowitz, H. (2011). The triple helix: Science, technology and the entrepreneurial spirit. *Journal of Knowledge-Based Innovation in China, 3*(2), 76–90.

Ferrandiz, J., Fidel, P., & Conchado, A. (2018). Promoting entrepreneurial intention through a higher education program integrated in an entrepreneurship ecosystem. *International Journal of Innovation Science, 10*(01), 6–21.

Fetters, M. L., Greene, P. G., & Rice, M. P. (2010). *The development of university-based entrepreneurship ecosystems: Babson College* (pp. 15–44).

Edward Elgar Publishing Limited, UK. https://www-elgaronline-com.ezp roxy.lib.swin.edu.au/view/9781849802635.00011.xml

Galvão, A. R., Marques, C. S. E., Ferreira, J. J., & Braga, V. (2020). Stakeholders' role in entrepreneurship education and training programmes with impacts on regional development. *Journal of Rural Studies, 74*, 169–179.

Godley, A., Morawetz, N., & Soga, L. (2019). The complementarity perspective to the entrepreneurial ecosystem taxonomy. *Small Business Economics*, 1–16.

Guerrero, M., Urbano, D., Fayolle, A., Klofsten, M., & Mian, S. (2016). Entrepreneurial universities: Emerging models in the new social and economic landscape. *Small Business Economics, 47*(3), 551–563.

Hancock, S. (2011). The development of university-based entrepreneurship ecosystems: Global practices. *Studies in Higher Education, 36*, 373–374.

Hayter, C., Lubynsky, R., & Maroulis, S. (2017). Who is the academic entrepreneur? The role of graduate students in the development of university spinoffs. *The Journal of Technology Transfer, 42*(6), 1237–1254.

Ho, Y.-P., Singh, A., & Wong, P.-K. (2010). *The development of university-based entrepreneurship ecosystems: National University of Singapore*. Edward Elgar Publishing Limited, UK. https://www-elgaronline-com.ezproxy.lib.swin.edu. au/view/9781849802635.00017.xml

Hruskova, M., & Mason, C. (2020). *Mapping entrepreneurship support provision in entrepreneurial ecosystems*. Paper presented at the Australian Centre for Entrepreneurship Research Exchange 2020 Conference, Adelaide, Australia.

Hsieh, R.-M., & Kelley, D. (2020). A study of key indicators of development for university-based entrepreneurship ecosystems in Taiwan. *Entrepreneurship Research Journal, 10*(2).

Isenberg, D. (2010, June). How to start an entrepreneurial revolution? *Harvard Business Review*, 41–50.

Jayathilake, H. (2020). The impact of unemployed youth on national development in Sri Lanka. *Journal of Emerging Issues in Economics, Finance and Banking, 9*(1), 2985–3005.

Johnson, D., Bock, A. J., & George, G. (2019). Entrepreneurial dynamism and the built environment in the evolution of university entrepreneurial ecosystems. *Industrial and Corporate Change, 28*(4), 941–959.

Jones, P., & Jones, A. (2014). Attitudes of Sports Development and Sports Management undergraduate students towards entrepreneurship. *Education & Training, 56*(8/9), 716–732.

Karwowska, E. (2019). Creating shared value by the university. *Social Responsibility Journal, 17*(1), 30–47.

Kirby, D. (2004). Entrepreneurship education: Can business schools meet the challenge? *Education & Training, 46*(8/9), 510–519.

Leydesdorff, L. (2000). The triple helix: An evolutionary model of innovations. *Research Policy, 29*(2), 243–255.

Lindquist, M. J., Sol, J., & Van Praag, M. (2015). Why do entrepreneurial parents have entrepreneurial children? *Journal of Labor Economics, 33*(2), 269–296.

Link, A. N., & Sarala, R. M. (2019). Advancing conceptualisation of university entrepreneurial ecosystems: The role of knowledge-intensive entrepreneurial firms. *International Small Business Journal, 37*(3), 289–310.

Maritz, A., Perenyi, A., de Waal, G., & Buck, C. (2020). Entrepreneurship as the Unsung Hero during the current COVID-19 economic crisis: Australian perspectives. *Sustainability, 12*(4612), 4612.

Martin, B. C., McNally, J. J., & Kay, M. J. (2013). Examining the formation of human capital in entrepreneurship: A meta-analysis of entrepreneurship education outcomes. *Journal of Business Venturing, 28*(2), 211–224.

Matlay, H. (2009). Entrepreneurship education in the UK. *Journal of Small Business and Enterprise Development, 16*(2), 355–368.

Miller, D., & Acs, Z. (2017). The campus as entrepreneurial ecosystem: The University of Chicago. *Small Business Economics, 49*(1), 75–95.

Ministry of Sustainable Development. (2018). *Sri Lanka Voluntary National Review on the Status of Implementing Sustainable Development Goals.* https://sustainabledevelopment.un.org/content/documents/19677FINAL_SriLankaVNR_Report_30Jun2018.pdf

Morris, M., Kuratko, D., & Pryor, C. (2013). Building blocks for the development of university-wide entrepreneurship. *Entrepreneurship Research Journal, 4*(1).

Nabi, G., & Liñán, F. (2011). Graduate entrepreneurship in the developing world: Intentions, education and development. *Education & Training, 53*(5), 325–334.

Neck, H. M., Meyer, G. D., Cohen, B., & Corbett, A. C. (2004). An entrepreneurial system view of new venture creation. *Journal of Small Business Management, 42*(2), 190–208.

O'Brien, E., Cooney, T. M., & Blenker, P. (2019). Expanding university entrepreneurial ecosystems to under-represented communities. *Journal of Entrepreneurship and Public Policy, 8*(3), 384–407.

Powell, P., & Walsh, A. (2018). Mutualising the university: Achieving community impact through an ecosystem. *Journal of Lifelong Learning, 64*(5), 563–583.

Rauch, A., & Hulsink, W. (2015). Putting entrepreneurship education where the intention to act lies: An investigation into the impact of entrepreneurship education on entrepreneurial behavior. *Academy of Management Learning & Education, 14*(2), 187.

Redford, D., & Fayolle, A. (2014). *Stakeholder management and the entrepreneurial university.* Edward Elgar Publishing.

Ricci, R., Colombelli, A., & Paolucci, E. (2019). Entrepreneurial activities and models of advanced European science and technology universities. *Management Decision, 57*(12), 3447–3472.

Rice, M. P., Fetters, M. L., & Greene, P. G. (2014). University-based entrepreneurship ecosystems: A global study of six educational institutions. *International Journal of Entrepreneurship and Innovation Management, 18*(05).

Rothaermel, F. T., Agung, S. D., & Jiang, L. (2007). University entrepreneurship: A taxonomy of the literature. *Industrial and Corporate Change, 16*(4), 691–791.

Secundo, G., Del Vecchio, P., Simeone, L., & Schiuma, G. (2019). Creativity and stakeholders' engagement in open innovation: Design for knowledge translation in technology-intensive enterprises. *Journal of Business Research, 119*, 272–282.

Spigel, B. (2016). Developing and governing entrepreneurial ecosystems: The structure of entrepreneurial support programs in Edinburgh, Scotland. *International Journal of Innovation and Regional Development, 7*(2), 141–160.

Spigel, B. (2017). The relational organization of entrepreneurial ecosystems. *Entrepreneurship Theory and Practice, 41*(1), 49–72.

Spigel, B., & Harrison, R. (2017). Toward a process theory of entrepreneurial ecosystems. *Strategic Management Society, 12*(1), 151–168.

Stam, E. (2015). Entrepreneurial ecosystems and regional policy: A sympathetic critique. *European Planning Studies, 23*(9), 1759–1769.

The World Bank. (2021). *Sri Lanka Country Overview*. The World Bank Group. https://www.worldbank.org/en/country/srilanka/overview

United Nations. (2020). *The 17 Goals*. United Nations Department of Economic and Social Affairs. https://sdgs.un.org/goals

Wadee, A. A., & Padayachee, A. (2017). Higher education: Catalysts for the development of an entrepreneurial ecosystem, or … are we the weakest link? *Science, Technology and Society, 22*(2), 284–309.

Walmsley, A. (2018). *Entrepreneurship in tourism*. Taylor & Francis.

Webber, D. J., Kitagawa, F., & Plumridge, A. (2020). Student entrepreneurial propensities in the individual-organisational-environmental nexus. *Economic Issues, 25*(1).

Wright, M., Siegel, D., & Mustar, P. (2017). An emerging ecosystem for student start-ups. *The Journal of Technology Transfer, 42*(4), 909–922.

Yi, G., & Uyarra, E. (2018). Process mechanisms for academic entrepreneurial ecosystems: Insights from a case study in China. *Science, Technology & Society, 23*(1), 85–106.

University-Based Entrepreneurship Ecosystems: The Role of the Sustainable Family Business Theory and Entrepreneurship Education

Edgar Rogelio Ramírez-Solís, Lucía Rodríguez-Aceves, and Verónica Ilián Baños-Monroy

1 Introduction

Entrepreneurship is still a promising tool for sustainable development in any country. For this reason, it has attracted the attention of researchers to find models and frameworks that explain and promote such phenomena. Therefore, studies discussing the interaction between entrepreneurship and universities have increased in recent years (Gibb & Haskins, 2013; Tarling et al., 2016). Studies claim that demographic characteristics (e.g.

E. R. Ramírez-Solís (✉) · L. Rodríguez-Aceves · V. I. Baños-Monroy
Tecnológico de Monterrey, Guadalajara, Mexico
e-mail: edgar.ramirez@tec.mx

L. Rodríguez-Aceves
e-mail: lucia_rodriguez@tec.mx

V. I. Baños-Monroy
e-mail: veronica.banos@tec.mx

© The Author(s), under exclusive license to Springer Nature Switzerland AG 2022
G. J. Larios-Hernandez et al. (eds.), *Theorising Undergraduate Entrepreneurship Education*,
https://doi.org/10.1007/978-3-030-87865-8_16

gender, perceived skills) and family background are essential variables that influence the university students' inclination towards entrepreneurship (Keat et al., 2011; Mustapha & Selvaraju, 2015). Besides, family influence is an essential factor that provides students with background experience and motivation to lead entrepreneurial activities (Bagheri & Pihie, 2010). This idea is supported by Anderson et al. (2005), who agree that social relations and networks play an essential role in developing promising entrepreneurs.

In the same line, Robson and Bennett (2000) establish that families and friends usually act as the preferred source of advice for small-medium enterprise owners. Family businesses are also known to inspire fresh graduates by providing a supportive environment that gives them resources to start a business after graduation. For example, parents play an essential role in developing students' entrepreneurial self-efficacy by encouraging them to get involved in their family owned businesses to foster their entrepreneurial intention (Bagheri & Pihie, 2010; Saiz-Alvarez et al., 2020). Some researchers demonstrated that students rely on informal sources such as family members, colleagues, social networks, and the same universities they are enrolled in (Greene & Saridakis, 2007; Mustapha & Selvaraju, 2015) for support and guidance in developing new business.

Universities have played a significant role in human capital formation and the production of new knowledge. Therefore, aiming to encourage family business education, degree-granting programmes that institutionalise family business in their curricula emerged in several notable business schools in recent years (Sharma et al., 2007). Moreover, family business centres and family business Institutes affiliated with well-known universities proliferated. At the same time, entrepreneurship became the third mandate of universities (Etzkowitz, 2001). As a result, university-based entrepreneurial ecosystems (U-BEEs) emerged as good detonators of sustainable development.

According to Jansen van de Zande et al. (2015), a U-BEE is "the organizations and climate that support students to build a successful enterprise." The core of a U-BEE is the students' startups and the University's exertions to generate, develop, nurture, promote, and commercialise such ventures (Shil et al., 2020). The U-BEE's conceptualisation is based on the entrepreneurial ecosystem approach (Mason & Brown, 2014; Moore, 1993), where several actors interact with each other integrating highly qualified human capital. This interaction also facilitates the access to resources needed in the creation of new ventures (Rodríguez-Aceves et al., 2019). Among such actors and elements, it is possible to identify incubators, accelerators, private and public funds, technology transfer offices, entrepreneurship events (bootcamps, pitch competitions, and networking), entrepreneurship professors and mentors, and undergraduate students in their role of entrepreneurs. From this perspective, the phenomena are analysed as a social process embedded in broader contexts, aiming to explain how the regional economic and social factors influence it (Bahrami & Evans, 1995).

Even though the importance of the interaction between family businesses and the U-BEEs, little is known about these two issues' relationship. Consequently, it is not well understood how U-BEEs can increase their support for the creation of family business spin-offs or the consolidation of family firms and vice versa, how family firms can contribute to U-BEEs. It is well-known that a considerable number of undergraduate students in business schools are related to a family business and are precisely preparing to step into and take a protagonist role in the short run. Therefore, entrepreneurial education represents a suitable element that may connect both systems, U-BEEs, and family businesses.

We aim in this chapter to explore how entrepreneurship education can connect elements of U-BEEs with the Sustainable Family Business Theory (SFBT) as a way to define the role of family firms in the U-BEEs and vice versa. The SFBT is suitable to be considered because it describes a dynamic, behaviour-based, multidimensional theory of family businesses that accommodates complex family/firm interactions (Zachary et al., 2013).

Therefore, in this chapter, we review the fundamentals of the SFBT, the development, and recent contributions of this approach. Afterwards, we offer an overview of entrepreneurship education. Then, we present current conceptualisations of U-BEEs. Finally, we propose a model in which entrepreneurship education may connect SFBT and U-BEEs.

2 The Sustainable Family Business Theory

A systems perspective is not a new approach to the study of family businesses (e.g. Tagiuri & Davis, 1996); however, literature has focused on whether family businesses are more accurately viewed as a single or dual system of family and business. The Sustainable Family Business Theory (SFBT) allows both points of view (Stafford et al., 1999).

Current family firm theories focus on the dynamics of the relationship between family members, based on love and trust that, in the long term, are perceived as adaptive capacity. A central premise of the SFBT is that "the use of resource patterns during times of stability creates adaptive capacity for challenges during times of change or unexpected internal and external disruptions" (Danes, 2015, p. 187).

SFBT was first developed by Stafford et al. (1999) and later refined in several studies (Danes et al., 2008, 2009). This theory argues that family businesses can be understood as resource systems and processes that produce results that affect family businesses' long-term viability. In other words, the family business is a connection point where the resources and procedures at the family level are intermingled with the resources and strategies at the company level to produce results (Mallon et al., 2018). SFBT is a theory based on the resources and interpersonal processes used to achieve the family business's long-term sustainability (Danes et al., 2008). For family business members, the company can be a source of income and, at the same time, the context of family activity and a source of family pride and identity (Shepherd, 2003).

SFBT is founded in Systems Theory. "The fundamental concepts of General Systems Theory related to families are the mutual influence of system components, hierarchy, limits, equifinality, and feedback" (Stafford et al., 1999, p. 199). In a word, reliance on parametric methodologies has hampered the development of sustainable family business theory by limiting empirical research on the mutual influence of system components (i.e. resources) and the possibility of equifinality of multiple combinations of elements leading to the same result. For example, parametric methodologies such as regression are adequate for determining the net effects of independent variables but not for understanding how several independent variables interact or combine to produce multiple pathways to the same result (Gudmunson & Danes, 2013).

A fundamental principle of SFBT is that short-term achievements and long-term sustainability depend on the support of functionally stable and strong families. The model defines family capital as the set of total resources of the owner families composed of human, social, and financial capital (Danes et al., 2009). According to the SFBT, family capital is more than the sum of individual capital because it can be combined in different circumstances (Oughton & Wheelock, 2003).

SFBT has two general assumptions that distinguish it from many other theories that have been applied to family businesses: (a) family is rational versus an irrational system; and (b) family is not in competition with business. In contrast to traditional models of firm and entrepreneurial success that focus on the business and portray the family as a component of the firm's environment, SFBT, Family, and firm are represented in equal detail, as is their interplay in achieving mutual sustainability. SFBT finds entrepreneurship in both business and owning family within the community's social context (Olson et al., 2003).

Traditional business performance literature is based on the assumption that individuals make economic decisions without considering their context. In opposition to this conventional perspective, the SFBT establishes that entrepreneurship within the family's social context and its social network are the core where family members initiate and grow their ideas (Danes et al., 2008). One of the main propositions of SFBT is that there is a positive symbiosis between the family, the firm, and the community host, which is, of course, productive for both the firm and the community (Stafford et al., 2010). In this chapter, we propose that U-BEEs, conceptualised as social processes occurring as a part of one Supra System, could be a fundamental link between family, businesses, universities, and communities.

3 University-Based Entrepreneurship Ecosystems (U-BEEs)

Entrepreneurship ecosystems can vary by technology, network intensity, and organisational support. However, ecosystem conceptualisations generally focus on networks' role and their function to provide firms with resources and information to navigate in a competitive environment. Hayter et al. (2018) proposed that the efficacy of academic entrepreneurship ecosystems depends on constituent elements' interconnectivity and their collective ability to provide information and resources for new firms' success. Nevertheless, the ecosystem concept has only recently been used within the context of academic entrepreneurship. Some authors anticipate the emergence of ecosystem perspectives, focusing on individual and inter-organisational networks (O'Shea et al., 2004).

Even though some authors believe that there is no reason to sustain that formal education in entrepreneurship leads to more successful firms (Isenberg, 2014), universities have responded with various strategies to what entrepreneurship education requires to improve the businesses. In the 1980s, the study of university-based entrepreneurship was mainly focused on the technology transfer process through patents and licensing (Siegel & Wright, 2015). In 2001, Etzkowitz suggested that entrepreneurship had become the third mandate of universities. Consequently, over the years, universities have developed new approaches to teaching and encouraging entrepreneurship among their students, faculty, and staff (Rodríguez-Aceves et al., 2019). In these programmes, the focus was the student and its involvement in real entrepreneurial scenarios, developing in the process competencies such as critical thinking and decision making in complex environments (Mandel & Noyes, 2016). According to Greene et al. (2010), a more recent and impactful approach incorporates an entrepreneurial mindset and a skill set for entrepreneurs, resource providers, suppliers, customers, and policymakers that are somehow related to the University. In this comprehensive approach that embraces a set of stakeholders, an entrepreneurship ecosystem perspective is pertinent.

In 2010, Fetter et al. coined the term University-Based Entrepreneurship Ecosystem (U-BEE), conceptualised as a multistakeholder environment in which entrepreneurs are centered on a field of university-related resources surrounded by supporting or contributing stakeholders that ultimately results in outputs and outcomes.

Due to their relevance, U-BEEs have attracted the attention of various scholars. Previous studies on U-BEEs address its key components (Perkmann et al., 2013; Rideout & Gray, 2013), interaction enablers (Silveyra, Rodríguez-Aceves et al., 2021), assessment methods to develop strategies for successful U-BEEs (Meyer et al., 2020), and analysis of U-BEEs key elements like university-based venture development organisations (VDOs) (Hsieh & Kelley, 2019; Yang et al., 2018). Furthermore, U-BEEs have been studied in resource-constrained contexts (Bedő et al., 2020), in developed economies (Lahikainen et al., 2019), as well as their expansion into under-represented communities (O'Brien et al., 2019).

U-BEEs main components are entrepreneurship courses, engagement with alumni entrepreneurs, incubators, prototyping services, funding support, and technology transfer services (Perkmann et al., 2013; Rideout & Gray, 2013). Moreover, according to Siegel and Wright (2015), the critical elements influencing the success of a U-BEE are (1) the creation of incubators/accelerators and science/technology/research parks to support technology transfer and entrepreneurship, (2) substantial growth in the number of entrepreneurship academic courses and programmes on campus, (3) the establishment and growth of entrepreneurship centres, (4) a rise in the number of entrepreneurs on campus to stimulate commercialisation and startup creation, and (5) a rapid increase in alumni support, including alumni commercialisation funds and student business plan competitions.

Although there is substantial literature in U-BEEs, to our knowledge, little attention has been paid to understanding how family businesses can play an enriching role in such arrangements. In Business Schools, it is common to find undergraduate students preparing to step into the family business who have a particular profile in terms of the resources they have at hand, such as previous experience, contacts, and funds. Whose interactions within the U-BEEs are inevitable. Due to the importance of both the U-BEEs and the family business's social and economic sphere, it is relevant to understand their interrelationships. In line with Siegel and Wright (2015) and Hameed and Irfan (2019), who affirm that U-BEEs can further improve their effectiveness through substantial growth in the number of entrepreneurship academic courses and programmes, we believe that entrepreneurship education can be the bridge between both Systems. Thus, in the following section, we present how entrepreneurial education may become the link between the SFBT and U-BEEs.

4 ENTREPRENEURSHIP EDUCATION

Nowadays, entrepreneurship education (EE) research has grown exponentially (Hameed & Irfan, 2019; Solomon, 2007). However, the areas of "what" should be taught and "how" still lack both consensus and devoted attention (Sirelkhatim & Gangi, 2015). EE in universities is highly relevant because entrepreneurs who create an enterprise within a university have a higher impact on their ecosystem's economic development (Silveyra, Herrero et al., 2021; Von Graevenitz et al., 2010) and perform better in contrast to entrepreneurs outside a university (Godsey & Sebora, 2010). This is because academic institutions provide entrepreneurs with skills, attitudes, knowledge, and entrepreneurial competencies such as business opportunity recognition and assessment, risk management, creative problem solving, value creation, and using networks (Balan et al., 2018; Morris, Webb et al., 2013; Piperopoulos & Dimov, 2015). Today, three aims may approach EE: learning to understand entrepreneurship, learning to become entrepreneurial, and learning to become an entrepreneur (Hytti & O'Gorman, 2004; Seikkula-Leino et al., 2010). Aligned with the latter, learning to become an entrepreneur may occur through formal and informal EE in diverse environments (Edwards & Muir, 2005).

Sexton and Smilor (1984) define EE as a formal-structured instruction that conveys entrepreneurial knowledge and develops in students-focused awareness relating to opportunity recognition and new ventures. Formal structured instruction is usually guided by well-defined aims, goals, and objectives of a specific programme (Mwangi, 2011). Formal EE commonly occurs within education institutions at different school levels, starting from primary school but most prominently at the university level (Edwards & Muir, 2005).

Another approach is out-of-school EE which is characterised as an informal instruction and is essential in youngster's development. Informal education takes place naturally, is disorganised, and non-systematic (Rogers, 2007). Within the family environment, informal education is not programmed and scheduled and does not require assessment so that continuity can occur at any time (Rogoff et al., 2016). The role model and parents' daily attitude and the intensity of communication between children and parents in family life are fundamental (Inanna et al., 2020). In the entrepreneurship education context, informal education forms youngsters' character both physically and spiritually. Consequently, informal EE provided by the family is carried out between parents and children in the domestic environment or the family business environment, in which parents offer knowledge, experience, and skills to their children.

One of the objectives of informal EE provided by the family is to prepare the next generation to step up in the family business to become corporate entrepreneurs. Corporate entrepreneurship (or intrapreneurial activities) allows family firms to preserve their legacy and react to changing customer demands. Particularly in small- and medium-sized firms and family firms, the level of corporate entrepreneurship is primarily affected by their managers, who are often members of the owning family. Regarding formal EE at the university level, "students are criticized for their inability to handle the ambiguity of high rates of change facing many industries today" (Bell et al., 2018, p. 233), while that ability is a prerequisite for corporate entrepreneurship and a firm's success.

Despite the apparent relevance of these constructs (corporate entrepreneurship and EE), we lack an understanding of how informal EE inside a family business could be a complementary approach to formal EE within the universities, and training can help future family managers build up the required entrepreneurial capabilities (Wiedeler & Kammerlander, 2021).

5 TOWARD A NEW CONCEPTUALISATION OF U-BEEs BASED-ON SFBT

SFBT is based on Systems Theory, the Social Capital proposed by Bourdieu (1986), and the Resource-Based View (Barney, 1991). The SFBT approach recognises family capital's potential (including social capital) to have simultaneous positive or negative effects on business performance (Danes et al., 2008; Dyer, 2006). Danes and colleagues (2009) concluded that resilience processes are more critical to the company's sustainability than capital availability.

High levels of social capital create greater flexibility, allowing family firms to address better internal and external disruptions (Danes & Brewton, 2012). Increased social capital builds trust that promotes cooperation and team collaboration (Bourdieu, 1986) and attracts another family human and financial capital resources. The family's adaptive capacity, seen as family capital, is combined with its social capital in a way that creates and strengthens a type of resilience that facilitates the transport of resources during the change between the "porous boundaries" of the family and the company (Rodriguez & Zapata, 2019). Adaptive capacity or resilience sustains companies when disruptions occur, either in the family or in the company (Yang & Danes, 2015).

Studies about family businesses "require a theory that recognizes the heterogeneous nature of both the family and the business, which need not only direct structures and processes in both systems, but also consider structures and processes necessary in times of stability and change" (Danes, 2015, p. 185). SFBT is inclusive in these characteristics (Danes & Brewton, 2012; Danes et al., 2008; Stafford et al., 1999). SFBT controls both family and business structures while emphasising heterogeneity of processes and links them to family business processes (Danes et al., 2007). In the framework of the SFBT, "sustainability of the business over time is its primary result rather than (...) profits because its essential principle is that sustainability is a function of successful business performance and healthy family functioning" (Danes, 2015, p. 185).

The SFBT seeks to identify the resources, constraints, processes, and business transactions most likely to lead businesses and families to achieve sustainability (Stafford et al., 1999, p. 203). Although research has been conducted on the independent effects of human, social, and financial capital (e.g. Chang et al., 2009; Danes et al., 2009), to our knowledge, no study has confirmed any configuration of these resources that improve the results of family businesses (Mallon et al., 2018).

One of the most critical resources is intellectual capital (which includes human, structural, and relational or social capital) because any investment in intangible assets and knowledge-based resources is crucial for the wealth-creation process of companies. Under the Resource-Based View, human capital is the most valuable and complex kind of resource to duplicate because it results from complex social structures that have been realised over time (Dawson, 2012). Increasing the human capital in a family firm is essential to prepare the later generation using formal and informal entrepreneurship. A recent study found that the later generation in family firms was positively related to intellectual capital performance (Ginesti & Ossorio, 2020).

Through formal and informal EE, attitudes can be modified to change the intention to carry out a particular behaviour or action (McNally et al., 2016). The heirs tend to receive an informal transfer of business knowledge and methods in the family (Zellweger et al., 2011). This process of human capital transfer (mainly formed by the set of conversations, parent education, social networks, and practical experience) is complemented by the formal education obtained in HEIs (higher education institutions), connecting in this way both systems: U-BEEs with Family business (Saiz-Alvarez et al., 2020).

Therefore, we propose the following model (Fig. 1) to show the connection between the Family Business and U-BEE Systems. In System

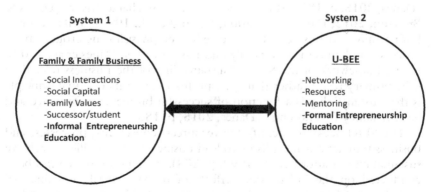

Fig. 1 The relationship between family business and U-BEE systems

1, the family business capital and its process flow are central in the SFBT, referring to the inventory and flow of the package of family owned resources, made up of human, financial and social capital (Danes et al., 2009). The SFBT assumes that "business and family systems are functional subsystems of the family business system and identify parallel family capital resources and interpersonal ones plus resource processes" (Danes, 2015, p. 187). It also assumes that experience in one system informs the other system because the focus on inventory and flow of resources over time leads in the short term the achievements of the family and the company and, in the long term, the sustainability of the family business (Danes, 2015, p. 187).

On the other hand, in System 2, the U-BEE is integrated by all the interactions within the HEI and its stakeholders such as mentors, professors, entrepreneurs, internal and external organisations, etc. We propose that the core element of this relationship is the formal (given by the HEIs) and informal (provided by the family) entrepreneurial education.

New ventures or startups, generally led by younger generations, are built through knowledge-based resources, including the social capital that must connect to other capitals and capabilities (Brush et al., 2001). In response to uncertainty, the new venture must be a learning organisation, requiring teaching by mentors, advisers, entrepreneurial leaders, and research to solve uncertainties. It must engage in outreach to access expertise and resources that do not reside in the venture (Rice et al., 2014).

As we mentioned earlier, the U-BEE's conceptualisation in literature is based on the entrepreneurial ecosystem approach, where actors facilitate access to resources for young entrepreneurs. Companies and startups are central actors in U-BEEs and can be classified by a variety of attributes, for example, whether they are family owned and managed or not. The importance of such recognition derives from the value generated to both systems, in two directions, back and forth. In one direction, for example, via the development and alignment of specific programmes offered by incubators or accelerators aiming to provide particular support to the family firms (i.e. succession plan, institutionalisation, protocol) may promote their consolidation and growth. In the other direction, U-BEE and its actors may be enriched by family businesses' expertise, contacts, and even by their funds as sponsors of open innovation challenges that encourage new ventures.

Based on all of the above, we understand U-BEE as a set of university actors (i.e. students, staff, teachers, community, graduates) who intentionally carry out entrepreneurial activities (such as teaching, consulting, financing, generation of networks) and depend on internal areas (i.e. incubators, accelerators, technology transfer offices, family business centres) that link with external organisations (such as government offices, business associations, family firms) aiming to support the creation of new high-impact businesses in the community.

Understanding and intentionally designing and implementing initiatives that enhance the interrelation between these systems (family firms and U-BEEs) are a relevant task. Above all, it is essential to recognise the importance of family businesses in U-BEEs.

6 Conclusions

Universities vary substantially in the extent to which entrepreneurship has been embraced as an academic discipline or central area of study and in their relative investments in developing learning environments that support the pursuit of entrepreneurial activity (Matlay, 2008; Morris, Kuratko et al., 2013). As previously mentioned, the university climate can serve to constrain and enable entrepreneurial behaviours (Welter & Smallbone, 2011). The purpose of U-BEEs is to become a rich pool of knowledge-based resources, networking possibilities, and even financial capital that are needed to successfully venturing within a family business (Guenther & Wagner, 2008; Zhao et al., 2005).

In this chapter, we explore a new conceptualisation of the U-BEEs, based on the SFBT. We use the primary systems involved in its operation: family firms (adding its human, financial and social capital) and universities (with its networking of different departments, mentors, and general guidance) to explain a launch platform for the entrepreneur's new ventures.

Family guidance is an essential factor that provides experience and motivation for students to become entrepreneurs. Moreover, Family businesses are providers of a supportive environment which nurtures graduates with information and resources to start their own business (Bagheri & Pihie, 2010). Furthermore, U-BEEs provide students and graduates with social relations and networks that complement what is offered by family members, playing an essential role in developing promising entrepreneurs.

As we have mentioned, the SFBT only considers the resources and the links between the different resources that are intimately interwoven between family business and family. However, the SFBT does not consider the heir or successor as an element that, in turn, is part of other systems as U-BEEs. There is also a disconnection between the family business system and the university system; with our proposed U-BEE definition, we want to fill this literature gap.

We believe that it is essential that subsequent research focuses on the individual, as we have already stated in the paragraphs above. Family businesses have to be seen as the base and source of future entrepreneurs who will study in universities that will provide them with their U-BEEs' resources, thus generating a virtuous circle where the individual, family business, family, and university benefit.

Due to the importance of family businesses in emerging economies (Nordqvist & Melin, 2010), more training for all students should be integrated into academic programmes. We believe that, in any university, it is necessary to incorporate students from all disciplines (i.e. business, engineering, humanities, design, medicine) into a U-BEE.

References

Anderson, A., Jack, S., & Drakopoulou, S. (2005). The role of family members in entrepreneurial networks: Beyond the boundaries of family firms. *Family Business Review, 18*(2), 135–154.

Bagheri, A., & Pihie, Z. A. L. (2010). Role of family leadership development of university students. *World Applied Science Journal, 11*(4), 434–442.

Bahrami, H., & Evans, S. (1995). Flexible re-cycling and high-technology entrepreneurship. *California Management Review, 37*(3), 62–89.

Balan, P., Maritz, A., & McKinlay, M. (2018). A structured method for innovating in entrepreneurship pedagogies. *Education+ Training, 60*(7–8), 819–840.

Barney, J. B. (1991). Firms resources and sustained competitive advantage. *Journal of Management, 17*(1), 99–120.

Bedő, Z., Erdős, K., & Pittaway, L. (2020). University-centred entrepreneurial ecosystems in resource-constrained contexts. *Journal of Small Business and Enterprise Development, 27*(7), 1149–1166. https://doi.org/10.1108/JSBED-02-2020-0060

Bell, R., Filatotchev, I., Krause, R., & Hitt, M. (2018). From the guest editors: Opportunities and challenges for advancing strategic management education. *Academy of Management Learning Education, 17*, 233–240.

304 E. R. RAMÍREZ-SOLÍS ET AL.

Bourdieu, P. (1986). The forms of capital. In J. G. Richardson (Ed.), *Handbook of theory and research for the sociology of education* (pp. 241–258). Greenwood.

Brush, C. G., Greene, P. G., & Hart, M. M. (2001). From initial idea to unique competitive advantage: The entrepreneurial challenge of constructing a resource base. *Academy of Management Executive, 15*(1), 64–78.

Chang, E. P. C., Memili, E., Chrisman, J. J., Kellermanns, F. W., & Chua, J. H. (2009). Family social capital, venture preparedness, and start-up decisions: A study of Hispanic entrepreneurs in New England. *Family Business Review, 22*(3), 279–292.

Danes, S. M. (2015). Family context and new venture creation. En K. Randerson, C. Bettinelli, G. Dossena y A. Fayolle (Eds.), *Family entrepreneurship: Rethinking the research agenda* (pp. 195–210). Routledge Taylor & Francis.

Danes, S. M., & Brewton, K. E. (2012). Follow the capital: Benefits of tracking family capital across family and business systems. In A. L. Carsrud & M. Brännback (Eds.), *Understanding family businesses: Undiscovered approaches, unique perspectives, and neglected topics* (pp. 227–50). Springer. https://doi.org/10.1007/978-1-4614-0911-3_14

Danes, S. M., Stafford, K., & Loy, J. T. C. (2007). Family business performance: The effects of gender and management. *Journal of Business Research, 60*(10), 1058–1069. https://doi.org/10.1016/j.jbusres.2006.12.013

Danes, S. M., Lee, J., Stafford, K., & Heck, R. K. Z. (2008). The effects of ethnicity, families and culture on entrepreneurial experience: An extension of sustainable family business theory. *Journal of Developmental Entrepreneurship, 13*(3), 229–268.

Danes, S. M., Stafford, K., Haynes, G., & Amarapurkar, S. S. (2009). Family capital of family firms: Bridging human, social, and financial capital. *Family Business Review.* https://doi.org/10.1177/0894486509333424

Dawson, A. (2012). Human capital in family businesses: Focusing on the individual level. *Journal of Family Business Strategy, 3*(1), 3–11.

Dyer, W. G. (2006). Examining the "family effect" on firm performance. *Family Business Review, 19*, 253–273.

Edwards, L. J., & Muir, E. J. (2005). Promoting entrepreneurship at the University of Glamorgan through formal and informal learning. *Journal of Small Business and Enterprise Development, 12*(4), 613–626.

Etzkowitz, H. (2001). The second academic revolution and the rise of entrepreneurial science. *IEEE Technology and Society Magazine, 20*(2), 18–29.

Fetters, M., Greene, P. G., & Rice, M. P. (Eds.). (2010). *The development of university-based entrepreneurship ecosystems: Global practices.* Edward Elgar.

Gibb, A., & Haskins, G. (2013). *Developing the entrepreneurial university of the future: Key challenges, opportunities and responses.* In A. Fayolle & D. T. Redford (Eds.), *Handbook on the entrepreneurial university* (pp. 25–63). Edward Elgar.

Ginesti, G., & Ossorio, M. (2020). The influence of family related factors on intellectual capital performance in family businesses. *Journal of Management and Governance.* https://doi.org/10.1007/s10997-020-09510-4

Godsey, M. L., & Sebora, T. C. (2010). Entrepreneur role models and high school entrepreneurship career choice: Results of a field experiment. *Small Business Institute Journal, 5,* 83–125.

Greene, F. J. & Saridakis, G. (2007). Understanding the factors influencing graduate entrepreneurship, research report 007/2007. National Council for Graduate Entrepreneurship (NCGE). http://www.ncge.com/. Accessed September 2020.

Greene, P. G., Rice, M. P., & Fetters, M. L. (2010). University-based entrepreneurship ecosystems: framing the discussion. In *The development of university-based entrepreneurship ecosystems: Global practices* (pp. 1–11). Edward Elgar.

Gudmunson, C. G., & Danes, S. M. (2013). Family social capital in family businesses: A stocks and flows investigation. *Family Relations, 62*(3), 399–414. https://doi.org/10.1111/fare.12017

Guenther, J., & Wagner, K. (2008). Getting out of the ivory tower–new perspectives on the entrepreneurial university. *European Journal of International Management, 2*(4), 400–417.

Hameed, I., & Irfan, Z. (2019). Entrepreneurship education: A review of challenges, characteristics and opportunities. *Entrepreneurship Education, 2*(3), 135–148.

Hayter, C., Nelson, A., Zayed, S., & O'Connor, A. (2018). Conceptualizing academic entrepreneurship ecosystems: A review, analysis and extension of the literature. *The Journal of Technology Transfer, 43.* https://doi.org/10.1007/s10961-018-9657-5.

Hsieh, R. M., & Kelley, D. (2019). A Study of Key Indicators of Development for University-Based Entrepreneurship Ecosystems in Taiwan. *Entrepreneurship Research Journal, 10*(2), 1–17.

Hytti, U., & O'Gorman, C. (2004). What is enterprise education? An analysis of the objectives and methods of enterprise education programmes in four European countries. *Education & Training, 46,* 11–23.

Inanna, I., Rahmatullah, R., Haeruddin, M. I. M., & Marhawati, M. (2020). Silk weaving as a cultural heritage in the informal entrepreneurship education perspective. *Journal of Entrepreneurship Education, 23*(1), 1–11.

Isenberg, D. (2014). What an entrepreneurship ecosystem actually is. *Harvard Business Review.* Retrieved from https//hbr.org/2014/05/what-an-entrepreneurial-ecosystem-actually-is

Jansen, S., van de Zande, T., Brinkkemper, S., Stam, E., & Varma, V. (2015). How education, stimulation, and incubation encourage student entrepreneurship: Observations from MIT, IIIT, and Utrecht University. *International Journal of Management Education, 13*(2), 170–181.

Keat, O. Y., Selvarajah, C., & Meyer, D. (2011). Inclination towards entrepreneurship among university students: An empirical study of Malaysian university students. *International Journal of Business and Social Science, 2*(4), 206–220.

Lahikainen, K., Kolhinen, J., Ruskovaara, E., & Pihkala, T. (2019). Challenges to the development of an entrepreneurial university ecosystem: The case of a Finnish university campus. *Industry and Higher Education, 33*(2), 96–107. https://doi.org/10.1177/0950422218815806

Mallon, M. R., Lanivich, S. E., & Klinger, R. L. (2018). Resource configurations for new family venture growth. *International Journal of Entrepreneurial Behaviour and Research, 24*(2), 521–537. https://doi.org/10.1108/IJEBR-06-2017-0184

Mandel, R., & Noyes, E. (2016). Survey of experiential entrepreneurship education offerings among top undergraduate entrepreneurship programs. *Education + Training, 58*(2), 164–178. https://doi.org/10.1108/ET-06-2014-0067

Mason, C., & Brown, R. (2014). Entrepreneurial ecosystems and growth oriented entrepreneurship. *Final Report to OECD, Paris, 30*(1), 77–102.

Matlay, H. (2008). The impact of entrepreneurship education on entrepreneurial outcomes. *Journal of Small Business and Enterprise Development, 15*(2), 382–396.

McNally, J. J., Martin, B. C., Honig, B., Bergmann, H., & Piperopoulos, P. (2016). Toward rigor and parsimony: A primary validation of Kolvereid's (1996) entrepreneurial attitudes scales. *Entrepreneurship & Regional Development, 28*(5–6), 358–379.

Meyer, M. H., Lee, C., Kelley, D., & Collier, G. (2020). An assessment and planning methodology for university-based: Entrepreneurship ecosystems. *The Journal of Entrepreneurship, 29*(2), 259–292.

Moore, J. F. (1993). Predators and prey: A new ecology of competition. *Harvard Business Review, 71*(3), 75–86.

Morris, M. H., Kuratko, D. F., & Cornwall, J. R. (2013). *Entrepreneurship programs and the modern university*. Edward Elgar.

Morris, M. H., Webb, J. W., Fu, J., & Singhal, S. (2013). A competency-based perspective on entrepreneurship education: Conceptual and empirical insights. *Journal of Small Business Management, 51*(3), 352–369.

Mustapha, M., & Selvaraju, M. (2015). Personal attributes, family influences, entrepreneurship education and entrepreneurship inclination among university students. *Kajian Malaysia: Journal of Malaysian Studies, 33*, 155–172.

Mwangi, S. M. (2011). The contribution of entrepreneurship education course in enhancing management skills of informal entrepreneurs. *Journal of Education and Vocational Research, 2*(3), 86–92.

Nordqvist, M., & Melin, L. (2010). Entrepreneurial families and family firms. *Entrepreneurship & Regional Development, 22*(3–4), 211–239.

O'Brien, E., Cooney, T. M., & Blenker, P. (2019). Expanding university entrepreneurial ecosystems to under-represented communities. *Journal of Entrepreneurship and Public Policy, 8*(3), 384–407.

Olson, P. D., Zuiker, V. S., Danes, S. M., Stafford, K., Heck, R. K., & Duncan, K. A. (2003). The impact of the family and the business on family business sustainability. *Journal of Business Venturing, 18*(5), 639–666.

O'Shea, R. P., Allen, T. J., O'Gorman, C., & Roche, F. (2004). Universities technology transfer: A review of academic entrepreneurship literature. *Irish Journal of Management, 25*, 11–29.

Oughton, E., & Wheelock, J. (2003). A capabilities approach to sustainable household livelihoods. *Review of Social Economy, 61*(1), 1–22+130. https://doi.org/10.1080/0034676032000050248

Perkmann, M., Tartari, V., McKelvey, M., Autio, E., Broström, A., D'este, P., & Sobrero, M. (2013). Academic engagement and commercialisation: A review of the literature on university–industry relations. *Research Policy, 42*(2), 423–442.

Piperopoulos, P., & Dimov, D. (2015). Burst bubbles or build steam? Entrepreneurship education, entrepreneurial self-efficacy, and entrepreneurial intentions. *Journal of Small Business Management, 53*(4), 970–985.

Rideout, E. C., & Gray, D. O. (2013). Does entrepreneurship education really work? A review and methodological critique of the empirical literature on the effects of university-based entrepreneurship education. *Journal of Small Business Management, 51*(3), 329–351.

Rice, M. P., Fetters, M. L., & Greene, P. G. (2014). University-based entrepreneurship ecosystems: A global study of six educational institutions. *International Journal of Entrepreneurship and Innovation Management, 18*(5–6), 481–501.

Robson, P., & Bennett, R. (2000). SME growth: The relationship with business advice and external collaboration. *Small Business Economics, 15*(3), 193–208.

Rodriguez, A., & Zapata, A. (2019). Caracterización teórica de la identidad co-emprendedora de pares-socios. *Pensamiento & Gestión, 46*, 222–261.

Rodríguez-Aceves, L., Mojarro-Durán, B., & Muñíz-Ávila, E. (2019). University-based entrepreneurial ecosystems: Evidence from technology transfer policies and infrastructure. In *Handbook of research on ethics, entrepreneurship, and governance in higher education* (pp. 455–475). IGI Global.

Rogers, A. (2007). Looking again at non-formal and informal education towards a new paradigm. In *Appeal of non formal education paradigm (0-79)*. Retrieved from https://pdfs.semanticscholar.org/d054/2cb45b8fa57e7f77ef 82c6665974614dd9ff.pdf

Rogoff, B., Callanan, M., Gutierrez, K. D., & Erickson, F. (2016). The organization of informal learning. *Review of Research in Education, 40*(1), 356–401.

Saiz-Alvarez, J. M., Rodríguez-Aceves, L. A., & Silveyra León, G. (2020). Does parental gender influence the entrepreneurial intention in heirs? *Journal of Small Business & Entrepreneurship*, 1–20.

Seikkula-Leino, J., Ruskovaara, E., Ikavalko, M., Mattila, J., & Rytkola, T. (2010). Promoting entrepreneurship education: the role of the teacher? *Education+ Training, 52*(2), 117–127.

Sexton, D., & Bowman, N. (1984). Entrepreneurship education suggestions for increasing effectiveness. *Journal of Small Business Management, 22*(2), 18–25.

Sharma, P., Hoy, F., Astrachan, J. H., & Koiranen, M. (2007). The practice-driven evolution of family business education. *Journal of Business Research, 60*(10), 1012–1021.

Shepherd, D. A. (2003). Learning from business failure: Propositions of grief recovery for the self employed. *Academy of Management Review, 28*, 318–328.

Shil, M., Shahriar, M. S., Sultana, S., Rahman, S. N., & Zayed, N. M. (2020). Introduction to university based entrepreneurship ecosystem (U-BEE): A model case study from Bangladesh. *International Journal of Entrepreneurship, 24*(1).

Siegel, D. S., & Wright, M. (2015). Academic entrepreneurship: Time for a rethink? *British Journal of Management, 26*(4), 582–595.

Silveyra, G., Herrero, Á., & Pérez, A. (2021). Model of teachable entrepreneurship competencies (M-TEC): Scale development. *The International Journal of Management Education, 19*(1), 100392.

Silveyra, G., Rodríguez-Aceves, L., & Villegas-Mateos, A. (2021). Enablers to fostering interactions during entrepreneurship events within university-based entrepreneurship ecosystems (U-BEEs). In M. Ramirez-Pasillas, C. Fernandes, & J. J. Ferreira (Eds.), *The role of universities and their entrepreneurial ecosystems in advocating sustainability*. Degruyter.

Sirelkhatim, F., & Gangi, Y. (2015). Entrepreneurship education: A systematic literature review of curricula contents and teaching methods. *Cogent Business & Management, 2*, 1052034.

Solomon, G. (2007). An examination of entrepreneurship education in the United States. *Journal of Small Business and Enterprise Development, 14*(2), 168–182.

Stafford, K., Bhargava, V., Danes, S. M., Haynes, G., & Brewton, K. E. (2010). Factors associated with long-term survival of family businesses: Duration analysis. *Journal of Family and Economic Issues, 31*(4), 442–457.

Stafford, K., Duncan, K. A., Dane, S., & Winter, M. (1999). A research model of sustainable family businesses. *Family Business Review, 12*(3), 197–208. https://doi.org/10.1111/j.1741-6248.1999.00197.x

Tagiuri, R., & Davis, J. (1996). Bivalent attributes of the family firm. *Family Business Review, 9*(2), 199–208. https://doi.org/10.1111/j.1741-6248.1996.00199.x

Tarling, C., Jones, P., & Murphy, L. (2016). Influence of early exposure to family business experience on developing entrepreneurs. *Education+ Training, 58*(7–8), 733–750.

Von Graevenitz, G., Harhoff, D., & Weber, R. (2010). The effects of entrepreneurship education. *Journal of Economic Behavior & Organization, 76*(1), 90–112.

Welter, F., & Smallbone, D. (Eds.). (2011). *Handbook of research on entrepreneurship policies in central and eastern Europe.* Edward Elgar.

Wiedeler, C., & Kammerlander, N. (2021). Learning the ropes of entrepreneurship: Understanding internal corporate venturing for family firms from an entrepreneurial learning perspective. *Review of Managerial Science, 15*, 669–703. https://doi.org/10.1007/s11846-019-00354-3

Yang, Y., & Danes, S. M. (2015). Resiliency and resilience process of entrepreneurs in new venture creation. *Entrepreneurship Research Journal, 5*(1), 1–30. https://doi.org/10.1515/erj-2013-0076

Yang, S., Kher, R., & Lyons, T. S. (2018). Where do accelerators fit in the venture creation pipeline? Different values brought by different types of accelerators. *Entrepreneurship Research Journal, 8*(4), 20170140.

Zachary, R. K., Danes, S. M., & Stafford, K. (2013). *Extensions of the sustainable family business theory: Operationalization and application.* Edward Elgar.

Zellweger, T., Sieger, P., & Halter, F. (2011). Should I stay or should I go? Career choice intentions of students with family business background. *Journal of Business Venturing, 26*(5), 521–536.

Zhao, H., Seibert, C., & Hills, C. (2005). The mediating role of self-efficacy in the development of entrepreneurial intentions. *Journal of Applied Psychology, 90*, 1265–1272.

Digital Skills and Entrepreneurial Education in Malaysia: Evidence from Experiential Learning

Zatun Najahah Yusof, Najib Murad, and Borhannudin Yusof

1 INTRODUCTION

This paper will look at the push by Malaysia to develop entrepreneurs and support graduates who exhibit entrepreneurial tendencies. Studies on entrepreneurial education in Malaysia are more focused on the condition of the system (Cheng et al., 2009; Shamsudin et al., 2016) and entrepreneurial intention (Trivedi, 2017; Pirzada & Khan, 2013). There is less empirical evidence of entrepreneurial education using experiential learning with an emphasis on digital business. The Organisation

---

Z. N. Yusof (✉)
University of Strathclyde, Scotland, UK
e-mail: zatun.yusof@strath.ac.uk

N. Murad
University of Stirling, Scotland, UK
e-mail: a.n.murad@stir.ac.uk

B. Yusof
Universiti Malaysia Terengganu, Kuala Terengganu, Malaysia
e-mail: borhan@umt.edu.my

© The Author(s), under exclusive license to Springer Nature Switzerland AG 2022
G. J. Larios-Hernandez et al. (eds.), *Theorising Undergraduate Entrepreneurship Education*,
https://doi.org/10.1007/978-3-030-87865-8_17

for Economic Co-operation and Development (Lakeus, 2015) defined entrepreneurship education (EE) as focusing more on the specific context of setting up a venture and becoming self-employed. A study by Hytii and O'Gorman (2004) found that if the objective is to enhance understanding of entrepreneurship, a good delivery is through a traditional approach such as lectures and seminars. This is mainly due to its effectiveness in delivery to large groups in short periods. Secondly, if the objective is to develop individuals' entrepreneurial skills, a method like industrial training should be used. Finally, if the creation of entrepreneurs is the objective, an effective technique is by using a controlled environment to facilitate experiments, through methods such as role play or business simulation. Solomon et al. (2002) found that the use of experiential learning is widespread and diverse in its application. This experiential learning is positively accepted among entrepreneur educators and researchers (Higgins & Elliott, 2011; Mason & Arshed, 2013; Wenninger, 2019) as supporting learning on how to learn (Kolb & Kolb, 2009), where the approach promotes holistic techniques and a focus on the action and experience of the learner.

Saptono et al. (2020) indicated the need to learn digital business transformation in e-commerce. It can be further highlighted that education affect skills and the ability to manage the business (Suparno et al., 2019) in the twenty-first century. It should be noted that the learning environment of an entrepreneurship classroom should consider current business trends and future growth areas. Hence, it is important to consider digital literacy in curriculum development.

The implication and challenges of digital literacy will be explored in this study. The focus will be the experience of Universiti Malaysia Terengganu (UMT) in delivering EE through the development of students' digital literacy skills. The development of the entrepreneurship course at UMT is based on a template developed by the Malaysia Higher Education Ministry, which focused on developing digital literacy among undergraduate students. This study intends to bring to the fore examples of practice-based EE developed at and delivered by UMT which hopefully will contribute to the broader discussion on entrepreneurial education design. To do this, the study draws on relevant theoretical perspectives and extended to conceptualise the experiential learning and digital literacy landscape to develop a better understanding and framework of the issues in management education and entrepreneurship practices contexts and to facilitate further research agenda in EE.

2 Experiential Learning

Twenty-first century EE is said to be moving towards experiential learning as part of the teaching approach (Hagg & Kurczewska, 2016). Various authors indicated effective EE should be linked to experiential learning (Kolb, 1984), entrepreneurial training (Gibb, 1999), work-related learning (Dwerryhouse, 2001), and action-learning (Smith, 2001). Solomon et al. (2002) found that the use of experiential learning is widespread and diverse in its application. This experiential learning is positively accepted among entrepreneur educators and researchers (de Villiers Scheepers et al., 2018; Hagg & Kurczewska, 2016; Higgins & Elliott, 2011; Mason & Arshed, 2013; Wenninger, 2019) as supporting learning on how to learn (Kolb & Kolb, 2009), where the approach promotes holistic technique, emotional intelligence, and focus on the action and experience of the learner. Building on Kolb's experiential learning model, Corbett (2005) argues that entrepreneurship requires different types of learning at different stages of the entrepreneurial process. These should include convergent, assimilative, divergent, and accommodative learning at different stages of the entrepreneurial development stages such as preparation, incubation, and evaluation. To provide an entrepreneurial environment to the students, universities must be able to formulate or design and develop a curriculum that would fulfil the students and industries demands. However, this would be a challenge when the learning environment changes from physical to online learning in response to a crisis (Covid) where there is a lack of clear guidance on how entrepreneurship educators should react. Furthermore, there are limited studies on students' perception of the effectiveness of online active learning and online entrepreneurial experiential learning towards their learning experience and digital literacy development.

3 Digital Literacy

The term digital literacy originated from Gilster (1997) who defined it as the ability to understand and use information in multiple formats from a wide range of sources when it is presented via computers. Law et al. (2018, p. 6) defined digital literacy as "the ability to access, manage, understand, integrate, communicate, evaluate and create information safely and appropriately through digital technologies for employment, decent jobs and entrepreneurship. It includes competencies that are variously referred to as computer literacy, ICT literacy, information literacy and media literacy". Recent work by Ayyildiz et al. (2021, p. 16) summarised that "digital literacy is innately a broad term encompassing varying dimensions of being conscious again stretching to various extents about the raison d'être; the role and function of digital technologies and those of any related resource in relation to everyday situations". Learners face the challenges of digitising systems, big data, and the swift flow of information that demand them to be skilled in information technology and ready to be competent in the world of work later (Wilson et al., 2017). This impact can also be seen in entrepreneurship, innovation, and development through digitisation that is at the heart of today's society.

Sariwulan et al. (2020) found two interesting elements relating to digital literacy. The first is that there is a significant and positive influence of digital literacy on the performance of small-medium enterprise (SME) entrepreneurs. This means the higher the digital literacy knowledge, the higher the performance of SME entrepreneurs. Secondly, there is a significant and positive influence of digital literacy on entrepreneurial skills. Hence, the role of education is important in preparing would-be entrepreneurs with the right skill sets. Universities need to respond actively to this shift towards digitisation and respond accordingly with changes in current practice as Morris and Liguori (2016) claimed that current pedagogy in entrepreneurship is far behind the practice of entrepreneurship in the real world. The challenge here is in developing students' digital literacy skills in entrepreneurship courses, which in turn enable would-be entrepreneurs to adapt to the development of technology. The development and increased use of online technologies including social media require a rethinking of EE on how to incorporate technologies into the curriculum.

4   Digital Literacy and Challenges in Entrepreneurship Education

There exists little evidence linking Malaysia's entrepreneurship teaching with the development of digital literacy. This can be said of most EE globally and this is a possible future area that can be explored separately. The market for the digital economy is growing as new technologies make processes in businesses easier and allow businesses to be competitive. As highlighted by the Confederation of British Industry (2019),

ICT/Digital literacy was among the top 3 skills deemed important by businesses (CBI, 2019). Students that can demonstrate this skill are more likely to secure employment than those that are unable to do so. Tan et al. (2010) found that urban Malaysian youths are proficient in computer and technological skills through regular and frequent engagement with web-based digital contents and resources. On the other hand, they do not use these skills for critical reading, analysis, and evaluation of digital contents. Being capable of using technologies both in a meaningful and purposeful fashion for academic and scientific purposes are among those critical skills (Carpenter et al., 2020) missing from Malaysian youths.

The growth in digital economy requires an effective approach in supporting learning how to learn and teaching entrepreneurship (Gibb, 2002). The World Bank (2018) highlighted the issue of digital entrepreneurship need to be addressed for Malaysia to ensure its growth in digital economy. The report highlighted Malaysia's education system is not ready to provide the right skills for the countries to move forward in the digital economy. This raises concerns among policymakers including those in the higher education sector. To address the digital entrepreneur skills gap and transition into the global trend in growth of digital business, policymakers in Malaysia have developed Malaysia's National Digital Strategy Plan 2018–2025. This framework is aimed at supporting and accelerating digital literacy among future graduates. Further to this, The Malaysia Education Blueprint 2015–2025 for Higher Education highlighted the importance and priorities of digital literacy, critical thinking, and problem-solving skills in helping students navigate the twenty-first century job market. To meet the expectation of future-ready graduates, public higher education institutions in Malaysia are expected to introduce emerging technology competencies in their education programmes as stipulated in the National Policy on Industry 4.0. HEIs, therefore, are required to develop a holistic approach (MOHE, 2018) and modernise their curriculum through the introduction of digital learning technologies. The MOHE is encouraging HEIs to provide more experiential learning that would contribute towards improving entrepreneurial absorptive capacity and develop entrepreneurial intention (Ajzen, 1991) among university students. This is expected to enhance skills development which has been identified as crucial for Malaysia in the digital economy. Based on Malaysia's Department of Statistics (2020) data, unemployed graduates in Malaysia accounted for 5.29 million people, which constitutes nearly 33% of total labour force (15.6 million people). This is one of the most acute issues facing graduates as they leave higher education.

The impact of Covid-19 is expected to further reduce employment opportunities for graduates and potentially affect transferable skills development among current university students as fewer employers are actively recruiting graduates. The unemployment rate in Malaysia has increased by up to 5.1% (DOSM, 2020) in the first quarter of the year 2020 report and this can be attributed to the Movement Control Order (MCO) restriction put in place to counter the spread of Covid-19.

In addressing current knowledge and research gaps of EE and digital literacy in Malaysia, two objectives have been set for this study. The focus of this paper is to explore the introduction of digital literacy skills in EE at UMT and document student participants' experience on the course. This will contribute to educators and governments understanding of the inclusion of such skills development on an HEI course. Firstly, how do entrepreneurial educators incorporate the concept of digital literacy and experiential learning in EE? Secondly, to what extent do undergraduate students in EE programmes perceive their digital literacy knowledge and skills had improved because of the development experience on the entrepreneurial course? The paper thus includes a stated purpose of contributing towards the development of a more experiential approach to EE in line with Kolb (1984) and Gibb's (1999) works. The main difference is the focus on the ability of students to adapt to the development of the technology world through the type of business they develop.

5   METHODS

A case study approach has been used to investigate entrepreneurial learning phenomenon within an undergraduate entrepreneurship course at University Malaysia Terengganu (UMT), a public Malaysian university. Other than individual assessment (test), students were required to work in a group and submit a written report and present their digital business in front of panels (entrepreneurial educators). Entrepreneurship students were introduced to entrepreneurial skills and theory, and digital business applications including digital marketing, search engine optimisation, mobile application, digital communication, and managing a business on a digital platform. The experiential learning incorporated the need for students to create an online business idea, launch and manage the business, write a business report and pitch their business. The learning outcomes and assessment grade reports from the 2020 cohort were used for analysis along with the student feedback review on the entrepreneurial course at the end of the semester. A thematic analysis was used to analyse the text data, and this is commonly used in entrepreneurial education's literature (Mason & Arshed, 2013; Pittaway & Cope, 2007) while descriptive analysis was used to analyse the exploratory data.

Case Study: UMT Entrepreneurship Education

The discussion earlier on Malaysia's national plan found that EE is a central dimension in accelerating entrepreneurial culture and mindset for the country. The compulsory entrepreneurship course at public HEIs is now the main subject component for every undergraduate student to graduate. It is also part of the national agenda to develop entrepreneurial skills in all the higher learning education system, leading to the growth of holistic graduates and job creators.

The Centre for Foundation & Continuing Education (PPAL) in UMT is responsible for providing all the university core courses for undergraduate students, including the entrepreneurship course. The EE undergraduate course in UMT is delivered through the Department of Basic Knowledge & Entrepreneurship (JIDK). Revisions to the EE course were made in early 2019 to adapt to the MOHE model. In doing so, teaching staff have to complete the Training of Trainer (TOT) e-ommerce course delivered by Malaysia Digital Economy Corporation (MDEC), a government agency facilitating and providing environment support for digital business. Further to this, an internal TOT session was delivered to all entrepreneurship educators in the department. This highlighted that the role of educators is becoming challenging and extending beyond the traditional teaching role.

The Basic Entrepreneurship course (MPU3223) is a compulsory course for every undergraduate student at UMT which has 30-degree programmes. To cater to these programmes' needs, the course is delivered every semester. Students join the course according to their programme structure. This typically entails first-year students undertaking the course in either the first or second semester of their study. However, there are variation to this on some programmes where the programme structure requires the course to be delivered in the students' final year of study.

The course aims to develop an entrepreneurial mindset among students and has three main learning outcomes;

1. understand the basic concept of entrepreneurship;
2. develop an entrepreneurship mindset via entrepreneurship activities exposure; and
3. demonstrate entrepreneurship skills via digital platforms.

The key learning outcomes are met through four key areas of focus. Firstly, the teaching introduces the basic entrepreneurship concept which includes entrepreneurship definition, process, characteristics, opportunity, innovative business models, business ethics, and challenges. Secondly, fundamental business concepts are taught including business entity (business registration), market analysis, marketing, strategic management, business planning, financial management, financing, cybersecurity, and intellectual property. Thirdly, the concept of digital business is taught including fundamentals of search engine optimisation (SEO), online advertisements, copywriting, creative content development, launching a small business with social media platforms (Facebook, WhatsApp and Instagram), the website for businesses, mobile applications, and email marketing. Finally, teaching focuses on developing an entrepreneurial mindset and skills including an opportunity for discovery and creation, knowledge sharing and transformation, the value of networking, problem-solving, resource constraints, competitiveness, and passion.

The course is delivered over 14 weeks where the syllabus includes a group project, an individual project, a presentation, a business and industrial talk event, and both formative and summative assessment. The Covid-19 pandemic had little impact on the course where delivery continued through remote delivery on the Oceania platform (virtual learning environment). However, there were concerns raised by students in relation to limited social experience and engagement with peers, educators, and industries that influenced the effectiveness of their learning and co-learning. The course structure is illustrated in Fig. 1.

Students are provided access to the GoEcommerce platform hosted by MDEC, the lead agency in driving the digital economy of Malaysia. GoEcommerce is an online entrepreneurial platform with the tools to help businesses monitor and manage their business efficiently. The GoEcommerce platform is a government initiative to facilitate EE in HEIs.

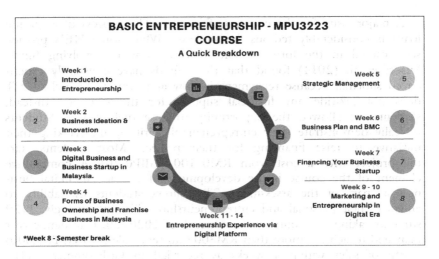

Fig. 1 Structure of basic entrepreneurship course

Currently, 19 out of 20 Malaysian public HEIs have access to the GoEcommerce platform on their entrepreneurship courses. The platform includes micro-credential online courses delivered by MDEC which are available through free access for all registered students. Students are provided links to the courses and participate in their own time. This entrepreneurial digital platform allows students the ability to update business records such as sales reporting and level of business which also acts as a database and monitoring mechanism of students' progress for educators.

During the first week, students are required to form a group consisting of 5–8 people (depending on the size of the class). Students work on group tasks and discussions facilitated by the teaching team during their 2 hours workshop every week. GoEcommerce was used to support entrepreneurial students to register, record, and monitor their business activities (including sales) as well as additional learning material and certification for business solution. Furthermore, students were introduced to the role of the Companies Commission of Malaysia (SSM) and encouraged to register their business with the Commission. The intention is that the business can be continued once students complete the course. This also supports creating entrepreneurial mindsets and intention among university students.

A major issue for the course is financing. The process of acquiring loans is considerably tedious for students. While some HEIs provide seed capital in the form of soft loans by way of revolving funds, Yusoff et al. (2014) found that these funds have constantly experienced shortfall because repayment is slow and erratic. As such, UMT does not provide any financial support for the students. Instead, students are allowed the opportunity to raise their capital. Students typically demonstrate their entrepreneurial spirit by undertaking their initiative to raise financing for their project. Most students start the project with a cost from RM0–100 (GBP0-20). A competitive element of the course is the development of the actual digital business as part of the assessment. This allows students the ability to enhance their personal and entrepreneurship skills. Interestingly, 1129 students taking the course in Semester 1 of 2020/2021 academic year managed to achieve more than RM300,000 (equivalent to GBP60,000) worth of sales within 4 weeks as recorded in GoEcommerce platform.

Participants

The sample consists of undergraduate students from UMT, a public university on the east coast of Malaysia ($N = 304$) who have completed the entrepreneurial course as part of their studies in 2020. A survey questionnaire was designed in the English language on an online survey platform which the entrepreneur educators shared with their current and former students. A total of 304 students completed the survey, representing a 38% response rate from 800 potential participants. The majority of participants are female (74%) in their first year of study (53%). There are variations in the distribution of the students by their subject discipline from psychology (19%), business and management (18%), engineering (18%) to marine biology (6%). This reflected the different programme delivered by the university and the compulsory requirement of the entrepreneurship course set by the MOHE. There were just over 30% of students with family owned businesses. Data were gathered from July to November 2020.

Measures

There are six items used to measure entrepreneurial concepts among the students. This used Barringer and Ireland (2008) ideas on entrepreneurship and the characteristics of successful entrepreneurs such as "entrepreneurship is about recognising opportunity and transform into meaningful outcome including wealth creation"; "entrepreneurial behaviour includes innovation and creativity"; and "entrepreneurial process involves idea generation, validation, managing and growing the business". Five items based on the learning outcomes of the course were used to measure knowledge of the digital business and e-commerce elements. These included "I am confident to do copywriting for advertising and marketing business online" and "I am confident on creative content development". Twelve items were used to measure transferable and employability skills derived from Evans and Yusof (2020) such as teamwork, communication, IT and digital skills, organisational skills and commercial awareness. A Likert scale of 1–5 was used to measure the response options (entrepreneurship, digital business learning experience, and employability skills) with scale one defined as "strongly disagree" and scale five as "strongly agree".

6 Results

Entrepreneurial and Digital Business Knowledge

Table 1 shows descriptive statistics on how university students perceived their entrepreneurial knowledge and digital business had improved as a result of participating in the entrepreneurship course and engaging in entrepreneurial learning activities. The result indicated a higher score of reliability ($\alpha > 0.9$) and is consistent among all sampled students. It is interesting to find that over 80% of the students acknowledged their understanding of the concept of entrepreneurship had changed and significantly removed some "entrepreneurship myths" such as entrepreneurs are profit-oriented; entrepreneurs are born and not made (Table 1): "Entrepreneurship can be learnt and made/develop" (90.1% tend to agree); "Entrepreneurs are motivated not only by money but also by sense of social responsibility" (88.2% tend to agree).

Furthermore, the dimension of pedagogy in EE is challenging with debates on how to effectively teach entrepreneurship. To measure this, the learning outcome was used to look at to what extent students effectively

Table 1 Entrepreneurial and digital business knowledge

	Mean	SD	Strongly agree/agree (%)
Entrepreneurial knowledge ($\alpha = 0.94$)			
Entrepreneurship is about recognising opportunity and transform into meaningful outcome including wealth creation	4.07	0.82	81.9
Entrepreneurship can be learnt and made/develop	4.32	0.83	90.8
Entrepreneurs are motivated not only money but also sense of social responsibility	4.31	0.87	88.2
Entrepreneurial behaviour includes innovation and creativity	4.35	0.86	89.1
Entrepreneurial firms contribute towards economic and social impact of local and national development	4.26	0.83	87.8
Entrepreneurial process involves idea generation, validation, managing, and growing the business	4.34	0.83	89.1
Digital business knowledge ($\alpha = 0.91$)			
I am confident to do copywriting for advertising and marketing business online	3.67	0.84	56.9
I am confident on creative content development	3.85	0.78	66.8
I am confident using Facebook for digital business	3.94	0.81	72.4
I am confident using Instagram for digital business	3.95	0.82	74.3
I am confident on how to set-up an e-commerce/digital business	3.83	0.85	63.2

learned, absorbed, and used their learning knowledge through their active participation in the digital business activities. This is reflected in a student-centred on action-oriented teaching model (Hägg & Gabrielsson, 2019). The findings (Table 1) indicate that over 70% of students claimed they are confident using social media (Facebook and Instagram) as a platform for doing digital business (e-commerce). This indicated that students (young adults in this survey) are comfortable participating in social media which corresponds with the latest survey by the Department of Statistics (2020) on ICT Use and Access by individuals and households. The survey reported that 97.1% of internet users in Malaysia used social media to participate in social networks and it is in the top five most popular activities. Just over half of the students perceived that they are confident with their knowledge and capability on digital business marketing "I am confident to do copywriting for advertising and marketing business online". This activity requires creative writing skills, data analysis, and digital marketing understanding. Students in business and management perceived that they excelled in this task compared to those in science-based subject studies, e.g. biological science and marine; engineering and technology; computing and statistic; and physical and environmental science. Interestingly, students reflected that they are confident in setting up an online business after completing the course (63.2%). This finding also highlights that these students can pursue online businesses (opportunity) and shows a good level of self-efficacy that contributed towards entrepreneurial competencies.

Career Aspiration and Entrepreneurial Intention with Experiential Learning

Alongside high perceived growth of the entrepreneur's knowledge base, the findings revealed that students highly rated the importance of their experiential learning with preparedness for a future career (86.1%) and intention to become an entrepreneur (81.6%). This suggests that the active involvement in experiential learning from exposure to theoretical knowledge, embedded practices in real environment and interaction with others such as group members, customers, suppliers, and educators accelerated students' certainty of plans and encouraged entrepreneurial intent. This corresponds to the Malaysian government agenda in promoting digital business among young entrepreneurs. This also supports Duval-Couetil and Long (2014) findings on the benefits of EE for undergraduate's future career and entrepreneur's mindset during uncertain labour markets (de Villiers Scheepers et al., 2018).

The Perceived Value of the Experiential Learning Process

The findings (Fig. 2) suggest students' experiential learning process in different learning settings and activities are perceived to be of importance. High involvement in active experiential learning was perceived to support students in acquiring entrepreneurial knowledge (86%) and contribute towards preparation for summative assessments such as the exam and report (78%). This finding is important for the learning process where

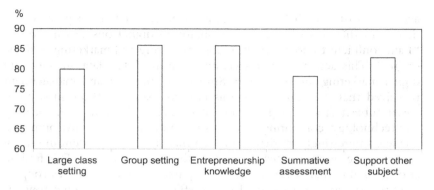

Fig. 2 Perception of experiential learning by learning activities

students were exposed to real business practice, absorb knowledge (from lectures, workshops, business talk), and convert these to a different form of action such as learning in other subjects.

Figure 3 presents a cross-category comparison of perceived entrepreneurial learning gained. The category of students with high

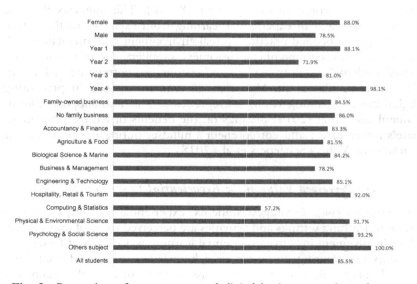

Fig. 3 Perception of e-commerce and digital business experience by category of student

perceived experiential learning is defined as those who attached important and strongly important value to the demand of experiential learning after completing the course. Students were asked "In large class setting, how important is your learning through active involvement e.g. e-commerce project"? Following on from Hawtrey (2007) approach. A Likert scale of 1–5 was used to measure the responses with scale one defined as "very unimportant" and scale five as "very important". In a group setting, students perceived its high importance as compared to a large class setting. This is expected as the digital business project required students to work as a group. There are small differences of 10% between female and male students. Interestingly, students in Computing and Statistics found the digital business experience less valuable (57.2%) compared with other subjects' specialism (all over 78%). This may suggest students found the course business content challenging and less relevant for them. The findings on digital knowledge revealed over 50% perceived confidence with the element of advertising and digital marketing (Table 1). When asked (open-ended question) on what a student would do differently if given more time on the project, the majority highlighted "I would change the advertising and packaging"; "doing more promotion"; and "learn more about digital marketing". This shows students experienced similar challenges to that of small businesses and provide a signal for educators to focus more on this key dimension for future learning cohorts and teaching method.

The impact of Covid-19 was also mentioned by students where they wanted to "open a stall"; "selling in open store or business carnival"; and "selling face-to-face". This goes against the course focus of the digital business. This issue was highlighted as a challenge for first-year students. This is expected due to students' limited ability to socialise (social experience) apart from online event due to national movement control. This limitation supported recent findings from the Office for National Statistics (2020) survey on the impact of Covid on student's social experience and satisfaction.

The development of individual transferable skills is considered important for students. Students were asked to rate their IT and digital skills against their future career aspirations based on learning experience and knowledge gained from the entrepreneurial course. The findings indicated 89.2% of students perceived IT and digital skills can contribute towards their career aspiration. There were no significant differences among the different category of students where each category scored over 80% on the value of entrepreneurial experiential learning towards their future career. This result is expected and reflected digital knowledge gained as displayed in Table 1. Data from open-ended questions highlighted how students improved their communication and self-confidence while working as a team. Other transferable skills analysed indicated teamwork and communication including presentation and report writing were perceived to be highly valued and mostly gained (both at 91.4%) from their involvement in the digital business project. This reflected the activities and assessment for the course. This was followed by attention to detail, analytical skill, and creative thinking all at 89.8%; project management (88.8%); time management (89.5%); organisational skill (88.5%); positive energy (88.5%); numerical confidence (85.9%); and commercial awareness (84.5%). The transferable skills gained are considered beneficial for graduate employability and are regularly highlighted by employers (Evans & Yusof, 2020).

Moreover, students found their entrepreneurial experiential learning is a process where students apply knowledge into practice, solving business problems, and learn to develop and grow their business. The narrative findings gathered from open-ended questions: "what is the most challenging aspect and/or difficulties you experienced in this course?" indicated that most students found difficulty in attracting and selling products to their intended market. Most cited "It's hard to find customer"; and difficult to use "online advertising at Facebook". Managing the business is recognised as a challenging activity by students: "it is difficult to control the budget"; "finding supplier"; and "packaging and delivery to customer on time". Nevertheless, students acknowledged the experience of being an entrepreneur through "I get experience to do real business"; "making money"; "customer satisfied with the product"; "it's made me feel good"; and "create a business for first time". All these indicated students' contentment with the course and activities on the course.

To summarise, evidence suggests that a predominant effect of linking digital business skills in EE with an experiential learning approach provided a positive test of entrepreneurial experience for teaching undergraduate students. However, resource availability (e.g. experience educators, an interactive entrepreneurial digital platform such as GoEcommerce) can be a major limitation in operationalising effective teaching and creating a positive student experience.

Future research on linkages between digital literacy and EE is needed to explore the extent to which changes in the learning environment and entrepreneurial pedagogy practice are reported. This will contribute towards more evidence-based research to build and improve the teaching and learning approach in EE. The UMT case provides policy reflection on the commitment of the government in providing infrastructure support to nurture and accelerating the growth of graduates' entrepreneur.

7 CONCLUSION

This study demonstrates and provides empirical evidence of EE practices and their influence on improving digital literacy skills among entrepreneurial students in the context of Malaysia during a challenging pandemic crisis. The evidence of how the entrepreneurial educator reacted (Ratten & Jones, 2021) to changes in the learning environment during the crisis and moving to online learning while maintaining an experiential learning focus serves as an exemplar for other entrepreneurial educators. The study found evidence of the contribution of EE towards the improvement of students' digital literacy and skills that could enhance the entrepreneurial process and aspiration (Duval-Couetil & Long, 2014) in digital business. This was evident across the respondents' feedback apart from those students on computing and statistics programmes. Embedding experiential learning with a digital business application in EE improves the entrepreneurial pedagogy and corresponds with the growth of digitisation, which is crucial for SMEs. Student's perception of EE with online experiential learning proved to be high (Fig. 3) and acknowledged improvement of their digital literacy.

The adoption of digital business in an entrepreneurial course demonstrated in this study exhibits an effective learning experience (e.g. real experience of creating, launching and managing digital business) and its perceived value in enhancing the entrepreneurial mindset and development of further digital skills among undergraduate students. The results indicate that blending digital business with entrepreneurship theory facilitated student learning and provided real experience of being digital entrepreneurs. This provides essential transferrable skills for university students for their future career aspirations and entrepreneurial intentions. However, the availability of resources and capability of entrepreneur educators to adopt this approach should be considered.

The study contributes towards the theoretical understanding of a blended experiential learning approach of EE in Malaysia. It offers practical recommendations for educators and highlights the significant role entrepreneurial educators played in supporting the national agenda towards digital economies and accelerating "digital entrepreneurs" intention, thus developing employability skills among graduates. The changing role and level of involvement of educators from a traditional practitioner (teacher) to facilitator, mentor, gatekeepers, and a certain extent as learners have been highlighted.

Furthermore, this study complements existing research on how entrepreneurial educators respond to crisis (Langston, 2020; Ratten & Jones, 2021) by utilising the concept of digital business and experiential learning in a changing learning condition that affects EE. The Malaysian case provides evidence of how entrepreneurship educators react and shift away from traditional methods and contribute towards improving EE practices (Liguori & Winkler, 2020; Winkler, 2014). This also provides educators and practitioners with a new perspective on changes in EE in Malaysia. More so, the case provides insight into the way the current business model is shifting by adapting to the growth of digital application and technologies in the twenty-first century digital economy. The understanding of entrepreneurial knowledge and digital business among students and its link with digital literacy is deemed among the first in EE literature and experiential learning. This will help to design more proactive and reflective learning and teaching methods in EE as well as enhancing the experience of students.

Finally, the digital world as it is today provides an opportunity for business growth to individuals with the know-how to thrive and exploit it. The development of digital literacy and the character of entrepreneurship will greatly help the progress of economic development. The contribution of this study based on a combination of experiential learning and digital literacy developments in the understanding of the development and creation of viable digital businesses by students. The advantage of emerging markets, like Malaysia, is in its ability to build new systems from the ground up, without the impairment of legacy systems. This also allows entrepreneurial educators a better understanding of the market needs in developing viable entrepreneurial courses.

References

Ajzen, I. (1991). The theory of planned behavior. *Organizational Behavior and Human Decision Processes, 50*(2), 179–211.

Ayyildiz, P., Yilmaz, A., & Baltaci, H. S. (2021). Exploring digital literacy levels and technology integration competence of Turkish academics. *International Journal of Educational Methodology, 7*(1), 15–31. https://doi.org/10.12973/ijem.7.1.15

Barringer, B., & Ireland, R. D. (2008). *What's stopping you?: Shatter the 9 most common myths keeping you from starting your own business.* FT Press.

Carpenter, J. P., Rosenberg, J. M., Dousay, T. A., Romero-Hall, E., Trust, T., Kessler, A., Phillips, M., Morrison, S. A., Fischer, C., & Krutka, D. G. (2020). What should teacher educators know about technology? Perspectives and self assessments. *Teaching and Teacher Education, 95*, 1–13. https://doi.org/10.1016/j.tate.2020.103124

Cheng, M. Y., Chan, W. S., & Mahmood, A. (2009). The effectiveness of entrepreneurship education in Malaysia. *Education+ Training.*

Confederation of British Industry. (2019). *Education and learning for the modern world: CBI/Pearson Education and skills survey report 2019.* https://www.cbi.org.uk/media/3841/12546_tess_2019.pdf. Accessed 10 August 2020.

Corbett, A. C. (2005). Experiential learning within the process of opportunity identification and exploitation. *Entrepreneurship Theory and Practice, 29*(4), 473–491.

de Villiers Scheepers, M. J., Barnes, R., Clements, M., & Stubbs, A. J. (2018). Preparing future-ready graduates through experiential entrepreneurship. *Education+ Training.*

Department of Statistics. (2020). *Report of special survey on effects of Covid-19 on economy and individual (round 1).* Department of Statistics.

Department of Statistics Malaysia, DOSM. (2020). *Principal statistics of labour force, Malaysia, second quarter (Q2) 2020.* Accessed 10 August 2020.

Duval-Couetil, N., & Long, Z. (2014). Career impacts of entrepreneurship education: How and when students intend to utilize entrepreneurship in their professional lives. *Journal of Business and Entrepreneurship, 26*(1), 63–87.

Dwerryhouse, R. (2001). Real work in the 16–19 curriculum: AVCE business and young enterprise. *Education and Training, 43*(3), 153–161.

Evans, C., & Yusof, Z. N. (2020). The importance of part-time work to UK university students. *Industry and Higher Education.* https://doi.org/10.1177/0950422220980920

Gibb, A. (1999). Can we build effective entrepreneurship through management development? *Journal of General Management, 24*(4), 1–21.

Gibb, A. (2002). In pursuit of a new 'enterprise' and 'entrepreneurship' paradigm for learning: Creative destruction, new values, new ways of doing things and new combinations of knowledge. *International Journal of Management Reviews, 4*(3), 233–269.

Gilster, P. (1997). *Digital literacy.* Wiley Computer Publications.

Hägg, G., & Gabrielsson, J. (2019). A systematic literature review of the evolution of pedagogy in entrepreneurial education research. *International Journal of Entrepreneurial Behavior & Research*.

Hagg, G., & Kurczewska, A. (2016). Connecting the dots: A discussion on key concepts in contemporary entrepreneurship education. *Education Training*, 58(7), 700–714.

Hawtrey, K. (2007). Using experiential learning techniques. *The Journal of Economic Education*, 38(2), 143–152.

Higgins, D., & Elliott, C. (2011). Learning to make sense: What works in entrepreneurial education? *Journal of European Industrial Training*.

Hytti, U., & O'Gorman, C. (2004). What is enterprise education? An analysis of the objectives and methods of enterprise education programmes in four European countries. *Education Training*, 46(1), 11–23.

Kolb, A. Y., & Kolb, D. A. (2009). The learning way: Meta-cognitive aspects of experiential learning. *Simulation & Gaming*, 40(3), 297–327.

Kolb, D. A. (1984). *Experiential learning: Experience as the source of learning and development*. Prentice Hall.

Lakeus, M. (2015). *Entrepreneurship in education—What, why when, how* (Entrepreneurship 360 Background paper). http://www.oecd.org/cfe/leed/BGP_Entrepreneurship-in-Education.pdf

Langston, C. (2020). Entrepreneurial educators: Vital enablers to support the education sector to reimagine and respond to the challenges of COVID-19. *Entrepreneurship Education, 3*, 311–338. https://doi.org/10.1007/s41959-020-00034-4

Law, N., Woo, D., de la Torre, J., & Wong, G. (2018, June). *A global framework of reference on digital literacy skills for indicator 4.4.2* (UNESCO Information Paper No. 51). Available at http://uis.unesco.org/sites/default/files/documents/ip51-global-framework-reference-digital-literacy-skills-2018-en.pdf. Accessed 25 April 2021.

Liguori, E., & Winkler, C. (2020). From offline to online: Challenges and opportunities for entrepreneurship education following the COVID-19 pandemic. *Entrepreneurship Education and Pedagogy, 3*(4), 346–351. https://doi.org/10.1177/2515127420916738

Mason, C., & Arshed, N. (2013). Teaching entrepreneurship to university students through experiential learning: A case study. *Industry and Higher Education, 27*(6), 449–463.

Ministry of Higher Education Malaysia, MoHE. (2018). *Framing Malaysian higher education 4.0 future-proof talent*. https://drive.google.com/file/d/1081nH3_BgS_BSQYzFuvp8kWieRcr5s7t/view. Accessed 10 August 2020.

Morris, M. H., & Liguori, E. (2016). Preface: Teaching reason and the unreasonable. In *Annals of entrepreneurship education and pedagogy—2016* (pp. xiv–xxii). Edward Elgar. https://doi.org/10.4337/9781784719166

Office for National Statistics. (2020). *Coronavirus and the impact on students in higher education in England: September to December 2020.* Accessed 8 May 2021.

Pirzada, Kashan and Khan, Fouzia. (2013). Measuring relationship between digital skills and employability. *European Journal of Business and Management,* 5(24). Available at SSRN: https://ssrn.com/abstract=2382939

Pittaway, L., & Cope, J. (2007). Simulating entrepreneurial learning: Integrating experiential and collaborative approaches to learning. *Management Learning,* 38(2), 211–233.

Ratten, V. and Jones, P. (2021). Covid-19 and entrepreneurship education: Implications for advancing research and practice. *The International Journal of Management Education,* 9(1), 100432. https://doi.org/10.1016/j.ijme.2020.100432.

Saptono, A., Wibowo, A., & Shandy, B. (2020). Factors influencing intention to establish business (start-up) students' a digital. 12(8), 73–91.

Sariwulan, T., Suparno, S., Disman, D., Ahman, E., & Suwatno, S. (2020). Entrepreneurial performance: The role of literacy and skills. *The Journal of Asian Finance, Economics and Business,* 7(11), 269–280. https://doi.org/10.13106/JAFEB.2020.VOL7.NO11.269

Shamsudin, S. F. F. B., Al Mamun, A., Nawi, N. B. C., Nasir, N. A. B. M., & Zakaria, M. N. B. (2016). Policies and practices for entrepreneurial education: The Malaysian experience. *The Journal of Developing Areas,* 50(5), 307–316.

Smith, P. (2001). Action learning and reflective practice in project environments that are related to leadership development. *Management Learning,* 32(1), 31–48.

Solomon, G., Duffy, S., & Tarabishy, A. (2002). The state of entrepreneurship education in the United States: A nationwide survey and analysis. *International Journal of Entrepreneurship Education,* 1(1), 65–86.

Suparno, Wibowo, A., Mukhtar, S., Narmaditya, B. S., & Sinta, H. D. (2019). The determinant factors of development batik cluster business: Lesson from Pekalongan, Indonesia. *The Journal of Asian Finance, Economics, and Business,* 6(4), 227–233. https://doi.org/10.13106/jafeb.2019.vol6.no4.227

Tan, K. E., Nga, L. Y., & Kim, G. S. (2010). Online activities and writing practices of urban Malaysian adolescents. *System,* 38(4), 548–559.

Trivedi, R. H. (2017). Entrepreneurial-intention constraint model: A comparative analysis among post-graduate management students in India, Singapore and Malaysia. *Int Entrepreneurship and Management Journal,* 13, 1239–1261.

Wenninger, H. (2019). Student assessment of venture creation courses in entrepreneurship higher education—An interdisciplinary literature review and practical case analysis. *Entrepreneurship Education and Pedagogy,* 2(1), 58–81. https://doi.org/10.1177/2515127418816277

Wilson, C., Lennox, P. P., Hughes, G., & Brown, M. (2017). How to develop creative capacity for the fourth industrial revolution: Creativity and employability in higher education. *Creativity, Innovation and Wellbeing, 184.*

Winkler, C. (2014). Toward a dynamic understanding of entrepreneurship education research across the campus–social cognition and action research. *Entrepreneurship Research Journal, 4*(1), 69–93.

World Bank. (2018). *Malaysia's digital economy: A new driver of development.* https://www.worldbank.org/en/country/malaysia/publication/mal aysias-digital-economy-a-new-driver-of-development. Accessed on 8 August 2020.

Yusoff, M. N. H., Zainol, F. A., & Ibrahim, M. D. (2014). Entrepreneurship education in Malaysia's public institutions of higher learning—A review of the current practices. *International Education Studies, 8*(1), 17–28.

Experiential Learning in Online Entrepreneurship Education: Lessons from an Undergraduate Entrepreneurship Course

Mavis S. B. Mensah, Keren N. A. Arthur,
and Enoch Mensah-Williams

1 INTRODUCTION

The global Coronavirus pandemic and its ravaging effects on human lives have led to a heightened urgency for educational institutions to adopt e-learning and reduce face-to-face instruction (FTFI). Since the first reported case in December 2019 in Wuhan, China, the pandemic had claimed two million, four hundred forty-six thousand and eight

---

M. S. B. Mensah (✉) · K. N. A. Arthur · E. Mensah-Williams
Centre for Entrepreneurship and Small Enterprise Development, School of Business, University of Cape Coast, Cape Coast, Ghana
e-mail: mmensah@ucc.edu.gh

K. N. A. Arthur
e-mail: keren.arthur@ucc.edu.gh

E. Mensah-Williams
e-mail: emensah-williams@ucc.edu.gh

© The Author(s), under exclusive license to Springer Nature Switzerland AG 2022
G. J. Larios-Hernandez et al. (eds.), *Theorising Undergraduate Entrepreneurship Education,*
https://doi.org/10.1007/978-3-030-87865-8_18

lives as of 20th February 2021 (World Health Organisation, 2021). Following the discovery of direct human contact as a primary transmission mode, world bodies and national governments have sanctioned protocols, including reduction in face-to-face interactions, as part of measures to halt the spread of the virus and mitigate its negative impact on society. Compliance with this directive is much more urgent in the education sector, especially in entrepreneurship education, where FTFI, rather than e-learning, has largely been the norm.

In entrepreneurship education, scholars allude to the limited use of e-learning and advocate for research to address the near absence of the much-needed insights for effective online teaching and learning (Liguori & Winkler, 2020). FTFI normally accounts for as high as between 60–80% time and focus in entrepreneurship education (Dhliwayo, 2008; Liguori & Winkler, 2020). Liguori and Winkler (2020) concur to scholarly arguments that online entrepreneurship education "...has failed to gain widespread adoption, in part, because contemporary approaches to entrepreneurship education stress the need for deliberate practice, real-world immersion, and experiential approaches" which lend themselves much more to FTFI (p. 348).

Globally, the use of experiential pedagogical techniques has been found to have positive impact on learners' entrepreneurial intention, acquisition of entrepreneurial skills and involvement in entrepreneurial activity (Boahemaah et al., 2020; Noyes, 2018). As the global pandemic forces entrepreneurship educators to adopt e-learning, the question of how to foster experiential learning arises, particularly, at the undergraduate level, where learners are mostly young and less experienced (Muduli et al., 2018). Kolb's experiential learning theory (ELT) postulates that knowledge and skill gaining is most effective when it is based on personal and environmental experiences (Kolb, 1984; Kolb & Kolb, 2017; Olokundun, 2018). Consistent with the ELT, this research adopted Hockerts' (2018) definition of experiential learning as learning from reflections on one's actual experiences resulting from interactions with instructors, other learners and the real world.

In light of the uncertainty associated with experiential learning in online entrepreneurship education, the purpose of this study was to explore the feasibility of experiential learning in online entrepreneurship education and how it can occur. The study relied on data from an undergraduate entrepreneurship course that was delivered online from 2nd July 2020 to 30th July 2020, at the University of Cape Coast (UCC), Ghana.

Prior to the pandemic, UCC, like other educational institutions in Ghana, relied heavily on FTFI. Although UCC had an online learning management system (LMS), it was not fully operationalised until April, 2020 when the government of Ghana directed all tertiary education institutions to close down and use e-learning in course delivery. The dawning reality is that e-learning has come to stay and will form an important part of the medium of instruction in Ghana's education system. Finding answers to the question of how to foster experiential learning in online entrepreneurship education is very much timely.

The next section is a review of related literature. This is followed by the research methodology and results. Discussions are presented together with a proposed model of online experiential learning in entrepreneurship education. The paper ends with conclusions together with recommendations, limitations and suggestions for future research.

2   LITERATURE REVIEW

Experiential Learning Theory

Learning is the process whereby knowledge is created through the transformation of experience (Kolb, 1984). According to Miettinen (2000), the concept of experiential learning is a cognitive enterprise in the field of adult education which is best illustrated in Kolb's (1984) experiential learning model (ELM). The model illustrates four main learning abilities of concrete experience (CE), reflective observation (RO), abstract conceptualisation (AC) and active experimentation (AC). Miettinen (2000) elaborates the ELM by stating that for learners to engage in effective learning, they must be able to involve themselves fully, openly and without bias in new experiences (CE); reflect on and observe their experiences from many perspectives (RO); create concepts that integrate their observations into logically sound theories (AC); and use these theories to make decisions and solve problems (AE).

Although Kolb developed his ELM from prior theories including that of Dewey, the ELM emphasises personal cognitive experience in the classroom, whereas Dewey's theory of reflective thought and action goes beyond personal and psychological experience to also embrace real-life experiences (Miettinen, 2000). Similar to Kolb (1984), Rogers (1969) stressed personal and cognitive involvement as the key elements of experiential education while Wolfe and Byrne (1975) accentuated the inductive nature of experiential learning using the trial and error concept.

Experience and reflection are two important aspects of experiential learning. Experience according to Dewey (1925 as cited in Hohr, 2013) refers to feeling, enliving and conceiving. Hohr (2013) draws upon Dewey's conceptualisations and defines feeling as the basic mode of experience where action, emotion, cognition and communication constitute an original unity. According to Hohr (2013), enliving is aesthetic experience and constitutes the lifeworld, as a person-in-world experience, whereas conceiving refers to the isolating and abstracting understanding of the world with even greater distance between action, emotion and cognition.

On the other hand, reflection according to Boud et al. (1993, p. 9 as cited in Beaudin & Quick, 1995) "...consists of those processes in which learners engage to recapture, notice and re-evaluate their experience, to work with their experience, to turn it into learning". Beaudin and Quick (1995) opine that reflection is a process that needs to be actively pursued after every learning experience and, in some cases, during the learning event. Hockerts (2018) also cautions on the need for in-class reflections after student's experiences in real-life situations to ensure that effective learning takes place.

Bergsteiner et al. (2010) stress that in experiential learning, individuals create knowledge from experience rather than just from received instructions. Therefore, in line with constructivism, learners should have the opportunity to learn from personal and group experiences as well as from feedback. Miettinen (2000) argues that reflection on group experiences provides rich learning experiences. Kolb (1984) also emphasises the importance of feedback in the ELM, for example, in the re-collections of participants which he describes as here and now experience. According to Beaudin and Quick (1995), experiential learning can occur in multiple settings—namely in real-life situations, in the learner's day-to-day life experiences and in classroom settings.

In that regard, various activities and teaching methods have been found to be associated with experiential learning on a continuum of learning typologies starting from concrete/active phase to abstract/passive stage, specifically, doing an activity, watching an activity, hearing about an activity and reading an activity (Bergsteiner et al., 2010). Elucidation of Kolb's ELM by Bergsteiner et al. (2010) and Byker (2016) shows that activities such as lecture examples, laboratories, readings, writings, fieldwork and audio-visuals foster CE. RO is achieved, for example, through thought questions, case studies, group discussions, presentations and written-response activities (Neck & Greene, 2011; Olokundun, 2018). Furthermore, AC can occur through lecture, text readings, model building and critiquing, projects and discussions (Bergsteiner et al., 2010; Kolb & Kolb, 2017). Lecture examples, projects (e.g. storytelling and movie making), laboratories, fieldwork and case studies have been found to foster AE (Bergsteiner et al., 2010; Olokundun, 2018). The categories are not mutually exclusive. For example, instructional methods recommended for active experimentation can also give students the opportunity to have concrete experience, reflect and conceptualise learned experiences.

Experiential Learning in Entrepreneurship Education

In entrepreneurship education, scholars interpret experiential learning differently with one school of thought emphasising Dewey's position on real-life experiences (Dhliwayo, 2008; McCarthy & McCarthy, 2006; Noyes, 2018) while another school gives priority to both personal cognitive experiences and real-life experiences (Neck & Greene, 2011; Olokundun, 2018). For example, McCarthy and McCarthy (2006) stress that in experiential learning, students must have direct personal encounter with the phenomenon that is being studied and must make real decisions rather than merely thinking about it. Similarly, Noyes (2018) explains experiential learning with emphasis on direct experience and action outside the classroom. On the contrary, Hockerts (2018) draws upon Kolb (1984) to define experiential learning as learning from reflections on one's actual experiences resulting from interactions with teachers and other learners, in addition to interactions with the real world.

The varied interpretations of experiential learning have resulted in disparities in what constitute experiential instructional approaches in entrepreneurship education. For researchers like Dhliwayo (2008), whose major pre-occupation is to produce practicing entrepreneurs, lecturing is simply inappropriate for entrepreneurship education and must be changed. However, Hägg et al. (2016) caution that experience is a philosophical construct as well as a common everyday practice; hence, it is both a theoretical and existential concept. Blenker et al. (2008, p. 55) also argue that "No matter whether the teaching is for or about entrepreneurship, some sort of theoretical foundation is useful..." because theory advances knowledge and improves practice (Fiet, 2001). The onus lies with the educator to ensure an appropriate blend of theory and practice and the degree of self-directed/student-centred learning in entrepreneurship education, as informed by the educator's instructional philosophy (Muduli et al., 2018).

Although experiential learning is said to originally be a domain of adult learning (Miettinen, 2000), its effectiveness at the undergraduate level is well-established (Boahemaah et al., 2020; Tete et al., 2014). To achieve learning effectiveness, Beaudin and Quick (1995) stress the need for instructors to discriminate in the kind of experiences they create for learners by deciding on the appropriate experiential delivery methods and creating conditions that positively influence the quality of the learner's future experiences. There is also a general concern that reflection is seldom encouraged in entrepreneurship education (Hägg et al., 2016; Hockerts, 2018). Therefore, Hägg et al. (2016) entreat instructors to give adequate attention to student's reflection since it is through reflection that actual learning occurs.

Nonetheless, the physical classroom setting has been a major teaching and learning environment in entrepreneurship education with limited online activities (Hockerts, 2018; Liguori & Winkler, 2020). The Coronavirus pandemic has heightened the exigency of online entrepreneurship education but there remains the unanswered question of how experiential learning can occur in virtual entrepreneurship courses/programmes. This study seeks to contribute to the emerging research on experiential online entrepreneurship education.

3 Methodology

The study adopted a qualitative research approach to understand the dynamics involved in promoting experiential learning in an online undergraduate entrepreneurship course. Dana and Dana (2005) emphasise the need for such deep-level investigations in entrepreneurship research because they lead to a holistic understanding of concepts under investigation. Specifically, the narrative research design (Wolgemuth & Agosto, 2019) was employed. This design involved pulling together information from recorded online lecture videos and discussion forums on the UCC LMS to tell the story of undergraduate students' exposure to experiential learning in an online entrepreneurship course.

The e-learning course was aimed at equipping final-year undergraduate business students with fundamental competencies necessary for pursuing intrapreneurship and new venture creation in the short, medium or long term. It was a required course for the students. Enrollment in the course was 29. The course was originally designed to be delivered via FTFI. Nevertheless, events surrounding the outbreak of the Coronavirus pandemic necessitated a transition to an e-learning delivery mode comprising synchronous and asynchronous teaching methods. Thus, the implementation of the course on the LMS was a first-time experience for both students and the facilitator.

The structure of the course involved five online lectures conducted over a period of five weeks, via Google meet. Prior to the commencement of the course, self-study resources comprising five lecture slides and six subject-related videos were uploaded onto the UCC LMS. Students were required to review the uploaded documents as part of preparations for the online lectures. For each week, students participated in a two-hour lecture. During the lectures, students engaged with the course by watching visual aids such as lecture slides and photographs, listening to the facilitator and peers and speaking about issues discussed. Students were also required to complete activities on UCC's LMS for four hours. Students also participated in three online discussion forums following the completion of specific offline exercises, namely self-assessment exercise, creativity exercise and resource mobilisation exercise, in real-life situations.

Using feedback from a self-completed questionnaire, the self-assessment activity required students to think deeply about their entrepreneurial traits; and to make decisions on how they will capitalise on their strengths and overcome their weaknesses, moving forward. The creativity exercise involved the application of innovation concepts learnt in the online lecture to real-life problem-solving. Students were required to identify an existing product that, in their opinion, fell short of market expectations, give reasons for their choice and offer an innovative solution that could serve as an entrepreneurial opportunity. The resource mobilisation activity involved students' assessment of the resource needs for a chosen business concept and the creation of a resource mobilisation plan to secure the resources from individuals in their network. Students were tasked to identify individuals on their mobile phones and contact them with regard to their intention to start the chosen entrepreneurial initiative for which they needed resources.

340   M. S. B. MENSAH ET AL.

A document review guide served as the main data collection instrument. Table 1 depicts how experiential learning was operationalised in the guide. In total, four categories of documents were reviewed including course participation report, activity completion report and discussion forum posts generated from UCC's LMS as well as recordings of the online lectures. These documents were chosen by taking into account the characteristics of "authenticity, credibility, representativeness and meaning" suggested by Scott (1990). All recorded online lectures and forum posts were considered for the analysis.

Data were collected within a period of two weeks from 16th to 29th November 2020. However, the researchers occasionally re-visited UCC's LMS and the recorded videos to verify information throughout the data analysis process, which lasted for a month. Thematic data analysis was

Table 1 Operationalising experiential learning

Dimensions	Variables	Sources
Learning through the senses: by sight, hearing, feeling	Watching and listening to audio-visuals Listening to lecture examples Reading an activity/text Reacting to issues raised in group discussions/expressing oneself in discussions	Kolb (1984) Miettinen (2000) Bergsteiner et al. (2010) Kolb and Kolb (2017)
Learning through cognitive action	Critiquing projects and discussions Asking questions and making follow-ups Answering thought questions Engaging in written-response activities Doing presentations Solving problems Creating concepts, plans Contributing to group discussions and debriefing/reflection sessions, etc.	Bergsteiner et al. (2010) Hägg et al. (2016) Hockerts (2018) Olokundun (2018)
Learning through physical involvement in real-life activities	Fieldwork	Bergsteiner et al. (2010) Neck and Greene (2011) Olokundun (2018)

Source Authors' Compilation (2020)

carried out (Creswell, 2014; Grbich, 2007). It was done manually by reducing the data through open and axial coding, displaying the data using tables to identify emerging themes and drawing of conclusions (Miles & Huberman, 1994; Schutt, 2012).

4 RESULTS

The feasibility of experiential learning in online entrepreneurship education was evaluated by examining the extent and nature of students' participation in the course through the senses, mind and the real world. Two virtual learning environments were explored: namely online lecture and online discussion forums.

Online Lecture

Analysis of the extent to which students accessed the uploaded lecture slides prior to the online lecture revealed that students accessed the slides more in comparison to subject-related videos. Most students, ranging from 13 to 18 per week out of 29 enrolled students, downloaded the lecture slides each week. Nevertheless, students' participation with regard to accessing the self-study resources was generally low in week four.

Students' participation in the online lectures varied with a minimum attendance of 11 students in week one and a maximum of 19 students in week two. Aside attendance, students engaged with the course by watching visual aids such as lecture slides and photographs, listening to the facilitator and peers and speaking about issues discussed. Generally, few students asked questions with a range of three to seven students speaking, except in one lecture where no student asked a question.

Despite the low number of students who spoke in class, findings showed that students who spoke, mostly did so voluntarily. Between two to five students contributed willingly to general discussions on the topic. While five students readily responded to questions posed by the facilitator, two students only answered questions when called upon by the facilitator. Overall, there was evidence to suggest some student–student and student–facilitator interaction. In one example, a student was able to make a decision about the creative behaviour of an individual in photographs displayed. However, several follow-up comments and questions yielded no change in the student's ability to offer a convincing justification for her decision until another student jumped in to bail her out.

Online Discussion Forums

Three online discussion forums were used to encourage experiential learning. Each of these online discussion forums was based on different activities; namely, entrepreneurial self-assessment, resource mobilisation and creativity exercises (see Sect. 3 above for more details).

Self-Assessment Exercise

A total of 23 out of 29 students visited the online self-assessment discussion forum. Results showed that the number of views fluctuated between two and 52 views per student with one student recording 92 views throughout the course. Of the number that visited the forum, 17 posted the outcome of their assessment on the discussion forum. Posts on the forum totalled 28 with the number of posts per student alternating from one to three on average. However, one student was observed to have nine different posts on the forum. Posts comprised students' submissions on forum activities (new posts) as well as questions and comments on the submissions of other students and that of the facilitator (follow-up posts). Findings showed that most of the self-assessment posts (17 out of 28) were new posts. Follow-up posts totalled 11.

Submissions were generally thoughts on the assigned task with one person observed to have used the platform to ask a question. All but one of the follow-up posts comprised comments and questions made by the facilitator to students. The only follow-up post submitted by a student was a response to the facilitator's follow-up question. Further, one of the submissions identified was discovered by the facilitator to be plagiarised text. Although the facilitator through two follow-up posts drew the student's attention to this, there was no feedback or re-submission of the post by the student.

Most students (14 out of 16) in reflecting on their entrepreneurial traits made reference only to the scale of the self-assessment questionnaire. For instance, forum submissions from two students were: "Considering a total score of 74% on the self-assessment, I have satisfactory ability to be an entrepreneur"; "With a score of 66% I fall into the assessment category of having a satisfactory ability to be an entrepreneur". Almost all of the respondents (15 out of 16) justified their arguments making reference to specific line items in the questionnaire. One student expounded: "I believe my assessment summarises my ability to maintain high standards for customer service and responsiveness that will be reflected in the results of my work". Another student stated: "my strength in terms of entrepreneurship includes determination, relationship building, risk-taking and hardworking".

None of the respondents explored the question of why they ranked themselves strong or weak in specific entrepreneurial traits. In a few cases, students made reference to past experiences, their motivations for having an interest in entrepreneurship and the implications of their weaknesses; but these illustrations were not clear. For one student, further details, on a previous entrepreneurial engagement, were only provided in response to follow-up questions by the facilitator.

Creativity Exercise

Findings from the study showed that 22 out of 29 students participated on the discussion forum via views. Out of this number, 18 students posted on the forum. While number of views per student ranged from two to 52, number of posts per student varied from one to five. Posts on the forum totalled 20, most of which were new posts (17 out of 20) with only a few follow-up posts (3 out of 20). Follow-up posts comprised two posts from students and one post from the facilitator. One of the student follow-up posts was in response to the facilitator's question while the second was initiated by the student to express his lack of understanding of a given task. There was no evidence of the facilitator responding to the student's query. One of the submissions on the forum was later found to be plagiarised text.

More than half of the students (13 out of 18) who contributed to the forum on the creativity exercise exhibited a fair ability to apply knowledge acquired in class to the assigned task. For these respondents, findings showed links between the solutions mentioned and several of the innovation types discussed in class. In student responses, emphasis was placed on describing the characteristics of the product with a few adding text on the uses and health benefits. Despite this, most responses (12 out of 18) either offered no explanation on what the problem was with the identified product or gave explanations of the problem but were unclear. Only in a few cases (3 out of 18) were respondents able to address the issue of fit of solution with the identified problem. This was evidenced in one example where the student proposed an idea of pureeing and packaging pepper as a solution to a supply side problem of short shelf-life; a solution which related to the product and marketing innovation concepts learnt in class.

Results showed that some follow-up posts by the facilitator led to improvements in the depth of students' reflection. One student's initial submission was very generic and appeared to be plagiarised text which the facilitator did not identify. Nevertheless, follow-up questions by the facilitator on the submission led the student to re-think and provide more details. Therefore, while the initial submission mentioned generally that "a new market will be considered so as to gain competitive advantage", follow-up questions led to the provision of details that "the product will be targeted to nursing mothers with a targeted market share of 70%". Justifications were also given for why these individuals will be interested in the offering.

Resource Mobilisation Exercise

Results from the analysis indicated that 21 out of 29 students visited the resource mobilisation discussion forum. More than half of the students who viewed the forum (17 out of 21) posted a comment or question. Number of views per student stretched from one to 45, while number of posts per student extended from one to eight. In total, 17 new posts were observed, one of which was found to be plagiarised text. Follow-up posts also totalled eight, five of which were by the facilitator. The remaining three follow-up posts were submitted by students in response to follow-up posts by the facilitator. Only two out of the five students responded to queries made by the facilitator.

Most submissions on the resource mobilisation activity (14 out of 17) reflected a poor understanding of the resource needs of the chosen businesses as students' submissions were shallow. For example, one student lumped all the required resources under three categories, namely physical, human and financial resources with no details on what the specific needs were. Additionally, students' list of resources required for pursuing their identified business opportunities focused mainly on operational resources such as utensils, raw materials, equipment, with a few students highlighting cash and explicit job roles which fall under financial and human resources, respectively. Most of the resource mobilisation plans presented on the forum (15 out of 17) lacked deep thinking about the objectives, targets, strategies and timelines associated with the proposal.

It was observed that there were resource mobilisation plans that could be considered fairly well thought through. One respondent explained: "Madam Amishawu, who deals in purchasing and selling of groundnut, has agreed to supply me with groundnut on credit to be paid in installments for the next six months while Mr. Razak has agreed to give me an interest free loan of GHC 20,000 to be paid back in two years". Another student highlighted: "The poultry farmer is willing to give me GHC 40,000 in return for 200 bags of maize after harvesting which will be used in managing the farm. Additionally, the regional best farmer, Mr. Kwakye, is willing to offer his farm inputs such as the planter, harvester and tractor at a fee of GHC 200 each per acre". These quotes and others on the online discussion forum showed that students who exhibited a deeper level of thinking emphasised timelines and conditions under which the resources sought would be given; for example, interest rate, type of financing option and discounts for repeat purchases. Some of these details were provided only after further probing by the facilitator through follow-up posts.

5   Discussion of Findings

Focusing on the extent of participation and the nature of student interactions in two virtual learning environments, the results of the study demonstrate the feasibility of experiential learning in online entrepreneurship education. It is evident from the results that the online lecture and the online discussion forums provided opportunities for experiential learning by students through active participation in new experiences, reflection on and observation of the experiences from many perspectives, integration of observations into logically sound theories and use of the theories to make decisions and solve problems (Kolb, 1984; Miettinen, 2000). The learning experience was made possible through students' engagement in online learning activities via sight, hearing, speaking and writing, with feedback from the facilitator (Bergsteiner et al., 2010; Hockerts, 2018).

The occasions for learning by sight in the online lectures were mainly through lecture slides and illustration cards which the facilitator used in the course of the lectures. Hearing occurred by listening while students spoke by asking or answering questions and making contributions to discussions. Downloading of self-study resources is also an indication of students' physical involvement by sight and hearing as they had to review uploaded lecture slides and reading materials and watch subject-related videos as part of preparations for the online lectures. These insights show that students had primary experience in the form of material interaction with the physical and social environment (Miettinen, 2000). Thus, online lecture, in contrast to arguments by Dhliwayo (2008), has the potential to foster both theoretical and practical learning in line with arguments by Hägg et al. (2016).

Experiential learning theory postulates that student-centred/self-directed learning is paramount to experiential learning because learners gain new experiences by doing an activity, watching an activity, hearing about an activity and reading an activity in a classroom setting or in real-life situations (Bergsteiner et al., 2010; Byker, 2016; Hockerts, 2018). According to findings from this study (e.g. comparison of the number of downloads of self-study resources with the attendance at online lectures), students engaged in self-directed learning (Hägg et al., 2016) as much as they did in online lectures.

Nevertheless, not all students engaged in the online lectures by speech, that is, by asking questions, responding to questions or making comments. This means that they may have missed opportunities of enriching their experience as Byker (2016) illustrates that speaking, for example, through presentations deepens an individual's ability to understand and reflect on issues. In addition, the results that students engaged in forum discussions and jumped into discussions, in the online lectures, to help each other to understand concepts, reinforces the importance of group discussions and group reflections. Miettinen (2000) argues that reflection on group experiences provide rich learning experiences. Similarly, Byker (2016) identifies group discussions and presentations as valuable activities for encouraging concluding actions under reflective observation.

The findings on students' engagement on the forums showesd that not all students who visited the online discussion forums posted on the forums. Thus, students who visited the forums may have had the opportunity to learn via sight, that is, by reading the submissions of others. However, the experience of those who did not post will fall short of the experience that one gains by participating via text (posting on the platform). According to illustrations by Bergsteiner et al. (2010) and Byker (2016), writing enhances one's reflection in ways that sight or hearing may not be able to achieve.

It is also evident from the findings that students' learning process entailed opportunities for personal and group reflections through discussions. It is well-established that actual learning takes place through reflection (Beaudin & Quick, 1995; Hägg et al., 2016). Therefore, results on the limited discussions among students and the low quality of students' personal reflections on the forum point to limited learning experiences of students in the study. It is possible that missing details on the rationale behind their forum submissions would have emerged through extensive discussions with the facilitator and with peers, making group reflection also necessary.

In relation to the finding on multiple views, it can be argued that the online discussion forums provided an environment that allowed for easy reference and re-collection by students. That is students could re-look at their own submissions, that of their colleagues and that of the facilitator, permitting recall in the learning process. This form of reflection on action, as well as reflection on feedback from the facilitator, is important in fostering experiential learning (Hägg et al., 2016; Hockerts, 2018).

The multiple posts by students also meant that the facilitator had to address a lot more people on the forum than in the online lecture. However, there were differences in the number of follow-ups by the facilitator in each of the forums. It was observed that forums that occurred in the early parts of the course had more follow-ups than those that were set up later in the course. This situation may be due to factors such as time constraint and fatigue considering the personalised nature of addressing issues on the platform and the number of students who engaged on the platform. This may be a reason why the results show that some students' plagiarism skipped the attention of the facilitator.

Findings on improvements in some students' reflection due to the facilitator's follow-ups highlight the importance of effective oversight and positive reinforcement by the facilitator (Kolb, 1984; Miettinen, 2000). There were opportunities for this kind of reinforcement in the online lecture through questioning by the facilitator. Nevertheless, feedback from the facilitator and the asynchronous nature of the forum appear to have enabled more students to engage in discussions on the forum in comparison to the online lectures as there were more posts on the forum than students' contributions in the lectures.

A Model of Online Experiential Learning as Physical Involvement and Cognitive Involvement

On the basis of the foregoing discussions, we proffer online experiential learning (OEL) as physical involvement and cognitive involvement (Fig. 1), following Bergsteiner et al.'s (2010) advice not to mix learning

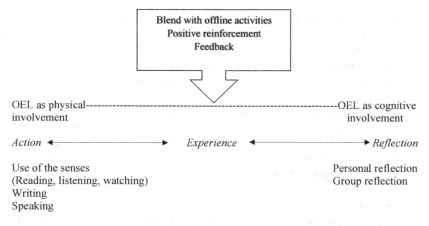

Fig. 1 Online Experiential Learning (OEL)

typologies with activity typologies since that can cause confusion and meaningless results. Physical involvement connotes action while cognitive involvement entails the use of the senses to tap into one's own experiences and those of others through, for example, reflective observation, abstract conceptualisation and active experimentation in the course of the learning process (Kolb, 1984; Miettinen, 2000).

Experiential learning theory, in its variant forms, for example, by Dewey (1925 as cited in Hohr, 2013) and Kolb (1984), underscores the importance of action, experience and reflection occurring in an interactive continuum in the teaching and learning process. Per the definition of experience by Dewey (1925 as cited in Hohr, 2013) and Hohr (2013), action is experience and comprises in-class and outside classroom activities such as listening, watching, writing and speaking (Bergteiner et al., 2010; Byker, 2016; Kolb & Kolb, 2017), all of which connote physical involvement. Opportunities for personal and group reflection via discussions entail cognitive involvement (Fig. 1).

According to the ELT, and as shown in Fig. 1, students gain experience through action, whereas actual learning takes place through reflection upon the experiences (Hägg et al., 2016; Miettinen, 2000). Nonetheless, the effectiveness of OEL would depend upon the presence of positive reinforcement, feedback and a blend of online learning experiences with experiences from real-life situations (Fig. 1). The higher role of facilitator feedback implies lower student–teacher ratio in OEL. Reinforcement on the online forum may also require some incentives due to the asynchronous nature of the forum, which does not allow students and facilitators to engage in real time.

6 Conclusions

This study has demonstrated what counts as experiential learning and how it can occur in online entrepreneurship education. Based on the key findings, it is concluded that online experiential learning in entrepreneurship education is possible through students' physical involvement and cognitive involvement in the online teaching and learning process. However, positive reinforcement, consistent feedback and a blend of online learning experiences with experiences from real-life situations are indispensable to the effectiveness of students' experiential learning. Moreover, lower student–teacher ratio is imperative to ensuring adequate feedback on asynchronous online platforms while grading of student engagement on such platforms may be a necessary reinforcement to encourage extensive participation. This study employed a cross-sectional data and relied on only two online teaching platforms. This limits the scope of the findings. Longitudinal studies and data from multiple online platforms may also provide additional rich insights.

References

Beaudin, B. P., & Quick, D. (1995). *Experiential learning: Theoretical underpinnings*. High Plains Intermountain Center for Agricultural Health and Safety.

Bergsteiner, H., Avery, G. C., & Neumann, R. (2010). Kolb's experiential learning model: Critique from a modelling perspective. *Studies in Continuing Education, 32*(1), 29–46.

Blenker, P., Dreisler, P., Færgemann, H. M., & Kjeldsen, J. (2008). A framework for developing entrepreneurship education in a university context. *International Journal of Entrepreneurship and Small Business, 5*(1), 45–63.

Boahemaah, L., Xin, L., Dobge, C. S., & Pomegbe, W. W. (2020). The impact of entrepreneurship education on the entrepreneurial intention of students in tertiary institutions. *International Journal of Management, Accounting and Economics, 7*(4), 123–146.

350 M. S. B. MENSAH ET AL.

Byker, E. J. (2016). Assessing experience: Performance-based assessment of experiential learning activities. In D. Polly (Ed.), *Evaluating teacher education programs through performance-based assessments* (pp. 261–280). IGI Global.

Creswell, J. W. (2014). *Research design: Qualitative, quantitative and mixed methods approaches* (4th ed.). Sage.

Dana, L. P., & Dana, T. E. (2005). Expanding the scope of methodologies used in entrepreneurship research. *International Journal of Entrepreneurship and Small Business, 2*(1), 79–88.

Dhliwayo, S. (2008). Experiential learning in entrepreneurship education. *Education+ Training, 50*(4), 329–340.

Fiet, J. O. (2001). The theoretical side of teaching entrepreneurship. *Journal of Business Venturing, 16*(1), 1–24.

Grbich, C. (2007). *Qualitative data analysis: An introduction.* Sage.

Hägg, G., Kurczewska, A., McCracken, M., & Matlay, H. (2016). Connecting the dots—A discussion on key concepts in contemporary entrepreneurship education. *Education+ Training,*

Hockerts, K. (2018). The effect of experiential social entrepreneurship education on intention formation in students. *Journal of Social Entrepreneurship, 9*(3), 234–256.

Hohr, H. (2013). The concept of experience by John Dewey revisited: Conceiving, feeling and "enliving." *Studies in Philosophy and Education, 32*(1), 25–38.

Kolb, A. Y., & Kolb, D. A. (2017). Experiential learning theory as a guide for experiential educators in higher education. *Experiential Learning & Teaching in Higher Education, 1*(1), 7–44.

Kolb, D. (1984). *Experiential learning.* Prentice Hall.

Liguori, E., & Winkler, C. (2020). From offline to online: Challenges and opportunities for entrepreneurship education following the COVID-19 pandemic. *Entrepreneurship Education and Pedagogy, 3*(4), 346–351.

McCarthy, P. R., & McCarthy, H. M. (2006). When case studies are not enough: Integrating experiential learning into business curricula. *Journal of Education for Business, 81*(4), 201–204.

Miettinen, R. (2000). The concept of experiential learning and John Dewey's theory of reflective thought and action. *International Journal of Lifelong Education, 19*(1), 54–72.

Miles, M. B., & Huberman, A. M. (1994). *Qualitative data analysis: An expanded sourcebook.* Sage.

Muduli, A., Kaura, V., & Quazi, A. (2018). Pedagogy or andragogy? Views of Indian postgraduate business students. *IIMB Management Review, 30*(2), 168–178.

Neck, H. M., & Greene, P. G. (2011). Entrepreneurship education: Known worlds and new frontiers. *Journal of Small Business Management, 49*(1), 55–70.

Noyes, E. (2018). Teaching entrepreneurial action through prototyping: The prototype-it challenge. *Entrepreneurship Education and Pedagogy, 1*(1), 118–134.

Olokundun, A. M. (2018). Experiential pedagogy and entrepreneurial intention: A focus on university entrepreneurship programmes. *Academy of Entrepreneurship Journal, 24*(2). http://eprints.covenantuniversity.edu.ng/12801/1/Experiential%20Pedagogy.pdf

Rogers, C. R. (1969). *Freedom to learn: A view of what education might become* (1st ed.). Merrill Publishing Company.

Schutt, R. K. (2012). *Investigating the social world: The process and practice of research.* Sage.

Scott, J. (1990). *A matter of record, documentary sources in social research.* Polity Press.

Tete, M. F., Limongi, R., De Almeida, M. I. S., & Borges, C. (2014). Experiential learning as teaching strategy for entrepreneurship: Assessment of a Brazilian experience. *International Journal of Innovation and Learning, 16*(4), 428–447.

Wolfe, D. E., & Byrne, E. T. (1975). Research on experiential learning: Enhancing the process. *Business Games and Experiential Learning in Action, 2*, 325–336.

Wolgemuth, J. R., & Agosto, V. (2019). Narrative research. In *The Blackwell encyclopedia of sociology.* https://doi.org/10.1002/9781405165518.

World Health Organisation. (2021). *COVID-19 dashboard.* https://covid19.who.int/?gclid. Accessed 20 February 2021.

Conclusion: Entrepreneurship Education for an Undergraduate Audience—A Review and Future Directions

Guillermo J. Larios-Hernandez[iD], Andreas Walmsley[iD], and Itzel Lopez-Castro

Theorising Undergraduate Entrepreneurship Education incorporates philosophical and pedagogical aspects of entrepreneurship education (EE) research, evoking some of the potential outcomes that can be expected from teaching techniques, curricular and extracurricular programmes. From a philosophical viewpoint, while authors in this title introduce a mixture of theoretical perspectives to undergraduate entrepreneurship education (UEE), such as behaviourism, cognitivism, constructivism, and new perspectives such as humanism, these positions turn out to be largely

---

G. J. Larios-Hernandez (✉) · I. Lopez-Castro
Universidad Anáhuac, Mexico, Mexico
e-mail: guillermo.lariosh@anahuac.mx

I. Lopez-Castro
e-mail: itzel.lopez@anahuac.mx

A. Walmsley
Plymouth Marjon University, Plymouth, UK
e-mail: awalmsley@marjon.ac.uk

© The Author(s), under exclusive license to Springer Nature Switzerland AG 2022
G. J. Larios-Hernandez et al. (eds.), *Theorising Undergraduate Entrepreneurship Education*,
https://doi.org/10.1007/978-3-030-87865-8_19

complementary, strengthening the theoretical foundation of EE in higher education (HE). To elaborate on such approaches vis-à-vis pedagogical aspects, some of the chapters have discussed EE methodologies, strategies and teaching techniques, the combining role of pedagogy and andragogy, as well as original proposals such as odigogy, which is directly concerned with HE students and their stage of life.

Additionally, and extending beyond general pedagogical considerations, authors make practical recommendations with direct implications for the delivery of EE in the classroom. These recommendations extend across curriculum and instructional design, didactic methods, mentoring, the role of experiential education and learning spaces. In that sense, some of the chapters invite the reader to reconsider new EE practices in HE, such as the use of novel online resources, the role of play and the purpose of learning spaces as proper environments for knowledge acquisition. In that regard, the role of teachers and other stakeholders turns out to be instrumental especially as they may accompany the student along the entire process of reflecting and learning. Finally, the book reflects on the outcome of UEE, desired and actual, assessing its effects on employability, competencies and identity.

Looking forward, the question, as ever, is where do we go from here? How can we as educators and scholars support the further development of EE, its theory and practice? On the one hand this text is further evidence that the subject is continuing to evolve, becoming theoretically more robust, drawing on a wider range of disciplines and theoretical insights to support its development and extending its geographical spread also. On the other hand, there are still many unanswered questions, and room for impactful research to find its place, not least because the world evolves and EE must evolve with it or become an irrelevance. That being so, scholarly views extend across a variety of EE themes (Gabrielsson et al., 2020), and all these research approaches become conditionally distinct when targeting HE students, this being the main focus of these chapters. The book, by focussing on the undergraduate student, has deliberately tried to place the student and their needs centre stage.

As expressed repeatedly in this title, undergraduates embrace generational and psychological needs that distinguish them from other groups, namely, their nascent professional experience, evolving identity and age-related ambitions. Hence, EE cannot ignore these qualities, inasmuch as they represent natural developmental requirements in HE students, and since EE continues to grow in most university curricula, we as researchers must necessarily feel compelled to try to understand teaching and learning models that may lead to better educational effectiveness. Naturally, this goal poses the problem of defining what we mean by 'effectiveness'. While the field of entrepreneurship typically refers to processes of ideation, opportunity identification and new venture creation, UEE acquires a more comprehensive perspective, training students to think and act entrepreneurially, as a professionalising skill that helps them create future value, for themselves and for society. In that sense, initial conditions for the development of such a mindset depend on educational techniques that take into account the stage of development of this group of, typically, young students.

However, and following on from these points, as social scientists we recognise temporal and spatial constraints in our work. Not only is entrepreneurship influenced by context (Spilling, 1996; Welter, 2011) so is entrepreneurship education. For a number of reasons this is an important consideration, we feel, for the future development of the field because what has been tried and in many respects tested in a 'Western' context may not necessarily apply in others. Additionally, the transitional stage in which most Western HE students find themselves, i.e. emerging adulthood, is also a mutable culture-dependent construct (Arnett, 2000), in that cultural norms may influence young people's identity and ambitions. Perhaps, this is why researchers in this book have concurrently supported practice, experience and reflection as core drivers of UEE, but differ in how UEE expresses in particular geographies or university programmes. In other words, the vastness of interpretations about how to implement UEE in specific contexts invites scholars to take a systemic viewpoint, in which EE is influenced too by the surrounding ecosystem.

The whole idea of an entrepreneurship education ecosystem (e.g. Brush, 2014, 2021) is contingent on the idea of context. In economics, the notion that institutions, whether regulatory, normative or cultural (North, 1990; Scott, 2001) play a critical role in determining economic behaviour is a long-standing one. In entrepreneurship itself, there is growing interest in the area of entrepreneurial ecosystems (Wurth et al., 2021) whose core idea is premised on interdependencies within a system. Entrepreneurship whose end goal is the creation of a new venture involves economic, sociological, psychological and administrative perspectives (Bula, 2012). In order to succeed, the entrepreneur is necessarily associated with functional elements of an entrepreneurial ecosystem, namely, other start-ups, venture capital, incubators, and accelerators, intrapreneurship programmes, among others. Such an ecosystem extends its influence to help develop EE from early stages in HE. This is an area we believe may attract increasing interest and drive developments in the field.

The temporal dimension is fundamental to EE and to many of the contributions in our book. Entrepreneurship itself is premised on change, on innovation, on novelty and on problem-solving. It is impossible to avoid claims in the media that we are living in an era of rapid change, technologically yes, but also at a societal level. The natural environment is changing rapidly too with the impact of human behaviour ever more apparent and, alas, frequently detrimental to it. Changing trends, patterns of behaviour, societal values and politico-economic systems are all macro-level factors that will have implications for what happens at a micro-level, what happens in the entrepreneurial classroom. This is the world today's undergraduates are faced with. There are more opportunities, but also fewer certainties. How is it possible to navigate such a terrain? Here EE can play a decisive role in supporting youth, including but not limited to aspiring entrepreneurs, live more meaningful, fulfilled lives (whatever that means for the individual).

Clearly, not everyone is looking to start their own business. However, as a consequence of this changing environment, EE nowadays involves competencies necessary for every professional, whose work environment demands knowledge as well as creative and social skills. This is one of the aspects where EE differs from business education. While a business programme is typically based on causal reasoning, following logical, linear patterns with predictable results, entrepreneurship education allows for effectual reasoning to be developed (Sarasvathy, 2001; Smolka et al., 2018). Effectual reasoning involves a discovery process, through which hypotheses are identified, which are iteratively tested in the market, and seeks to understand the reality of an opportunity before its development; learning in EE arises through the analysis of such a practical experience.

Still, we recognise that entrepreneurship education will continue to focus on business start-up; this does in our view lie at its core and provides distinctiveness (Neck & Corbett, 2018). What we are likely to see however is a continued expansion of EE into non-business disciplines in a quasi 'EE for all' approach. This has been advocated for some time (e.g. Gibb, 2002) and yet there is still much work to do in defining the 'what' and the 'how' of EE and we believe this book has provided some pointers in this regard with its undergraduate setting. In many respects contributors provide refreshing insights by reminding us of our intellectual provenance; EE simply ignores at its own peril past achievements in the area of educational theory development—we are not starting from a clean slate. At the same time, EE scholars can break into new ground with implications that extend beyond EE and we can find aspects of this in the chapters that comprise this text. In practice, EE has made the move beyond the business school, it remains to be seen to what extent its scholars can mirror this.

As some scholars have identified in articles such as Günzel-Jensen and Robinson (2017) or Neck and Greene (2011), EE is not solely about motivating students with stories about successful personalities, but about the development of the mind and skills necessary for creating value. It is about cultivating decision making, not just achieving the expected business outcome, about reflection on the entrepreneur's experience, which may cause a degree of perplexity, under uncertain conditions and knowledge, about how to seek solutions to our problems. In the case of HE, getting to understand the behaviour and psychology of the young university student becomes relevant if better entrepreneurial minds are to be developed, considering that EE is essentially a structure of methods, involving a frame of mind that embraces leadership, that could and should be used when running all types of organisations (Greenberg et al., 2011).

In all of this, the question of impact of our scholarly endeavours is unlikely to go away. Pfeffer and Fong (2002) some time ago warned about the scholarship of management discipline moving further away from actual practice of management. The threat of this happening in EE is perhaps not as acute as it is in the management discipline, and yet we should be reminded that in an increasingly cost-conscious, market driven HE sector we will be questioned about the relevance of our research to the so-called real world. HEIs in many countries are having to demonstrate research impact as a return on investment-type consideration (Hughes et al., 2019). The question of research impact is an intricate one, and it is not our intention to enter any kind of full-blown discussion here as to the pros and cons of committing to the 'impact agenda'. What we point to though is the need for more evidence of what works and in which contexts, which is something we surely need more of in EE. We also need to be asking (and answering) questions about who value is created for (Jones et al., 2020)? The issue of the wider, i.e. beyond academia, impact of scholarship in EE is, ultimately, a legitimate one.

REFERENCES

Arnett, J. (2000). Emerging adulthood: A theory of development from the late teens through the twenties. *American Psychologist, 55*(5), 469–480. https://doi.org/10.1037/0003-066X.55.5.469

Brush, C. (2014). Exploring the concept of an entrepreneurship education ecosystem. In S. Hoskinson & D. Kuratko (Eds.), *Innovative pathways for university entrepreneurship in the 21st century* (Vol. 24, pp. 25–39): Emerald Group Publishing.

Brush, C. (2021). Entrepreneurship education ecosystems: the case of Babson College. In H. Neck & Y. Liu (Eds.), *Innovation in global entrepreneurship education. teaching entrepreneurship in practice* (pp. 2–17).

Bula, H. O. (2012). Evolution and theories of entrepreneurship: A critical review on the Kenyan perspective. *International Journal of Business & Commerce, 1*(11), 81–96.

Gabrielsson, J., Hägg, G., Landström, H., & Politis, D. (2020). Connecting the past with the present: The development of research on pedagogy in entrepreneurial education. *Education + Training, 62*(9), 1061–1086. https://doi.org/10.1108/ET-11-2019-0265

Greenberg, D., McKone-Sweet, & Wilson, H.J. (2011). *The new entrepreneurial leader: Developing leaders who shape social and economic opportunity.* Berrett-Koehler.

Gibb, A. (2002). In pursuit of a new 'enterprise' and 'entrepreneurship' paradigm for learning: Creative destruction, new values, new ways of doing things and new combinations of knowledge. *International Journal of Management Reviews, 4*(3), 233–269. https://doi.org/10.1111/1468-2370.00086

Gibb, A. (2008). Entrepreneurship and enterprise education in schools and colleges: Insights from UK. *International Journal of Entrepreneurship Education, 6*, 101–144.

Günzel-Jensen, F., & Robinson, S. (2017). Effectuation in the undergraduate classroom: three barriers to entrepreneurial learning. *Education + Training, 59*(7–8), 780–796. https://doi.org/10.1108/ET-03-2016-0049

Hughes, T., Webber, D., & Nicholas, O. R. (2019). Achieving wider impact in business and management: Analysing the case studies from REF 2014. *Studies in Higher Education, 44*(4), 628–642. https://doi.org/10.1080/03075079.2017.1393059

Jones, C., Penaluna, K., & Penaluna, A. (2020). Value creation in entrepreneurial education: Towards a unified approach. *Education & Training, 63*(1), 101–113. https://doi.org/10.1108/ET-06-2020-0165

Neck, H. M., & Corbett, A. C. (2018). The scholarship of teaching and learning entrepreneurship. *Entrepreneurship Education and Pedagogy, 1*(1), 8–41. https://doi.org/10.1177/2515127417737286

Neck, M. N., & Greene, P. G. (2011). Entrepreneurship education: Known worlds and new frontiers. *Journal of Small Business Management, 49*(1), 55–70. https://doi.org/10.1111/j.1540-627X.2010.00314.x

North, D. (1990). *Institutions, institutional change and economic performance.* Cambridge University Press.

Pfeffer, J., & Fong, C. T. (2002). The end of business schools? Less success than meets the eye. *Academy of Management Learning and Education, 1*(1), 78–95. https://doi.org/10.5465/amle.2002.7373679

Sarasvathy, S. D. (2001). Causation and effectuation: Toward a theoretical shift from economic inevitability to entrepreneurial contingency. *Academy of Management Review, 26*(2), 243–263. https://doi.org/10.5465/amr.2001.4378020

Scott, R. W. (2001). *Institutions and Organizations.* Sage.

Smolka, K. M., Verheul, I., Burmeister-Lamp, K., & Heugens, P. P. M. A. R. (2018). Get it together! Synergistic effects of causal and effectual decision-making logics on venture performance. *Entrepreneurship Theory and Practice, 42*(4), 571–604. https://doi.org/10.1177/1042258718783429

Spilling, O. (1996). The entrepreneurial system: On entrepreneurship in the context of a mega-event. *Journal of Business Research, 36*(1), 91–103. https://doi.org/10.1016/0148-2963(95)00166-2

Welter, F. (2011). Contextualizing entrepreneurship—Conceptual challenges and ways forward. *Entrepreneurship Theory and Practice, 35*(1), 165–184. https://doi.org/10.1111/j.1540-6520.2010.00427.x

Wurth, B., Stam, E., & Spigel, B. (2021). Toward an entrepreneurial ecosystem research program. *Entrepreneurship Theory and Practice.* https://doi.org/10.1177/1042258721998948

INDEX

A

Abstract conceptualisation (AC), 335, 348
Accelerator, 258, 260, 264
Action-learning, 313
Action-oriented methods, 238
Action research, 212, 214, 223
Active experimentation (AC), 335, 337, 348
Active learning, 234, 239, 245, 313
Activity and experience oriented learning process, 230
Adult learning, 73, 77, 82, 338
Adventure Education, 239
Alumni entrepreneurs, 279, 280, 284, 285
American University Center for Innovation, 257
Andragogy, 20, 23, 25, 34, 40, 42, 45, 233–239, 241–243, 245
Andragogy in Practice Model, 237
Annals of Entrepreneurship Education and Pedagogy, 255, 256, 266

Appropriation (of tools and concepts), 52, 57, 63
Assessments, 272, 280, 281, 284–286
Autonomous learning, 237
Autonomy, 104, 106, 108, 110

B

Barriers to student and practitioner learning, 222, 230
Becoming, 16, 18, 22, 29
Behaviourism, 159
Being, 16, 18, 21, 25, 28, 29
Business start-up, 99, 100, 105, 106, 108, 109

C

California State University, 259
Career development, 108, 109
Career(s), 98, 102–105, 109, 110
Career trajectories, 197, 202
Cases, 259, 260, 266

© The Editor(s) (if applicable) and The Author(s), under exclusive license to Springer Nature Switzerland AG 2022
G. J. Larios-Hernandez et al. (eds.), *Theorising Undergraduate Entrepreneurship Education*,
https://doi.org/10.1007/978-3-030-87865-8

362 INDEX

Case study research-thick, rich
entrepreneurial learning insight,
220
Childhood development, 69, 71, 77,
90
Classroom play, 73
Co-creating external business
environment, 230
Co-Curricular Programs, 263, 265
Cognition, Cognitive competence,
139, 140, 143, 150–152
Cognitive involvement, 336, 347–349
Cognitive load theory (CLT), 34, 35,
37–39, 41
Community, 15, 71, 81–83, 85, 90
Compassion, 161, 162, 167
Competence model, 20
Competency/ies, 97, 99, 100, 107,
108, 116–119, 123, 124, 126,
174, 177, 234, 236, 245
Competency Based Learning, 239
Competition, 261, 263–265
Complex strategic learning task, 212
Concrete experience (CE), 335, 337
Construction play, 73, 84
Constructivism, 50, 51, 63, 159, 160,
164, 166
Constructivist, 180
Continuum of play, 83
Convergent thinking, 117, 119, 123,
126, 128
Cooperative Learning, 239
Corporate Entrepreneurship, 3, 298
Courage, 81–83, 90
Courses, 257–260, 263, 266
Covid, 313, 325
Co-Working, 263
Creative, 72, 77, 86, 87, 90, 91
Creativity and innovation capability,
225
Creativity exercise, 339, 342, 343
Creator Pedagogy, 259

Critical Thinking Based Learning, 239
Culture, 81, 82
Curiosity, 81–83, 90
Curricular Programs, 257
Curriculum development, 312

D
Deliberate practice, 238
Deliberative mindset, 145, 150
Demand model, 20
Design Thinking, 60, 63, 239, 260
Desired Student Outcomes, 80
Development, 160, 161, 163–165,
167
Dialogic system, 15
Didactic method, 126
Digital business, 311, 312, 315–318,
320–323, 325–328
Digital economy, 314, 315, 318, 328
Digitalisation, 107
Digital literacy, 312–315, 316,
327–328
Digital skills, 321, 325, 327
Digitisation, 314, 327
Discussion forums, 338, 339, 341,
342, 345–347
Distinctiveness of small enterprises,
212, 213, 226
Divergent thinking, 117, 119, 123,
126, 128
Diversity, 261
Double stimulation, 52–54, 57,
61–63
Dual approach, 241
Dual space, 126

E
E-commerce, 312, 317, 321, 322,
325
Economic development, 174
Ecosystems, 295

Educating would-be and existing entrepreneurs, 212

Educational philosophy, 158, 160, 164

Educational process, 15, 17, 18, 26

Educational theory, 158

Education in entrepreneurship, 234, 241, 245

E-learning, 333–335, 339

Emergent adulthood (EA), 34

Emergent adults, 34, 40, 44, 45

Emerging adulthood (EA), 117, 118

Emerging adults, 118, 121, 122, 233, 235, 243

Emotional intelligence, 313

Empathy, 138, 150–152

Employability, 98, 100–103, 105–109

Employability skills, 321, 328

Employed roles, 196

Employment, 313, 315

Enhancing student capacity to learn, 222

EntreComp, 100, 101, 107

Entrepreneurial Behaviour, 138

Entrepreneurial ecosystem, 273, 275–277, 286

Entrepreneurial Ecosystem Approach, 292, 301. *See also* University-based Entrepreneurship Ecosystems (U-BEEs)

Entrepreneurial education (EE), 311, 312, 317

Entrepreneurial environment, 313

Entrepreneurial Identity, 195, 197, 198, 201, 202, 205

Entrepreneurial identity, students, 16, 29

Entrepreneurial Intention, 174

Entrepreneurial Intention (Bagheri & Pihie, 2010; Liñán & Chen, 2009), 292

Entrepreneurial journey, 141, 143

Entrepreneurial knowledge, 321, 323, 328

Entrepreneurial learning, 217, 220, 223, 224, 226, 229, 316, 321, 324

Entrepreneurial learning space, 16–18, 20, 21, 23–25, 27–29

Entrepreneurial Mindset (EM), 100, 119, 120, 137–140, 142, 143, 146, 149, 151, 152, 318, 319, 327

Entrepreneurial process, 313, 327

Entrepreneurial strategy, 262

Entrepreneurial thinking, 149

Entrepreneurial training, 312, 313

Entrepreneurial university, 273, 275

Entrepreneurship, 71, 74–91

Entrepreneurship course, 334, 338

Entrepreneurship curriculum, 272, 279

Entrepreneurship education (EE), 15, 16, 50–52, 55, 56, 62, 63, 115, 126, 157–159, 161–168, 173, 177, 191, 193–195, 198, 203, 205, 255, 256, 264–266, 271–282, 284–286, 297, 298, 300, 312–314, 316–318, 321, 323, 327, 328, 334, 335, 337, 338, 341, 345, 349

Entrepreneurship education–content and delivery, 219

Entrepreneurship Education and Pedagogy (EE&P), 256, 266

Entrepreneurship education in the U.S., 266

Entrepreneurship education scene, 18

Entrepreneurship educator, 15–20, 22–29, 74, 76, 80, 90, 312, 313, 320, 327

Entrepreneurship pedagogy, 255

364 INDEX

Entrepreneurship programs, 257–259, 266
Entrepreneurship students, 75, 81
Entrepreneurship Theory and Practice (ETP), 256, 266
Equipping undergraduates for unknowable change environments, 229
Essential knowledge, 234, 241, 244
Exercises, 259, 260, 266
Expansive learning, 61
Experience, 334–338, 343, 345, 346, 348, 349
Experiential, 257, 259, 266
Experiential learning, 34, 42, 44, 117, 119–124, 126, 193, 194, 198, 202, 204, 205, 311–313, 315, 316, 323, 324, 326–328, 334–338, 340–342, 345–347, 349
Experiential learning model (ELM) (Kolb, 1984), 335
Experiential learning theory (ELT), 334, 335, 346, 348
Experimentation within learning process, 217, 224
Explanatory style, 147, 148, 152
Exploratory Play, 85, 87
External environment–unpredictable and unknowable, 214

F

Face-to-face instruction (FTFI), 333–335, 339
Facilitator, 44, 75, 164, 280, 284, 328, 339, 341–345, 347, 349
Faculty, 260, 262, 264
Family business, 261
Family business capital, 301
Family Capital (Danes et al., 2009). *See* Family business capital

Family owned resources, 301. *See also* Intellectual capital
Feedback, 336, 339, 342, 345, 347–349
Fieldwork, 337
Films, 261
Finance, 257, 261, 262, 265
First-year students, 35, 37, 38, 40, 41, 43, 44
Five core practices of entrepreneurship education, 71
Fixed mindset, 145, 146
Flipped Classroom, 239
Flux-zone, 243, 245
For approach, 175, 177, 243
Formal structured instruction of Entrepreneurship Education, 298
Fostering core undergraduate skills and abilities, 212, 220, 222, 225, 230
Framework, 16, 23, 26, 28, 29
Fun, 72, 76, 77, 79, 80, 82, 83, 90, 91
Future of work, 108

G

Games, 70, 73, 76–78, 83, 90
Gender, 261, 265
Generation theory, 104
Georgetown University, 259, 264
Graduates, 98, 100–102, 104, 108–110
Grove City College, 257, 260, 263, 264
Growth mindset, 145, 146, 148
Guidance, 34, 37, 38, 40, 41, 44, 45
Guiding principle for playful teaching, 79, 80

H

Heutagogy, 20, 23, 25

Higher education (HE), 98, 101, 116, 117, 233–238, 241, 243, 245, 312, 315, 316
Higher education policy, 98
Holistic technique, 312, 313
Human capital, 101, 292, 300
Humanism, 159–166, 168

I
Identity, 16, 21–24, 26, 28
Identity capital, 21
Identity theory, 22
Incubator, 263, 264
Individual and Inter-organisational Networks (O'Shea et al., 2004), 295
Informal instruction of Entrepreneurship. *See* Out-of-school entrepreneurial education
Information-based perspective, 237
Institution, 15, 18, 24, 26, 29
Instruction, 34, 37, 38, 41, 42, 44
Intangible assets, 300
Intellectual capital, 300
Intrapreneurial activities. *See* Corporate Entrepreneurship
Investing, 261, 264

K
Knowledge-based resources. *See* Intangible assets
Knowledge society, 101

L
Labour market, 103, 106, 108, 109
Learning, 70, 71, 74, 76, 80, 82, 83, 88, 90, 91, 158–160, 162–167
Learning and assessment vehicles, 227

Learning environment, 312, 313, 318, 326, 327
Learning experience, 336, 345–347, 349
Learning management system (LMS), 338–340
Learning organisation–in the small business context, 226
Learning process, 127, 128
Learning process and practices, 217, 230
Learning space, 117, 121, 123, 124, 126, 128
Learning stages, 234
Learning theory, 334, 346
Learning-to-learn capability, 220, 221, 230
LEGO® Serious Play® (LSP), 75
Living learning community, 264

M
Malaysia, 311, 314–317, 320, 327, 328
Management education, 312
Marketing, 262
Mediation, 52
Mental room, 17, 26
Mentoring, 234, 238, 241, 243, 245
Mentorship, 117, 122, 124
Miami University, 258, 260
Micro enterprises–challenges and benefits, 213
Mindset, 234, 238, 240, 241, 243–245
Minimum viable product (MVP), 261
Mixed profile, 234, 238
Model Canvas, 58, 62

N

Networking, 165, 264, 274, 276, 293, 318. *See also* Social Capital (Bordieu, 1986)
New ventures, 17, 120, 174, 179, 182, 274, 293, 298, 301
Non-linear, 177, 181, 182
North Carolina State University E-Clinic, 257
Novice learners, 35, 37, 40, 41, 44, 45
Nudge, 41, 42

O

Objectivist knowledge, 159
Odigogy, 34, 35, 40, 42, 44, 45, 243
Online entrepreneurship education, 334, 338, 345, 349
Online learning, 313, 327
Online lecture, 338–341, 345–347
Out-of-school entrepreneurial education, 298
Outward Mindset, Open Mindset, 149, 151
Owner managed enterprises – best entrepreneurship practice, 212

P

Parents, 272, 279, 282, 283, 285, 286
Pareto 80/20 principle, 58, 62
Pedagogical practices, 280
Pedagogy, 34, 40, 45, 167, 174, 233–238, 241–243, 245, 259, 266
Permanence, Pervasiveness, Personalisation, 147
Personal Construct Theory [PCT] (Kelly, 1955), 212, 214
Personal Construct Theory as research and teaching vehicle, 220

Personal construing–simple and complex learning, 221, 230
Personal values, 158
Perspective, 71, 75, 78, 81, 83, 89
Philosophy, 158, 159, 162, 163
Philosophy of Play, 78, 79, 90
Physical involvement, 345, 347–349
Physical room, 17
Plagiarism, 347
Play-based activities, 83
Playful, 71, 73, 77–79, 81, 82, 86, 90
Play in adult learning and higher education, 73
Play in early childhood development, 70
Practice, 334, 337
Practice of entrepreneurship, 77
Problem-based, 175, 176, 178, 180, 181, 183–185
Problem-Based Learning, 239
Process-based, 175, 177, 178, 183–185
Professional identity, 195, 197, 199, 203, 205
Professional identity theory, 22
Profile, 234–236, 243, 245
Program outcomes, 256

R

Real-life, 335–337, 348, 349
Real-world experience, 20, 21
Reflection, 22, 28, 175, 180, 182, 185, 334, 336–338, 344–348
Reflective and meaning-eliciting tools, 222, 225
Reflective learning, 328
Reflective observation (RO), 335, 346, 348
Reflexivity capability, 228
Relational capital. *See* Social Capital (Bordieu, 1986)

INDEX 367

Resource-Based View (Barney, 1991), 299, 300
Resource mobilisation exercise, 339, 344
Responsibility, personal, 20
Reversal effect, 34, 35, 38, 40–42, 44
Role of play, 70, 73
Roles, 15, 16, 27

S
Safe space, 25, 28
Scaling, 261
Self-assessment, 22
Self-assessment exercise, 339, 342
Self-determined learning, 185
Self-directed learning, 181, 194
Self-employment, 196, 198
Self-managed learning, 192–194, 203, 205
Self-reflective, 22
Self-study resources, 339, 341, 345, 346
Sensemaking, 81, 82, 86, 90
Service Learning, 239
Shared approach, 234, 236, 237, 241, 243, 244
Shared learning space, 25, 28
Signs, 53
Simulation and Gamification, 239
Simulations, 76, 77
Sir Ken Robinson, 70
Skills, 98–100, 102, 103, 105–110, 312, 314–316, 318, 320, 321, 323, 325–327
Small business entrepreneurs, 213, 224
Small business strategic management model, 226
Small business strategic management practice, 212, 230

Small Enterprise Education and Development Program (SEED), 260
SMEs, 102, 106, 109
Social Capital (Bordieu, 1986), 299, 300
Social entrepreneurship, 161, 167, 257, 258, 261, 262, 265
Social identity theory, 22
Social origin of cognition, 56
Society, 161, 168
Sri Lanka, 272, 278–281, 283, 286
Stakeholder engagement, 272, 274, 279, 281, 286
Stakeholders, 271–277, 279–286
Startups. *See* New ventures
Storytelling, 239, 260
Strategic control in uncertain operating environments, 216
Student as 'man the scientist', 218
Student-centred approach, 237
Student consulting, 259, 263
Student entrepreneur, 234, 235, 237, 238, 240, 245
Students, 97–100, 102, 104, 106–108, 272, 273, 275–277, 279–281, 284
Study abroad, 264, 266
Subjective knowledge, 166
Sustainability, 51, 294, 301
Sustainable Family Business Theory (SFBT), 293–295, 299, 301, 303
Symbolic play, 84
Systems Theory, 294, 299

T
Taxonomy of play, 72
Teaching effectiveness, 158
Teaching method, 120, 121, 126
Team academy, 192, 194, 195, 197, 205
Team-based, 192, 193, 200

Team Entrepreneurship graduates, 197, 199, 203, 204
Team Entrepreneurship pedagogy, 203
Team learning, 193, 205
Technology commercialization, 263
Technology entrepreneurship, 262
TeleCC project, 57
The $10 Reality Check, 87, 88
The future of play in entrepreneurship education, 89
The Paper Shirt, 84
The state of play in entrepreneurship education, 75
The Word Hack, 86
Theory, 335, 338
Theory of planned behaviour, 272, 282–285
Through approach, 236, 258
Tools, 52, 53, 55, 57–63
Toward a more playful teaching philosophy in entrepreneurship education, 77
Transformative learning, 19–21, 25, 28
Typologies, 336, 348

U

Ultimate Football League, 88
Undergraduate education, 52, 62, 63
Undergraduates, 122, 128, 201
Undergraduate students, 312, 316, 317, 320, 326, 327
United Kingdom, 98

United States Association for Small Business and Entrepreneurship (USASBE), 256–258, 266
United States entrepreneurship education, 256, 266
Unit of analysis, 52, 53, 58, 60, 62
Universiti Malaysia Terengganu (UMT), 312, 316, 317, 320, 327
University/ies, 98, 101, 102, 109
University-based Entrepreneurship Ecosystems (U-BEEs), 271, 273, 293, 295, 297, 300, 301, 302, 303. *See also* Entrepreneurial Ecosystem Approach
University-Based Venture Development Organizations (VDOs), 296
University of Missouri Kansas City Regnier Institute, 258
Utah State University, 260

V

Vygotsky, Lev, 51–57, 62, 63

W

Work-related learning, 313
World of 'live' small business practice as teaching-assessment vehicle, 212

Z

Zone of proximal development (ZPD), 51, 52